THE GRAND OLD MAN OF MAINE

CIVIL WAR AMERICA

Gary W. Gallagher, editor

The Grand Old Man *of* Maine

SELECTED LETTERS OF

JOSHUA LAWRENCE CHAMBERLAIN,

1865–1914

Edited by Jeremiah E. Goulka

Foreword by James M. McPherson

The University of North Carolina Press

Chapel Hill and London

© 2004 The University of North Carolina Press

All rights reserved

Set in Minion type by Tseng Information Systems

Manufactured in the United States of America

The paper in this book meets the guidelines for
permanence and durability of the Committee on
Production Guidelines for Book Longevity of the
Council on Library Resources.

Library of Congress Cataloging-in-Publication Data

Chamberlain, Joshua Lawrence, 1828–1914.

[Correspondence. Selections]

The grand old man of Maine : selected letters of Joshua
Lawrence Chamberlain, 1865–1914 / edited by Jeremiah E.
Goulka ; foreword by James M. McPherson.

  p. cm. — (Civil War America)

Includes bibliographical references and index.

ISBN 0-8078-2864-5 (cloth : alk. paper)

1. Chamberlain, Joshua Lawrence, 1828–1914—
Correspondence. 2. United States—History—Civil War, 1861–
1865—Personal narratives. 3. Generals—United States—
Correspondence. 4. Governors—Maine—Correspondence.
5. Bowdoin College—Presidents—Correspondence. 6. College
presidents—Maine—Correspondence. 7. Veterans—Maine—
Correspondence. I. Goulka, Jeremiah E. II. Title. III. Series.

E467.1.C47A4 2004

974.1′041′092—dc22   2003024972

Frontispiece: Chamberlain on horseback in a Portland,
Maine, parade (Courtesy of the Pejepscot Historical Society)

08 07 06 05 04   5 4 3 2 1

To my family

CONTENTS

MAPS & ILLUSTRATIONS

Joshua Lawrence Chamberlain has become a modern Civil War icon almost on a par with Ulysses S. Grant and William T. Sherman for the Union and Robert E. Lee and Stonewall Jackson for the Confederacy. This was not always true. Indeed, before Michael Shaara's novel *The Killer Angels* won the Pulitzer Prize for fiction in 1975, few except the most devoted Civil War aficionados had ever heard of Chamberlain. Shaara's portrait of the courageous college professor who joined the Union army in 1862 and led a bayonet charge that saved Little Round Top on July 2, 1863, catapulted Chamberlain into a fame that grew exponentially with Ken Burns's PBS documentary *The Civil War* in 1990 and the feature film and television miniseries *Gettysburg* in 1993–94. Today Chamberlain is one of the best-known Civil War figures, and the place where his 20th Maine fought at Little Round Top is the most visited site at Gettysburg National Military Park. For his leadership there, Chamberlain was later awarded the Congressional Medal of Honor.

The dramatic action at Little Round Top deserves all the attention it has received. But this attention does ironic injustice to Chamberlain. Shaara's novel and the movie *Gettysburg* end with Lee's retreat from the battlefield, and thus ends most readers' and viewers' knowledge of Chamberlain. (Michael Shaara's son Jeffrey's sequel to his father's novel, *Last Full Measure*, has reached only a fraction of the audience that *The Killer Angels* has enjoyed.) Chamberlain went on to become one of the most remarkable soldiers of the Civil War. He was wounded six times, twice almost fatally, and had five horses shot under him. He rose to command a brigade during the grueling overland campaign from the Wilderness to Petersburg in 1864. Leading his brigade in an assault on Confederate trenches at Petersburg on June 18, 1864, he was shot through both hips, a wound considered mortal at the time of the Civil War. Ulysses S. Grant personally promoted Chamberlain to brigadier general on the field—one of only two such occasions in the war—so he could die at that rank.

But Chamberlain defied predictions and recovered. He returned to lead his brigade—and eventually a division—in the final campaign from Petersburg to Appomattox. At the battle of Quaker Road on March 29, 1865, he took another bullet, this one just below the heart, where it would have killed him had it not been deflected around his ribs by a leather case of field orders in his pocket. He suffered two cracked ribs and a bruised arm but continued to lead his troops in several more fights during the next eleven days until the surrender at Appomattox. The impact of the bullet, though, had temporarily stunned him to a deathlike pallor, and for a second time some Northern newspapers carried a notice of his death. Chamberlain lived another forty-nine years in almost constant pain from his Petersburg wound. His favorite warhorse, Charlemagne, who was also shot three times, likewise lived to a ripe old age.

Few other Civil War soldiers could match this record. In other respects also Chamberlain was truly sui generis. His father had wanted him to follow a military career; his mother wanted him to become a clergyman. His mother appeared to win; young Lawrence (as his family called him) graduated Phi Beta Kappa from Bowdoin College and earned a B.D. from Bangor Theological Seminary. In 1855 he accepted a position at Bowdoin as professor of logic and natural theology, succeeding Calvin Stowe, whose wife, Harriet Beecher, had written *Uncle Tom's Cabin* while Chamberlain was a student at the college. In 1861 Chamberlain became professor of modern languages at Bowdoin. But he grew restless in those halls of ivy as war engulfed the nation. Although he was thirty-three years old and the father of three children, he considered it his duty to fight. To dissuade him, in August 1862 Bowdoin offered him a two-year sabbatical in Europe. Chamberlain tentatively assented, but went instead to the state capital and accepted a lieutenant colonelcy in the 20th Maine. He was not the only college professor in the Union army, but he was surely the only man in either army who could read seven languages — at least these seven: Greek, Latin, Hebrew, Arabic, Syriac, French, and German.

When Chamberlain returned to Maine in 1865, he wanted no part of his previous professorship at Bowdoin. He had already taught almost every course offered there. His war experiences had broadened his horizons — and his ambitions. After a stint as acting president of the college in 1865–66, he accepted the Republican nomination for governor. He was elected by a landslide and reelected three more times, twice by the largest margin in the state's history. His last two years as governor were marred by bitter controversies over temperance and capital punishment, however, and Chamberlain wearied of the strife. Thereafter he repeatedly sought higher office — a senatorship, or ambassadorship, or other prominent federal position — but something always intervened to deny him these prizes.

In 1871 Chamberlain's sense of duty impelled him to accept a unanimous call of the trustees to become president of Bowdoin, a position he held until the board finally accepted his third attempt to resign in 1883. As president, he modernized the curriculum by instituting new courses in science and engineering, social sciences, and modern languages. These innovations provoked opposition from some alumni and trustees—especially Congregational clergymen—who feared that Chamberlain was secularizing Bowdoin, tearing it up from its Christian roots and repudiating the wisdom of the past embodied in a classical curriculum. Similar controversies arose at other colleges and universities that undertook to modernize the curriculum in such a fashion—most notably at Harvard, where Charles Eliot became the national leader in this effort.

At Bowdoin this process became entwined with another controversial innovation by Chamberlain—the introduction of required military drill for all students. In the belief that the United States must never again be as unprepared for war as it had been in 1861, the army offered drill instructors to colleges that wished to establish what amounted to an early version of ROTC. Chamberlain's war experiences had persuaded him of the need for military preparedness. He instituted required drill in 1872. But student opposition flared into open rebellion in 1874, forcing Chamberlain to make the program voluntary and offer gymnastics as an alternative. Most students chose gym. Opponents of Chamberlain's curricular innovations benefited from the opposition to military drill, and the economic depression following the panic of 1873 made it difficult to raise money for expensive facilities for science and engineering courses. By 1881 these programs had been discontinued. In 1883 Chamberlain, suffering great pain and debilitation from a flare-up of his Petersburg wound, resigned as president.

Chamberlain's efforts to modernize Bowdoin appear to have been a failure. But it would be more accurate to say that he was ahead of his time. As Chamberlain's successor as president, William DeWitt Hyde, put it in 1914 after Chamberlain's death, he had "advocated the very reforms, using often the very phrases, that are now the commonplaces of progressive educational discussion—Modern Languages, Science, Classics in translation, political and social science, research and individual instruction." As he had in war, so in peace Chamberlain survived defeats to witness the final triumph of his cause.

From 1883 until his death, Chamberlain became involved in a number of business enterprises, including railroads, real estate development in Florida, and promotion of the new technology of electric power. Repeated surgical operations to ease the pressure and drain the abscess caused by his Petersburg wound achieved only temporary relief. From the time he returned home after the war until his wife Fannie (Frances) died in 1905, Chamberlain's war wounds and experiences put a physical and psychological strain on their marriage that almost led to divorce on one occasion.

Like many other Civil War veterans, Chamberlain became increasingly active in efforts to promote commemoration and remembrance of the war. He joined virtually every veterans' organization and became president of several. He lectured frequently on war subjects and wrote scores of articles and one book. Chamberlain played a large part in preparations for the fiftieth anniversary commemoration of Gettysburg in July 1913—the largest reunion of Blue and Gray ever held—but his health was too precarious for him to attend, much to his disappointment. Eight months later he died of his wounds at the age of eighty-five.

Virtually forgotten for sixty years (except in Maine), Chamberlain is now famous in Civil War circles. Yet most of the attention—and the bulk of the several biographies that have been published in the last ten years—focus almost entirely on the war years. Chamberlain's important careers as governor, educator, and chronicler of the war for half a century after Appomattox remain little known. This skillfully edited collection of Chamberlain's postwar letters—a labor of love as well as of careful scholarship by Bowdoin alumnus Jeremiah Goulka—is therefore an invaluable addition not only to the corpus of Chamberlain biographies but also to our understanding of the war, the Gilded Age, and the construction of Civil War memory. These letters reveal not Chamberlain the icon, but Chamberlain the man—as husband, father, son, brother, politician, educator, businessman, historian, and flawed as well as admirable human being.

James M. McPherson

❧ ACKNOWLEDGMENTS

I began this book as a college sophomore and managed to finish it during spare moments in law school. Young and inexperienced, I had no idea what I had gotten myself into. Fortunately, many wonderful individuals came to my aid and lit my path. I hope that these expressions of thanks can begin to address the depths of my gratitude.

First and foremost, I must thank Professor James M. McPherson of Princeton University for his prescient guidance and continuing willingness to aid the development of this book. His advice for shaping the text and finding a publisher were great rays of sunlight to a college student. Thanks also to Peter Hayes of Northwestern University for his foundational advice on how a college student might write and publish a book.

Many scholars took time from their busy schedules to read and critique the introduction and parts of the manuscript. I would like to thank Fitzhugh Brundage, Eric Foner, the late John Pullen, Dan Levine, Sarah McMahon, Merrill Peterson, Patrick Rael, Nina Silber, and Brooks D. Simpson, as well as my colleagues in the history department at the University of Edinburgh and my fellow panelists at the 2000 American Historical Association annual meeting, Alice Fahs, Stuart McConnell, and David Blight, for their insights and encouragement.

At the University of North Carolina Press, I would like to thank everyone with whom I had the privilege to work: Gary Gallagher, David Perry, Mark Simpson-Vos, Ron Maner, Kathy Ketterman, Vicky Wells, Laura Gribbin, and Liz Gray, my copyeditor, for their insights, experience, professionalism, and spirit of cooperation. Thanks also to the anonymous reviewers for their extremely useful suggestions for improvements to the manuscript.

I owe a debt of gratitude to my research assistants for their hard work when law school kept me away from the Bowdoin College library. Thank you, John Hoffman, Noah Jackson, Lindsey Wilkinson, and Scott Logan.

Along the way, I received a great deal of assistance from librarians and archivists across the country, especially Susan Ravdin of Bowdoin College Special Collections, and Julia Colvin and Erik Jorgensen of the Pejepscot Historical Society in Brunswick. Thanks to Richard Lindemann and his staff at the George J. Mitchell Department of Special Collections & Archives at Bowdoin College; Amy Poland, Deborah Smith, and Kate Higgins of the Pejepscot

Historical Society; Nicholas Noyes of the Maine Historical Society Library in Portland; Muriel Sanford of the Special Collections Department at the Raymond H. Fogler Library, University of Maine at Orono; Leslie Morris at the Houghton Library and Ellen Shea of the Arthur and Elizabeth Schlesinger Library, both at Harvard; Elizabeth B. Dunn of the Rare Book, Manuscript, and Special Collections Library, Duke University; Nan J. Card of the Rutherford B. Hayes Presidential Center; Danielle Moon in Manuscripts and Archives at Yale; Julia Hunter at the Maine State Museum; Bill Copeley of the New Hampshire Historical Society Library; Jean Aroeste of the Princeton University Library; D. Scott Hartwig of Gettysburg National Military Park; Frank Boles of the Clarke Historical Library at Central Michigan University; John Rhodehamel and Gayle Barkley of the Huntington Library in California; David Wigdor of Manuscripts and Archives at the Library of Congress; Patricia Burdick in Special Collections at Colby College; Steven J. Wright at the Civil War Library and Museum in Philadelphia; Karen Jania of the Bentley Historical Library, University of Michigan; Lynn Randall of the Maine State Law and Legislative Reference Library; Christine Ameduri at Gettysburg College; the librarians at the Historical Library of the Yale School of Medicine for their guidance on nineteenth-century home health remedies; and the librarians and staff at the Maine State Archives, the New-York Historical Society, the Historical Society of Pennsylvania, and the National Archives. I thank these libraries for kindly providing permission to publish the letters included in this volume.

I must also thank the many friends who chided me into actually finishing the book. You know who you are, but special thanks to the ones who pestered me most: Ajay Maker, Adair Gordon-Orr, Adam Mossoff, Joshua Walker, Jeff Widmayer, Jon and Dave Raksin, Paul Malmfeldt, Pamela Jaffe, and Jackie Zinn.

Finally, thanks to my family. My extended family—grandmothers, aunts, and uncles (especially Rob)—helped immensely, even if sometimes only asking, again and again, how the book was progressing. Most of all, thanks to my parents, Ann and Jim, and sister, Sarah, for your generous support and encouragement of an unusual extracurricular activity. Without you this book would not exist.

Little Round Top: They fired their last rounds. His men looked to their colonel. To fail to hold their position "at all costs" would be unthinkable — the loss of the Union left flank. "Not a moment . . . to be lost! Five minutes more of such a defensive, and the last roll-call would sound for us! Desperate as the chances were, there was nothing for it, but to take the offensive. I stepped to the colors. The men turned towards me. One word was enough, — 'BAYONET!'"[1]

A memory to last a lifetime, one to make civilians at home hold their manhood cheap. It was vivid, heroic, romantic, knightly, emotive, historically significant. Some lucky soldiers had more than one such moment. As William Tecumseh Sherman wrote, "To be at the head of a strong column of troops, in the execution of some task that requires brain, is the highest pleasure . . . a grim one and terrible, but which leaves on the mind and memory the strongest mark."[2] In these grim and terrible pleasures, Joshua Lawrence Chamberlain redefined himself from a country professor to a soldier. The Civil War was his defining moment and the source of his legacy of glory. It forever changed the world he lived in, his sense of self, and the opportunities open to him. Indeed, his finest memories did more than that. Chamberlain made them his benchmark for his personal expectations and aspirations. For this he would suffer.

It would have been hard for him to have done otherwise: Chamberlain was revered as his state's greatest hero for the entirety of his long postwar life, a life that lasted until the eve of the First World War. He was the citizen-soldier writ large, a hero in an age that worshiped heroes. Unlike many one-event heroes, Chamberlain could list Little Round Top; his battlefield promotion at Petersburg; his leadership at the Quaker Road, White Oak Road, and Five Forks; and his selection to receive the official surrender of the infantry of the Army of Northern Virginia at Appomattox. He had been thrust into greatness and he rose to the occasion, rapidly outgrowing his cloistered rural worldview to become a peer and friend to many of the nation's notables, a natural selection for one of the limited number of regular army colonelcies, and the obvi-

1. Chamberlain, "Through Blood and Fire at Gettysburg," reprinted in *Bayonet*, 33. See also Goulka, "Defining the Meaning."
2. Sherman, *Memoirs*, 898.

ous choice for governor of Maine. He was the "Grand Old Man of Maine," the "Hero of Little Round Top," who was elected governor with record-breaking majorities four terms in a row, who ran the college where he had studied, who saved Maine from civil war in 1880.

It was only natural that he would yearn for a continuation of his heroic life; the public encouraged, even demanded, it. Laudatory, near worshipful, newspaper reports frequently greeted him: "Sections may have their grand old men, but never were, are not and never will be, [any] grander than Maine's hero soldier, ex-governor, and greatest orator, Gen. Joshua L. Chamberlain."[3] His self-identity and self-worth responded accordingly. The degree to which Chamberlain met his Civil War service benchmarks determined his sense of continuing personal success. Predictably, the more frustrated he felt, the more he turned to history and reminiscence.

Because the Civil War so profoundly influenced postwar America, this volume of Joshua Lawrence Chamberlain's postwar letters is very much about the various influences of the war and its memory. As historians frequently note, historical memory (both natural and cultivated) plays a powerful role in individuals' and peoples' lives. Just as we are surprised to see classical or medieval ruins in an old painting, the past plays both a fundamental and an enigmatic-romantic role to the historical individual. To Civil War veterans, their war experiences and their memories of these experiences (in both the congruence and dissimilitude between them) were vital to their understanding of their world and of themselves. No one can skim even the most superficial study or novel of the Gilded Age without being astounded at how the Civil War loomed over later life. And not just in the South. Historical memory is the most prominent theme in Chamberlain's correspondence.

It is not the only theme, of course. The letters in this volume have been selected from hundreds of extant letters both to present a substantial look at Chamberlain's postwar life—his family relationships, his career and the decisions that shaped it, and his personal interests—and to highlight the predominant themes in his life and correspondence: the memory and commemoration of the Civil War, the military history of the Civil War, state and national politics in the second half of the nineteenth century, the politics of veterans and pensions, and the modernization of Bowdoin College and higher education. Intertwined throughout is the theme of Victorian manhood and masculinity. The letters are presented chronologically. This introduction will provide some analysis and historical context for the themes in the correspondence, but it will allow Chamberlain's letters to speak for themselves.

3. Quoted in Smith, *Fanny and Joshua*, 311.

This collection responds to a gap in Chamberlain scholarship. Chamberlain's Civil War career and letters have received a great deal of attention since Michael Shaara's novel *The Killer Angels*, Ken Burns's documentary *The Civil War*, and the movie *Gettysburg*, but his postwar life lay only superficially inspected for decades. A mere forty-nine pages cover that many years in the definitive biography, Alice Rains Trulock's *In the Hands of Providence: Joshua L. Chamberlain and the American Civil War*.[4] It has only been with the publication of the late John Pullen's short *Joshua Chamberlain: A Hero's Life and Legacy* and the limited run of Diane Smith's delightfully detailed *Fanny and Joshua: The Enigmatic Lives of Frances Caroline Adams and Joshua Lawrence Chamberlain* that the years after Appomattox have received significant treatment.[5] With the growth of Civil War historical memory as a field of historical inquiry and the increased interest in Chamberlain's postwar life — often taking the form of hagiography or overenthusiastic responses to that hagiography — a volume of his postwar letters takes on especial interest.

CHAMBERLAIN AND VICTORIAN MANHOOD

It is a commonplace that notions of manhood, masculinity, male roles, and male values have shaped American men and society,[6] but it is impossible to understand Chamberlain without understanding his notions of manhood. His masculine values exerted great sway on both his public and private lives.

Like most boys who grew up in a religious New England family,[7] Chamberlain was trained to aspire to a certain type of manhood. This was a principled, sentimental, chivalric manhood with a focus on service, honor, and knightly action.[8] Stories of Old Testament generals like his namesake Joshua and John Bunyan's *Pilgrim's Progress* were drummed into children's ears; adults read Byron and Sir Walter Scott.

Chamberlain's aspirational notions of masculine values developed through the course of his life. There is the vigorous manhood illustrated in the oft-told vignette about his father's instructions for overcoming seemingly insurmountable obstacles: "Do it! That's how." While a student at Bowdoin, Chamberlain developed a focus on "duty" that would guide his career

4. Chapel Hill: University of North Carolina Press, 1992.

5. Mechanicsburg, Pa.: Stackpole Books, 1999; Gettysburg: Thomas Publications, 1999.

6. See, for example, Rotundo, *American Manhood*; and "Body and Soul."

7. Philip Paludan suggests that religion shaped the North's vision of the Civil War more than any other influence. Paludan, *A People's Contest*, 339, 350–52.

8. For an interesting study of Victorian interpretations of the Middle Ages, see Girouard, *The Return to Camelot*.

choices.[9] He was, for example, an avid student of about fourteen languages, including Greek, Latin, German, Old Norse, and Provençal, with their classical and medieval literature of heroic myth and epic. And then there was the war.

Chamberlain's correspondence shows that he actively embraced Victorian definitions of masculinity. In his view, "Manhood is one of the noblest of God's gifts or manifestations."[10] When planning the centennial celebration of Senator Hannibal Hamlin's birth, he instructed that "some reference to his robust manhood should be made."[11] When Chamberlain wished to impress upon the outgoing governor of Maine that he would not allow armed men in the statehouse during the "count-out" crisis of January 1880, he told him that "My honor is pledged in this."[12]

As a man of God, a scholar, and a soldier, Chamberlain consciously cultivated the Victorian notions of manhood that he had always been taught to embrace. He saw himself as a Christian knight in dutiful errantry. As the eminent historian of chivalry, Johan Huizinga, wrote, "The conception of chivalry as a sublime form of secular life might be defined as an aesthetic ideal assuming the appearance of an ethical ideal."[13] This chivalric, dutiful Victorian masculine morality that Chamberlain was trained to believe and that he cultivated in himself was of such pervasive importance to him and the course of his life that one cannot hope to understand him or his letters without recognizing its influence.

CHAMBERLAIN AND CIVIL WAR HISTORY AND MEMORY

Without that recognition it is also impossible to understand the role of the Civil War in Chamberlain's life after Appomattox. Civil War veterans felt that they had participated in an extraordinary historical event that would shape their world for decades to come, one that connected them with their revolutionary forebears. They had made history and were revered as heroes.

Indeed, it is notable how frequently veterans used the word "History" (often capitalized) throughout—and especially toward the end of—the American Civil War. They were conscious of making history, of taking part in an event that was destined for legend. For supporters of the Union, it dawned a bright new era. The most prominent historian of the day, George Bancroft,

9. 23 Jan. 1856, J. E. Adams to Chamberlain, BSC. Bibliographical abbreviations follow citations of letters not included in this volume. All other letters cited can be found herein.

10. 10 Nov. 1905 to Munford.

11. 25 June 1909 to Burrage.

12. 7 Jan. 1880 to Garcelon.

13. Huizinga, *Waning of the Middle Ages*, 69.

declared that the Civil War settled all the major issues of the day by destroying slavery, preserving the Union and republican government, and vindicating the principles of constitutional government.[14] Henry Adams predicted that the war would infuse Americans with new, cleaner habits: they would quit drinking, especially at bars and taverns, and start brushing their teeth, washing their hands, wearing clean clothes, and taking on new, responsible life challenges, believing "that they have a duty in life besides that of getting ahead, and a responsibility for other people's acts as well as their own."[15] As soldiers declared that the war was now "a matter of history," they knew they would be the ones to write that history.[16]

And write that history they did.[17] There was a burst of interest in Civil War history during the conflict's immediate aftermath, partly due to the excitement of victory and defeat, and partly to avoid the tough questions that followed—Reconstruction, unemployment, inflation, revelations of wartime corruption—by focusing on the clear morality play of battle. As veterans struggled to adapt to their old home lives and to find work, many immediately turned to history.

This burst of interest passed as veterans and the country moved on, but as veterans entered middle and old age, as disappointments with the ambivalent fruits of war, their own lives, and their children's lives developed, they turned to reminiscence. During the 1880s and 1890s, Civil War reminiscence became a pastime, with lectures and reunions of old soldiers filling calendars, and memoirs and histories pouring off presses like so much water.

In such climates, Chamberlain was a natural star. He was the romantic hero of both Little Round Top and the official surrender of the Army of Northern Virginia. He was the professor-turned-officer honored by the likes

14. Pressly, *Americans Interpret Their Civil War*, 57.

15. Quoted in Smith, *Trial by Fire*, 588.

16. Indeed, the Society for the Preservation of Unpublished History was already in action on the battlefield during the spring of 1865. Davis, *Camp-fire Chats*, 344.

17. Paul Fussell considers the First World War to be the first truly literate war, partly because many British soldiers were armed with the *Oxford Book of English Verse*. Fussell, *The Great War*. A comparison of the works he analyzes with those discussed by Edmund Wilson in *Patriotic Gore* shows that even though the later war inspired more examples of fiction of high literary quality, Civil War soldiers, armed with their Bibles, were surprisingly literate, as the sheer quantity of their writing suggests. Even the barely literate often wrote powerfully, such as Bartlett Malone in his diary, *Whipt 'Em Everytime*. Though their works are usually the literary inferiors of those by Fussell's authors, Civil War soldiers rarely sank to similar depths of cynicism. For them, the Victorian outlook often survived the trenches.

of Ulysses S. Grant and Charles Griffin. He was a spellbinding orator, this former professor of rhetoric and oratory; indeed, he was orator of the Military Order of the Loyal Legion of the United States (MOLLUS) and the Society of the Army of the Potomac. Notably, rhetoric encompassed the field of history at the time. His career as a scholar gave him the patina of objectivity, and his scholarly interest in history fueled his research. Among Civil War historians and memorialists, Chamberlain held a special position.

During the first surge of interest in Civil War history, Chamberlain was adrift in Brunswick. At war's end, he had written to his sister Sarah that he was not "disturbed" about the "exceedingly uncertain state" of his future, for he had "plenty of 'strings to my bow', or in better words, Providence will both open & guide my way."[18] One option was to return to Bowdoin, though he professed to maintain the same fear of returning to the ivory tower that he had expressed at the beginning of the war:[19] while home on medical leave during the last winter of the war, he had informed his father that when the war ended, he intended to resign his professorship and "throw myself on the current of affairs, and either remain in the military service (as is most congenial to my temperament) or strike into some other enterprise of a more bold and stirring character than a College chair affords."[20] The offer of a military post — though a great honor — turned out to be less than bold and stirring: either western garrison or southern Reconstruction duty. Hoping for something better to come along, Chamberlain had turned down the prestigious collectorship of the Port of Bangor. But nothing else presented itself, so, in need of respite, he returned to teaching. He was terribly bored. To ease the transition, he lectured and began collecting records to write a history of the V Corps of the Army of the Potomac, but a call from the Republican Party would put the project on hold indefinitely.

For Chamberlain, the second surge of his interest in the history of the war began in earnest after his tenure as governor of Maine and president of Bowdoin College had ended with mixed feelings and after his hopes for a Senate seat or high office in the Hayes administration had been quashed. Frustrated by civilian life's failure to offer many moments of heroic duty (or to reward him when it did), he turned back toward the time when life was more generous to him. He was a prolific writer, orator, and organizer. He wrote articles and chapters on Fredericksburg, Gettysburg, Petersburg, the Quaker and White Oak Roads, Five Forks, Appomattox, Lincoln, and the

18. 6 June 1865 to his sister, in Chamberlain, *Through Blood and Fire*, 200–201.
19. 10 Oct. 1862 to Fannie, in ibid., 23–25.
20. 12 Feb. 1865 to his father, in ibid., 147–48.

Grand Review of the Army of the Potomac.[21] Invitations arrived from periodicals ranging from Hearst's popular magazines to the prestigious *North American Review*; Houghton Mifflin offered to publish anything Chamberlain wrote.[22] He wrote a history of the final days of the war, *The Passing of the Armies: An Account of the Final Campaign of the Army of the Potomac Based Upon Personal Reminiscences of the Fifth Army Corps*, which was published posthumously. He delivered countless lectures and Decoration Day (Memorial Day) addresses to countless groups on Civil War subjects.[23] His research work, editing work, and organizational work increasingly dominates his later correspondence.

Thinking about the war not only gave Chamberlain an opportunity to bask in his past glories and satisfy his scholarly proclivities, but it kept him connected with the "boys." He was extremely active in numerous veterans' societies and committees. He served terms as president of the 20th Maine Society, the Association of Maine Soldiers and Sailors, and the Society of the Army of the Potomac, and as commander of the Maine divisions of MOLLUS and the Grand Army of the Republic (GAR). He was a member of the Executive Committee of the Maine Gettysburg Commission, which prepared a volume to commemorate the state's role at Gettysburg, published in 1898.[24] In 1913 he chaired the commission, which organized the state's participation in the celebration of the battle's fiftieth anniversary. He also chaired the Maine committee to fund a memorial to honor Union women in Washington, D.C.

These groups were fraternal, delightfully social, and served myriad other purposes. Chamberlain legitimately saw at least some of them as historical societies, such as the commission that produced *Maine at Gettysburg*. The goal of a historical society was not just to record, however, but to remember and to teach. Here enters the romance of Civil War historical memory and the torturous path to sectional reconciliation. Nominating Rutherford B. Hayes to be commander-in-chief of MOLLUS, he stated that

> [MOLLUS] is most truly a Historical Society. Noble records that have been made are to be nobly kept. The power of noble deeds is to be preserved

21. Many of these are reprinted in *Bayonet*.

22. 7 Jan. 1879, *North American Review* editor-in-chief Rice to Chamberlain, YUL; Trulock, 494 n. 59.

23. On the concept of Decoration Day, see Blight, *Race and Reunion*, Chapter 3. Some of Chamberlain's lectures are reprinted in *Bayonet*.

24. Chamberlain was involved with the histories of the 20th and 16th Maine Regiments in *MAG*.

and passed on to the future. And what better recognition of our own place and service, what brighter link in the continuity of our own history, . . . than that . . . the head of our Society [be] . . . one who was called to the exercise of highest authority in realizing its consummation, and securing its consequences: [who] guide[d] the final steps in the restoration of the Civil Order, the reconstruction of disabled States and the regeneration of the Republic.[25]

Much of the correspondence illustrates this interplay between history and historical memory.

≈CHAMBERLAIN, VETERANS POLITICS, AND PENSIONS

The continuing influence of the Civil War upon national life is evident in his statement nominating Hayes. The war not only influenced (or outright created) many of the questions of the day, but it partially determined how the questions were addressed and who would address them. Some Republican regulars waved the proverbial "bloody shirt"; political prominence, even mere candidacy, often depended on one's Civil War record. On visiting Washington, Chamberlain wrote to his sister that "Self-seeking marks too many faces, & all the strifes of peaceful times — less noble often than those of war, — are seen here in their little play."[26] To Ellis Spear, he wrote that there "is a tendency now-a-days to make 'history' subserve other purposes than legitimate ones. 'Incidental' history, even if true in detail can be made to produce what used to be called in our logic 'suggestio falsi.'"[27]

The belated awarding of Medals of Honor provides a good example. Originally intended to honor "such noncommissioned officers and privates as shall most distinguish themselves by their gallantry in action, and other soldier-like qualities, during the present insurrection," the medal was extended to officers in 1863. When an 1890 rule allowed the belated award of the medals — with a mere recital of facts and a report from a commanding officer or witness required for substantiation — they were doled out promiscuously: 1,400 in eight years.[28] Chamberlain campaigned against such largesse: "The curious transformation of the rear rank to the front now that it is profoundly peaceful and safe [in Washington], is quite noticeable all along the line, and

---

25. Enclosure to 2 Nov. 1888 to Hayes, RBH.
26. 29 Jan. 1882 to Sae.
27. 27 Nov. 1896 to Spear.
28. *Deeds of Valor*, 1:frontispiece, 1.

makes a fellow of my temperament reluctant to put in any claim for recognition of any kind."[29] Naturally, he still wanted his due, rightly believing himself deserving of recognition and afraid of being conspicuously left out, but he wanted the medal to be "held sacred—not to be bought or sold, or recklessly conferred."[30] He may have influenced the striking of 911 awards from the Medal of Honor roll (including several hundred given to members of the 27th Maine merely for reenlisting) and the 1918 legislation that significantly raised the standard for awarding future medals.[31]

Accordingly, political veterans guarded their reputations assiduously. Chamberlain was no different. When William Oates, his adversary at Little Round Top, proposed to build a monument to his 15th Alabama in a location that would have implicitly suggested that the Alabamians had pierced the 20th Maine's lines, Chamberlain engaged in a heated battle to ensure that the monument would be located accurately.[32] He also carefully staved off a rebellion from within the 20th Maine's ranks over who actually led the charge.[33]

Postwar allies also supported each other's records. Chamberlain revoked permission to publish his favorable review of Franklin Haskell's book on Gettysburg when he "noticed the strictures on the conduct of [Alexander] Webb's brigade in that battle. General Webb is my very special friend."[34] This could reach even to the absurd: Chamberlain somehow managed to praise Ambrose Burnside as a "most deserving commander."[35]

The accuracy of his historical works thus begs the usual questions about narratives from memory, especially battlefield memories. Chamberlain thought deeply about the war, both critically and romantically. To the modern reader, his analyses are both fascinating and perhaps a touch too close to the action to be impartial. Battlefield haze and political purposes may have sometimes challenged a perfect impartiality. But, then again, impartiality regarding the war was almost heresy, and Chamberlain would have no part of that. He did recognize the difficulties inherent in his work, though: "I am perfectly aware that in my account, which only claimed to present things as they appeared to me,—which is perhaps a narrow point of view, although in some ways useful,—there must be errors even in statements of 'past' concerning

29. 18 May 1893 to Webb.
30. Chamberlain, *The Passing of the Armies*, 298.
31. See, for example, Pullen, *A Shower of Stars*, 171–81.
32. See Pullen and forthcoming works by LaFantasie for Oates's point of view.
33. See 27 Nov. 1896 to Spear.
34. 3 May 1910 to Hunt; see also 31 Mar. 1910 to Hunt.
35. 19 Oct. 1910 to Burrage.

'the other side'. . . . What I wish is to get the truth as far as possible—the 'whole truth' I fear is out of reach."[36]

Political veterans used veterans' groups to promote their careers and parties. One minor method was "patriotic education," to encourage teaching in a way that would glorify them and deprive alleged Copperheads of glory. Chamberlain edited *The American Sentinel: A Patriotic Illustrated Monthly*, which began running in 1898.[37]

The real utility of veterans' organizations to the Republican Party was to procure pensions. As veterans aged, those in politics quickly realized that the fastest way to their fellow veterans' votes was to secure them pension and patronage benefits from the government. Aging veterans, some of whom still suffered lingering effects of the war, naturally welcomed such benefits—even more so as the depression of the 1890s set in. Republicans resuscitated the long moribund Grand Army of the Republic to lobby Congress for veterans' benefits. Northern veterans (or at least their organizations) believed that they were entitled to honor and worship—and pensions. Congress acted accordingly, creating America's first entitlement program by passing legislation such as the Arrears Act of 1879 and the Dependent Pension Act of 1890, providing over $1 billion in pension benefits to veterans.[38]

During the two decades surrounding the turn of the century, numerous acts were proposed to reactivate volunteer generals and sometimes colonels in order to immediately retire them with generous regular Army pensions. These plans offered political veterans and their friends an opportunity to line their own pockets and secure additional honors (though, to be sure, veterans such as Chamberlain were deserving and needful). The delineation of beneficiaries among these ranks varied from bill to bill, but they naturally tended toward inclusiveness.

As health problems brought on by his war wounds made it increasingly difficult to earn a living, Chamberlain wanted a share of any benefits. He felt deserving and needful; his wounds were the scourge of his life and the cause of his death. Perhaps to protect his sense of dignity, he wanted his pension to be an honor, not a mere payout under some entitlement or political patronage program. Just as he had disdained the many hundreds of brevets doled out during the final months of the war and the hundreds of medals of honor handed out in the 1890s, Chamberlain refused to support or be included in

36. 10 Nov. 1905 to Munford.

37. See McConnell, *Glorious Contentment*, 167, 224–26; Rotundo, *American Manhood*, 232–35.

38. McConnell, *Glorious Contentment*, 138–53.

a "promiscuously" wide, money-grabbing bill. His sense of dignity forbade retirement acts to include anyone who had not commanded a division "in the field in actual operations of war" (though he only barely met this requirement himself).[39]

Although he often demonstrated a realistic understanding about any given bill's prospects in Congress, Chamberlain frequently refused to show support when politically appropriate. His outright opposition to the largesse of most bills proposed by veterans' groups like the GAR debilitated him when his private pension bills were eventually introduced: the groups (even those of which he was a charter member and senior officer) repaid his opposition by ignoring his bills, consigning them to oblivion in committee.[40] Chamberlain's arrogance in not supporting a bill whose breadth would reach beyond those of only the very highest degree of accomplishment cost him dearly.

🙡CHAMBERLAIN AND LEADERSHIP

In the Civil War, Chamberlain found success in a certain style of leadership. After the war, he sought to parlay that success into civilian forms of dutiful leadership. Soon after he returned to Maine in 1865, he was thrust into the interim presidency of Bowdoin and then into the race for governor. He never turned back. His impressive list of leadership roles — governor, college president, railroad executive — belies his creeping sense of disappointment with civilian leadership roles.

Chamberlain's difficulties as a civilian leader stem at least in part from his particular type of military leadership experience. As a regiment, brigade, and, briefly, division commander, his role was to use his tactical thinking to achieve assigned objectives that were products of more senior officers' strategic thinking. Battlefield tactics are not about compromise or spin.

Chamberlain recognized this. As he told his sister, "I am staggered by seeing both sides of a question. I never could be a partisan leader — a man of one idea. I see the whole combination, & am perplexed till the time comes for me to *strike* in — I can go in then & see 'clear as a quill.'"[41] Chamberlain believed that this circumspect approach had a strong moral foundation. Well as this may be, his attitude and style were not the stuff of which effective political leaders are made.

Chamberlain may have believed that executive politics would offer him an opportunity for administrative leadership akin to his military role. He won

39. 4 Dec. 1909 to Andrews. See also 29 Jan. 1910 to Hale.
40. See, for example, 29 Jan. 1910 to Hale; 14 June 1906 to Warren.
41. 21 Mar. 1872 to Sae.

the governor's seat by a landslide in the September 1866 elections and went on to win two more (one-year) terms, once in the largest victory in Maine history, and then an unprecedented fourth term. Republicans and Democrats both encouraged him to seek a fifth term under their banners. His politics were marked by a desire to modernize Maine's economy and a diligent effort to responsibly enforce the law, an effort that often beleaguered him.

Once the Fourteenth Amendment was ratified, the most controversial political issues of the day were temperance and capital punishment, issues whose partisans were not to be placated by someone of a moderate, nonpartisan, balanced, and intellectual temperament. In the 1850s, Maine had become the first state to enact prohibition. Dissatisfied with the mere requirement that local police officers enforce the "Maine law," the powerful temperance minority wanted a new constabulary dedicated to the suppression of illegal liquor and its trade. The constabulary, a forerunner of modern state police forces, was seen as draconian by a large part of the population, but Chamberlain took an ineffective noncommittal stance on it. Outraged by Chamberlain's proposed candidacy for an unprecedented fourth term and his refusal to support the constabulary, radicals in the temperance wing bolted the Republican party and ran their own candidate in 1869. Chamberlain's sheer popularity easily overwhelmed both the temperance and the Democratic candidates, but Chamberlain's handling of the constabulary issue tarnished his effectiveness in other matters.[42]

Maine had waffled on capital punishment for years. Statute law required a year to elapse after sentencing before the governor could set an execution date if he did not pardon or commute the sentence first. Past governors had asked the legislature to clarify the law with an eye to abolishing the death penalty, but the legislature always chose the safer path of silence. Governors responded in the same vein, delaying sentences indefinitely. Aside from one execution ordered by Chamberlain's predecessor Samuel Cony for a particularly heinous crime, there had been no executions in Maine since 1837.[43]

The capital sentencing of Clifton Harris, a freedman who had emigrated to Maine, where he brutally raped and murdered two elderly women, brought the issue to a head. Harris had turned state's evidence and implicated a white man, Luther Verrill, as a coperpetrator, but then he recanted and claimed to have acted alone. A statewide uproar followed when Verrill was acquit-

42. Chamberlain won 51,314 votes to the Democrat's 39,033 and the temperance candidate's 4,735. Barton, "Chamberlain: Governor of Maine," 81.
43. *Maine*, 384.

ted; Harris was an ignorant freedman who was pitied by many. Chamberlain threatened to actually order his execution if the legislature did not clarify the law, which legislators, of course, preferred not to do. So Chamberlain ordered the execution. It was bungled, Harris died a slow death by strangulation, and Chamberlain was excoriated by all sides.[44] Though Chamberlain was always a popular figure, Maine's voters often deemed him ineffective as a political leader.

Even so, Chamberlain's administration was not without accomplishment, such as some useful development of Maine's resources and the development of an agricultural academy that was the precursor to the University of Maine at Orono. Both political parties wanted him to run for a fifth term. The public continued to adore him and encouraged him to seek a fifth term or run for the U.S. Senate. After refusing to appoint himself to finish William P. Fessenden's Senate term — and so place himself in a strong position to run for reelection as a popular incumbent — he launched a halfhearted senatorial campaign against his appointee, the powerful Lot M. Morrill, in 1870, pending the seating of the state legislature and the end of Fessenden's term in 1871. However, his failure to cultivate, or even ally with, the state party leadership consistently blocked any hopes he might have had of a seat in the Senate.

Chamberlain moved into a different form of leadership at Bowdoin, which will be discussed below. But Lot Morrill's resignation from the Senate in 1876 to become secretary of the treasury during the last year of Grant's administration drew Chamberlain back into the maelstrom of his senatorial ambitions. He pushed for the governor's appointment to fill out Morrill's term, but party boss Rep. James G. Blaine got the nod.

His disdain for the party's leadership caused him to exult in Rutherford B. Hayes's decision to link himself with the independent wing of the Republican Party and bring men like Carl Schurz into power. As he wrote Hayes, "the prestige of personal despotism in politics is broken, and . . . the true relations of the several branches of the government are in a fair way to be restored. Honest men will take courage, & will stand together, and stand by you, in this reconciliation & regeneration of the Country."[45] Civil service reform looked like a real possibility, and southern home rule (which northern intellectuals supported, hungering for sectional reconciliation and an end to the corruption endemic in Radical Reconstruction) was promised. Chamberlain believed that in spite of Hayes's unpopularity with the Maine Republican

44. See Barton, "Chamberlain: Governor of Maine," 55–66.
45. 19 Jan. 1878 to Hayes.

leadership, the national party was purified and would offer him high office. Again he found disappointment, though he did enjoy a trip to Europe as a commissioner on education.

Chamberlain's correspondence suggests that he brought on his frustration and disappointment by deeply desiring high office while steadfastly refusing to play partisan politics or openly ask for a role and risk rejection. One particular political event did offer him a rare reprieve from civilian drudgery, a rare moment to shine again. In January 1880, Maine faced an election crisis that threatened to touch off civil war. Though the complicated and dramatic politics of the 1879 election "count-out" crisis demands more space than can be given here, a brief description follows.[46] Maine's constitution required gubernatorial candidates to win by a majority at the polls; a mere plurality would be resolved in the new legislature. In 1878, incumbent Republican Selden Connor won 44 percent to Democrat Alonzo Garcelòn's 22 percent and Greenbacker John Smith's 34 percent. Thrown into the legislature, the Democrats and Greenbackers combined as "fusionists" to elect Garcelon.

The following year the scene was similar. In the September 1879 election, Republican Daniel Davis won 49 percent to the unwelcome incumbent's 15 percent and the Greenbackers' 34 percent, but the Republicans won a large enough majority in the legislature to ensure Davis's victory there. To block the Republican majority from electing Davis, Governor Garcelon's executive council took action. Responding to accusations of vote tampering, it set out on a campaign of its own administrative tampering, using technicalities to strategically void ("count-out") whole towns' election rolls in order to elect a fusionist legislature.

With armed bands and popular outrage centering on Augusta, Governor Garcelon called Chamberlain in to protect the state's institutions as commanding general of the state militia. Chamberlain faced what he called "another Round Top," and he reveled in it.[47] Death threats mounted; both parties excoriated him in the press; both parties tried to bribe him with the offer of Hannibal Hamlin's soon-to-be-open Senate seat. Chamberlain staved off disorder until the Maine Supreme Judicial Court could identify the legitimately elected legislators and government could continue.

The public proclaimed Chamberlain savior of the state's constitutional government and encouraged him to run for the Senate. Again his ambition surged, but it was yet another halfhearted campaign in which he refused to

46. For more on this fascinating episode, see Pullen; Graham, "Month of Madness"; and Chamberlain Association of America, *Joshua Lawrence Chamberlain Supplement*.
47. 15 Jan. 1880 to Fannie.

really extend himself and risk rejection, hoping that the office would seek the man. Even so, it may have been futile because this time the party sought to bury him for his treacherous refusal to support them during the crisis (even though his impartial handling of the crisis had allowed them to take power legitimately). Crestfallen, Chamberlain looked to the new and exciting world of business. It was a risky chance for wealth, fame, and service.

Following his eventual resignation from Bowdoin, business would have been a natural option, considering that politics was no longer a possibility (though he did seek an ambassadorship during Arthur's presidency), and offers of college presidencies or professorships no longer appealed to him. The power of Chamberlain's name made him a commodity for letterheads and fund-raising. Over the next several years, he became the president or senior officer of numerous New York companies, mostly railroads and technological development concerns such as the Kinetic Power Company, which made improved urban transit engines, and of Florida development companies, thinking that the climate would improve his health. He was president of the Homosassa Company, the Kinetic Power Company, the Mutual Town & Bond Company, the Ocala and Silver Springs Company, and the Lillian Mining Company; he was vice president of the Florida West Coast Improvement Company and the Silver Springs, Ocala and Gulf Railroad; and his list of titles ran on. His involvement in each company varied. Because he was active in so many ventures, several of which were interconnected, it is difficult to gauge his exact activity in each. For some he only raised seed investment, whereas he actually operated some of his Florida ventures.[48]

Lecturing, veterans' meetings and reunions, and his health prevented Chamberlain from giving his full attention to even one company for any length of time. His Florida ventures may have received more of his attention when he was there due to the state's isolation. Though business leadership might have more closely paralleled his military leadership than anything he had yet tried, it does not appear that he ever fully engaged or understood business. The travel, though a hardship, seems to have pleased him, and New York excited him. Spending time in Florida both fulfilled his old missionary instincts and was good for his health — until a bout of malaria prostrated him. His need to feel a sense of duty or service was powerful, and this did something to satiate it.

Chamberlain's frustration as a civilian leader led him to jump at oppor-

48. His business correspondence is for the most part too mundane for inclusion in this collection. The Frost Papers at Yale and the Pejepscot Historical Society offer a treasure trove for the interested reader.

tunities when war broke out. The first time this happened he was governor of Maine — he offered his services in the Franco-Prussian War![49] More in line with his character was his offer of services for the Spanish-American War: "I cannot but think that my day is not yet over for the service of my Country. You gentlemen in Congress and in the offices of the Government, are in your right places: I desire to be in mine."[50]

As his health and wealth faded toward the end of the century, Chamberlain sought a patronage position. Again politics played its role, and his refusal to engage in a partisan game prevented him from receiving what he — and many others — considered his due. The most important administration post in the state, and therefore the top patronage position, was the collector of customs for the Port of Portland. Party leaders were fully cognizant of Chamberlain's fame, so to keep the office from him wholesale would have been dangerous, but they did not want to give him the top spot.[51] Instead they gave him the number two role, the surveyorship.[52]

With hundreds of Maine's most prominent citizens supporting him for the collectorship, Chamberlain viewed being offered the lesser role as a significant insult.

> What I aspired to, and received the splendid support of a large and powerful portion of our citizens for, was the Collectorship. . . . It is concerned not only with the collections of the customs; but it represents the party in power; it represents the Government in its authority and dignity: it represents the President among the people . . . . It has been thought promotion even for Governors. I am free to say I thought myself equal to these things. The Surveyorship has nothing of this character or history about it. It is essentially an obscure office, tending to keep one out of notice, as well as out of responsibility.[53]

Adding to the pain was the knowledge that he needed the easy job, and he needed the money. Disappointed by the role and physically weakened by his wounds, Chamberlain reveled in one aspect of the post: it allowed him to focus on Civil War history and his memories of successful leadership.

49. 20 July 1870 to King Wilhelm.
50. 22 Apr. 1898 to Frye.
51. See, for example, 20 Nov. 1899 to Hale.
52. Pullen describes the duties of the surveyor at 152–55.
53. 26 Dec. 1899 to Richards.

In 1862, Chamberlain announced that he would never again return to academia. "Let me say no danger and no hardship ever makes me wish to get back to that college life again. I can't breathe when I think of those last two years. Why I would spend my whole life in campaigning it, rather than endure that again."[54] Even though teaching was merely a fallback in 1865, and even though he often pronounced himself profoundly bored and frustrated by it, education would always remain a fundamental part and passion of Chamberlain's life, and he had the great good fortune to be involved in the dramatic years of educational reform of the second half of the nineteenth century.

Chamberlain held myriad academic posts. He was an educator in the regular sense as a professor of Rhetoric and Oratory, and chair of Modern Languages before the war, chair of Rhetoric and Oratory until becoming governor, and Edward Little Professor of Mental and Moral Philosophy and professor of Political Science and Public Law afterward. During his time at Bowdoin, he somehow managed to teach nearly every course there as well as to devise a few new offerings of his own. As an administrator, he served as interim president of Bowdoin in 1865 until he became governor and as president of Bowdoin from 1871 to 1883; he remained a trustee until his death. He also presided over the Stimson Institute for Artist-Artisans in the early 1890s. In addition, he was a member of numerous scholarly organizations in fields ranging from religion and philosophy to political science and Egyptology.

His was not a prolific career in terms of scholarly publication, but, then again, his was an unusual career. He did have several published articles and addresses to his credit on a multiplicity of topics including philosophy ("The Two Souls"), political theory ("American Ideals"; "Society and Societies"; "Sovereignty and Sacrifice in Political Society"; "Ruling Powers in History"), law ("The Law and Right of Property"), Maine history ("Maine, Her Place in History"; "DeMonts and Acadia"; "Maine," in *Encyclopaedia Britannica*, 9th ed.), and education (his inaugural address, "The New Education"; the introduction to *Universities and Their Sons*, a series that he also edited; his 1879 report to the State Department on education in Europe). He also presided over *New England Magazine* and *The American Sentinel: A Patriotic Illustrated Monthly*.[55] His career *was* prolific when it came to Civil War history, and his appeal as an orator and writer must have been at least partially due to the fact that he was a scholar.

54. 10 Oct. 1862 to Fannie, in Chamberlain, *Through Blood and Fire*, 23–25.
55. Pullen, 114.

Though modern liberal arts education has its roots in the German-inspired seminar system developed at universities such as Johns Hopkins and the University of Chicago after Chamberlain's retirement from academe, these roots could only take hold following a series of foundational steps. The most important of these was the secularization of the academy. From this, many other changes might follow.

As the influence of the clergy waned in postwar America, so too did it wane at Bowdoin. When Chamberlain was first hired in the 1850s, Bowdoin was a rigorously Congregationalist college. By the early 1870s, it had eased its sectarian connections to the extent that Chamberlain wished to make clear the "fact [that] there is no College—which is a Christian College at all—that is so little sectarian as Bowdoin."[56] Sectarian strife certainly existed, but this was the strife of changing times.[57]

Part and parcel with secularization was a broadening in the purposes of a college education. Before the war, colleges and universities prepared students for careers in the ministry, the law, the military, medicine, politics, or academia. After the war, the proportion of students drawn to the pulpit and other traditional disciplines plummeted as occupations such as business and engineering became highly regarded career options. Faced with financial troubles and this shift in career focus, Bowdoin was desperate for new leadership.

This presented Chamberlain with a fantastic opportunity. Prior to the Civil War, he had been hounded as a radical for his pedagogical theories;[58]

56. 21 Jan. 1873 to Stephen Coburn. Also see 19 Sept. 1876 letters to Mason and Wheeler for discussions of the growing secularization of Bowdoin. Bowdoin did not become officially secular until 1908.

57. See, for example, 9 Oct. 1872 to Henry B. Smith.

58. As a professor in the broad, multisubject department of Rhetoric and Oratory, he had had ample opportunity to experiment in his own classes. Word of his microreforms reached the faculty at large, however, and they pushed him out of his beloved department into the narrower field of Modern Languages. Chamberlain would not budge, however, so the college bribed him to accept by offering him tenure, the department chair, the highest pay grade, and a European sabbatical. It was a battle that severely diminished Chamberlain's contentment in academia. See Mar. 1861? to Sae, UMO.

Legend has it that the sabbatical was offered in an attempt to prevent Chamberlain from going to war. The evidence suggests, however, that Chamberlain had already accepted the chair of Modern Languages, with its inducements, by early 1861. In March 1861, Chamberlain complained to his brother Thomas about his "double work" (teaching and department administration), and in June, Americus Fuller reported to Oliver O. Howard that Chamberlain had told him that he intended to wait until the short war was over to take his sabbatical. 4 Mar. 1861 to Thomas Chamberlain, BSC; 15 June 1861, Fuller to Howard,

now he was positively encouraged to be a strident reformer. This was an extraordinary chance to develop his theories. In an 1859 letter to Professor Nehemiah Cleaveland, he explained and defended his educational philosophy.[59] Chamberlain argued that a "College course" should offer a "liberal education—not a special or professional one." It should not purport to give a "*finished* education," but should give a "general outline . . . involving such acquaintance with all the departments of knowledge and culture . . . as shall give some insight into the . . . powers by which thought passes into life." In being introduced to "each of the great fields of study," a student may "experience himself a little in all." Within this framework, the role of Chamberlain's Department of Rhetoric and Oratory would be to nurture analytic thinking and self-expression to help give "growth and grace and vigor to the mind." For "what every man most cherishes and most sensitively regards . . . is the expression of himself—the outward manifestation of the thoughts and feelings which are most real, most characteristic, most sacred to him." The goal should be, he thought, to "let a man come out . . . till we see what manner of plant he is: then, when he can bear it without bleeding to death, nip, prune, check by degrees till you begin to see the glorious form growing out before you into the shape and symmetry God meant for it."

To accomplish this, professors needed to change the way they interacted with students. He did not find the usual routine—"themes written, faithfully corrected, returned, and burned"—effective, so he devised a system "for the sake of 'getting at' the student's mind (and heart too, for he has one) and . . . securing the practical use and application of the suggestions." Juniors would spend a fortnight every term with him, individually, editing their themes into real papers. Then students would make their traditional oral presentations, "thus returning to the old practice of 'original declamations,' which is a valuable exercise." (It certainly had been for him.)

Chamberlain had tried to employ this pedagogy in his own courses. One of these was a popular senior elective on the history of English language and literature. His syllabus began with a detailed study of the historical origins of the language and then proceeded to cover the great authors, poets, and orators of the language, medieval and modern. When students ran into confusion

---

BSC. Confusion arises because Chamberlain used his sabbatical as his means of joining the Army of the Potomac in 1862 when the faculty refused to grant him leave to go to war. They feared having to find and train a new scholar—and the conservative Congregationalists feared that the college president would hire someone they found distasteful.

59. 14 Oct. 1859 to Nehemiah Cleaveland, BSC.

over such things as "manners and customs now obsolete," they performed independent research and presented historical papers to the class. He worked with each student closely to "get at" his mind.

Now Chamberlain could employ his theory freely and openly. For instance, he outlined a new approach to teaching political philosophy. His plan was to "begin, after the general college course has given the student some knowledge of ancient & medieval history, & take up the history of the development of Society, Government & Constitutional liberty then Political Ethics, or the abstract principles involved in political society, & finally Constitutional Law, Jurisprudence, Political Economy, & Social Science."[60] He spurred the interest in political science at the college and introduced new electives.

As ever, the Civil War had its influence. The growth of industry during and after the Civil War and its importance in winning the war gave new prestige to business, science, and engineering. Agricultural academies such as the one Chamberlain helped develop as governor appeared on the landscape. He opened new departments, introducing new courses in science and engineering. He created a two-year Masters program in Letters, Science, and Philosophy. He set up a coeducational summer school course in science; in his inaugural address, he had even hinted at generally admitting women.[61] In the process, he doubled the size of the faculty. Chamberlain's correspondence shows that, like the presidents of other prominent universities, he devoted an increasing proportion of his time to fund-raising to open and maintain the expensive new departments.[62] He created Bowdoin's first endowment and built Memorial Hall.

As part of the broadening of collegiate education, Chamberlain relaxed social discipline. He stripped the faculty of much of their social policing roles and chose to treat his students "like gentlemen," holding "a man's word of honor as better than foreign testimony."[63] He eased the social code, which he believed to be overly strict, including its policy of making "good behavior" a prerequisite for candidacy for honors.[64]

60. 29 Feb. 1878 to Samuel H. Blake, PHS.

61. Chamberlain, "The New Education."

62. For illustration, his 1873 fund-raising goals were: $100,000 for the general fund, an endowed presidency at $50,000, half a dozen endowed professorships at $30,000 each, one or more dormitories at $25,000 each, with rent to accrue to the college, and the establishment of a scientific department for $250,000. See 24 Mar. 1873 to John Pike, PHS.

63. Chamberlain quoted in Hatch, *History of Bowdoin College*, 131. A liar, however, was "rotten at heart and good for nothing."

64. Calhoun, *A Small College in Maine*, 191; Trulock, 342–43.

Another vestige of the Civil War was a lingering belief that the North had been unprepared for conflict and that this had led to slaughter through incompetence. This militated toward advanced preparation for future conflict, so students were to be trained in engineering and science. And Chamberlain thought that all young men should have at least a rudimentary knowledge of military science, so he instituted a program to teach military science and tactics.[65]

The reaction to the "drill," as it was known, was somewhat predictable. At first, the boys enjoyed playing soldier, but when it became a routine they found it an annoying waste of time and money. They resented having their college turned into a military academy. Complaints mounted until the junior class finally refused to participate; the two lower classes joined in the rebellion.

It was an ugly moment at Bowdoin. Chamberlain felt personally snubbed. What may have saddened him most was a discovery that his students did not share his martial definition of manhood. Perhaps he thought his effort to develop students' independence and self-expression had backfired on him. In strict military style, he expelled all the rebels—a full three-quarters of the student body—and threw the college into a terrible crisis.[66] In the end, all but three of the rebels were readmitted upon swearing an oath to the college. The drill lived on as an elective until its demise from lack of enrollment a couple of years later. Ironically, it was ahead of its time. In the 1890s, drills founded under GAR's auspices became popular nationwide and were the progenitors of modern ROTC programs.[67]

The drill rebellion was the end of Chamberlain's honeymoon as president. His authority had been questioned, and the depression of 1873 slowed the flow of donations, threatening the existence of the new departments. Science and engineering students feared that Bowdoin would close the new programs, so they began to preemptively transfer to the Massachusetts Institute of Technology and similar schools, as did some faculty. Chamberlain had to watch his cherished engineering and science departments wither and die. Though he had been given a mandate for change, there had been too much change too fast, and as funding slowed, the boards of trustees and overseers and the faculty turned reactionary. Sectarian politics returned to haunt him. In addition, since most of Maine's most prominent men were Bowdoin alumni, the clois-

65. See 16 Sept. 1872 Regulations for the Interior Police and Discipline of the Bowdoin Cadets.
66. See 28 May 1874 to the fathers of the drill rebels.
67. McConnell, *Glorious Contentment*, 199, 230–32.

ter did not protect Chamberlain from his foes in state politics.[68] His two prior attempts to step down had been rebuffed, but the enmity he had engendered and his poor health led the college boards to accept Chamberlain's resignation from the presidency in 1883. As he warned Bowdoin professor Henry Johnson, "however pleasant and useful the life of a College Professor may be, that of a President, in I may say any of our common or best New England colleges even, is about the most thankless wearing and wasteful life that can be undertaken."[69]

Throughout his life, Chamberlain's relationship with Bowdoin was one of intense caring. Chamberlain was almost everything an alumnus could be: holder of bachelor's, master's, and honorary doctorate degrees; instructor, professor of nearly every subject, chair of departments and holder of endowed chairs; overseer; trustee; president of the alumni society; and president. The students worshiped him, and he loved them back. Stories abound of them meeting him at the depot, of swarming him at his gate, of constantly paying calls on Fannie and him, of joining them for holidays.[70] He loved and cherished the college, yet academic politics were always distasteful to him, and the failure of his reforms to hold during his tenure saddened him — but he could still joyously celebrate his successor William DeWitt Hyde's success in seeing through the lasting birth of the modern Bowdoin during Hyde's long years of patient guidance.

In addition to his continuing activities at Bowdoin and his continuing historical writing and lecturing, Chamberlain made one last stab at educational administration in the 1890s. As Chamberlain's frolics with business speculation in New York and Florida faded with their hopes of riches, he was well placed for a new adventure. Around this time, several robber barons-turned-philanthropists were founding vocational schools for ambitious urban working-class youth. A variation on this theme was Jonathan Stimson's Institute of Industrial Arts. Stimson's avant-garde art school sought to introduce new techniques for art education, such as favoring live models to the traditional plaster casts. The *New York Times* called it "the most vital American Art School and by all odds the best in this country."[71] Chamberlain began a fund-raising campaign, and he tried to open a summer school extension at Domhegan, his seaside summer home near Brunswick at Simpson Point.[72]

68. Sen. William Frye merged the two currents of sentiment against Chamberlain by accusing him of taking the college Unitarian. Smith, *Fanny and Joshua*, 260.

69. 6 Feb. 1884 to Johnson.

70. See, for example, 28 Nov. 1877 to the student body.

71. Quoted in Wallace, *Soul of the Lion*, 279.

72. See 14 Feb. and 23 Mar. 1893 to Andrew Carnegie.

Unfortunately his poor health kept him bedridden and the depression of 1893 dried up funds. He returned to Maine and turned again to the Civil War.

CHAMBERLAIN AND HIS FAMILY

Many of the letters in this volume are to Chamberlain's family, and, indeed, family was of paramount importance to him. His wife Fannie, his daughter Grace, his sister Sae, and his mother received the bulk of his epistolary attentions. His mother and sister lived in his native Brewer, which he was not able to visit as often as he would have liked. There is relatively little correspondence with his son Wyllys or his brother Tom, both of whom appear to have been disappointments to him, but he did see more of them than the others because they worked with him at times. He doted on his daughter Grace and her children. It is unclear whether he managed to modulate his favoritism for her and how this may have affected Wyllys, who never married or became truly independent.

Chamberlain's relationship with Fannie was often a difficult one.[73] They were both romantics and tended toward jealousy. The war profoundly altered their marriage. Chamberlain may have resented the fact that Fannie did not support his decision to go to war and did not participate in soldiers' aid societies while he was gone. Meanwhile, his prolonged absences regenerated her native independent streak, and she began traveling, visiting her family often, sometimes without leaving word as to her whereabouts. The war was his defining moment, and she had not been part of it—a disconnect that would affect both of them. Their marriage was forever changed.

Whereas before the war Fannie had been able to rein in Chamberlain's missionary impulses and keep him in Brunswick, now his fields of opportunity were broad. It is not clear how attentive Chamberlain was to Fannie's thoughts on his ambition and career decisions, but his acceptance of jobs in Augusta, New York, Florida, and Portland suggest either that her opinions did not carry a definitive weight with him or that she was content with their geographical separation.

The hardest period of the marriage was his return from the war and his tenure as governor. Their seventeen-month-old daughter Gertrude had died in April 1865. The Chamberlain who reentered Fannie's life was different from the man whom she had married. He was a proud man with a "habit of command" that may have been difficult to endure, a returned soldier who was confused, bored, and in desperate need of surgery. His Petersburg injuries must have affected his sexual capabilities. As he wrote in 1866, "There is not

73. See Smith, *Fanny and Joshua*; and Smith, "The Reconstruction of Home."

much left in me to love. I feel that too well. The last six months experience has finished me."[74] They considered divorce and attempted separation.[75] In the end, they settled for de facto separation: Fannie refused to go to Augusta with him. As the years passed, they continued to spend considerable amounts of time apart, with Chamberlain absent even on some holidays[76] and Fannie often in Boston. To these separations we owe the quantity of his letters to Fannie. He also found escape in his continuing Civil War life, reuniting with the "boys" and reminiscing in speech or print.

Though their marriage was often a difficult one, these difficulties should not be overstated. There are reminders in the correspondence that the tenderness they had once felt during their courtship returned in recurrent waves. From Florida, he wrote: "How I should delight to have you here . . . I am sure we should find worthy & profitable themes for converse, & even nature would please me better by having more *body* in it then!"[77] Eager to impress during the count-out crisis, he wrote from Augusta: "I wish you were here to see & hear."[78] In Fannie's last years, as her blindness set in and her health failed, there was a poignant rapprochement. To ease his grief after Fannie's death in 1905, Chamberlain would once again find solace in Civil War memory.

74. 23 Mar. 1866 to Fannie.
75. 20 Nov. 1868 to Fannie.
76. 27 Nov. 1877 to his mother, UMO.
77. 20 Oct. 1885 to Fannie.
78. 9 Jan. 1880 to Fannie.

For biographies of Chamberlain, the best place to start is Alice Rains Trulock's *In the Hands of Providence: Joshua L. Chamberlain and the American Civil War* (Chapel Hill: University of North Carolina Press, 1992). For the period covered in this volume, see the late John J. Pullen's *Joshua Chamberlain: A Hero's Life and Legacy* (Mechanicsburg, Pa.: Stackpole Books, 1999), an insightful work by the man who is most responsible for reviving modern interest in Chamberlain. The most detailed and freshest biography is Diane Monroe Smith's comprehensive *Fanny and Joshua: The Enigmatic Lives of Frances Caroline Adams and Joshua Lawrence Chamberlain* (Gettysburg: Thomas Publications, 1999). Willard M. Wallace's *Soul of the Lion* (1960; reprint, Gettysburg: Stan Clark Military Books, 1991), the first full-length biography and the only one by an academic, is still highly valuable. The dual biographies by Mark Perry, *Conceived in Liberty: Joshua Chamberlain, William Oates, and the American Civil War* (New York: Viking, 1997), and Michael Golay, *To Gettysburg and Beyond: The Parallel Lives of Joshua Lawrence Chamberlain and Edward Porter Alexander* (New York: Crown, 1994), are interesting, entertaining, but less insightful and less well researched than the above works. Thomas Desjardin has written a short biography, *Joshua L. Chamberlain* (Gettysburg: Greystone Communications, 1999).

There is an increasing body of studies of specific aspects of Chamberlain's life. George Thomas Barton's "Joshua L. Chamberlain: Governor of Maine, 1867 to 1871" (M.A. thesis, University of Maine at Orono, 1975) comprehensively covers Chamberlain's gubernatorial career. Jennifer L. Smith analyzes Chamberlain and Fannie's marriage in her chapter "The Reconstruction of Home: The Civil War and the Marriage of Lawrence and Fannie Chamberlain," in Carol Bleser and Lesley J. Gordon, eds., *Intimate Strategies of the Civil War: Military Commanders and Their Wives* (New York: Oxford University Press, 2001), 157–76. Chamberlain's role in the fascinating "count-out" crisis is featured in John Graham's "Month of Madness: Maine's Brush with Civil War" (M.A. thesis, University of New Hampshire, 1981).

The enthusiastic celebration of Chamberlain's legend, which has often lacked moderation, has brought on a backlash, including writings such as Glenn LaFantasie's "Joshua Chamberlain and the American Dream," in Gabor S. Boritt, ed., *The Gettysburg Nobody Knows* (New York: Oxford University

Press, 1997), 31–55; and Edward G. Longacre's spotty *Joshua Chamberlain: The Soldier and the Man* (New York: DaCapo, 1999). Controversies from Chamberlain's day have been revisited in William B. Styple's edition of Holman Melcher's writings, *With a Flash of His Sword: The Writings of Major Holman S. Melcher 20th Maine Infantry* (Kearny, N.J.: Belle Grove Publishing, 1994); Abbott Spear et al.'s edition of *The Civil War Recollections of General Ellis Spear* (Orono: University of Maine Press, 1997); and LaFantasie's soon to be published book-length study of the battle for the battle of Little Round Top.

Chamberlain wrote and spoke prolifically. Many of his most interesting works have been reprinted in recent years. There are several reprint editions of his one monograph, *The Passing of the Armies: An Account of the Final Campaign of the Army of the Potomac Based Upon Personal Reminiscences of the Fifth Army Corps* (1915). Stan Clark has published a collection of several of his lectures and papers entitled *"Bayonet! Forward": My Civil War Reminiscences* (Gettysburg: Stan Clark Military Books, 1994). Many of Chamberlain's Civil War letters are reprinted in Mark Nesbitt's edition, *Through Blood and Fire: Selected Civil War Papers of Major General Joshua Chamberlain* (Mechanicsburg, Pa.: Stackpole Books, 1996).

Excellent works that have insightful sections addressing the immediate return from war include Charles Royster's *The Destructive War: William Tecumseh Sherman, Stonewall Jackson, and the Americans* (New York: Alfred A. Knopf, 1991); Phillip S. Paludan's *A People's Contest: The Union and Civil War 1861–1865*, 2nd ed. (Lawrence: University Press of Kansas, 1996); and Stuart McConnell's *Glorious Contentment: The Grand Army of the Republic, 1865–1900* (Chapel Hill: University of North Carolina Press, 1992). For a discussion on academic research on readjustment to civilian life following the war, consider James Marten's article "Exempt from the Ordinary Rules of Life: Researching Postwar Adjustment Problems of Union Veterans," *Civil War History* 47 (March 2001): 57–70. For studies of Union veterans in the postwar years, consider Stuart McConnell's *Glorious Contentment*; Mary R. Dearing's *Veterans in Politics: The Story of the GAR* (Baton Rouge: Louisiana State University Press, 1952); and Cecilia Elizabeth O'Leary's *To Die For: The Paradox of American Patriotism* (Princeton, N.J.: Princeton University Press, 1999).

For Civil War historical memory, David W. Blight's *Race and Reunion: The Civil War in American History* (Cambridge, Mass.: Belknap Press, 2001) is the definitive work. More narrowly focused studies include Thomas J. Pressly's *Americans Interpret Their Civil War* (Princeton, N.J.: Princeton University Press, 1954. Reprint, New York, Free Press, 1962); Nina Silber's *The Romance of Reunion: Northerners and the South, 1865–1900* (Chapel Hill: University of North Carolina Press, 1993); the articles in James M. McPherson and William

J. Cooper Jr., eds., *Writing the Civil War: The Quest to Understand* (Columbia: University of South Carolina Press, 1998); Merrill D. Peterson's *Lincoln in American Memory* (New York: Oxford University Press, 1994); and Edmund Wilson's *Patriotic Gore: Studies in the Literature of the American Civil War* (London: Andre Deutsche, 1962).

The best studies of postwar politics tend to be focused on specific periods. For Reconstruction, the ambitious should tackle Eric Foner's *Reconstruction: America's Unfinished Revolution, 1863–1877* (New York: Harper & Row, 1988); the weaker at heart (or tighter of schedule) should read his abridgement, *A Short History of Reconstruction: 1863–1877* (Harper & Row, 1990). For studies of the Gilded Age, see Morton Keller's *Affairs of State: Public Life in Late 19th Century America* (Cambridge: Harvard University Press, Belknap Press, 1977); and the essays edited by Charles Calhoun in *The Gilded Age: Essays on the Origins of Modern America* (Wilmington, Del.: Scholarly Resource Books, 1996). For the history of the liberal wing of the Republican party, see John G. Sproat's *"The Best Men": Liberal Reformers in the Gilded Age* (New York: Oxford University Press, 1968); or, for a more positive analysis, David M. Tucker's *Mugwumps: Public Moralists of the Gilded Age* (Columbia: University of Missouri Press, 1998). On the civil service reform movements and Rutherford B. Hayes, see Ari Hoogenboom's *Outlawing the Spoils: A History of the Civil Service Reform Movement* (Urbana: University of Illinois Press, 1961); *The Presidency of Rutherford B. Hayes* (Lawrence: University Press of Kansas, 1988); and *Rutherford B. Hayes: Warrior and President* (Lawrence: University Press of Kansas, 1995). Irwin Unger's *The Greenback Era: A Social and Political History of American Finance, 1865–1879* (Princeton, N.J.: Princeton University Press, 1964), is an excellent study of the Greenback movement before it reached Maine. C. Vann Woodward's works are the best look at the Hayes-Tilden dispute and the development of race and racial politics in postwar America. See *Reunion and Reaction* (Boston: Little, Brown, 1951); and *The Strange Career of Jim Crow* (New York: Oxford University Press, 2001). For the first decades of the twentieth century, see John M. Cooper Jr.'s *Pivotal Decades: The United States, 1900–1920* (New York: Norton, 1990).

An excellent modern work on the history of Maine is to be found in Richard W. Judd, Edwin A. Churchill, and Joel W. Eastman, eds., *Maine: The Pine Tree State from Prehistory to the Present* (Orono: University of Maine Press, 1995). The best and most modern history of Bowdoin is Charles C. Calhoun's *A Small College in Maine* (Brunswick, Maine: Bowdoin College Press, 1993), published for the college's bicentennial.

The letters selected for this volume are presented chronologically. Undated letters are included in the Appendix. Each letter is presented by its recipient's name:

TO ULYSSES S. GRANT

If the name is unknown or there is confusion regarding the recipient's identity, it is presented as:

TO UNKNOWN RECIPIENT

TO ULYSSES S. GRANT?

Footnote annotations provide contextual information about the individuals and events mentioned in Chamberlain's text. Individuals mentioned three or more times have short biographies in the Dramatis Personae section rather than in the footnotes. Most household staff are not given biographies, but they are included in the First Name, Nickname, and Household Staff Register.

The letters are presented in their entirety, lightly edited only when absolutely necessary. Editorial additions of missing words or parts of words are presented in brackets. Misspellings have been corrected with brackets. Punctuation has largely been regularized, with a number of stray periods and commas deleted. Chamberlain made frequent use of underscores where modern text would use em dashes; the modern form has been chosen for ease of reading. Where Chamberlain made corrections to his text, his corrections have been adopted except where his substantive word choice offers insights into his thoughts. Clearly gratuitous letters or repeated words have been deleted. Words crossed out in manuscripts are ~~canceled~~. Tentative reconstructions include a question mark inside the brackets. Hopelessly illegible words are denoted as [ill.] or [*n* words ill.]. Dates that are not included in the manuscript are presented in brackets. Contemporary spellings are respected. Abbreviated words are explained in the Glossary. For his handwritten letters, though Chamberlain did not use ampersands, I have used them because no other typed character catches the feeling of his cursive sign for "and."

Chamberlain's extant letters are often copies or first drafts. Drafts are obvious from the number of errors. Chamberlain sometimes used a typewriter. His clarity in keyboarding can be indicative of his health, although this is somewhat muddied by our knowledge that his typewriter at the Custom House was of much higher quality than his personal one.[1] The frequency of typographical errors is indicative of typed letters.

Holding libraries for the letters are identified in brackets at the end of each letter. Abbreviations for the libraries and frequently cited books can be found in the next section. The sesquicentennial *General Catalogue of Bowdoin College*[2] is so frequently used that citation of it is simply implied in annotations of Bowdoin graduates, faculty, and officers.

1. Bette Copeland, "Interview between Mrs. Bette Copeland and Mrs. Catherine Smith on General Chamberlain (During the 1970s)," <http://www.curtislibrary.com/pejepscot/csmith.htm> (11 Mar. 1999).

2. Wilder, *General Catalogue of Bowdoin College*.

Baillie	Laureen Baillie, ed., *American Biographical Index* (New York: K. G. Saur, 1993). This microfiche index contains entries from several biographical dictionaries. Unless otherwise specified, numbers identify specific fiche.
Bayonet	Joshua L. Chamberlain, *"Bayonet! Forward": My Civil War Reminiscences*, ed. Stan Clark (Gettysburg: Stan Clark Military Books, 1994).
BBGB	Roger D. Hunt and Jack R. Brown, *Brevet Brigadier Generals in Blue* (Gaithersburg, Md.: Olde Soldier Books, 1990).
BHL	George S. Morris Collection, Bentley Historical Library, University of Michigan, Ann Arbor, Michigan.
Bib Maine	Joseph Williamson, *A Bibliography of the State of Maine, 1821–1888*, 2 vols. (1896. Reprint, Augusta: Maine State Library, 1985).
BioDictGovr	Robert Sobel and John Raimo, eds., *Biographical Dictionary of the Governors of the United States*, 7 vols. (Westport, Conn.: Meckler Books, 1978).
BOL *(nnn/nn)*	*Encyclopaedia Britannica Online*. <http://www.eb.com:180/cgi-bin/g?DocF=micro/*nnn*/*nn*.html> 1998.
BSC	Joshua L. Chamberlain Papers, Oliver Otis Howard Papers, Henry Johnson Papers, George J. Mitchell Department of Special Collections & Archives, Hawthorne-Longfellow Library, Bowdoin College, Brunswick, Maine.
CC	Special Collections, Colby College, Waterville, Maine.
CMU	Oliver W. Norton Papers, Clarke Historical Library, Central Michigan University, Mount Pleasant, Mich.
CWD	Mark M. Boatner III, *The Civil War Dictionary*, Rev. ed. (New York: Vintage, 1991).
CWLM	MOLLUS Collection, Civil War Library and Museum, Philadelphia, Pa.
DAB	Allen Johnson, ed., *Dictionary of American Biography*, 30 vols. (New York: Charles Scribner's Sons, 1928).

DU   Rare Book, Manuscript, and Special Collections Library, Duke University, Durham, N.C.

EB   *The New Encyclopaedia Britannica*, 15th ed., 29 vols. (Chicago: Encyclopaedia Britannica, 1997).

GB   Ezra J. Warner, *Generals in Blue: Lives of the Union Commanders* (1964. Reprint, Baton Rouge: Louisiana State University Press, 1992).

GC   Special Collections, Musselman Library, Gettysburg College.

GNMP   William C. Oates Correspondence Scrapbook; 20th Maine Volunteer Infantry File, Gettysburg National Military Park, Gettysburg, Pa.

HL   John P. Nicholson Papers, Huntington Library, San Marino, Calif.

HU   Houghton Library, Harvard University, Cambridge, Mass.

LC   Joshua L. Chamberlain Collection, Manuscripts and Archives, Library of Congress, Washington, D.C.

MAG   Executive Committee of the Maine Gettysburg Commission, *Maine at Gettysburg: Report of the Maine Commissioners* (1898. Reprint, Gettysburg: Stan Clark Military Books, 1994).

Maine   Richard W. Judd, Edwin A. Churchill, and Joel W. Eastman, eds., *Maine: The Pine Tree State from Prehistory to the Present* (Orono: University of Maine Press, 1995).

MHS   Joshua L. Chamberlain Papers, Maine Historical Society Library, Portland, Maine.

MSA   Miscellaneous correspondence, Maine State Archives, Augusta, Maine.

MSL *(n)*   Maine State Law and Legislative Reference Library, <http://www.state.me.us/legis/lawlib/*n*.htm> 11 Mar. 1999. Without *(n)*, the information was kindly provided by Lynn Randall at the Library.

MSM   Maine State Museum, Augusta, Maine.

NA   Joshua L. Chamberlain Military Pension Records, Military Personnel File, and Military Service Records, National Archives, Washington, D.C.

NH   John B. Bachelder Papers, New Hampshire Historical Society Library, Concord, N.H.

OED   J. A. Simpson and E. S. C. Weiner, *Oxford English Dictionary*, 2nd ed. 20 vols. (New York: Oxford University Press, 1989).

OR   U.S. War Department, *The War of the Rebellion: A Compilation of the Official Records of the Union and*

	Confederate Armies, 128 vols. (Washington, D.C.: Government Printing Office, 1880–1901).
PHS	Joshua L. Chamberlain Collection; Joshua L. Chamberlain Letterbook, Pejepscot Historical Society, Brunswick, Maine.
Pullen	John J. Pullen, *Joshua Chamberlain: A Hero's Life and Legacy* (Mechanicsburg, Pa.: Stackpole Books, 1999).
RBH	Rutherford B. Hayes Presidential Papers, Rutherford B. Hayes Presidential Center, Fremont, Ohio.
SL	Chamberlain-Adams Family Papers, Schlesinger Library, Radcliffe Institute for Advanced Study, Harvard University, Cambridge, Mass.
Trulock	Alice Rains Trulock, *In the Hands of Providence: Joshua L. Chamberlain and the American Civil War* (Chapel Hill: University of North Carolina Press, 1992).
UMO	Chamberlain Family Papers; Fannie Hardy Eckstorm Papers, Special Collections Department, Raymond H. Fogler Library, University of Maine at Orono, Orono, Maine.
WhoAm	*Who Was Who in America*, Vol. 1: 1897–1942 (Chicago: Marquis Who's Who, 1981).
WhoAmH	*Who Was Who in America*, Historical Vol., 1607–1896 (Chicago: Marquis Who's Who, 1981).
YUL	Civil War Papers; Frost Family Papers; Lounsbury Papers; A. S. Webb Papers, Manuscripts and Archives, Yale University Library, New Haven, Conn.

THE GRAND OLD MAN OF MAINE

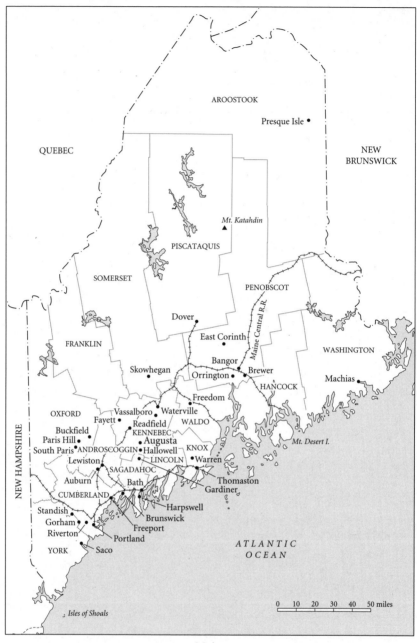

AROOSTOOK

Presque Isle •

QUEBEC

NEW
BRUNSWICK

Mt. Katahdin ▲

PISCATAQUIS

SOMERSET

PENOBSCOT

FRANKLIN

Dover •

East Corinth •

Bangor •

WASHINGTON

Skowhegan •

Orrington • • Brewer

HANCOCK

Machias •

Freedom •

Vassalboro • • Waterville

OXFORD

Fayett •

Readfield •

WALDO

Buckfield •

KENNEBEC

Paris Hill •

Augusta •

Mt. Desert I.

South Paris • ANDROSCOGGIN

Hallowell •

KNOX

NEW HAMPSHIRE

Lewiston •

LINCOLN • Warren

Auburn •

SAGADAHOC

Thomaston

CUMBERLAND

Bath •

Gardiner •

Standish •

Harpswell •

Gorham •

Brunswick

Riverton •

Freeport

ATLANTIC
OCEAN

Portland

YORK

Saco •

0   10   20   30   40   50 miles

Isles of Shoals

Maine

CHAPTER 1 ❧ THE RETURN OF THE HERO

With war's end, northern veterans slowly returned to their homes, where a long readjustment awaited them. Prematurely mustered-out, Chamberlain returned to a marriage strained by unwelcomed separation, the recent death of his seventeen-month-old daughter Gertrude Loraine, an urgent need for surgery, and few immediate job prospects. Despite his pledge never to return to his old life in academia,[1] little beyond garrison duty presented itself to Chamberlain on his arrival in Brunswick. It was some balm to be able to return to his beloved department of Rhetoric and Oratory rather than Modern Languages, but the interim presidency of Bowdoin College was also thrust upon him.

The public forum offered a welcome outlet from the harsh readjustment. Chamberlain reveled in the public's encouragement to dwell upon the war. He delivered numerous public speeches and gathered materials for a history of the V Corps. Soon the politicians would stop neglecting the state's great war hero and retrieve him from limbo.

❧ TO CHARLETON T. LEWIS

Head Quarters 1st Div. 5th A.C.
June 26 1865.

My dear friend,[2]

Your very kind letter was duly received. I thank you for the interest you take in my success. Indeed it is only for my friends sake that I care particularly for what we call success. For myself alone I have no especial ambition; but my friends are very dear.

No good to me becomes a joy till they share it.

So I have to thank you yet again in as much as you lay me under new obligations.

I was fully expecting to see you & Mrs Lewis[3] at our Grand Re-

---

1. 10 Oct. 1862 to Fannie; and 12 Feb. 1865 to his father, both in Chamberlain, *Through Blood and Fire*, 23–25, 147–48.

2. Charleton T. Lewis (1834–1904), a prominent New York lawyer, academic, and prison activist. DAB, 11:208.

3. The former Nancy McKeen (d. 1883) of Brunswick, granddaughter of Bowdoin president Joseph McKeen. Ibid.

view.[4] You could have made yourselves comfortable in my Camp, for a while, at least. But now I must look to some other time, and possibly, *place* for the pleasure of meeting you.

The old Army of the Potomac is gone.

Very few of the familiar faces are seen among us now. In a few days we expect to be broken up by explicit orders,[5] and distributed & assigned in widely different places. I have no idea of my own fate. To my great astonishment I learn that Genl. Meade has sent my name to the President with a few others— all by far my seniors & superiors—for the full appointment of Major General.[6] I appreciate the compliment at this time when the effort is to get rid of officers.

But my feeling now is that I shall return very soon to my private life. Soldiering in time of peace is almost as much against my grain as being a peace man in time of war.

My wounds too, I find, now that I am called on no longer to bear up against them, are very troublesome, and I need to be fitted at home a while.

Apropos of that, I thank you, from my heart for your friendly invitation to visit you on my return. If possible I shall not deny myself that pleasure. It is now my expectation to go North in the course of a month.

With many thanks for your kindnesses to my brother who always remembers them, and with warmest gratitude for the good thoughts & words of yourself & Mrs Lewis.

I am
very truly
your friend
J. L. Chamberlain

[YUL]

4. The final review of the Union armies took place in Washington on 23 and 24 May 1865.

5. It was officially disbanded two days later.

6. He received it, but it was withdrawn to be given to Sen. William Pitt Fessenden's son, as Maine's quota of major generals was full. See ca. 18 May 1893 to Webb. Chamberlain was, however, brevetted to the rank for his leadership at the Quaker Road, 29 Mar. 1865.

Head Quarters 1st Brigade 3d Div. Provis. Corps.[7]

July 6 1865.

Brig. Genl. L. Thomas
Adj't Genl U.S.A.[8]
General.

I have the honor to request that I be relieved from service in the field, & ordered to some duty in the State of Maine, or in Washington City, or wherever my services can be of most benefit, until I no longer require surgical treatment for my wounds.

I have been in the field for nearly three years, having had only four days leave of absence in that time, except when sent away for medical treatment.

I was very severely wounded last summer before Petersburg, & returned to duty before I was able to mount my horse, and since that time have been twice wounded in action, without leaving the field. The state of my wounds is such as to require care and attention. I shall be obliged to undergo a severe surgical operation as soon as the heat of summer is past.

I do not apply for a leave of absence, because I believe I am able to render full service, if placed in a favorable position, until the operation referred to can be performed; and I am unwilling to be off duty without absolute necessity.

There are at present two General officers in my [command] besides myself—Bvt Brig. Genl Gregory,[9] & Bvt. Brig Genl Root[10]—, so that I trust the interests of the service will allow my request to be received with favor.

I have the honor to be
Very respectfully
Your obdt. servant
J. L. Chamberlain
Bvt. Maj. Genl

7. In the shrunken place of the Army of the Potomac, the War Department created a "Provisional Corps," formed of one division from each of the II, V, and VI Corps, under VI Corps commander H. G. Wright. Chamberlain commanded one brigade. Confidential rumors spread that the new corps would be used by Sheridan to assist the French in their withdrawal from Mexico, but political circumstances made the plan obsolete and with it the Provisional Corps, which was disbanded in mid-July. Trulock, 329–30.

8. Lorenzo Thomas (1804–75). GB, 502–3; DAB, 18:441–42.

9. Edgar M. Gregory (d. 1871) of New York, promoted to major general for Five Forks. Baillie, 654.

10. Adrian Rowe Root (d. 1899) of New York. CWD, 708.

Comdg 1st Brig. 3d Div. Prov. Corps
late 1st Div. 5th Corps, A.P.

〰 TO ULYSSES S. GRANT

Portland, July 31st, 1865.

Lieut. General Grant,

General:

Learning that you are to be in town tomorrow, I respectfully solicit the honor of your presence at a reunion of the Graduates of Bowdoin College who have been in the war on Wednesday Evening.[11]

This would occupy but a small portion of your time, and would be exceedingly gratifying to all our citizens and especially to those on whose behalf I make this request.[12]

Very respectfully

Your obedient servant,

(Signed) Joshua L. Chamberlain,

Bvt Major General.

〰 TO LOT M. MORRILL

Brunswick Nov. 1st 1865

My dear Senator;

You were kind enough to mention to me when I had the pleasure of seeing you last in Washington, that the Secretary of War[13] had voluntarily spoken of me with the assurance that I should receive the appointment of Major General, for which I had been several times particularly recommended by my Superior officers, one of the last acts of Genl Meade, while the Army was about breaking up, being to send my name up for that promotion. Genl. Meade said there could be no possible doubt that, from the manner in which the recommendation went up, I should receive the appointment.

Instead of that however, I was suddenly mustered out of service while my

11. Trulock (330) misinterprets this letter as an invitation to Bowdoin's commencement. Grant had already accepted Oliver Otis Howard's invitation to commencement. The "reunion of Graduates" was an evening event to follow commencement. McFeely, *Yankee Stepfather*, 109; McFeely, *Grant*, 236; Calhoun, *A Small College in Maine*, 178–79.

12. Grant accepted the invitation, visited the Chamberlains, and attended the reunion. Trulock, 330.

13. Edwin M. Stanton.

wounds were in so bad a state that a surgical operation could not with safety be performed which is necessary to my even partial restoration to soundness.[14] If I had been off duty & lying about in Hospital or on sick leave I should not have been thus mustered out. I had no particular wish to be retained in service as a burden to the Government. But I did not exactly like the manner in which I received my congé, nor shall I ever feel that it was either kind or just.

Others have since been appointed to every grade, whose military record I am not afraid to have brought into comparison with my own.

I had neglected to secure any particular "influence" to keep myself "before the people" or the Government, and when the army in the Field broke up, I was suddenly unknown.

There are now but three or four weeks during which it is possible to receive such an appt. as I speak of, as I see they are still made. I write to ask you if this now empty honor, which I still esteem as a proper completion of my record, can be conferred on me. I am ashamed to be obliged to solicit as a favor what I have earned at the point of my sword. But as things are I do not hesitate to do so. I should not expect to hold this appointment at all, and should probably resign it at once after acceptance.

If this cannot be done; though I shall not easily be persuaded of this when I see it done almost daily—then I shall of course be obliged to put up with the indignity, and content myself with thankfulness that I have passed through this war at least without dishonor, that my life has been preserved through almost mortal wounds, and that the blood I have shed for my country has not been in vain.[15]

Very respectfully
your obdt. servt.
J. L. Chamberlain

[MHS]

14. Chamberlain was accidentally mustered out with the first group of generals, perhaps an inadvertent result of his above letter to Lorenzo Thomas. Besides wounding his pride, this deprived Chamberlain of confirmation of his recommended promotions to both brevet and full major general (perhaps opening the procedural window for withdrawing the promotion) and funds for needed surgery.

15. Pressured by Gov. Samuel Cony (1811–70), Sen. Morrill and the state delegation petitioned the president to restore Chamberlain to active service. With Grant's approval, Stanton restored his rank and changed his date of discharge to 15 January 1866. Trulock, 331–33, 510 n. 99.

Brunswick, Me. Nov. 10, 1865

Col. Jno. B. Bachelder[16]

My dear Sir,

Your circular respecting your visit to Gettysburg only reached me the last of the month, or I certainly should have joined you there. I happen to be possessed of some information or rather *knowledge*—in regard to the operations on the left, which I desire you to have to benefit you in your work.

Your map is a marvel, & I am relying upon it for a great deal of information.[17]

But the accounts of Col. [Joseph W.] Fishers brigade in connection with the holding or capture of Round Top which appear in the "History of the Reserves" and elsewhere I can assure you are without any warrant.[18]

I do not think Col. F. himself will claim that they are correct. If he does it will be no difficult matter to refresh his memory, & modify his judgment.

The accounts which now are studiously kept current by somebody do great injustice to a most gallant & deserving officer, who sealed his earnest devotion to his country's cause with his blood in the terrible days of "Spotsylvania." I am prepared to give you the *real* truth & very nearly the whole truth as to that affair. I was an eye & ear witness to the whole operation.

I suppose you wrote to Brig. Genl. Rice of New York,[19] [to get] at the truth, and as I have much material for your work, shall be glad to aid you in placing it at your disposal.

I sent a "circular" to your Boston address some time ago, which will inform you that I am engaged again in writing an official History of the 5th Army Corps.

I shall be glad to hear from you again at any time.

16. John B. Bachelder (d. 1894), a New Hampshire journalist and artist who became perhaps the foremost historian of the Battle of Gettysburg during his lifetime. Bachelder, *John Bachelder's History.*

17. On the creation of Bachelder's detailed map and history, see Blight, *Race and Reunion,* 187–89.

18. Joseph W. Fisher (1814–1900) of Pennsylvania commanded the 3rd Brigade, 3rd Division, V Corps, at Gettysburg. He claimed full credit for taking Big Round Top. BBGB, 203; CWD, 280; Smith, *Fanny and Joshua,* 278. Also see 25 Jan. 1884 to Nicholson(?).

19. New York's two Generals Rice (James and Samuel) died from wounds during the war. The North's other Generals Rice (Americus Vespucius, Samuel's brother Elliott, and Edmund) ultimately settled elsewhere, but one might have lived in New York at the time. CWD, 695–96; GB, 398–402; *WhoAm,* 1026.

J. L. Chamberlain
Bvt. Major General

[NH]

〜TO JOHN L. HODSDON

Brunswick Nov 11th 1865

My dear Genl,

Your favor in regard to my military history shall be forwarded in a day or two. I have never had time to make this out, as already requested from the Adjt. Genls office in Washington. But I will do so for *you*, at once.

John S. C. Abbott[20] has written me several times for my history to make an Article in his Series of "Heroic Men"![21] I couldn't have the face to do that, & can scarcely bring myself to brag to you of my own doings. I will send such official mentions as have been made in regard to my career with a little elucidation [three words ill.]

By the way I am at work too in History Making — or writing rather.

I enclose a circular.[22] There have been four Maine Regts. in the 5 Corps — gallant men all — and I want to get your Report for 64. in order to follow up the changes in their organization &c.

I have your 62 & 63.

The Regts are

{2[d] Infty

{6[th] do[23]

{20[th] do

{1[st] Sharpshooters

Very truly

your friend & servt

J. L. Chamberlain

Genl.

John L Hodsdon

Adjt. Genl.

[GSA]

20. John Stevens Cabot Abbott (1805–77), Bowdoin graduate and friend of Fannie's family, was a Congregational minister and prolific writer of popular, didactic histories and biographies. *DAB*, 1:22–23. His Civil War works are reviewed in Pressly, *Americans Interpret Their Civil War*, 37–39.

21. Abbott's series "Heroic Deeds of Heroic Men" ran in *Harper's Magazine* during the 1860s.

22. See below.

23. Abbreviation meaning "ditto."

Washington, D.C., Aug., 1865

General;

A History of the *Fifth Army Corps* is in course of preparation under the direction of a Committee of its late officers. It is designed to make this work authentic, impartial, and thorough; a record not merely of the Corps as a body, but also of the several organizations which have shared its vicissitudes, as well as of individuals who have borne a conspicuous part in its career.

Besides official reports and other ordinary data, more particular details — incidents of special services — personal reminiscences — would contribute to the interest and value of the work. Unusual facilities have already been afforded for collecting the requisite material; but it is desired to omit no means of securing every possible advantage in setting forth this Record of the old Fifth Corps.

Communications in furtherance of this design are respectfully solicited of you at your earliest convenience, and may be addressed to Brev't. Maj.-Gen. J. L. Chamberlain, Brunswick, Maine.
Genl John L. Hodsdon
Adj't. Genl of Maine.

[MSA]

TO JOHN L. HODSDON

Brunswick Nov 29 1865

Dear General.

I have to acknowledge the favor of your statement sent a few days since, and thank you for the abstract which you promise. It will be invaluable to me.

I want to be able to give the whole number Maine furnished to [the] National Service. All that we lost & if possible the number of the wounded.

I hope to see you for a moment soon.

truly yours

J. L. Chamberlain
Gen J. L. Hodsdon
Augusta

[MSA]

TO JOHN L. HODSDON

Brunswick Dec. 6th 1865

My dear Genl.

I have thought it best to send you a Book in which a *portion* of the papers I referred to are copied, & other authentic slips of paper pasted. — There are incidents of a merely formal nature which it would not be proper for me either to write myself, [or] (by that convenient process to which a flaming modesty so often resorts) to procure others to write for me. Time will bring them out. I prefer that my reputation should *improve* upon a better knowledge of fact rather than diminish.

I observe that in your Report I am spoken of as absent from my Regt. occasionally without any remark to the effect that I was at that time comdg. the Brigade. Indeed I am classed merely with Col Gilmore[24] as "absent," when in fact I was at that time leading my Brigade into Battle, & had my horse shot there. It is perhaps my own fault. I did not communicate to you every little point I happened to gain. You will see by reference to the book that the service at Gettysburg was of far more account than has been made of it here in Maine.

These things I know are mere inadvertencies. I wonder there are not more in a work so complicated & difficult as yours.

I refer to me this further. You observe I was recommended in April for a full Major Genl. That recommendation was favorably endorsed by Meade & Grant, & like others before only dropped at Washington. When the army broke up Meade & Grant made a particular nomination which I was assured would be favorably acted on. But the gentlemen at Washington had other views.[25]

The request has shown.

Very truly

your friend & servt.

J. L. Chamberlain

I never had but *four days* proper "leave of absence" during my service. At all other times when not in the field I had been ordered away for treatment of wounds &c, or on duty by order of the War Dept. I never shirked field duty. J. L. C.

[MSA]

24. Charles D. Gilmore succeeded to command of the 20th Maine when Chamberlain was shot at Petersburg. He never led it in a major battle. Pullen, *The Twentieth Maine*, 4, 239.

25. See 1 Nov. 1865 to Morrill.

Brunswick
March 20th, 1866.

Dear Fanny

I forgot to enclose the pictures of the children, as you desired me to do.

Please find them enclosed. This is the only one of Wyllys which is left. I have the original picture now, & can have more made if you desire it.

We are all at home now, & every thing is going on perfectly well. We have a girl in training. She promises well. Colored slightly, & married rather more. So she will be steady we think. Her husband is going to sea as cook or steward of a ship in a few days. All your things are under lock & key. Though our "Julia" is *perfectly [finest]*! I went to Vassalboro last evening & lecture in Augusta Saturday next.

I have been invited to give the opening address at the great Fair for the benefit of Soldier's orphans & widows to be held in Portland next month. Mrs Sampson also is frantic to have me speak for her cause — her "orphans home" too, & as the same address will do for both, I am going to try it.[26]

My flag came at last, all right.[27]

What do you think of the Dunlap house?[28] I have seen Mrs D. & she will sell I think for $4000. If I can sell for $2500, do you think it best to buy? Or would you give $5000 for Prof Upham's house?[29] We must get away from this I think, at any rate, or else buy the lot in front.

Coladnus[30] is off, & we have some order & decency now. Mother is much gratified at your remembrance of her by this donation to the Maine Miss [Esq?] Society, making her a life member. The political plots continue.[31]

26. Sarah Sampson (d. 1907), a former Civil War nurse, was an advocate for Maine veterans and their widows and orphans. Smith, *Fanny and Joshua*, 149, 179, 300–301, 333. Chamberlain's speech is printed in the *Eastern Argus* (25 Apr. 1866) and partially reprinted in Smith at 180–81.

27. Perhaps the 20th Maine battle flag that Chamberlain kept in his study.

28. There was a Dunlap house at 1 Federal Street and one on Maine Street facing Dunlap Street. American Association of University Women, "From the Falls to the Bay," 4.

29. Thomas Cogswell Upham (see Dramatis Personae) lived in the large white house at 179 Park Row (now the Elks Lodge) designed by Samuel Melcher III, architect of most of Bowdoin's early buildings and many of Brunswick's finest houses. Ibid., 2; *DAB*, 17:517–21.

30. One of Chamberlain's pets. He had many named after historical leaders, such as Tiberius Caesar, Henry of Navarre, and, of course, his horse Charlemagne. Smith surmises that Coladnus was a child's pronunciation of Collatinus Tarquinius, a Roman consul. Smith, *Fanny and Joshua*, 370 n. 8.

31. In the spring of 1866, Republican leaders courted Chamberlain to run for governor. These letters to Fannie show his outward reluctance to give in to their suit.

I hope you are having a good time & recd the check I sent for $100. Let me know when you want more.

I go to Dover N.H. on the 30th & may then take a run to Boston. I cannot make the Providence visit then or I would ask you to join me there. If you want to reach me on the 30th my address is care [of] Prof Thomas Tash[32] Dover N.H. Do make John some little present, & get something for Salome Field[33] again if you can. I wish you would make Sae a little present. I will send more money if you wish, to do it with.

Please give my warmest regards to the good people at Mrs Darling's & Mr Leland's.[34]

Daisy comes in & sends her love & says she hopes you are having a good time. Wyllys is growing finely & is a most noble boy. I like him v[ery] much. Aunty's[35] children are coming in May. I shall be glad to see the poor little things.

Tom speaks of John's attentions to you. Dont fail to acknowledge them. You are rather cool you know, about things.

Lawrence.

[MHS]

〜 TO FANNIE

Brunswick March 23^d 1866

Dear Fanny,

I suppose you never got the draft I sent for $100. as you say nothing of it. Please let me know at once that I may give notice at the bank.

I go to Augusta to day, and shall be in Dover N.H. next Friday. I can meet you in Boston after that, if you wish; or can even go for you to New York if you much prefer. Please let me hear. I think it quite likely I shall go to Boston at all events.

The children are well and happy. Wyllys goes to school to Miss Susie Melcher[36] & is much interested in the matter. Daisy's new dress is much praised by [every] body. She needed it v[er]y much.

As for me I have a bad cold, & have had rather a hard time of late. & many services & duties in prospect which prevent my resting much. The address at the opening of the orphans' Fair in Portland *falls* to me, am[on]g other things.

32. Thomas Tash (1819–89), Bowdoin graduate and overseer, was principal of Dover High School.

33. Unidentified.

34. Both are unidentified.

35. This aunt is unidentified. The "Aunty" or "Cousin D" who frequently cared for Chamberlain's children, is Deborah G. Folsom (d. 1866), but she never married.

36. Melcher is otherwise unidentified.

Frances "Fannie" Adams Chamberlain, 1865 (Courtesy of Bowdoin College)

Have as good a time as you can while you are away. There is not much left in me to love. I feel that too well. The last six months experience has finished me.

L.

[SL]

〰 TO FANNIE

Brunswick April 7th 1866

Dear Fanny

To tell you the whole truth we are getting rather lonesome without you. I am not going to revoke my permission for you to stay as long as you want to, but you will be very welcome when you do return. I feel a little babyish perhaps now because I am quite near being sick with a cold & influenza. I have had a suspicion of diphtheria but do not fear it now. Lottie Packard[37] is very dangerously sick with it. The children are well and stout as two little "bulls of Bashan." We are having very pleasant times, only you are wanting to our complete happiness.

I am full of cares and labors, & not being well for some few days past, have grown rather thin and pale. I am summoned to Augusta today by a dispatch—to see some of the gentlemen interested in having me nominated I suppose—I hate these things. I have been making Prof. Upham an offer for his house,[38] but I doubt if he takes it. How would you like to live in that house? Would you rather have ours put upon the "White" lot & the roof raised?[39] I prefer this place to Prof Upham's.—Captain Boutelle got a verdict against the teacher who whipped his boy. Carrie (Newman) Merrill[40] has a boy, & is not do[in]g very well, I hear.

Dr Dana & Dr Tewksbury of Portland,[41] your father & [Salome] Field[42] took tea with me last ev[enin]g. Let me hear from you soon.

37. Perhaps a member of Bowdoin professor Alpheus S. Packard Sr.'s family.

38. See 20 Mar. 1866 to Fannie.

39. In 1867, the Chamberlains moved their single-story Potter Street house to a lot facing onto Main (later "Maine") Street, across from the First Parish Church and the college. Certain that he would remain in Brunswick with a suitable salary, Chamberlain raised the house and built a new first floor under it in 1871. Trulock, 347–48.

40. Caroline Merrill, daughter of Bowdoin professor Samuel Newman and wife of shipmaster Leonard Merrill.

41. Probably Dr. Israel T. Dana, professor at the Medical School of Maine, and Dr. Samuel H. Tewksbury (1819–80), a Medical School of Maine graduate practicing medicine in Portland.

42. See 20 Mar. 1866 to Fannie.

With much love
Lawrence.

[SL]

≈ TO CHARLES H. SMITH

Brunswick, April 12, 1866.

My Dear General:[43]

I share with you most fully the solicitude expressed in regard to the pres-ent posture of our national affairs.[44] One year ago this very day, you and I were present at the surrender of the proudest army of the rebellion, when the banners of secession went down before the broad ensign of the Republic, the prestige of the national government was vindicated and restored, its power made invincible by victory, its authority acknowledged and the greatness of its future in the triumph of republican principles apparently as well assured as if it had been vouchsafed by a Divine decree.

But in the twelve month that has since elapsed, that promise has not seemed in a fair way to be fulfilled: that progress has not been made which we had so fondly hoped, in realizing the benefits of our dear-bought victory. We fought for that "more perfect Union," which the Constitution announced as its object: we fought for the completion of those great ideas which inspired the souls of our fathers; for the extirpation of that fatal Calhoun heresy which would destroy the very existence of our nationality, and in defence of a united and indivisible country. We fought for liberty, in its widest and best sense. In the language of an early Congress, "the rights for which we contended were the rights of human nature."

If we fail in attaining these ends then was the blood of our heroes poured out in vain, and our treasure worse than wasted. If this war has taught any one lesson more imperatively than another, it is that we should be slow to trust those who have been disloyal to the country, and that we should do justice to those who stood by her in the hour of danger and trial. It seems little else

43. Charles Henry Smith (1827–1902), a cavalry brigade commander who briefly served Machias in the state senate before taking a regular Army colonelcy in July. *DAB*, 17:249–50.

44. Chamberlain had not yet publicly touched upon the issue of Reconstruction, so some Republican newspapers suspected that he did not adequately side with the Radicals against Johnson. This open letter was Chamberlain's response; it succeeded. The *Bangor Daily Whig and Courier* reported that Chamberlain's views were "squarely upon the most advanced grounds occupied by Union men of the north." Barton, "Chamberlain: Governor of Maine," 10–12.

than absolute madness to hasten to reinvest with political power the very men who precipitated upon us the horrors of civil war; and little less than cowardly wickedness to turn our backs upon the millions whose humble and despised condition did not prevent them from befriending the country when it was most in need of friends, and yet this very madness and this very wickedness constitute to-day the main features of a policy urged upon the country with the full strength of the party which, pretending to oppose the war during its continuance, did in reality encourage and prolong it by a moral support, and now that the war is ended in a triumph so contrary to their predictions, seeks to rob that victory of the fruits we had supposed secure.

I know not how politicians may view this question. I am not in political circles; I have no hand in making platforms; nor am I skilled in party or partisan devices. But I know with unerring instinct how the soldiers who fought the battles feel upon this issue, and how the great popular heart of Maine, always patriotic, always true, will respond. The soldiers and the people as one, will demand that their mutual efforts and mutual sacrifices shall not have been in vain. They demand that traitors, whether pardoned or unpardoned, shall not be clothed with political power; they demand that no injurious discrimination shall be made against any men who participated in the struggle for the preservation of the country. Political power must be impartially enjoyed by loyal men, and by loyal men alone.

All must unite in demanding security for the future. Indemnity for the past we cannot obtain. The treasure expended in the war is gone, and the grave cannot give back its dead. We must not repine over the past, nor be disheartened by the inevitable; but we shall be most recreant to duty if we fail to provide wisely for the future. Secession must be repudiated with its debts and claims, its spirit and principle. We must have guaranties good and sufficient, against any future attempt to destroy this government, whether in the exercise of a pretended right by open war, or by the more artful and insidious assaults against the principles on which this nation was founded. These are points we cannot yield without danger and dishonor; and when the Southern States shall have complied with these conditions in good faith, they will be in a position to ask association and fellowship with the loyal commonwealths of the country which they deserted with such violence and scorn. Until that time, in my judgment, it is wise to hold them in strict probation.

In demanding these guarantees we ask nothing humiliating to those States — nothing which is not dictated by justice, and most accordant with honor. To day we have the power to enforce these guaranties, if we are resolute and true; if we falter and fail, we show ourselves less potent in council than on the

bloody deck and field. The high position taken by our congressional delegation on all the great questions growing out of the rebellion, should be, and I
make no doubt will be, fully supported by the loyal men of Maine, who in the
darkest hour of the conflict did not forsake their cause. We must not lower
this standard an inch, nor suffer it to be lowered by others. The struggle may
still be severe but we have faith in the right; for the hearts of the people are
in this cause, and they will stand by the flag till there shall be no doubt of its
integrity or its meaning — till triumphant through blood and tears, it shall be
recognized as the emblem of what is dear to humanity and right before God.

Pardon the length of this letter to which the importance of the topics
suggested has led me, and believe me as ever, your friend and servant,

J. L. Chamberlain

To Maj.-Gen. C. H. Smith, Eastport.

[*Kennebec Journal*, 27 April 1866]

TO DAVID A. BUEHLER

Brunswick Maine
August 21st 1866

D. A. Buehler,
Secretary Trustees,
Penna. Coll.[45]
Gettysburg, Pa.
My dear Sir;

I have to acknowledge the receipt of your favor of the 9th inst. informing
me of the vote of the Trustees of Pennsylvania College conferring upon me
the honorary degree of LL.D.

In accepting most gratefully this token of regard, allow me to say that I
deem it a distinguished honor to be thus connected with a College so highly
esteemed throughout the land for its sound scholarship, its evangelical spirit,
and its effective patriotism. And it is with peculiar pleasure that I associate
this honor with a place not only endeared to me by the most thrilling memories, but one forever precious in the heart of the Country, and immortal in
History.

With the assurance of my warm interest in your college, and with sincere
thanks to the Trustees and Officers thereof,

45. David A. Buehler was a lawyer, journalist, and trustee of Pennsylvania College
(later renamed Gettysburg College). Thanks to Christine Ameduri at Musselman Library
for this information.

I am

With high regard,

your obdt. servt.

J. L. Chamberlain

[GC]

⊗ TO THE TRUSTEES AND OVERSEERS OF BOWDOIN COLLEGE

Bowdoin College Nov 13th 1866.

To The Honorable

Board of Trustees & Overseers

Gentlemen;

The College Government finding itself without a President at the beginning of the year, I accepted, at the urgent solicitation of the Faculty, the charge of the Executive duties of that chair for the time being.

These duties were undertaken with extreme reluctance, as the care of my Professorship already gave me scarcely any time for responsibilities of a more public nature which came upon me at that time. An arrangement was made with Instructor Packard[46] to take the Sophomore class in Rhetoric: but the duties still left in my hands made my labors in College very severe. In consequence of this I have been obliged to employ a Private Secretary, and also to forego opportunities for Lectures and other public engagements which would have been of great pecuniary advantage.

I therefore respectfully ask that during the time of my service in this capacity my whole pay be made at least equal to the rate of the salary of President as now provided.[47]

I have the honor to be

very respectfully

Your obdt. Servt.

J. L. Chamberlain

[BSC]

46. Probably Alpheus Spring Packard Jr. (1839–1905), Bowdoin graduate and instructor and son of the elder Professor Packard. He became America's preeminent entomologist while teaching at Brown. *DAB*, 14:126–27.

47. $400 per quarter, as during his later presidency. Bowdoin complied with the request.

In executive government Chamberlain saw an opportunity for leadership more akin to his military role than anything else offered in civilian life. He defeated a prominent Democrat by a landslide in the September 1866 elections and went on to win two more terms by larger majorities and then an unprecedented fourth term. His policy was marked by a desire to modernize Maine's economy and a diligent effort to responsibly enforce the law. Administrative drudge work, the political crises brought on by the temperance movement and the capital sentencing of Clifton Harris, and Republican Party leaders' resentment of his impartial leadership style rid Chamberlain of the illusion that he would find the satisfaction of military leadership in state politics. Meanwhile, his marriage suffered. Still, the public adored him, and he was strongly encouraged to run for another term as governor — by both the Republican *and* the Democratic parties.

🌊 TO THE TRUSTEES AND OVERSEERS OF BOWDOIN COLLEGE

Bowdoin College
Brunswick, Me.
Nov. 13th 1866.

To The Honorable
Board of Trustees & Overseers,
Gentlemen;
   Having been called to discharge of a Public duty which may be considered incompatible with the continuance of my present relations to the College, I beg leave respectfully to tender my resignation of the Chair of Rhetoric and Oratory, — to take effect December 31st 1866, or at such other time as shall be agreeable to your honorable Bodies.
   I am,
   Gentlemen,
   With high respect and esteem
   Your obedient servant
   J. L. Chamberlain
   Prof. Rhet. & Orat.

[BSC]

State of Maine
Executive Department
Augusta, February 5th 1867.

To the Honorable
William H. Seward
Secretary of State:
Sir:—

I beg to avail myself of the opportunities afforded through your Department to ascertain whether there are to be found any heirs, or relatives, of George J. Summatt who appears from the rolls of our Army to have been born in Naumburg, Germany.[1]

He was formerly a First Sergeant in the Second Regiment United States Cavalry, and lately Captain in the First Regiment Maine Cavalry, and was killed in battle at Aldie Virginia June 17th 1863.[2]

There is a sum of money to his credit in the Treasury of this State, and it would be an act of justice to place this in the hands of his proper representatives.

I would therefore esteem it a favor if you would allow the officers of your Department in Germany to take such measures as may lead to the discovery of Captain Summatts heirs.

I am with high respect
Your obedient servant.
J. L. Chamberlain.

[PHS]

TO HANNIBAL HAMLIN, JOHN A. POOR, AND A. D. LOCKWOOD

State of Maine
Executive Department, Augusta, May 9, 1867.

Gentlemen:[3]—

I have examined with deep interest the preliminary Report of the Board of Commissioners on the Hydrographic Survey,[4] and assure you of my hearty

1. Administrative matters like this comprise the vast majority of Chamberlain's gubernatorial correspondence.

2. A minor skirmish in the Gettysburg campaign. CWD, 6.

3. Amos D. Lockwood (1811–84), Bowdoin's top private contributor in the 1870s, was a Lewiston manufacturer. For Hamlin and Poor, see Dramatis Personae.

4. In an effort to attract outside investment into Maine, Chamberlain proposed a survey of sources of water power. The legislature appropriated $3,300 to survey the state's southern rivers. Barton, "Chamberlain: Governor of Maine," 28.

approval of the general views therein set forth. The extent of your proposed researches will open a vast field of interesting material, and it is to be regretted that all the results cannot be fully brought within the limits of your final Report. Valuable as this material is, you will agree with me that in its arrangement and presentation for the work now in hand, everything must be strictly subordinated to the leading object of the Resolve, providing for a Hydrographic survey; and tempted as we might well be, to use this opportunity to make known the remarkable physical features and resources of our State, we must constantly bear in mind the practical character of our undertaking, and its evident intent to attract the attention of business men to the facilities of this State for manufactures, and the investment of capital, energy, and enterprize on our hitherto neglected waters.[5]

Our present work therefore from the beginning, should be shaped to that end, and the final Report, while it should undoubtedly be something more than the bald statistics of our water power — its reservoirs, volume and fall and general availability — should still in all that is collateral to the main design, be not different in treatment, style and bulk, from a rigid and well-arranged Digest. In these suggestions I have no doubt you will cordially concur.

I am impressed with the importance of the work now before you, and of the results which will necessarily accumulate under your liberal and energetic labors, and trust that in some form the State may have the benefit of them. She has reason already to congratulate herself on the ability and zeal, with which your Board has entered on its duties.[6]

I am, gentlemen, very truly, your friend and servant,

J. L. Chamberlain

To Hons. John A. Poor, A. D. Lockwood, Hannibal Hamlin, Commissioners of the Hydrographic Survey.

[MHS]

5. Poor had ambitiously proposed to survey sources of building supplies, soil fertility, and manpower, but the legislature's resolve only funded a survey of water power sources. Ibid., 29.

6. The survey located river power sources providing over one million horsepower. In 1868, Chamberlain proudly reported that the survey was in high demand and investment was rising. Ibid., 29–30.

State of Maine
Executive Department
Augusta Nov. 14th 1867.

W. W. Rice Esq.
Warden of State Prison,[7]
Sir:—
I would request you upon receiving convicts under sentence of death to place them in "solitary confinement," and if it is necessary to put them also at "hard labor"—as I am aware the law and the sentence in such cases indicate to help them separate from others who are under sentence of less degree. The reason for this is obvious, and I trust you will so understand my intention as not to take any course with such convicts which would embarrass me or you in the execution of the sentence, or which would produce an injurious effect upon the discipline or feelings of the prisoners generally in case the sentence were executed. It is my intention to take the responsibility of *disposing* of the cases which come under my jurisdiction, and not to shirk my duty and increase the embarrassments of my successors.

This is for your private information and guidance rather than for public notification; but it is proper for you to show this to the Inspectors of the Prison.

Very truly yours
J. L. Chamberlain.

[PHS]

≋ TO SAMUEL CONY

Brunswick Nov 30 1867

Hon Samuel Cony[8]
Augusta
My dear Sir,
When in Washington recently I got the Treasury Dept. to pass upon our war claim account then pending, and in its being allowed I forwarded to the Treasurer of Maine the U.S. Treasurer's draft for the acct. viz $10.682.23 which should properly appear in your accounts.

In response to my inquiries as to the time when the further examination of our claim could be taken up, I received the letter which I enclose. In con-

7. Rice is otherwise unidentified.
8. Chamberlain had appointed the former governor (see 1 Nov. 1865 to Morrill) to press Maine's war claims in Washington.

sideration of this, I think there is no occasion to incur further expenses at present in prosecuting this claim, and as all has been accomplished which any commission can now do, I would suggest that you make up a final Report at the close of the present year.

The State has reason to congratulate itself on the present state of her account with the General Govt. & such a Report would be exceedingly gratifying to our people.

Very truly yours

J L Chamberlain

[BSC]

〰TO JOSEPH H. POLLARD

State of Maine
Executive Department
Augusta Dec 27th 1867.

Joseph H. Pollard.[9]

I have your letter asking for a pardon. It is a manly letter and I like it, only I fear that you cannot stand against temptation. If I were to let you out now without any guaranty of good behavior which I could hold in my hands as security, I should fear that you would fall into bad company and not do yourself or me credit. You are capable of becoming a worthy and useful citizen, and I wish to help you to do so. I want to be able to look after you, and keep a hold on you; not for the purpose of catching you in fault, but of keeping you from fault.

Now you have been a soldier; and a good one, so far as I can learn, and I take more interest in you from that, and am not willing to have any injustice done you, nor to send you out into the world without helping you to break away from evil. Your prison associations have not probably done you much good, and I fear you are even less able than before to lead a good, honest, manly life.

But I like the way you write, and now I want to have you give me your solemn word of honor as a man, which I can keep on file and refer to, that you will leave off, or not return to, bad associations, and will try with all the manhood that is in you to become a good citizen.

Such you may be, and I will help you to do so.

I want to hear from you now as to what you mean and will promise to do.

If I am satisfied you will hear from me again.

9. Pvt. Pollard of the 8th Maine had deserted, been court-martialed, reenlisted, and again deserted.

J. L. Chamberlain
Governor of Maine

≈ TO ADOLPH SUTRO

State of Maine
Executive Department
Augusta June 4th 1868.

Adolph Sutro Esqr[10]
My dear Sir:

I have read with great interest your statements in regard to the Sutro Tunnel to the Comstock lode[11] in the State of Nevada, and am deeply impressed with the facts, arguments and suggestions therein presented.

When we consider the experience of other Countries — of Mexico on the one hand and Germany on the other — we cannot fail to see the immense advantage of an intelligent National encouragement of these great enterprizes which promote the public as well as private good, but are too expensive at the outset for private capital to undertake.

I have no doubt that the construction of the tunnel as you propose would be a measure not only of humanity towards the miners, but of public economy and profit, as I understand it you ask the credit or endorsement of the Government and propose to apply the proceed on completion, to the payment of interest and principal of all guarantees so granted, at or before maturity. This appears to me a proposition which may safely be accepted.

Believing that your enterprize will be a means of opening the rich resources of the Country, and thereby of meeting our present heavy indebtedness, & this in its immediate [two words ill.] remote results contribute to the [ill.] prosperity and honor of the Nation I cannot refrain from expressing my hearty interest of small avail as that may be in the success of the proposition you are now asking Congress to consider.[12]

With high respect
Your obedient servant
Joshua L. Chamberlain

10. Adolph Sutro (1830–98), a Prussian-born Gold Rush mining engineer. *DAB*, 18: 223–24.

11. America's richest deposit of silver. Sutro wanted to ease access to it by digging a tunnel. Ibid.

12. After years of fund-raising in America and Europe, Sutro opened his $6.5 million tunnel in 1869. It proved effective and made Sutro fabulously wealthy. Ibid.

State of Maine
Executive Department
Augusta August 27th 1868

To
Col A. W. Wildes.
Hon S. H. Blake.
Hon. S. G. Corser.
Railroad Commissioners.[13]
Gentlemen;

You have doubtless given attention to the many complaints against the Grand Trunk Railroad, and have taken such action as seemed proper in regard to it. I deem it my duty however to call to your notice the developments which have arisen from the recent accident at South Paris. From what I can learn of that occurrence it would seem to be but a natural result of the habitual condition of the track on that road. I have examined sketches of the present actual state of the track in several places, which I forward to you today. Such a state of things, imperiling life every hour, should not be permitted; and certainly demands the most rigorous measures on the part of the Commissioners. Section 2^d of Chapter 179, Public Laws of 1868 gives you ample powers; and if anything more is required than you feel authorized to do, I will cheerfully share the responsibility with you.

You could not, it is true, stop the train on that rail without serious inconvenience to our people, and damage to the business of Portland; but it may be necessary to resort to that decided measure to awaken the attention of the Company to the public demand and their own duty.

Very truly yours
J. L. Chamberlain

[PHS]

Augusta Nov 20 1868

Dear Fanny,

In the whirl of all this uproar of obloquy now hurled at me by the friends of Harris[14] & the rampant temperance men I find myself assailed by only one thing which distresses me.

13. Samuel H. Blake (1807–87) was a wealthy Bangor lawyer and prominent state politician. *Bib Maine*, 1:145. Wildes and Corser are otherwise unidentified.

14. Clifton Harris, a freedman whose January 1867 rape and murder of two elderly Auburn sisters had set off the capital punishment controversy embroiling Chamberlain.

On arriving here last night sick & worn-out, I had hoped that even if I could have no other care and nursing [I] would at least have that of sleep.

Things have now however come to that pass that I must trouble you by referring again to the suggestion I made to you some time since in regard to your making a confidant of unworthy persons. I have had abundant & concurrent testimony from many—all as much your friends as mine—that you were complaining to everyone who came into the house of my conduct & treatment of you. I have passed that over for a long time not thinking it worthwhile to notice it. When I found that you were still disposed to do this & in the last instance in a direction that would do you more harm than me, I ventured to give you the warning I did some time since. You received it with apparent kindness & I was satisfied. I then referred to it again just before I came away & you spoke in a way that made me nearly happy.

Now last night after I had gone to bed, Mr Johnson came in with a very distressed demeanor & begged me not to be angry with him but he saw such grief & ruin impending that he must tell me. Miss Courlaender[15] it seems is freely telling people that "you told her (& Mrs. Dunning also as well as everybody else) that I abused you beyond endurance—pulling your hair, striking, beating & ot[h]erwise personally maltreating you, & that you were gathering up everything you could find against me to sue for a divorce." Mr Johnson says this is doing immense harm, whether the *fact* is so or not & the bitter enemies who now assail me on public grounds will soon get hold of this & will ruin me. He is in great distress & begs me to do something—what he does not know.

You must be aware that if it were not *you* who were so clearly implicated in this business, I should make quick work of these calumniators. I fear nothing for myself. But you must see that whatever come upon me; comes upon you too with even more effect & for your sake I must again offer the suggestion that you act with wisdom and discretion.

If it is true (as Mr. Johnson seems to think there is a chance of its being) that you are preparing for an action against me, you need not give yourself all this trouble. I should think we had skill enough to adjust the terms of a separation without the wretchedness to all our family which these low people to whom it would seem that you confide your grievances & plans will certainly bring about.

You never take my advice, I am aware. But if you do not *stop this* at once it will end in *hell*.

15. Miss Courlaender was a Brunswick school teacher. Smith, *Fanny and Joshua*, 372 n. 12.

I am sorry to say this to you, when I have so entirely confided in you & have been so reassured of late in this confidence, as my interest in your matters & in your friends must convince you. Of course this has given me a troubled night & I am taking up the duties of the day wholly unfitted for them.

The thing come[s] to this, if you are contemplating any such things as Mr Johnson says — there is a better way to do it. If you are *not*, you must see the gulf of misery to which this confidence with unworthy people tends. You have this advantage of me, that *I* never spoke unkindly of *you* to any person. I shall not now do so to you. But it is a very great trial to me — more than all things else put together — wounds, pains, toils, wrongs & hatred of eager enemies

truly yours,

J. L. Chamberlain

[YUL][16]

🖋 TO HIS MOTHER

Augusta Jan 27 1869

Dear Mother;

I enclose $20 payt. for months board of Arthur,[17] who I hope is well, & not too much trouble to you.

I have not been quite well but am now improving much. There is quite a pressure of cares on me which I bear well. Great issues are sometimes in my hands but I always try to seek wisdom & strength from above.

I received a warm-hearted letter from [Mr.] Wells[18] in which he refers with great interest to a visit he made to you not long since.

Many are bitter on me about capital punishment but it does not disturb me in the least.

I had a very abusive & threatening letter from one "Jo Green" who says my sentiments remind him of the dogmatisms of Joshua the Great — (grandfather I suppose) — who says too that he used to see me as a little good boy playing up by *Murders* — who is the man. He writes from Washington D.C.

The poor fool whomever he thinks he is thinks he can scare me by terrible threats of vengeance. He is mistaken in his man. I do not think I have a particle of fear in me of anything that walks or flies.

I go on in the strength of conscious rectitude & you cant scare me.

Hoping that you and father are well.

16. Perry incorrectly cites this letter as at BSC. Perry, *Conceived in Liberty*, 460.
17. Likely a dog. Chamberlain was fond of Arthuriana. See 27 Jan. 1910 to Zell(?).
18. Wells is unidentified.

I am your loving son.

Lawrence

〰 TO THE MAINE REPUBLICAN NOMINATING COMMITTEE

Brunswick, April 27, 1869.

Gentlemen,—

I have to acknowledge the honor of your communication, in which you invite me to accept again the candidacy for the office of Governor.

After repeated elections to this high honor, the last time by the largest vote ever given by the people of Maine, I had deemed it my duty to relieve them from the embarrassment of further provision for me, by retiring to the privacy from which I was called by the cannon which menaced the life of the Republic. You are pleased however to convey to me in terms so flattering that I dare not appropriate them to myself, but with the testimony of names too potent to be disregarded, the intimation that I may still be of service to the State. You call me in the most sacred names—of service, of duty, of devotion. I hear the summons as the bugle-call to action, and I obey. Those whom I love it is right that I should also serve.

With a spirit chastened by the solemn and sacred memories which bind me to her history, and still strong in the faith of her cause, and exultant in the pride of her name, I shall deem myself honored, by any humble part to which the people of Maine may assign me in her on-coming bright career.

Your friend and servant,

Joshua L. Chamberlain

To Abner Coburn, Dennis L. Milliken, Nathan Dame, Noah Woods, Washington Long, J. P. Morse, George F. Shepley, George L. Beal, and Thomas S. Lang.[19]

["Governor C's Reply," *Kennebec Journal*, 5 May 1869]

19. Milliken (1804–79) of Waterville was a state legislator and member of the governor's council. Dame of Alfred had been Maine state treasurer during the Civil War. Woods (1811–91), a former Gardiner mayor and state legislator, was a railroad executive and attorney. Long is otherwise unidentified. Morse was a state senator from Bath. Gen. Shepley (1819–78) was a former U.S. attorney for Maine who would soon be appointed to the federal bench. Gen. Beal (1825–92) later served as Maine's adjutant general and treasurer. Lang was a state representative from Vassalborough. MSL; MSL (treas); *Biographical Encyclopedia of Maine*; DAB, 17:78–79; GB 26–27.

GOVERNOR OF MAINE { 29

≋ TO LOT M. MORRILL

Brunswick July 7 1869

Hon L. M. Morrill,
President Repub. State Convention
Dear Sir;

I accept the distinguished honor of the renomination as Candidate for Governor tendered me through you by the Republicans of Maine. It is a compliment which I appreciate no less, that the Resolutions of the Convention declare a public policy identical with the line of my life and labors hitherto.[20] It only remains for me to assure you of my earnest faith that the triumph of these liberal and vigorous principles will make our people prosperous and our State great.

Your friend & servant
Joshua L Chamberlain

[BSC]

≋ TO DAVID W. LEWIS

State of Maine
Executive Department
Augusta Dec. 2 1869.

David W. Lewis Esq.[21]
Macon, Ga.
Dear Sir;—

I have before me your favor of the 25th ult, in which you kindly invite me to attend the annual Fair of the Georgia State Agricultural Society at Macon.[22] I regret exceedingly that I shall not at that time be able to leave this State for so long a period as would be required to give myself the pleasure of meeting you.

I cannot however permit this opportunity to pass without assuring you of the deep interest which I feel in your undertaking, and my approbation of the wide and generous efforts [ill.] you are making to increase the interest, the

20. The party's resolutions focused on development of Maine's natural resources and compromised on enforcement of prohibition (leaving the temperance wing unsatisfied). See Barton, "Chamberlain: Governor of Maine," 67–86.

21. David W. Lewis (1815–85), a Georgia planter and cofounder of the Georgia State Agricultural Society, was a former Confederate legislator and future president of the North Georgia Agricultural College. Wakelya, *Biographical Dictionary of the Confederacy*, 284–85.

22. Chamberlain received many invitations to similar conventions and fairs, most focusing on economic development in the South and sectional reconciliation.

significance and the usefulness of the occasion. It is not indeed to be expected that the deep and strong feelings enlisted on the one side and the other in a civil war can be readily soothed into harmony and accord; nor that the momentous results of such a conflict in which the very constitution of Society, the system of social and industrial life, are Shocked and overturned, and in a brief space of time or without great deeds still of patience, self conquest, and earnest endeavor be formed into calm and settled order, and open all the genial courses of prosperity and peace.

But this desired end is to be brought about most effectually by such institutions and efforts as those which now so happily engage your attention. The considerations suggested by your occasion are worthy of the best thoughts and sympathies of every patriot throughout the Land. I cannot but hope it may serve to bring together persons & influences which shall powerfully tend to restore fraternal confidence and enterprise, and overrule and harmonize diverse and even discordant elements for the good of our whole people for the better bond of union and the future prestige of the Nation.

I have the honor to be
With high regard
Your obd't Serv't
Joshua L. Chamberlain.

[PHS]

〰 TO HIS FATHER

Brunswick Dec 17
1869

Dear Father,

I have to thank you for your letter so promptly conveying to me the agreeable intelligence of Sarah's happy deliverance from her perils, and the birth of another daughter of our House.[23] I am glad to hear of your health and hope for the pleasure of a visit from you during the winter. Wyllys is now proposing to go over Friday of next week — Christmas eve — & make you a visit. I am planning my affairs so as to see more of you during the coming summer.

Your aff son
Lawrence
Joshua Chamberlain
Brewer

[BSC]

23. Alice Farrington.

State of Maine
Executive Department
Augusta Dec 31 1869

Dear Fanny,

We are winding up the year, and I write to wish you a Happy New Year. I have been digging away at my Message,[24] here & at home, as the rush on me was more or less. I have had a severe rheumatism, so that I had to invade your little boudoir bed room so as to have a softer bed. I got a mortal cold by it though I had the furnace going a whole day before hand. However I am well enough now except [being] *tired*.

My Message will be long & dull but there is plenty of hard work in it.

I was expecting you almost every evening the last week when I was in Brunswick. You will stop there to get your things I suppose. I have looked out against rains. I shall go home again tomorrow to put the last touch on the message. Half expect to see you there. I came to Augusta Tuesday for good: though if you are in Brunswick I shall go there again Saturday. Let me know if you get this. Draw on me, or *leave* the bill at Stevens House if you find necessa[ry].

Wyllys happy as a king. I saw Rebecca [every] day when at Brunswick.

Very aff.y & anxious to see you again. Your old Guy
Lawrence[25]

[SL]

≈ TO THE MAINE STATE LEGISLATURE

Augusta March 10 1870

To the Senate
and House of Representatives

The Bill entitled "An Act additional to chapter 33 of the Public Laws of 1858 relating to the sale of intoxicating liquors" has been laid before me for approval.[26] Some of its provisions appear to be of so extraordinary a character

24. Chamberlain, *Address of Governor Chamberlain to the Legislature*.

25. Signed autographed noted by Grace below Chamberlain's signature: "Happy New Year. Daise."

26. After foolishly running its own candidate against Chamberlain in 1869, the temperance movement gave up its cherished constabulary and accepted a compromise bill that fined local police for failure to enforce the law and reduced the requirements for issuing a search warrant. Chamberlain was deemed victorious in the press. See Barton, "Chamberlain: Governor of Maine," 84–85.

as to suggest grave doubts of their propriety or good effect. But considering the remarkable circumstance that the Bill has passed both Houses without opposition I have given it my official signature.

Joshua L. Chamberlain

[BSC]

⚞ TO WILHELM I, KING OF PRUSSIA

Copy   Augusta July 20 1870

To His Majesty,
William. King of Prussia[27]
Sire,

The undersigned respectfully presents to your Majesty the tender of his services in the war now opening in Europe. He has the honor to refer to the fact that he has served through all grades from field officer to that of General of Division. His last two promotions were made on the field of battle under circumstances which warrant him in referring to them as testimony of his capacity. The office he now holds of Governor of the State of Maine he proposes to resign in case your Majesty shall be pleased to accept his service.

While no great principle of international right is involved in the present impending war, the honor of manhood is a point on which a soldier may well be sensitive. In this feeling & sympathizing with your Majesty's political & personal attitude, well acquainted with your language & admiring your people I tender the best service of my sword.

Your Majesty's most obedient servant
Joshua L. Chamberlain
late Major Genl. Bt. U.S. Army
Gov. & Comdr in chief of State of Maine

[PHS]

⚞ TO MARQUIS D. L. LANE

Brunswick
Aug 11 1870

My dear friend[28]

I got home last evening at midnight after a weeks absence, & thank you most cordially for your kind letter. I hasten to assure you that I do "think as

27. Wilhelm Friedrich Ludwig (1797–1888), the king of Prussia who, influenced by his chancellor Otto von Bismarck, had unleashed the Franco-Prussian War. "William I," BOL (640/27).

28. Marquis D. L. Lane was a Standish state senator. MSL.

much of you as I did last winter" & more too; and shall be glad to testify my friendship in every possible way.

I think it would be a good idea for you to return to the Senate. You under-stand the reasons why I had to pass by you and nominate Mattocks for County Atty,[29] & I trust [you] have not laid up any grudge against me, as certainly I have not against you. I know people wish you all sorts of good, & will support you for anything you desire. I think the Senate will be quite as well for you on the whole as the County Attorneyship.

Your request for Mr Paine[30] is duly noted.

I see it is still your opinion that I ought to run for Senator. I hate to but if I do, I dont like the idea of seeming to *ask* the people for something & being denied.

However we shall see.

truly your friend

Joshua L. Chamberlain

Hon M. D. L. Lane

Standish

[BSC]

✎ TO HIS FATHER

Augusta Nov 26 1870

Dear Father,

I only returned home late on the Evening before Thanksgiving and could not seasonably acknowledge your invitation for that day. The sudden sickness and death of Mr Arthur Folsom[31] called me to New York, & now occupies me much with business.

I should have enjoyed a Thanksgiving with you if I had a clear field for rest a day or two.

I shall now be much occupied for a couple of weeks & after that hope to run over and make you a little visit.

I saw Tom who seemed to have business enough on hand, but anxious lest he should be turned out of office. For one I dont care much if he is, for I doubt if his associations there now are profitable. I shall advise him to go into

29. Charles P. Mattocks (1840–1910), a former Civil War brigade commander, was Cumberland County attorney from 1870 to 1873. See Mattocks, *"Unspoiled Heart,"* xiv–xx, 285–89.

30. Paine is unidentified.

31. Perhaps a relative of Fannie's father's first wife, Sarah Ann Folsom Adams, or of Deborah Folsom ("Cousin D").

business with Mr Farms[32] in Boston in some way where his *business acquaintance* in New York will still be advantageous to him. I shall see him often, as I shall now have to visit New York frequently on Mr Folsom's estate. I saw Mr Willard of Worcester the portrait painter, and he wishes to know when he can most conveniently paint the portraits of you and mother for which I have engaged him.

I think a good light could be had for painting in the garret room — the old *boy's room.*[33] If you feel like it this winter & it would be convenient to have him there for a week or ten days in December or January I would like to know it.

I hope Sadies baby[34] is better & that she is comfortable.

Give my affectionate regards to Mother. The children & all of us are hearty & well, I send our best greeting. We have "hauled up" the *Wildflower* & made all snug for winter.

Your aff. son
Lawrence

[BSC]

〰 TO ABRAM TANBORN

Augusta, Maine.
December 8th 1870.

Abram Tanborn Esq.[35]
Bangor.
Sir.

In the peculiar condition of the case of Howard A. Cleaveland [*sic*] now a convict in the State Prison[36] it has been deemed expedient to take measures for a new trial by applying for a writ of error,[37] and anxious that the rights

32. Farms is unidentified.

33. The room where Chamberlain had prepared for his Bowdoin entrance exams.

34. Alice Farrington.

35. Cleveland's attorney.

36. Cleveland, an Orrington native, was convicted of murdering one Warren George, but his indictment did not explicitly charge him of first degree murder, a capital offense; it only mentioned the elements of that offense. In an effort to avoid execution, Chamberlain directed the Executive Council to ask the Supreme Judicial Court, "Did the jury by their verdict aforesaid find said Cleveland guilty of murder in the first degree, according to the provisions of the statutes in such cases made and provided?" The court ruled that it had. These letters represent Chamberlain's efforts to commute or redecide the case. *State v. Howard A. Cleveland*, 58 Maine Reports 564 (1870).

37. The common-law form of appeal predating the spread of the civilian mode of direct appeals. See Goulka, "The First Constitutional Right to Criminal Appeal," 167–70.

of the prisoner may be well and ably cared for I duly request you to assure & discharge the duties of counsel for the said Cleaveland, & proceed to take such steps as appear to you proper in the case.

I have notified the Chief Justice and the Attorney General[38] of my action in the matter.

Very truly yours

Joshua L. Chamberlain

Governor

[PHS]

TO THOMAS BRACKET REED

Augusta Maine.

Dec. 8th 1870.

To Hon. Thos. B. Reed

Attorney General of State.

Sir,

I have to inform you that it has been deemed proper to enter on measures for a new trial in the case of Howard A. Cleaveland, and that Abram Tanborn of Bangor has been requested to take charge of the interests of the prisoner and apply for a writ of error in the case. This information is given that you may guard the interests of the State in the matter as your duty may determine & require.

Very respectfully

J. L. Chamberlain

[PHS]

TO JOHN APPLETON

Augusta, Maine.

December 8th 1870.

To the Honorable

John Appleton, Chief Justice Sup. Jud. Court.

Sir.

Whereas the Executive Council, acting on the opinions of a majority of the Justices of the Supreme Judicial Court severally expressed, in answer to interrogations by the Council as to the Status of one Howard A. Cleaveland now a convict in our State Prison under sentence of death and believing that the verdict in said case was imperfect and does not warrant the capital execution of sentence in accordance with the terms thereof, have advised me to stay

38. John Appleton and Thomas Bracket Reed, respectively.

the said execution, and whereas it is my duty to see that the laws are faithfully executed; I therefore have deemed it expedient to have measures entered upon for a new trial in case of the said Howard A. Cleaveland, and have requested Abram Tanborn Esq of Bangor to take charge of the interests of the prisoner and apply to the Court for a *writ of error* in the case, and have notified accordingly the Attorney General of the State. I have taken these steps thus promptly lest the prisoner taking advantage of the impression produced by the informed indication of the opinion of the Court, might procure his release under a writ of *habeas corpus*,[39] and thus defeat the due administration of justice & escape the proper penalty for his crime.

This has appeared to me the only proper cause for the Executive under the peculiar circumstances of the case, & I trust it may meet with your approval & cooperation.

I have the honor to be
Very respectfully.
Your obdt serv't
J. L. Chamberlain.

[PHS]

꩜ TO JOHN A. POOR

Augusta Dec 19 1870

Dear Sir;

I would now be glad of any knowledge or suggestions at your command in regard to the site at Mount Desert as a Naval Station. I have found a singular want of interest in the matter on the part of those to whom I looked for cooperation in my efforts in the matter.

To enable me to embody the advantageous points of the case in a proper memorial, I would take it as a favor if you can now find the time (which was not at your disposal when I spoke with you last summer) to give me the results of your valuable knowledge & judgment in the matter.

If this involves expense to you it will be made up to a reasonable extent by me.

Very truly yours
J. L. Chamberlain

39. In addition to releasing detainees who are jailed but not charged (the aspect of the writ suspended by Lincoln), the writ of habeas corpus provides convicts with an opportunity to challenge convictions resulting from unconstitutional procedure. Chamberlain was concerned because writs of error lead to a new trial, whereas habeas corpus leads to outright release from prison.

Hon
John A Poor

≈ TO HENRY W. PAINE

Augusta Dec 27 1870

Hon Henry W Paine[40]
My dear Sir

The "Boston Journal" has a correspondent in Maine who, angry because I declined to make him my private secretary, has been indulging in personal abuse of me — puny & pitiful, it is true, for the most part, but at last taking a form which enables and compels me to put an effectual stop to it.

The "Journal" has recently published a letter of his in which direct charges are made against me (with others) amounting to the allegation of criminal & impeachable offences on my part.

I am sorry I have not a copy of the issue itself of the Boston Journal which contains the charge. You will be able to find it, no doubt.

I intend to make these parties understand that this sort of political campaigning "wont do," and in pursuance of this intention I now write to request and engage you to take charge of my interests in the case. I would desire you (if you approve of it) to take my letter enclosed to the office of the Boston Journal, & present it in such manner as you deem best, and to advise & institute such subsequent action as the course of the responsible parties may require in order to secure reparation.

I shall be altogether inclined to accept & follow your advice in the matter. Only I want it understood that I "mean business." I know it is "*mean business*" any way; but I mean a mean to an *end*.

If the Journal people understand the character & reputation of this correspondent they would doubtless ~~remove~~ discharge him. But that would not be enough to undo the outrage of justice in the case.

[MHS]

40. Henry William Paine (b. 1810), a former Hallowell legislator then practicing law in Boston.

Brunswick Me
Mar 7 1871

Majr. Genl.
O. O. Howard.
My dear General
I desire to express my grateful feeling in view of your triumphant vindi-cation from the calumnies of partisanship and falsehood.[41]
May God ever bless you as He has.
your friend
Joshua L. Chamberlain

[BSC]

41. Stating that he deserved the "gratitude of the American people," House Republi-cans had passed a resolution acquitting Howard of "groundless and causeless" charges brought in a Democratic inquiry into misuse of funds at the Freedmen's Bureau. Even so, the allegations so tarnished Howard's and the Bureau's public image that it was closed shortly thereafter. Carpenter, *Sword and Olive Branch*, 208.

After an uneven tenure as governor and a failed bid for the Senate, Chamberlain returned to Brunswick and again to Bowdoin—but this time it was different. Far from being a fallback, Bowdoin offered him a glorious mission, to revitalize and modernize the college. Here was an extraordinary opportunity for Chamberlain to serve the college he loved and an invitation to bring fruition to the educational vision that had met only frustration in earlier years. He energetically embraced his mandate, raising new funds, opening new departments, and offering new courses in science and engineering. He relaxed the sectarian aspect of the college and changed student life. He even started a military drill.

Meanwhile, President Rutherford B. Hayes's decision to link his administration with Carl Schurz's wing of the Republican Party revived Chamberlain's political optimism and ambition. Civil service reform looked like a real possibility, as did southern home rule, a notion supported by northern intellectuals. He also continued to seek new adventures to alleviate the creeping tedium of civilian life, to the extent his health allowed. One of these was the burgeoning Gilded Age world of business. And in January 1880, the electoral crisis gave Chamberlain a long-desired reprieve from civilian boredom.

TO GRACE

April 28/71

My darling Daisy

I go to South Paris today to lecture. How happy I should be to spend the Sabbath with you somewhere! There is too much going on however to allow me to be away Saturday & Monday. I am cleaning up about the grounds—planting my little farm, near Mrs Newman's[1]—putting the Yacht in order & superintending the repairs on the church. Meantime College matters have to be talked over & plans made about my future &c. So that all things considered I dont see that I can very well be absent this Saturday. It is a great deprivation to me not to see you; but then time is rapidly passing & you are coming home. I am glad you have a yacht dress—"red white & blue." We will have some good

---

1. A Mrs. Newman lived on Chamberlain's Potter Street.

times this summer. I want you to do *the best thing* about returning to Gorham.[2] When does the summer term *begin*, & *end? Perhaps* it may be better for *you* to remain another term. I want you to do true, but whether it will be right for me to ask you to sacrifice so much to my whims is a question. At all events I can have you twice a month for a yachting "spree" — whether your abiding place on shore is in Brunswick or Gorham. I have some doubts whether you would have the best discipline here, so much time is wasted in *waiting*: & you now need to push your studies, and place yourself under discipline & culture.

It is only the best thing for you that I seek.

Dont think I am too sober, & dont be bothered with dresses that are unbecoming & distasteful to you. I would be glad to have you come home Saturday if it were not for the loss of [*work*]. Let me know when you want anything.

Your loving
Father

[SL]

⫷ TO HIS MOTHER

Brunswick
Sept 8 1871

My dear Mother;

I have been full of business all day & it is almost twelve at night; but I will not miss my letter for the birthdays are never forgotten by me.[3] I have to thank you for many things; not the least of them is the right care & training which have given me a strong constitution & a cheerful mind.

I find everything working pleasantly in regard to my opening a larger field for the College to work in. It looks as if I could do some good here, and I can stand a great deal of hard work.

We are delighted at the expectation of seeing you with us so soon. I hope Father will come too.

Mr Willard came down, & wanted me to give you his invitation to go to his home in Sturbridge, Mass, (near Worcester) & have a new picture. I want you to go. It will only take a week, or less even. If you can you would enjoy it, I think. It is important to have a satisfactory picture of you & now is the time. If you go you are more than half way to New York.

2. Grace, then fourteen, may have been attending the State Normal School in Gorham, where Chamberlain gave his "Dead on the Field of Honor" lecture. *Bib Maine*, 1:503-4.

3. Chamberlain usually wrote his mother on his birthday. See also 8 Sept. 1887 to his mother.

I am sorry for Sae's baby,[4] & think she would be better off here.

Let us know when you are co[min]g.

All well & happy. Jenny is still here. Leaves Monday.

Your affectionate son

Lawrence

[BSC]

〰 TO SAE

Bowdoin College

Brunswick, Me. March 21 1872

My dear Sae,

I have not any "sleepy" afternoons — not even Sunday — I can tell you; but I am glad to snatch a moment in the very middle of the week to acknowledge your kind & most welcome note, & to assure you of any constant and strong interest in you & yours.

Do not think the many cares and vexations of life crowd out my better thoughts or chill my heart to its nobler needs. I think I cherish all things that are true & lovely and of good [report] no whit the less for a busy & burdened life which compels me to grapple with things that are neither of the virtues & beatitudes of the category referred to.

And I am sure my friends are as dear to me as ever, — & even more so.

Yes we are all "launched into life" — pretty well off shore too. Plenty of breeze I find, surely: & I go under reefed topsails now, & make all the headway I want to, at that.

I have not been graduated 20 years yet, and have made a good many voyages.

How I wish I could turn over to Tom some of the many "chances" I have to make a venture in something. Calls come to me every week; but his line is so entirely out of my course that I cant do him so much good as I could Horace or John, if they were living.

I am working him up now, however, into something — I hope. If I can ever get to New York I may be able to get him a better place. I am helping him into the "cyder" business now. Tom is a little too timid. He wants moral courage — self reliance. His lack however may be, & I think is, excess of a good quality — viz modesty, shrinking from dependence, yet not quite up to striking out for independence. That is not exactly what ails me. I am staggered by seeing both sides of a question. I never could be a partisan leader — a man of one idea. I see the whole combination, & am perplexed till the time comes

4. Alice Farrington.

Sarah "Sae" Chamberlain Farrington, ca. 1870
(Courtesy of the Pejepscot Historical Society)

for me to *strike* in — I can go in then & see "clear as a quill." I will see Tom through now, sure.

We want you to come & see us. Now this sloppy muddy weather is coming to plague you & we have not any of it here. Plenty of room for Alice & the whole kit. I want you to see my house.[5] We are settled pretty well now. The

5. Chamberlain had raised his house and built a new first floor under the old one in 1871. See also 7 Apr. 1866 to Fannie.

children are hearty as bucks, & all well but we who are a little worn. My love to Father & Mother & Charlie.

yours aff.

J. L. Chamberlain

[SL]

≫ TO HIS FATHER

Brunswick July 25 1872

Dear Father:

Returning home from a few day's trip among the Islands I found your favor with check for $515.—which you are kind enough to let me use for a while. It is very acceptable just now, as my principal income is in September when my "ship gets in."[6]

The extra expenses on my house this year crowd me a little, & my leaving business to take the college has involved some losses; but on the whole my affairs are very satisfactory. I would be glad to assist Tom, if I can in any way. Would like to have them come & make me a visit. Plenty of room now for a grand family gathering. I wish you would *all* come & stay a week, this summer. We could have a good time.

Your aff son

J. L. Chamberlain

We feel greatly indebted to Sae & Mother for their kindness to us during Commencement week. We are through now, & are going off for a week or ten days. J. L. C.

[UMO]

≫ DOCUMENT: BOWDOIN CADETS

REGULATIONS

FOR THE

INTERIOR POLICE AND DISCIPLINE

OF THE

BOWDOIN CADETS

1.   For instruction in Military Science, the students of Bowdoin College will be organized into a Battalion of four companies, under the Professor of Military Science and Tactics,[7] and will be officially styled the BOWDOIN CADETS. Each company will be commanded by a Cadet officer.

---

6. Chamberlain invested in commercial shipping. See 16 May 1873 to his father.

7. Maj. Joseph Prentice Sanger (1840–1926), a career soldier who would rise to the rank

2.   The officers and non-commissioned officers shall be appointed by the President of the College, from a list submitted by the Commandant of the Battalion. The selection will be made from those Cadets who have been most studious and soldierlike, and most exemplary in their general deportment. In general, the Officers will be taken from the Senior Class, the Sergeants from the Junior, and the Corporals from the Sophomore.

3.   The Captains will cause the men of the companies to be numbered in a regular series, including the non-commissioned officers, and divided into four squads — each to be put under the charge of a non-commissioned officer.

4.   Each Cadet Lieutenant will be charged with two squads. The 1st Lieutenant will have the first and second; the 2d Lieutenant the third and fourth. They will supervise the order and cleanliness of their squads, and will assist the Captains in the performance of all company duties when required.

5.   As far as practicable the men of each company should be quartered together.

6.   There will be a military exercise for instruction every day when the weather is favorable; Saturdays and Sundays excepted. Each exercise will continue at least one hour, and shall not exceed one hour and a half.

7.   There will be Guard Mounting and Dress Parade daily, when the weather permits, according to the forms prescribed in Upton's Infantry Tactics.[8]

8.   There will be an inspection of the Battalion under arms every Sunday morning, whenever the weather permits, according to the form prescribed in Upton's Infantry Tactics.

9.   No cadet shall be absent from any military duty whatever without the permission of the President, unless excused by a Surgeon, in consequence of sickness or disease.

HOURS FOR DAILY DUTIES

10. REVEILLE
    GUARD MOUNTING. 2 P.M., daily.
    DRILL. 1½ hour before Sunset.
    RETREAT. Sunset.
    SUNDAY INSPECTION. 9 o'clock A.M.

---

of major general, taught Military Science and Tactics as well as International Law at Bowdoin from 1871 to 1875.

8. Based on his Civil War experience, Emory Upton, the Army's foremost tactician, developed *A New System of Infantry Tactics, Double and Single Rank, Adapted to American Topography and Improved Firearms* (1867), also known as "Upton's Tactics." DAB, 19:128–30.

Uniform—Same as that now worn.

11. No Cadet shall, without permission from the Commandant of the Battalion, wear any article of his uniform except during the performance of military exercises, and upon occasions of public or private ceremony.

12. The hair to be short, and the beard neatly trimmed.

BADGES OF DISTINCTION

13. Cadets acting as officers and non-commissioned officers shall be designated as follows:—

Captain—Chevrons of four bars of single lace on each arm above the elbow, points up.

Lieutenants—Chevrons of three bars of single lace on each arm above the elbow, points up.

Adjutant—The Lieutenant's chevrons with an arc.

Quartermaster—The Lieutenant's chevrons with horizontal bar.

Sergeant Major—The Sergeant's chevron with an arc.

Q.M.[9] *Sergeant*—The Sergeant's chevron with horizontal bar.

First Sergeant—Chevrons of two bars, single lace on each arm above the elbow, points up with a lozenge.

Sergeant—Chevrons of two bars single lace on each arm above the elbow, points up.

Color bearer—The Sergeant's chevrons with stars.

Corporals—Chevrons of two bars of single lace on each arm below the elbow, points up.

Corporals of the Color guard—The Corporal's chevrons with a star.

ARMS AND ACCOUTREMENTS.

14. All arms and other public property issued to cadets shall be marked with their designated number. The Captains of companies at such times as they deem necessary, or the Commandant may direct, will examine and ascertain whether each cadet is in possession of the articles of public property which have been issued to him.

15. The arms or other public property issued to cadets shall not be taken from quarters except for duty. No cadet shall lend or exchange his arms or accoutrements, or use those of any other cadet.

16. No cadet shall alter his musket by scraping, filing, cutting or varnishing the stock, barrels or any other part of it, nor shall the lock be removed or taken apart, without the permission of the Commandant.

9. Quartermaster.

17.   When belts are given to a cadet the Captain will see that they are properly fitted to the body, and it is forbidden to cut or punch holes in any belt without his sanction, and even then not without his personal supervision.

18.   Cartridge boxes and bayonet scabbards will be polished with blacking.

19.   The utmost attention will be paid by the Commanders of companies to the cleanliness of the military clothing, arms, accoutrements and equipments of the cadets.

20.   When not in use, the arms will be placed in the arm racks, the stoppers in the muzzles, the hammers let down, and the bayonets in their scabbards; the accoutrements suspended over the arms, and the swords hung up by the belts on pegs. Whenever a cadet turns out in uniform under arms he will wear white gloves.

21.   The cadets will bear in mind that the arms, accoutrements, and other public property for college use, are obtained from the U. S. Government, and that the President of the College is personally responsible for their safe keeping. Cadets losing or damaging articles of public property, will be charged the full or proportionate value.

COMPLIMENTS.

22.   Courtesy among military men is indispensable to discipline. Respect to superiors should not be confined to obedience on duty, but will be extended on all occasions. It is always the duty of the subordinate to accost, or to offer the first the customary salutation, and of the senior to return such complimentary notice. Cadets when off duty, or when engaged in their ordinary College pursuits, will recognize the President and Faculty of the College by touching or raising the hat.

23.   When on duty, Sergeants with swords drawn will salute by bringing them to a present; with muskets, by bringing the left hand across the body so as to strike the musket near the right shoulder. Corporals out of ranks, and Privates, not sentinels, will *carry arms*; and salute in the same manner. These marks of respect will be paid Cadet officers whenever they appear in their uniforms. It is well to remark that in the military service a soldier is required to offer the customary salutes to an officer whenever he recognizes him, and whether he be in uniform or not.

CORRESPONDENCE.

24.   Written communications from a Commander to those under his command are usually made by his staff officers. In all other cases by the officer himself.

25.   In signing an official communication, the writer shall annex to his name his rank and corps. When he writes by order, he shall state by whose order.

26. Communication to or from a Commander, and those under his command, must pass through the Adjutant General, Assistant Adjutant General, or Adjutant on duty with it. All communications, whether from an inferior to a superior, or *vice versa*, are as a general rule to be passed through the intermediate Commanders. The same rule governs in verbal applications; for example, a Lieutenant seeking an indulgence must apply though his Captain, the Captain through the Adjutant.

27. All correspondence concerning military matters at Bowdoin College will be so regulated. The correct form of an official letter can be obtained by application to the Adjutant.

MISCELLANEOUS.

28. The offices of the Commandant, Adjutant and Quartermaster of the Battalion will be in No. 18 Appleton Hall. The hours of business will be published in orders.

29. Cadets are not allowed to visit this office except on duty.

30. The standing of cadets will depend on their merits in the various studies and exercises which may be prescribed; their prompt attendance at, and strict attention to the same; and the condition of their arms, accoutrements and military clothing.

31. All offences of cadets against military discipline shall be recorded according to the following scale: —

An offence of the first class counts 5.
   ″   ″   second   ″   3.
   ″   ″   third   ″   1.

Offences of the first class are — neglect of duty while on guard; absence without leave; disrespectful or insubordinate conduct; trifling with a sentinel; using profane oaths; wearing uniform except as prescribed, etc.; incivility as failing to salute. Offences of the second class are — Arms or equipments grossly out of order; not enforcing military regulations; reading on post; talking unnecessarily on post; trifling on post; slovenly appearance, etc.; ignorance of orders. Offences of the third class are — inattention under arms; laughing or talking in ranks; not in uniform when under arms, etc.

32. In the Freshman year offences do not count until October 10.

33. When a cadet shall have a total of numbers thus recorded exceeding 100 in six months, he shall be reported to the Faculty as deficient in military discipline.

34. Every member of the graduating class, upon completing his course of study, shall have a credit of 16.67 for each month which he shall receive no demerit, to be deducted from the demerit he may have received during his entire cadetship.

35. Immediately on the arrival of the Freshmen they will report in person to the Commandant of the Battalion for assignment to companies.

36. All students, who are excused from military instruction, will assemble in front of the chapel at the first call for Retreat or Parade, and answer to their names: the squad will be under the supervision of the Quartermaster or his Sergeant as may be ordered.

37. Company and class parade grounds will be designated in orders at the commencement of the Fall term. To the places so specified the companies or classes will repair, when required, at the *first call*, ready to *fall in* promptly when the *assembly* shall sound.

38. All cadets are presumed to be strictly on honor in the performance of military duty, and it is expected, and they are hereby required to report all offences which come under their observation.

39. The Professor of Military Science and Tactics, on duty at this College by authority of the United States Government, is the recognised Commandant of the Battalion, and will be obeyed and respected accordingly.

40. The foregoing Regulations having been approved by the Faculty, under authority of the Boards of Trustees and Overseers, are hereby published for the information and guidance of students; and it is expected that they will conform thereto in all matters of discipline, dress and instruction.

JOSHUA L. CHAMBERLAIN, President.

BOWDOIN COLLEGE, Sept. 16, 1872.

[BSC]

TO MARY LOW

Bowdoin College
Brunswick
Oct 9 1872

Miss Low;[10]

Dr. Brackett[11] has handed me your letter suggesting your entering our Medical School.

I perceive the reasonableness of your proposition, and regret that not having contemplated such applications we can not [make] such arrangements as would be fit & proper in the case.

---

10. Mary Low, the first woman to study at a New England all-male college, was a sophomore at Colby. She was valedictorian of the class of 1875. <http://www.colby.edu/about/index.html> (Dec. 2003).

11. Cyrus F. Brackett (1833–1915), professor and librarian at the Medical School. *WhoAm*, 127.

I am sure that with the high character & famed purpose you evince, how-ever, [you] will soon find these "equal times" which they so justly desire, either by building up new Colleges or by raising up the old ones.[12]

Very truly y[our]s

J. L. C.

[BSC]

≈ TO HENRY B. SMITH

[copy]   Brunswick

                                                    Oct 9 1872

My dear Professor Smith; — [13]

Some of our watchmen on the walls think Professor Morris[14] may have tendencies to Rationalism, or at all events may not be in strict accordance with "orthodox" faith.

I regard the chair of Philosophy as of more importance than the Presi-dency. We need a strong, sound man.

May I venture to ask for a word in confidence as to Prof. Morris. He has written me withdrawing his name as a candidate; but I never supposed he knew of our thoughts towards him. I have not yet answered his letter, and hope to hear such satisfactory accounts of him in all respects that I can insist upon retaining him.[15]

With thanks for your former kindness I am,

Very truly,

Your friend & servt.

Joshua L. Chamberlain

Rev Henry B. Smith, D.D.,

New York City

[BHL]

12. Chamberlain had hinted at coeducation in his inaugural address: "Women too should have a part in this high calling [of higher education and 'true life']. Because in this sphere of things her 'rights,' her capacities, her offices, her destiny, are equal to those of man. She is the Heaven-appointed teacher of man, his guide, his better soul." Cham-berlain, "The New Education." He opened some of the new summer science courses to women. Smith, *Fanny and Joshua*, 222, 233.

13. Henry Boynton Smith (1815–77), a professor at Union Theological Seminary, had been an instructor in philosophy and Greek at Bowdoin early in his career.

14. George S. Morris (1840–89) was an empirical critic of German Idealism at Michi-gan. Garraty and Carnes, *American National Biography*, 15:894–95.

15. Morris never taught at Bowdoin.

Brunswick. Maine.
Jan 20th 1873

Hon L. F. Kersey:[16]
My dear General;
   Recalling the very kind words you incidentally dropped in reference to Bowdoin College when I had the pleasure of last paying my respects to you, I believe it will not be displeasing to you if I make a frank statement of our condition and needs, and submit some matters both for your consideration and sympathics.

   I think it is apparent that the College has entered on a new career of usefulness and prosperity. Distinguished and even remarkable as her past history has been — both as to her usefulness to the State and Country, and as to the great eminence of her graduates, it is still true that for lack of anything like an adequate endowment, the College has not been able to keep pace with the advance of the times, in respect to the means and appliances for instruction in the higher branches of science and general learning.

   By a new adjustment and rearrangement of our forces however we have lately been able to offer facilities for the best and widest study, each as I believe in some respects to be better than are offered any where else. The result is seen in the fact that the number of students has nearly doubled in the space of little over a year, & a new & warm interest is springing up every where in the College.

   But now for the other side. We can not keep this up, and hold our own against the powerful influence of Colleges outside of the State, which surpass us only in pecuniary means, unless the strong men of Maine come to her support. If our leading men would do for Bowdoin what the men of Massachusetts without distinction of sect or party, are doing for Harvard,[17] we shouldnt fall much behind her in the good work we could do for young men & for society generally.

   Already liberal minded men, here and else where, are coming forward to express their approval of our new efforts. Hon. Peleg W. Chandler of Boston[18] is providing a Building for a Museum of Natural History which he says shall

---

16. Kersey was an otherwise unidentified wealthy Mainer.

17. Under Charles Eliot (1834–1926), Harvard led the nation in educational modernization.

18. Peleg W. Chandler (1816–89), a prominent lawyer, civic activist, and Bowdoin graduate who summered in Brunswick and married Prof. Cleaveland's daughter Martha Ann Bush. DAB, 3:615.

be the best in the Country, and these both in Massachusetts and in Maine are contributing generously to strengthen the undertaking to have a first rate College in Maine.

What we want next and most is a Laboratory of Chemistry and Physics, (that is, Natural Philosophy as we used to call it) and, General, I want you to build it and give it your name.

We regard you as perhaps the wealthiest man in Maine. We know you are one of her most distinguished citizens, & that what ever may be your wealth it does not exceed your generosity. I have a feeling that it might be a pleasure & satisfaction to you to place some of your resources at the disposition of the College for the purpose I have indicated. Certainly there is scarcely any way more sure to perpetuate your honored name in an act that shall be a service & a blessing for all time to come.[19] I am sure you will appreciate the motive which leads me to write this, and will believe me to be in this as in all other regards, your friend,

Joshua L. Chamberlain

[PHS]

TO JAMES W. BRADBURY

Brunswick. Maine.
Jan 20th 1873.

Hon J. W. Bradbury:[20]
My dear Sir;

It is hard to hold our own against the tide which is sweeping everything away to the great centres unless we can have a large endowment of the College very soon.

Our best Professors — those who are the life and marrow of the College — will surely be drawn away. I don't know that we can possibly help it now, with the best we can do, and the College in spite of us will go back.

I am pondering whether my duty to the College requires me to stay here & see all this good work we have begun languish & die out.

Nothing but a sense of duty & good faith towards the friends who have placed me here, makes me willing to work in a cause which looks likely to fail in the end, for want of suitable endowment.

Nothing has occurred here to depress me especially, for there is an in-

---

19. Kersey is not recorded as a major donor to Bowdoin. Sewall, *Conditional Subscriptions*; *Bowdoin College Donations and Funds, 1794–1898*.

20. Former senator James W. Bradbury (1802–1901), a Bowdoin graduate and trustee, pledged to give $2,000 by 1875. *DAB*, 2:547–48; Sewall, *Conditional Subscriptions*.

creasing interest on the part of the students & a greatly increasing tendency towards this College among young men who are fitting for a liberal course of study. But knowing as I do the small means we have to work with, the small capital we are doing business on—and knowing also that our best Professors will surely leave us before long—prosperous as we are in numbers, I feel that it is of the most pressing importance that we secure the countenance and aid of liberal men in our State. I have boldly written several of them, but see no results as yet.

If we go to the Legislature I think we ought to ask for fifty thousand dollars ($50,000) on condition that $200,000 more are raised—$10,000 to be paid by the State as fast as the sum of $40,000 is raised by private subscription.

I have conferred with some of our wealthiest men, & they advise the course, & say the propositions can be carried—both parts of it.

Mr. A. P. Gould of Thomaston,[21] Mr J. T. Hobson of Wiscasset[22] are among those who will aid us generously. I have been throwing together the materials of a memorial to the Legislature.

I encounter the question whether the Constitutional provision as to the power of the State over the College has ever been met as was attempted in the act of June 16th 1820. (Special Laws Maine. Vol. 1.) Will you please see whether we are barred?[23] I will come and see you soon. I go to the Boston dinner tomorrow.

Yours truly.

Joshua L. Chamberlain

[PHS]

≈ TO ABNER COBURN

Brunswick, Maine
Jan 20th 1873.

Hon. Abner Coburn,

My dear Governor;

I make no apology for writing to you in the interests of public education for I am well aware of your views on that subject, and think I shall have at least your commendation in what I now desire and propose.

I took this place, as you must know, simply because I thought I could

21. Albert Palmer Gould (1821–88), Thomaston lawyer and state representative, pledged $1,000. *Bib Maine*, 1:405; Sewall, *Conditional Subscriptions*.

22. Hobson, who is otherwise unidentified, is not recorded as a major donor to Bowdoin.

23. See 28 Jan. 1873 to Bradbury.

here soonest and best try the experiment of a *liberal course of study which should tend to the widest practical use in life*. The great demand of the times is that knowledge, instead of being turned inward, and shut up in the cloister, should face outward towards the real work of life.

I have tried to meet that demand here and have organized a Scientific Department, separate from the College Course, and vigorous and effective in itself. Many students have come in even in this brief space of time, and many more — a large number in fact — are to join us next term.

Indeed the effort is a thorough success, and has attracted attention all over the Country and been recognized in a substantial manner by the Scientific Department of the Government of the United States. Letters of inquiry and congratulation are coming in from nearly every state in the Union, and if I am enabled to carry the work on as I have begun, it will have a National reputation.

Now, Governor, I know that you will not consider me as "begging" or as representing any [ill.] interest, when I say that the movement is worthy of your attention and aid. With your patronage and name the School of Science and Art can be made powerful for good to this State and Nation.

The College here, with all its large appliances and able Professors, can furnish a great part of what we need. But it cannot do all. A very moderate degree of assistance however will be sufficient now. Prudence and caution should be used in all forward movements.

What I want is not mere temporary relief and support, but some sure reliance. I want the benefit of your patronage and influence. Others have given their names to Institutions whose success was by no means assured. I want yours to be given to one already past the stage of experiment, and sure to flourish. Let this be known as the *Coburn School of Science & Art*, and I am sure it would be a source of pride and gratification to the people of the State that a name already honored in the history should represent a vital element in her prosperity *for all coming time*.

You are naturally considering I doubt not, some measure of public benefit to represent your character after you are gone. Would it not be gratifying to see it extended upon under your counsels & guidance?

This is an opportune time. Ours of all similar efforts, appears to have touched the right chord in the public favor, and met the public demand. I should be glad to show you if you are so disposed, what we have done, and with your aid can do.

May I be encouraged by a word from you that shall look to a further consideration of the matter, with hope of future realization.

I am, Governor,
With highest respect and esteem
Your friend and servant.
Joshua L. Chamberlain

≋ TO STEPHEN COBURN

Brunswick. Maine.
Jan 21st 1873.

Hon. Stephen Coburn,[24]
My dear Sir;
Knowing that you are a man of generous views and public spirit, I have for some time been intending to bring to your notice a great public bene-faction, on which Governor Coburn and I have had some conference, and in which I know he feels deep interest. My unwillingness to add even a thought of care to his present heavy burden has prevented me from attempting to set the matter before him as its merits deserve. But I believe your influence with him and with other members of your family may be of great avail in realizing a measure of public benefit as important as anything that has ever been done for the good and glory of the State.

I beg therefore to submit a copy of two communications which formed part of our correspondence.

The desirableness of carrying out this plan of establishing a popular De-partment of Liberal and useful Learning is greatly increased by the assured success of our small beginning already. Distinguished men I have met in vari-ous parts of the Country have spoken, of their own accord, of the providential opportunity to meet a great need of Maine, which would be the occasion of the highest honor to the Governor and a perpetual blessing to the State. And some of our own best citizens, (not connected in any way with this Institution) have advised me to submit the matter again through you.

As to the two points which seemed to cause the Governor's hesitation, I suppose I need not now say anything of the objection that the Governor's estate was largely in lands not immediately productive. If that is still so, the representative value of any portion he should be pleased to place at the dis-posal of such an Institution as that proposed, would equally avail as a basis of operation.

24. Stephen Coburn (1817–82), an influential Skowhegan lawyer, was Abner Coburn's brother. *WhoAmH*, 181.

For the other point:—the sectarian character of "Bowdoin College,"—I wish I had an opportunity to disabuse the Governor's mind and all other minds. The fact is there is no College—which is a Christian College at all—that is so little sectarian as Bowdoin. She has always had Baptists, Methodists, Episcopalians or members of some other evangelical society in her faculty, as well as Congregationalists.

But the main thing is that I do not ask the Governor to endow *Bowdoin College*, but the *Coburn College of Science & Art*. There is a great need of such an Institution in the State. There is no reason why such an Institution should not take rank among the highest in the land. The advantage of having it in connection in certain respects, with Bowdoin College, is that we can avail ourselves of the great facilities gathered around the oldest and strongest College of the State, and economize our forces.

Every where else, except in Maine, distinguished and liberal-minded citizens are founding such schools of instruction. Here we need it, and the success which has already attended our new course here, shows that the State appreciates & avails herself of the opportunity thus granted. It seems to me that a very small part of the means at the Governor's disposal, the withdrawal of which neither he nor his family would feel in the least, would secure this grand enterprise from falling back, & be a perpetual & ever widening memorial of his character and name.

I am rejoiced to hear that the Governor is improving in health. I have always cherished a warm personal attachment for him, & would not urge this measure, did I not think it would if understood & realized, meet his judgment & approval.

If any suitable opportunity should occur, I beg that you will make known to the Governor the purport of this communication. I trust I may yet see him so restored as to be able to look into this matter which appears to me so beneficial & so grand in its results.

I am, my dear Sir, relying on your own liberal views for my pardon in taking so much of your time and attention, and I hoped that good may come of it beyond anything that you or I can now realize.

I am with high regard,

Yours truly

Joshua L. Chamberlain.

[PHS]

Brunswick. Maine.
Jan 28th 1873.

Hon. J. W. Bradbury.

My dear Sir;

Since writing you last,[25] I have examined the tenure by which Bowdoin College now exists, and its right to aid from the State of Maine. I am [cl]ear in the opinion that we are *barred* from receiving aid, under the constitutional provision.

You have doubtless perceived that action was commenced by the special act of June 16, 1820, looking to a relation of the College to the State of Maine which would enable the State to endow the College. That action however was never completed. It occurred to me when in Boston last week that we could in a few days obtain the requisite consent of Massachusetts, to complete their transfer of jurisdiction; but on reflection it appeared to me, quite doubtful whether such action is now desirable.

The College now holds by a tenure altogether peculiar, nothing like it in the Country. The consent and concurrence of these parties is now necessary to effect any change as to the powers & privilege of the College — viz the Trustees & Overseers of the College, the Legislature of Massachusetts & the Legislature of Maine. I have some doubts whether it may not be best to keep in this cleft of a rock, safe from political storms, & partisan influences. At any rate, I did not like to proceed in the direction formerly contemplated, without referring the matter once more to the Boards. It is a very important step, & should be considered.

At the same time I feel that it was a great mistake not to have effected the transfer of jurisdiction at the time it was undertaken. We should then have been & contained *the* College of Maine; & should have had aid & endowment from the State.

There is one way in which we have the matter in our hands without further consulting Massachusetts. That is by taking advantage of her Resolve of June 12, 1820 whereby any modifications of the act of separation relating to Bowdoin College, not affecting the right of Mass, which may be made by the Trustees & Overseers, with the consent & agreement of the Legislature of Maine, are *already ratified beforehand*.

But the whole matter needs care & deliberation.

Meanwhile we must have a large increase of our funds in some way, or we cannot retain an able Faculty, or draw in Students by offering proper facilities

25. 20 Jan. 1873 to Bradbury.

for successful study. All we need is *to keep up what we have now begun.* I take some satisfaction in reflecting that we have accomplished what we have, in fact, actually doubling the power of the College — in Faculty, students, means & appliances of instruction, without any serious inroad upon our capital.

I don't see how we can ask the State to finish Memorial Hall.[26] We had better wait till the whole question can be discussed by the Boards, & work meanwhile on *individuals*. This, however, must not be remitted for a day.

Yours very truly.

J. L. Chamberlain.

[PHS]

≈ TO JOHN D. LINCOLN, ET AL.

Brunswick April 9 1873

Dr J. D. Lincoln[27] & others

Committee &c

Gentlemen;

Finding that I was chosen upon a committee at the last Town[28] meeting to carry into effect the vote to erect a "Town Hall" "instead of" a "Soldiers monument," I beg to resign the place, or if the Committee have no right to accept the resignation, to decline to take part in its proceedings.

There was no legal right on the part of the Town meeting to raise money for an extraordinary purpose not specified in the Warrant.

A Town Hall is a very good thing, but it is not a "Soldiers monument," any more than it is a Bounty Broker's monument.

There being then nothing which in my view can legally be done by this committee, I take this method of relieving myself from any responsibility in the matter.

Very respectfully

your obt. servt.

Joshua L. Chamberlain

[BSC]

26. Memorial Hall, built haltingly between 1867 and 1882, honors Bowdoin's Civil War veterans. Calhoun, *A Small College in Maine*, 150.

27. John Dunlap Lincoln (1821–77), a Brunswick doctor. *Bib Maine*, 1:709.

28. Brunswick.

Portland, May 16 1873.

Dear Father;

Your kind favor was duly received. I have made inquiries about the Soldiers' lots, and find that they have all been sold years ago, & nobody can tell who bought them.

I will still try to keep a look out for some of them, or others.

We are all well, and would be glad to see you. I am sure you would all enjoy my splendid Green House—if you can call it *green* where there are over fifty different kind of flowers in full bloom.

It is the wonder of the town.

For myself I am almost ashamed to say I weigh 180 pounds. It looks as if I had a pretty easy time but that is not the case exactly. I have a perfect portrait of Mother taken from a Photograph enlarged. As soon as I can get it suitably framed I shall show it to all comers, and if you cant come here to see it, I will take it over to you.

I am still expecting Willard to paint a large one, as a mate to yours.

I hear from Tom occasionally and am trying to help him all I can. Sent the $100. as I said when I last saw you. Shall try to give him the fitting out of the Ship Bombay now due at *Boston*, though that will be a little awkward. It can be done I suppose. I own an eighth of her. Shipping is doing well now, & I am glad I did not sell out in hard times.

Hope all is going well with you all. I shall [have] more time to see you after July 15.[29]

Love to all

Your aff son

Lawrence.

[PHS]

Bowdoin College

To the July 8 1873

Trustees & Overseers:

Gentlemen;

When I assumed the duties to which you honored me on your election, I was aware that they involved difficulties and trials from which older and abler men than I had [retired?] in despair. I have exerted myself beyond any previous experience to be equal to this place and to meet your wishes. I hoped

---

29. Commencement was on 9 July that year.

to succeed, but I have not met my own expectation. A spirit seems to possess the College with which I cannot harmonize, and under which I cannot advantageously work.

I owe the world some better service, and it is my duty to seek it.

Grateful for the many kind and generous words with which you have endeavoured to support and aid me. I respectfully tender my resignation of the Presidency of Bowdoin College.[30]

Your obedient servant

J. L. Chamberlain.

[MHS]

⬿TO WILLIAM GAY WAITT

Bowdoin College

Oct 13 1873

Mr W. G. Waitt[31]

I am directed by the Faculty of this College to inform you that unless you immediately after this notice procure the Blouse & other articles of dress prescribed for use in the Drill you are *dismissed*, and will leave town by the first train.

Joshua L. Chamberlain

President.[32]

[BSC]

⬿DOCUMENT: STATEMENT ON BOWDOIN DRILL REBELLION

[ca. May 1874]

I do not feel called upon to discuss this trouble at length, or the causes which led to it. The outbreak was wholly unexpected by me, and I believe that, with half a dozen exceptions, it was entirely unpremeditated by the students. They had never shown more interest in the drill and never given so little trouble. The sudden change in their deportment has been attributed to the hardship of the drill and a consequent feeling of discontent and dislike. I do not believe it & know many who took part in the demonstration had no sympathy with its objects, in fact, who violated their sense of right and manliness in thus opposing the drill; therefore I deny that the class feeling which

30. His resignation was not accepted. See also his attempts of 26 June 1876 and 10 July 1883.

31. Waitt (1855–1909) was not dismissed; he graduated in 1876 and became a Boston lawyer.

32. An enclosed card reads: "With the Compliments of Joshua L. Chamberlain."

forced so many of the students into an attitude of hostility to the military department was an aggregate of the opinions of the individuals concerned, or was even an exponent of the honest sentiments of the majority. The greatest public misapprehension prevails in reference to the entire question and I hope steps will be taken towards removing the unjust suspicions at present resting on it.

It is alleged that the college has been converted into a military school, that its members are under unusual restraint and without the usual privilege of a hearing in cases of discipline; that they have been compelled to purchase a costly and useless dress; that an enormous amount of time is frittered away in needless drills and parades, and that a cordial hatred of all this and the many acts of injustice springing from it brought about an honest effort to save the college from military despotism and ruin. The answer to all this is that during the past 2½ years, but 8 students have been disciplined on account of trouble growing out of the ~~drill~~ military department and that neither of these was denied a full hearing: that during the past year not a student has attended more than 44 drills (the whole number) that not one of those drills has been over one hour and ten minutes in duration, and that the exercises were suited to the most effeminate and delicate of those taking part: that no student has been required to pay more than $6.00 for military equipment; that more time is devoted to study in Bowdoin College now than before the establishment of the military department and that dissatisfaction with the drill per se, was not wholly the Cause of the recent rebellion.

[BSC]

≈ TO ASA. D. SMITH

Bowdoin College
Brunswick, May 26, 1874.

Rev. A. D. Smith, D. D., President of Dartmouth College[33] —
My Dear Sir:—

It is freely asserted here among our students that the authorities of Dartmouth College have given assurance that students dismissed or expelled from this College for disobedience to its laws and requirements, particularly those pertaining to the Military drill, will be received and admitted at Dartmouth.

I cannot believe that a proposition so contrary to the comity and courtesy which has always marked the relations of our high institutions of learning, could have been authorized by you. Still it is important to be able to

---

33. Asa D. Smith (1804–77), the modernizing president of Dartmouth College. DAB, 17:239.

disbelieve and deny this on grounds sufficient to countervail the positive assertions which are rife here, and I beg you not to regard it as a discourtesy if I request you to give me an authoritative statement touching the point in question. The interests of Dartmouth no less than of Bowdoin seem to be involved. As an early answer is desirable, please telegraph the substance of your reply.

Awaiting this, I am,
Your friend and servant
Joshua L. Chamberlain

[Open Letter, MHS]

≈ TO UNIDENTIFIED RECIPIENT

Brunswick May 27 1874

My dear Sir:

We called up every man yesterday liable to drill and those who refused to obey the laws & requirements were sent home by first train. Ninety six were sent, but we have more men left in good standing than the whole number of students in College when I came here.[34] Meantime we have taken care that not a single regular College exercise shall be omitted. Every thing is going on "by the bell."

I did not find you at your house when I went over to see you while here. I wanted to speak about the Cabinet.[35] There is some difficulty in the fact that two professors must have access to it & control of it in certain respects, & there is an unfortunate tendency to jealousy between the parties so related which leads to little criminations & recriminations. No one was willing, under the circumstances, to take entire charge of the Cabinet so the best one could do was to pass a vote (last month) tha[t] the Cabinet should not be opened or visited except under the immediate supervision of some member of the Faculty, or that of yourself or some one by your authority.

Prof White[36] & I are the committee to prepare rules & regulations in regard to the care custody & use of the Cabinet, & we are ready to report.

I have been so tied down here with recitations, lectures &c that I have not been able to get off a single day, but have been pushing our subscription all I could far & near.

34. Bowdoin had grown from 126 students in 1848 to 309 in 1874. Bowdoin College, *Catalogue.*

35. Prof. Parker Cleaveland's prized fiefdom housing scientific and natural history specimens.

36. Charles Abiathar White (1826–1910), Josiah Little Professor of Natural Science at Bowdoin.

We must get our $100,000 & we will, I believe.

By the way, the "Advertiser" had a noble editorial on the "situation" here. I half thought you had a hand in it.

I shall come up & touch a point or two the moment I can leave. I have to steady the ship now for a time.

truly yours

J. L. Chamberlain

[BSC]

≈ TO FATHERS OF DRILL REBELS

Bowdoin College, May 28, 1874.

Dear Sir:

On the 26th inst. your son _____ in answer to a question put to him individually by an authorized Committee of the Faculty, positively refused to obey rules and regulations of the College, in so far as they related to the "drill." Thereupon he was directed to leave at once for home, there to await the action of the Faculty in his case.

The following is a statement of the circumstances which made this action necessary:

On Friday last, at the hour for drill, the greater part of the Sophomore and Freshman classes refused to report for duty. During the day it became known that a majority of the Junior, Sophomore, and Freshman classes had bound themselves by a written agreement to resist the drill at all hazards.

In the evening the Faculty met and appointed a committee of two to inquire into the cause and aim of this insubordination. The committee called several of the most prominent and reliable of the disaffected students and conversed with them fully and frankly with regard to their objections to the drill. The Faculty then appointed one of their number to meet each of the disaffected classes the next morning and endeavor to convince them of the wrong they were guilty of in combining to resist lawful authority; of the mistake they were making in choosing this way to abolish the drill; and of the misapprehension under which they appeared to be laboring in supposing that it was in the power of the Faculty to give up the drill, — that being a matter in which the Governing Boards only had a right to direct. But the students resolved to adhere to their former decision, and the Faculty, wishing to give abundant opportunity for better counsels to prevail, decided to wait until their regular meeting on Monday evening before taking decisive action, thus giving the students the whole of Saturday, Sunday, and Monday, in which to reconsider their action.

When the Faculty met on Monday evening, the students, for the express purpose as was afterward admitted of forcing an issue, sent in form announcements of their continued determination not to drill. (These were formally retracted the next morning, but this written withdrawal was accompanied by a verbal explanation that it was not to be understood as implying any change in the attitude of the students.)

It was clearly the duty of the Faculty to deal first of all with concerted rebellion against lawful authority, and a rebellion, too, of no ordinary magnitude, for in addition to their demand to be exempted from drill, it was well known that the disaffected students had bound themselves to leave in a body if their leaders were sent away.

The Faculty therefore decided as the first step to send home every man who persisted in his refusal to comply with all the requirements of the College, and in consequence of that decision, and your son's refusal, he has been sent home.

The next step which the Faculty decided upon, and which it is now my duty to announce to you, is as follows. If your son will sign the enclosed blank, renewing in good faith and without reservation his matriculation pledge of obedience to the Laws and Regulations of the College, and forward it to the President within ten days from date, he will be allowed to return and resume his place in his class, and this he will be expected to do without further delay. If he does not do this, he must consider himself by the act of refusal as expelled from the College at the expiration of the ten days. If he concludes to return to his duty, and his objections to the drill are not removed, he can at the end of this term, but not before, receive an honorable dismission and go to some other College.

It may be added that if the drill was a hardship and all other means of redress had failed (which the Faculty by no means admit), this method of obtaining relief (i.e. an honorable withdrawal from College) has always been open, and should have commended itself instead of the attempt which has been made to defy the authority which every student at his matriculation pledges his word of honor to obey.

The Faculty consider the matriculation pledge as one which of right takes precedence of all others in whatever concerns the relations of the students to the government of the College, so that in requiring your son to recede from his subsequent conflicting agreement with his classmates, the Faculty believe that they are not only requiring nothing dishonorable, but are pointing out the only course which is consistent with true and highest sense of honor.

The enclosed blank with your son's signature thereto must be received by the President by 7 o'clock P.M. on Monday the 8th day of June, or it cannot be accepted, reasonable allowance being made for unforeseen delay in delivery though the mails.

No other form than the printed one enclosed can be accepted.

By order of the Faculty.

Joshua L. Chamberlain

President of Bowdoin College.

[BSC]

≋ TO THE TRUSTEES AND OVERSEERS OF BOWDOIN COLLEGE
[July 1874]

To Boards of Trustees & Overseers

Bowdoin College.

Gentlemen;

In view of the present necessities of the College I hereby propose and offer to relinquish the sum now allowed me for rent, viz $300. until the finances of the College will warrant the payment of this without embarrassment.[37]

I am also authorized to say that Professor Packard offers to relinquish for the ensuing year the sum now paid him as Librarian, — viz $300.

Joshua L. Chamberlain

President.

[BSC]

≋ TO HIS MOTHER
Bruns. 4 July 74

Dear Mother;

More thanks than I can speak for the kind words. It seems as if I have not heard anything like them for a long time.

The Box I have not had time to look at. Have had to work 14 hours a day for three weeks. I am not very easily cast down & dont mean to be now. Just refused an honorable position at $6000 salary & plenty of time. I am going to carry this point here for I can do good. Am in the right place now.

Much love to Tom & Fa[ther] & Delia & all the rest. Will write when I get through.

I send a bold abstract of my "sermon" tomorrow PM. at 4.

With all my love

Lawrence

[BSC]

37. Payment recommenced in 1880. Trulock, 515 n. 41.

State of Maine
Head Quarters Volunteer Militia
9 P.M.
Sept 1 Tuesday Evening 1874

Dear Daisy:

We have had a working day of it & are now all safe & sound in camp. The men are singing stirring old army songs & seem happy. We had a beautiful parade at Sunset, & the Bands played an hour afterwards. Many people were here. Beautiful ladies were plenty. I succeeded in keeping my tent free. This morning I took a run over home. Went all over the house before I found any body. Mamma first—in Sadie's kitchen washing handkerchiefs, then one by one all the rest—well & happy. Many people called on you at the Bangor house[38] this morning, where the papers announced you were. They want you to come. But do as you please.

Let me hear from you at all events.

Your aff. [ill.]

Joshua jr.[39]

[BSC]

≋ TO ABNER COBURN

Brunswick Jan. 7, 1875.

Hon. Abner Coburn,

My dear Governor;—

I am sure I do not presume too much in returning to the matter of the Scientific School. What I have to propose I sincerely believe will reflect as much honor and advantage upon you, as you will therein confer upon the State.

I have been looking at the case of similar Schools in New Hampshire, Massachusetts, and Connecticut, and appreciate the great good they are doing. Each of these Schools has been founded by some liberal minded man in private life. It seems to me many things conspire here to make such a School as we might establish distinguished among them all. I feel confident that we should draw students from all over the Country. It is in your power to do what no other man in the State can do. And I know of no other way in which you can so well use [a] portion of the means in your hands. Allow me to submit an outline of what appears to me desirable and practicable. You are a business man and will like to see a definite proposition in plain words and figures.

38. Most likely the Farrington home.

39. This is a rare instance of Chamberlain signing his name as his father did.

The Coburn Scientific School of Maine.

This is to provide a liberal education for youth, in which prominence is to be given to the Modern Languages and to the Sciences and Arts most closely related to what are commonly called the useful pursuits in life.

Three Courses should be open to the choice of Students.

1. *Natural Science.*

Including Chemistry, Natural Philosophy, & Nat. History

2. *Engineering.*

Civil and Mechanical, also Surveying and Navigation.

3. *Select Studies.*

History and Political Science to have prominence.

The College is already able to provide buildings laboratories, apparatus, cabinets and libraries. Not less than $250,000. are already invested in means and appliances available for the ends proposed.

To equip such a School fully for present needs would require and cost the following

1. A Chair of Natural History	Salary	$2000
2. Chemistry, Nat. Philosophy.	"	2000
3. Engineering	"	2000
4. Instruction in Languages &c.	"	2000
5. A Chair of Mathematics	"	2000
Total annually		$10.000.

A portion of this instruction could be given by the present Professors in the College, so that not more than $7,500 a year will be regained for some time to come. The income therefore of $100,000 would well provide for the present wants of such a School, and the basis would be laid for an Institution that would rank among the best in the land. Nowhere else could that sum of money be invested so as to produce such beneficial results. Not a dollar of this will be wasted in experiments, or sunk in buildings. The period of experiment is entirely past. Every dollar spent here would go directly into the life of the School.

In the course of time there would doubtless be occasion for a larger endowment. Indeed the School should be well endowed; for I think it desirable that the tuition should be free. Actual expenditure of material, and wear and tear of apparatus, should be made good by equitable assessment upon Students. Should there be any excess of income beyond necessary expenses, I think it should be used to promote original investigation and individual application, on the part of both Students and Professors. We want them able to [go] farther and do better than merely to study other men's works, and repeat other men's thoughts. Our success has been so great that I cannot bear to see these laborious beginnings lost. I cannot see an enterprise conceived especially for the benefit of young men who have to make their own way in life, and which has attracted and quickened so many earnest young minds, fall to the ground and be extinguished, when Providence has put it into the powers of one of our most honored citizens to perpetuate this blessing and glory to the Commonwealth.

I have laid this before you thus freely, Governor, because I know the object is worthy, and the views are broad, and the plan cannot fail to strike you with favor. In such a cause I need not ask pardon for importunity. You will not consider it such. It is the opportunity which I present to you — or rather Providence presents — the same Power which enables you to respond to it, and in a manner worthy of it. It is befitting that you, reared in this State and rising by your character, abilities, and worth to the highest honors in her gift, should confer upon her this lasting honor and benefaction. It is a beautiful consummation of a noble career, that a name associated with one of the most momentous periods in the history of the Country, should be perpetuated in a public Institution, and still inspire her young men with the example of what integrity, loyalty, and liberality can do for the welfare of man.

In view of these things I do most earnestly hope that you will take measures to establish this School of Science and the Arts under the supervision of the President and Trustees of Bowdoin College — the oldest by a generation of the Colleges in the State and ranking already in many respects among the most honored in the land, and that you will do this now, while you may have the satisfaction of seeing it established under your own age and guided by your own hand, and of reaping in your own consciousness the rewards of well doing.

I am glad that Mr. Ezra Cornell[40] was spared to see the rich results of his liberal ideas and acts. Since I have been writing this, it is announced that Mr. John C. [Green] of New York, has just given $600,000 to found a Scientific department at Princeton College New Jersey.[41] It will take a far less sum

40. Ezra Cornell (1807–74), cofounder of Western Union and Cornell University. "Cornell, Ezra," BOL (145/18).

41. John Cleve Green (1800–1875), a lavish benefactor of Princeton who enlarged the campus, endowed professorships, built its first library building and first chemical laboratory, and founded the John C. Green School of Science. The current Green building

to do a similar good work here. Allow me to add that should it possibly be the case that you could not conveniently at once appropriate the whole sum necessary for the endowment of the School it would serve equally well if you could bestow the income of it and meantime provide for the principal sum in such a manner as you may deem proper.

Commending these things to your earnest consideration, and in the hope that your life may be long spared to us and grow richer as it ripens.

I am

With highest respect & regard

your friend and servant

Joshua L. Chamberlain.

[PHS]

〰 TO MISS CHARLOTTE

Brunswick, Mar. 9th 1875

Miss Charlotte; — [42]

The verses you sent me yesterday are indeed very beautiful, & I have considered not only their merit as such, but also the intent & bearing of them.

In this latter respect they would be very well, if attended by, or following, other acts or token of regret at an injury done. As things are, however, they are so incomplete and isolated when regarded as apology & reparation, that I am constrained by a sense of honor to tell you that I cannot accept them, & could only do so when their genuineness was attested by other corroborating acts.

Perhaps I should state one or two reasons more particularly.

1st. *Reparation should be made on the same ground where the offence was committed.* For example, a public insult cannot be atoned for by a private apology. Paul objected to being "thrust out privily" after he had been *openly* beaten & cast into prison uncondemned. Judas did not (privately) offer to *Christ* the thirty pieces of silver, but to the [irritated] hypocrites to whom the infamous betrayal had been made. So slander-makers cannot square the account by mere personal professions to their victim.

At any rate, they can not do that to *me*.

So then in this matter, I should feel very differently about your verses, if they had come after you had begun to do all you could to correct the mischief

---

was named for him after the School of Science burned down in 1928. Leitch, *A Princeton Companion*, 230–31.

42. Miss Charlotte is unidentified.

of your former statement & insinuations. I use both words; for I know very well that without any positive language mere negations—mere assumptions of ignorance—mere silence, may be made to serve much evil purpose, & a look or tone totally contradict the purport of words.

So then nothing but the most explicit & thorough *retraction* can avail to undo the mischief of a bad intent. Much of your unfortunate share in injuring me may have come by these *indirect* means, & will hence require even more labor in correction than if words alone had done the wrong. This poem which would be a graceful consummation, at present but adds to the offence, by the inconsistency of claiming a friendship while the effects of a betrayal of it are still allowed to sun on, unchecked & uncontradicted.

2^{d}. *The matter to which this apology reaches* (if it is indeed an apology) *affects another besides myself.* A friendship, valuable to me at least, is embittered by insinuations which, though *mockery & sacrilege* of the spirit they presume to approach, yet tarnish all they touch with their base suggestions. You have not been unfrank in one thing. You have done your best to damage each of us in the other's esteem. Still I care far more for the wounds inflicted in the innocent friend—hurt, I well know, solely because helping me—than I do for any distress I can feel at personal injury.

So I think if you have kindly thoughts, they should be turned in *that* direction. I feel compelled therefore to return the verses which bear a spirit of so sweet a charity that I wish for them a wider field.

As for the main matter, when I know as much of good words spoken, as I have of evil ones, I shall then think there is a spirit of friendship which I can respond to.

Perhaps this is as good an opportunity as I shall have to give notice, that I am not hereafter to be abused through my quiet & forbearance, but the line between friends & enemies will be found to have at least one sharp edge to it, so that people will be aware which side of it they are on.

This is my case: which I am sorry to have to state in this distinct manner to one of whom I have thought so highly; but it is a matter which admits of no other treatment. Not only am I wronged but truth is wronged, while I suffer any sentiments of kindness to tolerate misrepresentation. Yours as above

Joshua L. Chamberlain.

[SL]

Brunswick March 22ᵈ 1875

My dear Mr. Longfellow:

I am rejoiced to hear that you are to visit "old Bowdoin" with your class this year.⁴³ We will try not to make it uncomfortable for you.

My special object in writing is to ask you to make my house your "base of operations." You shall have freedom and quiet if you wish it. Moreover, I wish to add Mrs Chamberlain's compliments and beg you to do us the favor to bring one at least of your daughters with you.

This house was, I think, one of your homes while you were here; and it seems as if you ought to be here while you are in Brunswick.⁴⁴

If you can stay a few days after Commencement, I want to make up a pleasant party and take a look at Casco Bay and the Islands. I shall have a new Yacht just ready for sea at that time, and I think you would enjoy the trip.

With highest regard,
Joshua L. Chamberlain.

[HU]

≋ TO THOMAS W. HYDE

Brunswick Mar 7 1876

Genl T. W. Hyde
My dear Genl

The resignation of Senator Morrill is providential & places the Govern.⁴⁵ in a position of great responsibility. It is a critical time. The last few weeks has changed the complexion & probabilities of many things.

This is an opportunity & a test for the Govern. I hope he sees this & so then me. I believe he will act as he thinks *right* is.

I must not intrude upon him, but I may ask you to let me know how his mind is in the matter.

43. Longfellow returned to Bowdoin in 1875 for his fiftieth reunion, where he delivered "Morituri Salutamus," a poem he wrote for the occasion. See entry for Alpheus S. Packard in Dramatis Personae.

44. Longfellow had rented three rooms (now upstairs) where he had brought his first wife to live. When Chamberlain showed him the rooms, he apparently wept and declared that they looked just as they had when he wrote poems while gazing into the sitting room fireplace. Trulock, 349.

45. Governor: Brig. Gen. Selden Connor (1839–1917), a Republican, who would have to appoint someone to complete Lot Morrill's Senate term. GB, 88–89; *BioDictGovr*, 2:616–17.

Yours as ever
Joshua L. Chamberlain

[PHS]

〰️ TO GRACE

Bruns. 29 My 76

My dearest Grace—

I have been waiting long for your letter & now I have come home from faculty meeting *11.30 P.m.* & find it.

Thank you & bless you for it. (Private & confidential) I dont love you so much because you are my daughter—that is a mere plupical[?] law of time & earth—a mechanical [encampment]. *I* love *you* because you are a splendid soul & belong to *Eternity*. I should love you any way daughter—sister—*woman* more especially the *latter*. Dont consider this a Paternal epistle in which fathers say what is proper for fathers to say to daughters. I go back to first principles. Father & daughter is an arrangement of temporal & earthly law for the present sphere. If you were not a *woman* to command my *love*, you would not have it—daughter or no daughter. You do command it—& I want to tell you that is something *worth having*.

I am glad of all the things you tell me of. You do not tell me of *every thing* You have good reasons. I dont care what they are if they are not the miserable ones of "*afraid to tell my father.*" Let me tell you nobody will ever love you more or more deeply or widely than your *present addressor*!!

I love you as a father *properly* & *regularly*. I love you besides as a true, solid, genuine, splendid *woman*, whom if God had given to *me* I would have looked on as God's representative on earth—(*as a woman should be to a man*) & I would have been something more than I am.

If you dont like this burn it up, & me too. I am in a hurry, & have been *sick* ever since my return. I wrote you a long letter & *burned it*! It did me just as much good & you no hurt! God bless you for a sweet true woman—my joy & *hope*. If you want anything of me as a daughter let me know. Tear up & burn if you dont like. Written in 10 minutes after 3 days of small hell-torments. Confidentially,

Yours,

J. L. C.

[MHS]

Chamberlain, ca. 1878, while president of Bowdoin College
(Courtesy of the National Archives)

〰 TO THE TRUSTEES AND OVERSEERS OF BOWDOIN COLLEGE
To the Trustees & Overseers of Bowdoin College
Gentlemen:—
I hereby tender my resignation of the office of President, and of Professor of Mental & Moral Philosophy, [to] take effect at the close of the present College year.

In doing this I desire to express my profound sense of the distinguished honor you have done me in conferring these important trusts. That I have labored earnestly to fulfill them cannot be so fully realized by you, as it is by me. Indeed all that has actually been accomplished during the last five years does not yet fully appear, and some labor has perhaps been wasted. But I am happy to leave the College in so good a condition, as will be apparent if any one [is] so disposed to consider it. Our funds are nearly doubled: our Buildings greatly improved: our means of instruction and the number of our students largely increased: and we have every prospect of an unusually large entering class, and of continued additions to our funds. A new interest is also kindled among our alumni. So the prosperity of the College seems now assured, and such services as I could render it could I believe, be much more profitably employed otherwise.

Having been connected with the College in offices of instruction or of government ever since taking my second degree in 1856, I was well aware of the difficulties I should encounter, even had not the task been laid on me of establishing a new department of study without adequate means — without, indeed, any means at all. Some difficulties I have met with were unexpected and, I think, unnecessary, and some doubtless the result of my too sanguine & self-reliant spirit. However that may be I am willing to leave to time the justification not only of what I have done, but of what I have attempted and not been able to carry through.

I cannot close this communication, which closes so long — to me a life-long — service of the College, without tendering to you, both in your official and individual capacity, my warmest thanks for your strong support and generous friendship, and the assurance of my constant & deep interest in all that concerns the welfare of the College or yourselves.[46]

I am, Gentlemen,
With high respect
Your friend & servant
Joshua L. Chamberlain

Brunswick June 26 1876
[MHS]

46. In addition to the reasons presented in 19 Sept. 1876 to Mason[?], it is possible that Chamberlain hoped that resigning would make him available for political appointment. Like his earlier attempt (see 8 July 1873), this resignation was not accepted.

Brunswick Sept 11 1876

To the Selectmen

Brunswick:

Gentlemen,

It occurs to me that some extra police force may be needed in the vicinity of the Encampment this week.

We shall, I trust, be able to take care of our soldiers; but there are always some rowdies and roughs hanging about, who keep just outside the limits of military authority.

We shall have a guard on the main road north of the camp, and it seems to me that you will need a police patrol from that point to the foot of the mall. There should be a good understanding between the police and the officers of the guard, and I ask your cooperation in preserving order and peace and obedience to the laws during the encampment.

It would be well to have some officer at hand authorized to seize liquors offered for sale. We shall not permit such sales on the camp grounds but outside may give us trouble.

I should be glad of any advice from you — and any information in regard to the interests of good order may be communicated to the officers of the guard of Genl Mattocks[47] who will command the camp the first two [ill.] days or to me.

Very respectfully yours

Joshua L. Chamberlain

[PHS]

TO JAVAN K. MASON?

Brunswick Sept 19 1876

Rev. Dr. Mason,[48]

My dear friend,

Your kind letter assuring me of your continued confidence & support, and reaffirming your reasons for asking me to withhold my resignation as President of the College at the last Commencement, is received.

I need not say that I value your friendship and your good opinion. As I have said to you before, it is a comfort to deal with a true man.

47. Probably Charles P. Mattocks, see 11 Aug. 1870 to Lane.

48. Perhaps Javan Knapp Mason (b. 1817) a minister and prison reformer. *Bib Maine*, 2:98–99.

Nor can I deny that it is grateful to me to be assured by you that I am better understood and "appreciated" among the friends of the College than ever before, and that I am still thought to be of service here, or at any rate my leaving would show that I had been of some use to the College.

I knew this was a difficult place & that the "law" of the College was for the President to be opposed—I will not say abused—by both Faculty and Boards. That certainly has been the case ever since I knew anything about the College, & I expected my share. Some things, however, have been outrageous. I can trace them to certain political influences in a great degree. It has been thought necessary for the "good" of certain gentlemen prominent in politics that I should be "killed off" in every way. Some honest people have not seen this "devil's draw" in the matter, & have been misled.

I was not in position or disposition to disturb any body's ambition, but my principles & modes of action or possibly my knowledge of some men's actions [ill.], have been a source of disgust to some, also have been means of influencing many immediate friends of the College. But let this pass. It will come out right in the end.

I do not wonder that good people see much to be desired in improving the religious influences at Bowdoin. I am heartily with them in opinion and sympathy, & a *little beyond them* in *active effort* in this direction.

I shall not slacken my efforts while I hold this responsible position. As to my teachings I am aware that they deal with the most essential principles in the guidance of thought & the formation of character. I can only say to you that the teachings I give are from my earnest convictions, growing out of my study and experience of life, & I believe when they are better known they will be found in accordance with *sound doctrine*—whether in politics, philosophy or religion.

I thank you for your letter and am grateful for your good opinion.
Yours truly
Joshua L. Chamberlain

[PHS]

Brunswick Sept 19 1876

Rev. C. H. Wheeler
Missionary in Harpoot, Ty.[49]
Dear Sir:

Your favor written from Bangor came duly to hand, & I have also had sent to me yours to Prof Packard. We have felt some interest in your work and have been considering the matter of undertaking to secure a Lectureship, or at least some testimonial of our interest in your College. Prof Packard & I, surely, did all we could to bring out our people & give you a favorable reception here.

You may imagine my utter surprise when on stirring up the matter among our Professors I was met by the statement that you [had] been active since your visit here in denouncing not only our people but the College.

The statements were very strong as reported to me, such as that "the College was going to the Evil One." "It was making Infidels faster than anybody else could make Christians," and that "this would not be the case if President Harris[50] were here," and more to that effect.

Now you have got hold of an old cry. The "infidel" aphorism was started while Dr. Harris was here. I heard the charge when it was made, originally.

I do not think you took pains to ascertain the truth of this accusation, or that the remarks you indulged in were made in a friendly or courteous or Christian spirit. At all events you must see that this must somewhat dampen the ardor of any efforts we might be disposed to make in behalf of your particular cause.

The tenor of your letters, to be sure, does not correspond with the statements reported to me, but the source through which the latter came is of such a character that I cannot doubt their having some foundation in remarks you have made concerning the College.

I have no reason to have other than the kindest feeling towards you personally (& certainly I have the strongest interest in the great work in which you are engaged.) but if this is the disposition you cherish toward the College it is only fair for me to say that I do not intend to submit to having the College misrepresented & abused without some protest, & I, for one, am not pledged to such a non-combatant policy that I cannot repel [ill.] in a hostile blow.

49. Crosby Howard Wheeler (1823–96), a Bowdoin graduate, was founder and president of Euphrates College in Harput, Turkey.

50. Rev. Samuel Harris (1814–99), Chamberlain's predecessor, a distinguished theologian and Bowdoin graduate who had left for Yale in 1871 in order to return to teaching.

For the present this is the reply to your letter.

J L Chamberlain

[PHS]

≈ TO HENRY R. LINDERMAN

Brunswick Maine Jan 27 1877

Dr. Henry R. Linderman[51]

Sir:

I have the honor to receive your favor of the 24th inst. informing me that the President[52] has designated me as one of the Commissioners to examine the coins of 1876, and to say in reply that I will accept the service, and will be at the mint in Philadelphia on the 14th of February as directed.

Very respectfully

Your obedient servant

Joshua L. Chamberlain

[PHS]

≈ TO LOT M. MORRILL

Brunswick Jan 27 1877

Hon. Lot M. Morrill

Secretary of the Treasury

My dear Sir:

I have to acknowledge your kind dispatch, before replying to which I awaited the letter referred to & now received, which names me as one of the Commission to test the [ill.] of the coins for 1876.

I thank you for your kind thoughts, but were it not for your dispatch I certainly should decline; for if the service is a real one I am unfit for it, not being an expert, & if it is only formal, I cant afford to take it feeling that I am rendering no real service.

I should not have troubled you with this letter had you not thought it worth while to telegraph me asking me not to decline the appointment.

As this may indicate an importance in your mind attaching to the matter which I do not see in it, I have thought it best to accept; and in thanking you, beg you to know that this is my only reason, and not a desire for office!

I am, with high respect,

51. Henry R. Linderman (1825–79), first director of the U.S. Bureau of the Mint. DAB, 11:273.

52. Ulysses S. Grant. The presidential "lame duck" period lasted until March until 1933.

Your friend and servant
Joshua L. Chamberlain.

≈ TO RUTHERFORD B. HAYES

Brunswick Maine March 8ᵗʰ 1877

General R. B. Hayes
President of the United States:
My dear Sir:

I beg to express, for myself and on behalf of many others who are among the most thoughtful and able Republicans in this section of the Country, the great satisfaction we feel in the opening acts of your administration.[53]

A small part of that satisfaction is in the evidence that the views set forth in your letter of acceptance have suffered no shock, and that you stand the champion of honest peace and constitutional liberty. The hopes of the Country hang on the realization of those ideas.

When in the conduct of the campaign those principles as announced by you, were by some self-made and self-seeking leaders so significantly ignored — scarcely a reference to them or to you being made in the leading speeches here — and supplanted by the untimely arousing of m[o]re sectional hate, and the memories of a bitter war, and thus so far from hearing any principles suggested that were conservative and constructive we were compelled to listen only to appeals to forces disintegrating and destructive, those who had rejoiced in your nomination as restoring honor to the Republican party, were fearful of the results even of victory.

We had before us the remarkable spectacle of a management by which the success of the party might be interpreted as a support, not of its candidate and his principles, but of the ascendancy of those very leaders who had involved us in so many difficulties, and many of the best and firmest Republicans were only kept in heart by the hope that somehow *you* might succeed in spite of *them*. It was only loyalty to the principles expressed by you and by Mr Wheeler[54] which commanded the solid vote of the Republican party.

53. In his acceptance letter, Hayes linked his administration to the party's liberal wing and its reform agenda, including civil service and currency reform, and southern "home rule."

54. Rep. William Almon Wheeler (1819–87) of New York, Hayes's running mate and vice president. "Wheeler, William A(lmon)," BOL (637/50).

It is therefore with no common satisfaction that we recognize in your triumph that of your policy. Your opponents stand rebuked, and not you.

Nothing could more fully express our sentiments or command our cordial support than your Inaugural address. Nor could we desire a better guarantee of the wisdom, courage, and firmness of your administration than the selection of such gentlemen as Mr Schurz and Mr Evarts for the chief offices in your Cabinet.

I foresee the opposition you must encounter from that same element in the party which gave you so insincere a support in the canvass. I hope you will not yield to their assaults or their artifices, and I know I speak the thoughts of the best minds in this part of the Country when I assure you of the most hearty endorsement of the patriotic, broad, and Statesmanlike policy foreshadowed by your action thus far, and if an issue is made against you for this, the people will rally to your support in the most decisive manner.

Not being able at this time to pay my respects to you personally, I beg you to accept this assurance, which is made for no other purpose than to pledge you the sympathy and strength of many who having served the Nation and the State, have a right to express an interest in the settlement of the great questions of the day.

Your friend and servant
Joshua L. Chamberlain

[RBH]

≫ TO CARL SCHURZ

Brunswick Maine
April 5, 1877.

Hon Carl Schurz
Secretary of the Interior
My dear Sir:
Observing that some of the papers in this State which are most under the control of the present managers of the Republican party are manifesting a special hostility to you as well as to the policy of the President on the civil service and the southern question, and apprehensive lest from the apparent unanimity with which these managers were put in their place you might attach too much weight to these expressions and regard the Republicans of this State as not in sympathy with the Administration, I beg to assure you that these papers do not represent the best element, nor even, as I believe, the majority of the party at the present time, but only a power which by factitious means has gained a false eminence, and which under the just and firm policy of the President is already losing its hold.

I made bold to write the President when the uncalled for and insolent threats were made against him on his very first acts and utterances, and assured him of the hearty and unqualified support of the best minds in this section of the Country. In the accession of President Hayes the people representing the American ideas have triumphed over party; and the same people will stand by what is now understood to be the policy of the Administration.

It now looks as if hostility to that policy might call out a more active demonstration on the part of its supporters. If so, be assured the earnest convictions of reasonable men will carry the defence even to a reorganization of parties, and the lines will be drawn not between those who name themselves Republicans and those who were Rebels and Rebel sympathizers, but between those who support the President's policy and those who do not.

I had but an imperfect opportunity of conversation with you when honored by your presence at my house, but you may know that I have always been looked upon with much dislike by those who seek to make political or pecuniary fortunes out of the excitements of sectional war, because though firm in adherence to the great principles of the Republican party, I still believed in the purification of the Civil service, a constant regard for local self-government, and the subordination of the military to the Civil power in time of peace. It was my high respect for you as a bold champion of these principles which has led me to join with others like-minded in expressions of personal regard which may give some title to congratulate you on your triumph and that of the principles for which many of the best men have been ostracized.

My present position at the head of an important Institution of Learning does not give me so much freedom as I desire in taking an active part in politics, but it does not forbid me to instill sound doctrines into the minds of the young men who go out every year to the duties of citizenship; and my acquaintance in the Country will still enable me to give hearty and I hope effective support to the measures now so happily inaugurated.

The problem before the Government is a difficult one and it should have the best services of all right-minded men as it certainly shall have of

Yours most respectfully

Joshua L. Chamberlain

[PHS]

Bowdoin College
Brunswick Maine Apr 7th 1877.

Hon William M. Evarts
Secretary of State
My dear Sir:

I beg not to be candid and presumptuous in referring to the fact that your predecessor[55] has honored me by sending copies of the diplomatic correspondence of the United States and other papers relating to our Foreign relations, and in asking that this favor may be continued. I shall cordially agree to any condition you may think proper to annex, as these papers are of great interest and value to me.

I pretend to no other claim than that of a citizen studious of the country's character, and deeply interested in her history — past and present, unless you are good enough to regard as some pretext for the favor the circumstance that I had a responsible command in the army during the recent war for the Union, and have since served four terms as Governor of Maine, and am now President of this College where I am trying to direct attention to a more thorough study of the principles of Government and of Constitutional and International Law.

I regret to be obliged to introduce myself, but suppose I must do so in order to justify my request. Having said this you may pardon me if I add the expression of my most thorough, and I may well say triumphant satisfaction in the good Providence which has placed you in your present position and has led the President to take the just and noble and statesmanlike view he does of his duty and opportunity. I am not just now it is true "in politics"; but it is not, I trust, because the people of my state have parted company with me, but because I could not give my unqualified support to either of the "policies" that have been prosecuted by the great parties of the last six years.

Now I rejoice that I can; & I beg you to pardon me for saying even so much.

Your obdt. Servant
Joshua L. Chamberlain

[PHS]

---

55. Hamilton Fish (1808–93), Grant's secretary of state, a wealthy and influential New York politician and former senator. "Fish, Hamilton," BOL (210/14)

Brunswick Apl 28 1877

Hon

A. H. Rice

Governor of [Massachusetts] [56]

My dear Governor,

When I last saw you, you kindly asked if you could do anything for me. At that time my thoughts were not particularly awakened to having any thing done for me.

But I see the lines are going to be drawn here, and I for one mean to stand by the President. Being here in the College I can not help him as I might and would. I believe his policy, as I now understand it, is all that is going to save the Country or the party, and I want to be recognized that I can have some reason or excuse for stepping forward in to active politics.

What I would be glad to have you do is to write the President, if you can do so without interfering with any plans of your own — giving me such favorable mention as your own friendship, our common views, and what reputation I may have gained (if it has been worthy enough to come to your ears) may warrant.

I do not know that I want any office, in particular — nor in general — although I learn that highly influential friends in New England have already mentioned me for the French Mission, and if *anything* is to be said to the President I want it to be strongly substantiated. The *offer* of an office would do more good perhaps than the office itself. If I make myself understood, I hope I am not presuming too much in asking your kind offices.

Should this however in any way conflict with your own views, I beg you not to be troubled by thinking of my suggestion a moment.

If Gov. Noyes is to have the French Mission I dont know of anything I really would care for in the way of office. [57]

Very truly your friend

Joshua L. Chamberlain

[RBH]

56. Alexander Hamilton Rice (1818–95), a former congressman and paper magnate. *DAB*, 15:534–35.

57. Gen. Edward F. Noyes (1832–90) of Ohio did get the French mission. *DAB*, 13:587.

≋ TO THE STUDENT BODY OF BOWDOIN COLLEGE

Bowdoin College
Nov 28 1877

The President would be glad to have all Students who are in town Thanksgiving day spend the Evening at his house in a perfectly informal way where they will be made as much "at home" as possible.

[MHS]

≋ TO RUTHERFORD B. HAYES

(Confidential.)   Brunswick January 18 [187]8
To the President, Executive Mansion, Washington D.C.

Any compromise that rejects Murray[58] would be the triumph of your enemies, and put to shame your friends and supporters here. We cannot bear to see your strong following in Maine annihilated. Murray's nomination is the decisive test, and is vital to every interest you are endeavoring to maintain.

([ill.] J. L. C.) Joshua L. Chamberlain

[Telegram, PHS]

≋ TO RUTHERFORD B. HAYES

Brunswick Maine Jan 19 1878

To the President:

Honored & dear Sir:

I beg to say that the telegram I was constrained to send you last evening did not imply any unwillingness on the part of your friends to leave the matter in your hands without further importunity; but was prompted by the feeling here that the situation would probably be misrepresented to you, and a compromise proposed which seemingly conciliatory would yet save to your opponents the chief working power of the Machine—the Marshalship.

I well knew it was presumptuous to address you in that way, but the letters of solicitude almost amounting to agony that came in all day—not from the candidates but from the best representatives of your supporters here, together with the misgiving that I might have not done my duty in trying to make you fully aware of the situation, made me willing to risk my reputation for good judgment and patience—though not, I trust, my place in your esteem—for the greater sake of what seem to us the public importance of the issue.[59]

58. Bvt. Brig. Gen. Benjamin Bixby Murray Jr. (1828–1906), Maine's adjutant general, was a lawyer whom Hayes was considering for U.S. marshal for the District of Maine. BBGB, 438.

59. Hayes did indeed appoint Murray marshal. Ibid.

I am, with highest regard
Your servant & friend
Joshua L. Chamberlain

[PHS]

〜TO RUTHERFORD B. HAYES

Private   Brunswick Maine Jan 26 1878

To the President:

My dear Sir:

I deem myself greatly honored in the attention you have given to the suggestions which I was permitted to bring to your notice in regard to the recent Maine appointments.

Your friends, and they are increased in number by the very fact, are enthusiastic in their admiration for the manner in which you have maintained your position.

The effect, indeed, will be far wider and more important than even this genuine and warm feeling in one remote State. The whole Country will see that the prestige of personal despotism in politics is broken, and that the true relations of the several branches of the government are in a fair way to be restored. Honest men will take courage, & will stand together, and stand by you, in this reconciliation & regeneration of the Country. Nothing could be better than the nominations. I am assured however that Mr Webb will decline as soon as formal notice reaches him.[60]

In that case, and if — as I doubt not — you have good reasons for not nominating Mr Talbot, I beg to say that the appointment of neither of the gentlemen before named to you would be such as you would desire if aware of the exact merits of the case.

Mr Hale is a very worthy young man & not completely (as I am told) opposed to the principles of the administration. But he is young, & has not yet achieved that eminence in his profession which would entitle him to such a position.

The other candidate I am entirely confident is in no wise a suitable person for the place.

60. It is unclear to which appointment this letter refers. Among the potential nominees: perhaps Nathan Webb (1825–1902), U.S. attorney for the District of Maine and later a federal judge; probably artilleryman Bvt. Brig. Gen. Thomas H. Talbot (1828–1907), a Justice Department official under Grant; Hale is unidentified; for Mattocks, see 11 Aug. 1870 to Lane. Federal Judicial Center, *History of the Federal Courts* <http://air.jfc.gov/history/index_frm.html> (April 2001); BBGB, 603.

I am very sure that next to Mr. Webb in all points that you would regard most essential Genl. Charles P. Mattocks of Portland is the man fittest and worthiest for the place. His character, ability, professional standing, political honesty and manly support of the principles you are endeavoring to establish for the well-being of the Country, would render his appointment a *tonic* for public opinion and sentiment in political affairs.

I trouble you with this because I am anxious that you should understand the real merits of the question of candidates, and because of the importance which at this juncture attaches to every public act.

Assuring you of my thanks for your confidence, and my profound admiration for your courageous stand for the principles your earnest and true words have set so clearly before our people, and also of my hearty desire to render you all honor and aid in my power,

I remain

Your servant & friend

Joshua L. Chamberlain

[RBH]

TO WILLIAM M. EVARTS

Brunswick Maine
March 5 1878

To the Honorable
Wm. M. Evarts
Secretary of State
My dear Sir,

I am placed under great obligation by the proposal which you did me the honor to communicate in your dispatch of the 4th tendering me an appointment as Commissioner to the Paris Exposition.[61]

My ignorance of the nature of the duties assigned to that appointment and of the time at which it would be necessary to leave this Country, is the reason why I did not more promptly respond.

If I may speak freely with you, I did not want to be absent from the Country during what may prove to be an eventful summer with us politically. If the policy and *personnel* of the Administration are to be assailed within our own

61. Hayes appointed Chamberlain as a commissioner of education to the 1878 Exposition, where he prepared a report on education in the world, with an emphasis on France, that won a Bronze Medal from the French government. On the report and his time in Paris, see Wallace, *Soul of the Lion*, 250–53.

Party in the summer conventions, I have looked forward to it as my duty to "throw myself into the breach" in Maine.

But if the President does not deem that necessary, or if I have deemed it of too much importance,[62] I should be disposed to accept the honor tendered in your dispatch.

I presume I can get released here by the 5th of June. Would that answer your purposes?

Very respectfully

Joshua L. Chamberlain

[PHS]

≈ TO FANNIE

Brunswick Mar 6 '78

Dear Fanny,

Mr. Murphy[63] writes me you did not go to his house, & they were all much disappointed.

I do not know where to address you (as usual) but will try the St Germaine.

All well here. I go to Farmington Friday, & to Bangor & Foxcroft the week after, & to Portland & Freeport the week after that & to Andover Mass the week after *that*!

Do by all means call on Mr Briggs[64] in Boston & settle that matter.

I may go to Paris after all—am now corresponding with the Secretary of State about it.

If so I shall be sorry you have bought so many things, & expended so much money: for I should try to take you & Grace if I could possibly get money enough. It would cost $3000 for all of us—to go as I expect to if I go at all June 6th (a month *before* Commencement) & stay till Oct 1st 4 mos.

But do as you think best. Only it seems to me poor policy to pile more things into the house to shut up & leave liable to be burned up before we return.

You shall go, if you will be good!, & I want Grace to go. Wyllys can't.[65]

You might come over after I have been there a month & got acquainted, so as to take advantage of things.

---

62. It is possible that the administration viewed Chamberlain's enthusiastic support counterproductive in Maine.

63. Murphy is unidentified.

64. Briggs is unidentified.

65. Wyllys did ultimately join them. See 14 June 1878 to his parents.

I thot I ought to let you know what is *probably* to happen.

Some considerati[o]ns have led me to change my mind about the desirableness of my going.

Everything is right, here, so far as I know.

(I wish we could have foreseen this plan; as we would have saved at least $500 of the New York expenses.)

But all right, somehow—I suppose.

aff yours

J. L. C.

[SL]

≈ TO UNIDENTIFIED RECIPIENT

Brunswick Mar 17 '78

Hon [ill.]

My dear Sir,

Your favor of the 16th referring to the Greenback movement in Maine, and suggesting that I take a position on the currency question in harmony with the Republicans of the West in order to aid in giving direction and effectiveness to this movement, was duly received.

I fully agree with you that this movement is an expression of dissatisfaction with the course of existing parties, but as a positive issue in politics I do not see what the Greenback party proposes to do to relieve the distress of the country. I have no especial objection to the Greenback as currency representing the good faith, intention & ability of the government to pay it.

But how are the people to get Greenbacks into their hands unless they give an equivalent in value of some kind?

There does not seem to me good ground to stand on in the merely "incendiary" & denunciatory statements which, as far as I have seen, make up the appeals of the Greenback party in Maine.

As I understand matters an increase in the value of the currency is not going to help us out of our difficulty. I never believed in paying off the public debt in a hurry, but I would not increase it.

If our people who protest against the miserable work the leaders of the great parties have made would only they take some ground that could be defended, & some principle that could be made aggressive & result in real reform, we could then know how to take hold.

This movement may take a shape that has some other end than Greenbacks. We shall soon see the results of our silver bill, & new phases of the great financial questions will arise.

It seems to me we who wish better things should try to recover influence in the Republican party, & hold together by such organization as we can now effect, & endeavor to guide things so as to make that the party of true reform & truly expressive of the interests of the people.

I sympathise with the feelings of the new party but I do not think they have quite given us the chance to take hold with them yet.

Confidentially & hastily yours

J. L. Chamberlain

[PHS]

〰 TO THE TRUSTEES AND OVERSEERS OF BOWDOIN COLLEGE

Bowdoin College
June 13th 1878.

The undersigned respectfully represents that having been appointed a Commissioner of the United States to the Paris Exposition assigned to the Department of Education & Instruction with leave to report by the middle of June, he consulted the visiting Committee and members of the Board of Trustees, & officers of the Board of Overseers, who assented to his request to be allowed to leave the College on the first of June in order to accept this appointment. I now ask the formal assent of the Boards to this request for leave of absence. It was my expectation to return at the close of the Summer vacation, but as my departure has been delayed by duties it became necessary to render to the College before leaving I may desire to prolong my stay in Europe beyond that time, and I respectfully ask that provided I can make suitable arrangements for the instruction usually given by me at the opening of the Fall Term I may be allowed to be absent for a period not exceeding four weeks of that term.

Respectfully submitted

J. L. Chamberlain

President.

[BSC]

〰 TO HIS PARENTS

Steamer "England."
New York,
June 14 1878

Dear Father & Mother;

I reserved a day or two to run down & make you a little visit, but matters came in so heavily on me the last week I had to work day & night without interruption except for three or four hours sleep just before daylight.

We all are off for France, & are well & happy. It will be a great thing for the children to have this opportunity of seeing Europe with us, & we shall try to write you from *Tankerville Castle* & many other interesting places.[66]

I was very much disappointed not to see you once more before going, but it could not be done without neglect of College duties. I expect to be away about five months. My first address will be (for three weeks) care Messrs McCulloch[67] &cs.

No 41 Lombard St

London England

(5 cents U.S. postage)

next:\ U.S. Commissioner \

     \ Paris Exposition   \

      \ Paris   \

       \ France   \

        \ _____ (*5 cents* U.S. postage)

I am going to take a house in Paris, or near it, & *keep house*, with a French housekeeper. We can learn how they do it.

Wyllys is happy as a bird. The ship is magnificent — five thousand tons — & our cabin was the first choice.

We all send our dutiful & affectionate regards, with much love to dear Sadie, & wishing the best things for you & the best prayers from you for the welfare of all until our next happy meeting.

     Your affectionate son

     Joshua L. Chamberlain

H. W. Chamberlain

[BSC]

≫ TO RUTHERFORD B. HAYES

Brunswick Maine

Feb. 7 1879

     Dear Mr. President;

I appreciate the honor of your remembrance "by the token" of a copy of your Message to the Senate in the matter of the New York Custom House.[68]

---

66. Tancarville in Normandy, home of William the Conqueror's chamberlain, provider of the family name. The Chamberlains visited Britain, France, Italy, Switzerland, and Germany. Smith, *Fanny and Joshua*, 240.

67. Perhaps including Hugh McCulloch (1808–95), former and later secretary of the treasury, then a partner with Jay Cooke in a London banking house. "McCulloch, Hugh," BOL (363/70).

68. Cleaning up the New York Customs House was an integral part of his civil service

It would be presumptuous of me to characterize it: the sequel has proved the strength of your position and the conclusiveness of your reasons.

I congratulate you on the result. We are all rejoicing at your triumph,—not in the Senate merely, but in the recognition of the people.

Your servant & friend;

Joshua L. Chamberlain

[RBH]

〰 TO THE TRUSTEES AND OVERSEERS OF BOWDOIN COLLEGE

Bowdoin College July 8 1879

The undersigned, understanding that there is now a prospect of making permanent provision for the chair of [M]ental or Moral Philosophy, respectfully tenders his resignation as Edward Little Professor of Mental & Moral Philosophy.[69]

Joshua L. Chamberlain

[BSC]

〰 TO JAMES G. BLAINE

Brunswick
Dec. 29, 1879

Hon. James G. Blaine:

My dear Sir:—

I telegraphed Governor Garcelon[70] the day Governor Morrill's letter appeared, urging him as earnestly as I could to submit the disputed questions to the Court. I afterwards wrote him a letter to the same effect.[71]

As to the indignation meeting proposed here, it was my opinion that demonstrations of that sort had already been sufficient to impress upon the Governor the state of public feeling; and that what we now need to do is not to add to popular excitement which is likely to result in disorder and violence,

---

reform program and his "spectacular battle with Congress." Hoogenboom, *Rutherford B. Hayes*, 403.

69. Autographed note by another hand at bottom: "Read & accepted." See his previous attempt of 26 June 1876.

70. Alonzo Garcelon (1813–1906), a highly regarded physician and civic activist, was the outgoing Democratic governor. *WhoAm*, 438.

71. Gov. Garcelon submitted questions regarding the disputed 1879 election to the Maine Supreme Judicial Court, but he ignored the court's response. See 70 *Maine Reports* 560 (1879).

but to aid in keeping the peace by inducing our friends to speak and act as sober and law abiding citizens.

In my opinion there is danger that our friends may take some step which would put them in the wrong. That would be very bad. If wrong is to be done, let the responsibility of it rest with those who do it, and do not let those who are aggrieved seek redress in a way to shift upon themselves the burden of wrongdoing.

I deprecate all suggestions of bloodshed in the settlement of the question. Not only would that resort be deplorable, but the suggestion of it is demoralizing. I cannot bear to think of our fair and orderly state plunged into the horrors of a civil war.

I hope you can do all you can to stop the incendiary talk which proposes violent measures, and is doing great harm to our people. I cannot believe that you sympathize with this, and I am sure your great influence can be made to avail much now to preserve peace and respect for the law.

Pardon me for this, but I think the circumstances demand of me to make these suggestions.

Very respectfully yours,
Joshua L. Chamberlain

[PHS]

≈ TO UNIDENTIFIED RECIPIENT

Augusta, [January] 1[880]

My dear Sir:

I am well aware of the occasion you have to be anxious, and thank you for any positive information which may come to your knowledge.

I do not want to move the militia unless made necessary by a first blow against the peace. Who ever makes the first *move* may be held responsible for all the consequences whether foreseen or not.

Rest assured I am master of the situation as yet, & master of myself.

If you can keep people [quiet] outside & make them discourage wild rumors, & avoid crowding into the Capitol, I believe we can pull through the day in peace. [A]s I said I am "master of myself" — & believe my head is level, & that I see the whole situation. It is a critical time, & calm men must guide.

The Mayor & the Sheriff[72] are well posted & prepared, & I can command sufficient force at a short notice, for any emergency.

72. Charles Elventon Nash and William H. Libby, respectively.

Truly yours
J. L. Chamberlain
Major General[73]

[PHS]

≋ TO ALONZO GARCELON

Augusta Jan 6 1880

To His Excellency The Governor
Sir;
Upon such investigation as I am able to make, 1 do not find that the men on duty as a guard or police force in the State House[74] have any proper ~~authority~~ or *status* civil or military, to enable them to act in such capacity ~~which they appear to hold, either civil or military.~~ I do not feel authorized to give them any orders, & not desiring to assume such responsibility, I respectfully make this report of the situation.

With high respect
Your obedient servant
J. L. Chamberlain
Major Genl.

[MHS]

≋ TO ALONZO GARCELON

Augusta Jan 7 1880

His Excellency
Alonzo Garcelon
Governor;
After our good success today in having the peace so well kept,[75] I am sorry to learn that the men in the State House have taken arms again. I cannot think this has been authorized by you. I heard your order yesterday to have the arms boxed up, & the report to you that it had been done. I therefore with your assent published my card assuring the public that there were no armed men

---

73. Commanding the state volunteer militia. He had previously held, resigned, and again declined the position because the militia was underfunded, but the election crisis caused him to accept the position once again (with power to restructure the militia) on 2 Jan. 1880. Pullen, 89–90.

74. Garcelon had hired what Chamberlain regarded as a band of thugs to protect the State House.

75. The new legislative session opened on January 7th. The governor's term ended at midnight.

in the State House & that arms would not be taken without due cause and in a lawful manner.

My honor is pledged in this.

Moreover under your orders I am made responsible for public property in the State House & after 12 midnight the sole responsibility ~~will fall on me~~ appears to rest on me.

I beg therefore ~~to be relieved of this responsibility, or else that no man in the~~ and must therefore [ask that] no men in the State House be allowed to ~~take~~ touch the army ~~this~~ tonight, ~~we~~ will have the whole embarrassment relieved in the mor[nin]g.

[Very] respectfully
Your obt servt
J. L. Chamberlain
M. G.

[MHS]

≋ FRAGMENT TO FANNIE

Augusta Jan 7 1880

Dear Fanny:—

Every thing is confusion here yet, although I succeeded yesterday in getting a good many awkward things straigh[t]ened out.

But what vexed me is that some of our own people (Republicans) do not like to have me straigh[t]en things. [T]hey want to have as big a mess as possible. They actually blame me for dis arming the State House. The [very] ones who are [clambering] because it was armed.

We shall have no Gover—

[SL]

≋ TO FANNIE

Jan 9 1880

My dear Fan[n]y:

There is such confusion here—no Governor & no legislature—that to prevent positive anarchy & mob-law I have been obliged to assume the defence & protection of the Institutions of the State as you will see by my Proclamation to the people which you perceive bears a very quiet & *un*assuming mien.

I do not dare to leave here a moment. There would most assuredly be a coup d'etat, ending in violence & bloodshed.

I am determined that Maine shall not become a *South American* State.

I wish you were here to see & hear. But there is not a great crowd of ladies here I assure you.

I wish Carrie would give me a little more of an *outfit*. I came off in a great hurry. No one knows what will come next, & I cant tell when I can get home. For the last two days & nights I have scarcely slept.

It is a critical time & things are greatly mixed. But I know my duty thoroughly.

Thanks to a good Providence my health is quite good.

Hoping that you are all well & happy & not worried about me I remain yours most affectionately.

J. L. C.

[SL]

≋ TO JOHN APPLETON

Copy.   Augusta Jan 12 1880

Sent to midnight train

My dear Sir:—

Mr Lamson[76] has borne himself so honorably, & has aided so much in trying to bring about a peaceful solution, that I have come to entertain a high respect for him.

I earnestly hope it will be found that Lamson is entitled to be recognized. *In that case I can see a way out.*[77]

Of course the Court can only give the law: but where the "letter" is killing the "spirit," it might be possible to temper justice with mercy.

Sincerely yours

J. L. Chamberlain

(Later)

76. James B. Lamson of Freedom, Maine, was the former-Democrat-turned-Green-backer selected by the fusionist would-be Senate as its president. Pullen, 95; *Biographical Sketches*, 7.

77. Fusionists wanted Lamson recognized as Senate president, which, under the state constitution, would make him acting governor. Republicans feared that this would lead to recognition of the unelected fusionist legislators. Chamberlain refused to recognize him, but encouraged Lamson to submit his bid to the Supreme Judicial Court. Because he had been informed that many "counted-in" fusionists would resign their seats once the legislature was properly seated, Chamberlain thought that recognizing Lamson offered a way out. Typically, he did not publicize his apolitical reasoning, exposing him to attack from Republicans itching to fight. See 30 Dec. 1880 to Appleton on the political damage this letter caused him. Graham, "Month of Madness," 80–81.

The excitement is now terrific in bitterness. The fusionists swear they will resist with blood & fire if the ~~decision of the~~ Court sustains the ~~proposed~~ Republican programme. J. L. C.

[MHS]

Thursday mor[nin]g
15 Jan. [1880]

My dear Fanny;

Yesterday was another Round Top; although few knew of it. The bitter attack on me in the Bangor Commercial calling me a traitor, & calling on the people to send me speedily to a traitor's doom,[78] created a great excitement.

There were threats all the morning of overpowering the police & throwing me out of the window, & the ugly looking crowd seemed like men who could be brought to do it (or to *try it*). Excited men were calling on me—some threatening fire & blood & some begging me to call out the militia at once. But I stood it firmly through, feeling sure of my arrangements & of my command of the situation.

In the afternoon the tune changed. The plan was to arrest me for treason, which not bei[n]g a [j]ailable offence, I should be kept in prison while they inaugurated a reign of terror & blood. They foamed & fumed away at that all the evening. Mr Lamson kindly came to me & said he would be the one to sue out a writ of habeas corpus & have me set at liberty again.

That plan failed.

At about 11 P.M. one of the citizens came & told me I was to be kidnapped—overpowered & carried away & detained out of peoples knowledge, so that the rebels could carry on their work. I had the strange sense again—of sleeping inside a picket guard.

In the night Gen'l. Hyde of Bath came up with 30 men & Col. Heath[79] of Waterville with 50 men: sent for by Republicans I suppose & greatly annoying to me & embarrassing too.

I wish Mr Blaine & others would have more confidence in my military ability. There are too many men here afraid [for] their precious little pink skins.

---

78. Each party's newspapers accused him of siding with its adversaries, labeling him in headlines a "Republican Renegade," a "Fusionist Sympathizer," the "Serpent of Brunswick," a "Lawless Usurper," the "Tool of Blaine," and the "Most Dangerous Man in Maine." Ibid., 89.

79. Francis E. Heath (1838–97) of the 19th Maine, a lumber mill operator. BBGB, 275.

I shall have to protect them of course: but my main object is to keep the peace & to give opportunity for the laws to be fairly executed.

Do not worry about my safety. Make yourself as comfortable as you can at home.

If you are afraid, send word to the selectmen, or Mr. Thos K. Eaton[80] to have the police keep an eye to you & the house.

But I dont believe any body will think of troubling you.

Somebody else beside Annie ought to be in the house with you. Dont worry about me,

yours aff.

J. L. C.

[BSC]

~ TO JAMES G. BLAINE

Three P.M.
Augusta, Jan. 16 1880.

My dear Mr. Blaine.

I pay great deference to your judgment as to the imminence of peril.

A storm is raging around me here in the State House; & I have no doubt of the designs of wicked men inside of this building as well as outside.

But I do assure you, my dear sir, with the utmost deference to your opinion & also to your wishes that I can guarantee peace with the dispositions I have made, & which I hardly dare make generally known, lest the bad elements get wind of it and thwart my plans. But do be assured that the position shall be held & that all rights & privileges shall be yet fairly & lawfully vindicated. Neither force [nor] treachery nor trick shall get the mastery of the situation out of my hands.

I have means of knowing all that is going on all over the State, & shall be ahead if force is resorted to.

But, my dear sir, as to ordering out the Militia, I want to save the moral lesson for our people *if possible*, that in this State right shall be vindicated by peaceful measures & not by force, and I shall resort to that only in the last moment when everything else has failed.

Whoever first says *"take arms!"* has a fearful responsibility on him, & I don't mean it shall be me who does that.

Pardon the haste and nervousness of this; but the pressure & whirl here is enough to distract a man.

---

80. Eaton is an unidentified Brunswick police officer or resident.

I beg you to put confidence in me now, & do not think you will be disappointed.

Respectfully yours,

J. L. Chamberlain.

I have had to write this by snatches for the last 2 hours. J. L. C.

[PHS]

≫ TO DANIEL F. DAVIS

Headquarters First Div. M.M.,
Augusta, January 17, 1880.

To the Honorable Daniel F. Davis,[81]

Sir:

I have the honor to acknowledge the receipt of your communication informing me that you have been legally elected and duly qualified as Governor of Maine, together with a certified copy of the opinion of the Supreme Court upon the questions affecting the legality of the organization of the Legislature of 1880.[82]

As it is manifest that this opinion establishes the legality of your election, and that you are duly qualified as Governor, I have the honor to report to you that I consider my trust, under Special Order No. 45, as at an end.

I am, with highest respect, your obedient servant,

Joshua L. Chamberlain, Major General.

[MHS]

---

81. Daniel F. Davis (1843–97), a veteran and lawyer from East Corinth. *BioDictGovr*, 2:618–19.

82. A justice of the peace swore in the Republican legislators (both undisputed and counted-out) on January 12th, and they immediately posed questions to the Supreme Judicial Court on the legality of the election and the procedures used on the session's opening day. The court (which did include a Democrat) unanimously ruled in favor of the counted-out Republicans. See 70 *Maine Reports* 570 (1880). When the certified copy of the decision arrived from Bangor, where the court had deliberated in safety, Chamberlain recognized Daniel Davis and returned to Brunswick. Graham, "Month of Madness," 85, 90–93.

HEADQUARTERS First Div. M.M., }

AUGUSTA, January 17, 1880. }

General Orders }

No. 4. }

I.   As the Honorable Daniel F. Davis has been duly qualified as Governor of Maine, the trust devolved on me, by Special Order No. 45, Adjutant General's office, January 5, 1880, is at an end.

II.   Paragraph IV, of General Order No. 3. from these headquarters, is so far modified as to recognize the fact that all military authority now emanates from Daniel F. Davis, Governor and Commander-in-Chief.

III.   The General commanding cannot but express his grateful acknowledgments to Lieut. Col. John Marshall Brown, Major Frank E. Nye, Major Joseph W. Spaulding and Captain Edward E. Small,[83] of his staff, for the very able, prudent and efficient manner in which they have discharged the difficult and harassing duties demanded of them during the unprecedented disorders of the last twelve days, and the great service they have rendered to the State in preventing violence, and securing the impartial regard for the rights of all.

IV.   To Captain Henry M. Sprague, Company "C," First Regiment, Volunteer Militia, and Captain John W. Berry,[84] Richards Light Infantry, for their zeal, fidelity and constancy in the discharge of important duties, honorable mention is due.

V.   The General particularly commends the attitude in which the troops of this State have borne themselves in a crisis which so severely tested firmness and di[s]cipline, showing that no local or partisan feelings for a moment shook their loyalty to the constitution and the laws.

VI.   It would be unjust not to take the occasion to recognize the service rendered by the Honorable Charles E. Nash, Mayor of Augusta, who, with rare tact, impartiality and skill, has discharged the difficult task of preserving the peace and order of the Capitol and city, and who, with his police and the efficient aid of William H. Libby, Esq., Sheriff of the County, and his deputies, has made it possible to avoid all show of military force, and prevent any disturbance of the peace while we were passing through a most dangerous crisis in the history of this State.

---

83. Acting Asst. Adjt. Gen. Nye was a temporarily retired Army officer from Augusta. *WhoAm*, 909. Spaulding (1841–1919), a Civil War colonel, was a lawyer and editor of Maine's law reports. *Bib Maine*, 2:460–61. See 4 Oct. 1880 to Spaulding. Small is otherwise unidentified. For Brown, see Dramatis Personae.

84. Both are otherwise unidentified.

VII. The General also thanks the citizens of Maine, who, without distinction of party, have borne patiently the exercise of powers so unusual, and have strengthened his hands in the trying task laid upon him, of protecting property and rights in what might be called the absence of civil government.

Joshua L. Chamberlain, Major General.

Official.

Frank E. Nye

Major and Acting Asst. Adjutant General.

[MHS]

≈ TO FANNIE

New York, May 11, 1880

Dear Fannie:

Here I am; but it does not seem very natural here. The house itself is entirely changed. But then I am not here much except to sleep.

Genl Sheridan has been in the witness stand the two days I have been here & will be [t]omorrow probably, so that my evidence will not be given before Thursday & I shall very likely be kept under cross examination at least another day.[85] The cross-examinations are very searching & as my evidence will be important I expect quite an ordeal. I dislike very much to be away so long a time; but this is something I cant be absent from. We are bound to have the true history of this thing out now.

I had a warm greeting from Sheridan & Hancock & a great many others including *Gen Sickles* (your friend).

Some of the Rebel officers will be here soon.

I still hope to be through by the last of the week.

I am go[ing] to try to think out my Philadelphia oration. They expect a great deal I find, & I must not fall much below my work.

If you want me to get any thing here, there will be time I think to let me know.

yours aff

J. L. C.

[SL]

85. Chamberlain was in New York for the hearings reviewing Sheridan's decision to relieve Gen. Gouverneur K. Warren of command of the V Corps at the battle of Five Forks.

Brunswick Oct 4, 1880.

Genl. J. W. Spaulding,

Personal

Copy

My dear General;

I am now urged from all quarters to accept support for the U.S. Senatorship. Of course I can regard you as a right hand man, as you were in the crisis of last winter.[86]

Would your Senator, Mr. Lamson be as friendly to me as he was then?[87]

And do you see anything preposterous in my being a candidate before the people of Maine or the Republican party?[88]

Yours as ever

J. L. Chamberlain.

[MHS]

≋ TO CHARLES O. FARRINGTON

Copy   Bk. Oct. 8 1880.

C. O. Farrington Esq.

My dear Sir;—

I find that thoughtful & earnest Republicans not only in Maine but throughout New England are expressing th[ei]r desirableness of my being brought forward as a representative man of the conservative element of the party for the U.S. Senatorship.

---

86. Encouraged by the public and some Republicans to seek Hannibal Hamlin's open Senate seat (which each party had offered him in exchange for recognition of their gubernatorial candidate), Chamberlain began an epistolary campaign. He wrote legislators, politically connected friends, and individuals who had helped him in January, and he called in favors from appointees whose jobs he had helped secure, such as Benjamin Murray (see 18 and 19 Jan. 1878 to Hayes; 8 Oct. 1880 to Murray, MHS).

87. James B. Lamson, see 12 Jan. 1880 to Appleton.

88. Chamberlain's leadership during the election crisis once again made him a hero, and he might have won a direct election, but state legislatures selected senators until 1913. His impartiality created so much enmity in an already hostile Republican leadership that, in what may be his words, "For a long time—those who desired to secure office or contracts under the State or National Governments were obliged to represent themselves as not friendly to the General." Chamberlain Association of America, *Joshua Lawrence Chamberlain Supplement*, 26. The Republican legislature ultimately gave the seat to Rep. Eugene Hale, the party's floor leader in the State House during the crisis and a close ally to James G. Blaine.

Some thing different from former ways has got to be done or the party is doomed.

I am at present inclined to think favorably of their suggestion. I do not know how your representative Mr Nickerson[89] would feel, but I presume he & most of my old townsmen would be inclined to think favorably & to act firmly in the matter.

I would be glad to know how the matter stands in your vicinity, I should suppose our people would see that something ought to be done to give us a little more hold on the respect of the world or even of our own people.

If not too much trouble I wish you would put me in the way of getting at Mr Nickerson's feeling.

yours truly

J. L. Chamberlain

[MHS]

TO EPHRAIM FLINT JR.

Bk. Oct. 8 1880.

Hon Ephraim Flint.[90]

My dear Sir;—

I suppose I cannot be wrong in believing that you are in no wise changed from what you have always been, & that I have a right to rely on you as a firm friend, "first, last & all the time."

I am urged by many thoughtful Republicans to allow myself to be brought forward for the Senatorship, I presume you think this a proper thing to do, & would do all in your power to promote it, even if I said no word to you about it.

But I value your judgment, & would be glad to be advised by you in regard to the matter

I certainly can see no reason why either of the other candidates has so decided a [hold] on the office that an ordinary man like me might not presume to speak of the matter.

If the Republican party wants to vote me down they may do so without hurting my feelings

But there are principles which are going to triumph & there are men who are going to stand by me as well as I by them.

89. Jeptha H. Nickerson, a ship carpenter, was a Brewer Republican. *Biographical Sketches*, 12.

90. Flint had been Maine secretary of state from 1864 to 1867. MSL (SOS).

It is a matter of some importance now what sort of a man & what sort of ideas shall represent the Republican party in Maine.

Will you give me your views?

Truly yours

Joshua L. Chamberlain

[MHS]

≈ TO JOHN APPLETON

Brunswick Dec. 30th 1880.

Hon John Appleton LL.D.

My dear Judge;—

I see it asserted that Mr Charles Boutelle has a letter I wrote you regarding the solution of the dead-lock last winter.[91] This letter had reference solely to a proposition which Mr Lamson had agreed to make & to open the way to which he had prepared certain very fair questions to submit to the Court if they would recognize him sufficiently to answer them.[92]

It has since appeared that he *never sent you these questions at all.* As the who[le] thing was superseded by the subsequent action of the Republican members I did not think it worth while to write you again. My main object was accomplished through their measures,—the political rights of members were vindicated.[93]

As my letter was only a private one I naturally supposed I could wait until I could see you, and explain at leisure what bearing and aim my letter had. It had no reference whatever either to the "Fusion Legislature" nor to the Republican organization which soon afterwards propounded the questions to the Court which so effectually determined the issue.

No one can possibly understand my letter unless he knows a pretty important chapter of the "secret history" of that crisis. I cant very well explain it publicly without involving some friends neither you nor I nor even Capt. Boutelle would like to see placed in a more disagreeable position than they have already suffered.

I cannot believe that Capt. Boutelle has my private letter to you; but if there is an intention to use it to my disadvantage it might be better first to

91. See 12 Jan. 1880 to Appleton.

92. In an effort to crush Chamberlain, Boutelle had used the wording of his hastily drafted letter to suggest that Chamberlain had secretly recommended that the fusionists be recognized.

93. See 17 Jan. 1880 to Davis.

know the bearing and history of it, & the complications involved in its explanation which might result in injuring other parties more than it would me.

I have been desirous of seeing you but have not yet found an opportunity.
Sincerely yours
J. L. Chamberlain

[MHS]

〰TO JOHN APPLETON
Confidential   Brunswick Jan. 1 1881
Copy
My dear Judge
Your kind letter is received, and the fact is as I supposed.

The reason I am so reluctant to make a public explanation is that it must necessarily involve a friend whom I do not wish to have any more embarrassed than he is now — if you will let me name him to you confidentially — Judge [Libbey].[94]

The situation at the time I wrote that letter was peculiar. Let me (tho' too hastily) recount a few features.

I was informed on Saturday 10th of January by a gentleman of the highest standing who professed to speak by permission & authority from three Judges of the Supreme Court, that the Court were ready & desirous to have *me* put certain questions which they would answer in a certain way.

I had three reasons for not doing this.

1. I didn't like that way of doing such business
2. I doubted the binding force of, & general acquiescence in answers made to questions put by a military officer to whom the constitution gave no such right.
3. I had a still better reason.

Several leading Republicans had pointedly assured me (by authority again) that I might consult, and safely rely on & follow *Judge [Libbey]* who would represent the Court generally on the questions that were embarrassing me, or on which I needed advice. (Saturday or Sunday evening). I did consult him & was met by the remark, "I have been expecting you, and have examined the case pretty thoroughly & have formed my opinion." Lamson is *de facto* Governor & you have no other course but to recognise & obey him." My

94. Artemus Libbey (1823–94), the sole Democratic justice on the Maine Supreme Judicial Court. MSL (judge-c).

answer was "That is equivalent to saying that I have been a usurper all this week & very nearly a traitor." "Judge L: I do not say that, but your only safe course is to recognize him." My answer — "This is to beg the question & surrender the position. That act of mine would virtually give the government to the *Count-outers*."

We then discussed the matter at length & I finally made this statement.

"Judge, in view of the whole case I have concluded to take the responsibility of holding on where I am. I am a public officer charged with exceedingly important trusts & in a most critical time. It is my duty to know important unquestioned & notorious facts. Among these are the non-elections (conceded until the action of the Governor & Council) of certain "Senators" whose votes were necessary to Mr. Lamson's election. Knowing those facts I shall expect Mr. L. to satisfy me of the legality of his election, & this can only be done by a new utterance of the Court, & Mr L. must put the questions. If he is as you say *de facto* Governor, the Court's answer will make it apparent; if not, you will not answer him & I shall then know what to do next." On the Monday following Mr. Lamson called on me to "recognize" him & I declined in my letter made public Jan 12th, Lamson then came to me & said he acquiesced in my reasons & said the Republicans had recognized him fully by asking him to qualify them (or proposing to ask him) which he could not do unless he were at least de facto President of the Senate. He said I was the one refusing to recognize him. But he thought my reasons good. I told him it would embarrass me very much if he did qualify the Republican members, as then logically I should be obliged to surrender my special authority — & responsibility — & obey him. *He said he did not dare to have me do that*, & agreed to submit questions himself which would fairly test the case & abide by the answers of the Court.

I thought this a good way out & that is what I said to you in my note. But as you never saw the questions *which I* then supposed to have been sent (*night of 12th or 13th*, you did not understand my letter. I will send you a copy of Lamsons questions which I have.

Truly yours

J. L. Chamberlain

[MHS]

≈ TO ARTEMUS LIBBEY OR THOMAS W. HYDE?

Brunswick Jan 6 1881

My dear General:

I had no thought of your letter being published with my "interview." I sent a request such as the one I handed you to Genl Brown & asked him to add what he could in another letter & leave it with Mr Richardson[95] who already had yours (not for publication but for Mr R's *information*). Genl Brown seems to have believed I wished them published & it seems to [three words ill.] ~~also that he~~ so advised Mr R. I regret this very much, as it gives you ~~unnecessary~~ trouble & annoyance.

The reporter also seems to have misunderstood me. I did not mention your name in reference to the letter to Judge Appleton, nor Gen'l Brown's either. I said "that letter was seen by one or two gentlemen of high standing, Republicans." It was Mr *Lamson's questions* which I said Genl Spaulding saw.

I did not say that I *would* ask you to make a statement but that I *had* done so. I did not know, until I asked you last week, whether you saw my letter to Judge Appleton or not. It was a private, that is a merely personal letter.

Had it been in any way official, I should most certainly have consulted you in regard to it; and you are perfectly correct in saying I would not have written or sent such a letter without your knowledge.

I wish to say however that the letter, though personal, was in no way secret. It was personal because it would have been improper for me to have written an official letter on that subject, or to have addressed the Court upon it.

The circumstances are well known.

A distinguished Republican member of the Senate had risen in his place & moved "that the Senate do now adjourn in order that the President of the Senate (*Lamson*) may administer the oath to members of the House as required by the Constitution." (I take this as [given] by the Reporter of the Herald. I have not the Senate Journal before me now.) And the Republican members of the house had formally asked Mr. Lamson as President of the Senate to qualify them.

I saw no reason why I, in my situation, should not desire that the Court should decide on that matter before I acquiesced in this view; & in order to [do] that it was necessary that Mr Lamson's right to put such questions, & have them answered, should be recognized. I thought that the best way out ~~& think so now~~. There is no secret about it, & no offence that I can see.

I only wanted a *legal decision* of a question the Republicans had *assumed* in asking Mr Lamson to qualify the members of the House.

I am sorry you have been put to trouble, by what was in fact no fault or mistake of mine, but a misunderstanding of what I said ~~to the advertiser reporter~~.

You may make any use of this or any portion of it you please. I ~~shall write Mr. Richardson correcting the statement or do anything else you desire.~~

95. Richardson is unidentified.

But the baseness & indecency of some men is trying to one's faith in human nature.

Sincerely yours

Joshua L. Chamberlain

P.S. I perceive also that the printer left out the words "*I fully believe*" inserted in your letter where you refer to my intent & understanding in writing Judge Appleton. J. L. C.

[MHS]

TO JAMES A. GARFIELD

Brunswick June 14 '81

To President Garfield,

Honored Sir:

It has been suggested to me by a medical gentleman of much experience that the best treatment Mrs Garfield could have would be a summer on the coast of Maine.[96] Should that judgment commend itself to you I shall be very glad if it may be in my power to aid in the selecting [of] a suitable place, or in any way to contribute to your satisfaction in regard to the matter.

I beg also to add;—though not in any way the main object of this letter—that should it be pleasing to you to continue your visits to Educational Institutions in this direction, you would be most welcome at Bowdoin College during our Commencement week which is the second week of July (10th–14th). We expect President Chadbourne[97] here on Commencement day—the 14th.

With very high regard

your obt servt.

Joshua L. Chamberlain

[LC]

TO OLIVER OTIS HOWARD

Brunswick Aug 1 '81

My dear Genl Howard:

I must renew my invitation for our Reunion Aug. 25th 1881.[98]

All the old Maine soldiers want to see Genl Howard.

96. Lucretia Garfield (1832–1918) was bedridden with a mixture of exhaustion and malaria. She chose to recuperate on the Jersey shore, nursed by the president—where she would soon nurse him. Peskin, "Lucretia Garfield."

97. Paul Ansel Chadbourne (1823–83), president of Williams College.

98. The "Re-Union and Encampment" of the Association of Maine Soldiers and Sailors, of which Chamberlain was president: "It is expected that there will be a large gathering of the survivors of the late war who served in the army and navy of the United States

Will it reverse our respective stations of authority if I say you *must come*?
Cordially yours
J. L. Chamberlain

[BSC]

PETITION ON CIVIL SERVICE REFORM
TO UNIDENTIFIED RECIPIENT

New York September 16, 1881

Dear Sir

The recent murderous attack upon the President, the result of which is still in doubt,[99] but success in which under the present system might mean a redistribution of offices, has drawn attention everywhere to the imperative necessity of some effectual remedy for the abuses and dangers of patronage in the Civil Service. Such a remedy however, will be delayed until there is a general agreement upon measures.

To this end, it is respectfully suggested, that at any public meeting in your neighborhood to express the strong feeling which has been excited by the assault, or on other appropriate occasion, a resolution be introduced, asserting the paramount importance of the question of reform: and pointing out, that as the evils spring chiefly from personal influence upon minor appointments, the only effective remedy lies in annulling that influence, by providing that appointments shall be made for proved merit instead of personal favor, and that connection with the service in such offices shall be terminated only for legitimate cause, such as dishonesty, negligence, or inefficiency, but not for political reasons.

If this [suggestion] should meet your approval, it is hoped that for the common welfare you will interest yourself in the passage of such a resolution.

Yours respectfully,[100]

[RBH]

---

from the State of Maine, and distinguished military gentlemen from other sections of the country." 5 July 1881, BSC.

99. The frustrated office seeker Charles J. Guiteau shot President Garfield on 2 July 1881. Nursed by the first lady on the Jersey shore, Garfield held on until 19 Sept. 1881.

100. Signed by thirty-five luminaries, including Chamberlain, Rutherford B. Hayes, Charles F. Adams, and John Hay. Largely due to the assassination, Congress passed the Pendleton Civil Service Act of 1883, the zenith of the civil service reform movement — ironically signed into law by the Tammany Hall hack Chester A. Arthur.

Washington Jan 29 1882.

My dear Sister;

I am so far on my way home & write a word to let you know where my movements are leading.

I made quite a visit to Florida, & saw much there to invite energetic & resolute young men. There are great opportunities to get health & wealth, & also to do good, & help other people.

I was most warmly received by all sorts of people, & had many invitations to take positions of responsibility which naturally suit my temperament & aspirations. I always wanted to be at the head of some enterprise to transform the wilderness into a garden—both materially & spiritually—to be a missionary of civilization & of Christianity at once.[101] Here is a great chance to do it, & in my own Country, which is peculiarly dear to me. It would be a delight to me now to give my energies to bringing forward the true results of all our struggle & sacrifice for the Country, & to secure the blessing of so great a victory for the right.

As yet I have made no plans, for I owe a duty yet to the College, & must see that all fulfilled before I think of new fields.

Health surely could be favored & kept in that wonderful clime where the sea sands & corals have made a land of strange contrasts of soil, & the days & nights are glorious above, & the airs sweeping from the Atlantic & the Gulf keep a constant & delicious evenness of temperature.

I mean to take Fanny there next winter, & think it would cure her of all her ills.

It may be I shall have more to say & do about Florida by & by.

Friday I visited the battlefield of Petersburg & spent 4 hours in trying to identify the spot where I fell on the 18 of June 64 in leading a charge upon the Rebel works.

All is changed there now. What was a solid piece of works through which I led my troops is now all cleared field, & the hill side so smooth there is now grown up with little clumps of trees—marking some spots made more rich perhaps by the bloody struggles enacted on them. At last, guided by the rail road cut & the well remembered direction of the church spires of the city, I found the spot—or a space of 20 or 30 feet within which I must have fallen.

101. Perhaps to placate his parents' early ambitions for him—his mother wanted Lawrence to be a minister, his father a soldier—Chamberlain's initial ambition had been to become a missionary.

It is now a plowed field—too rich, I suppose, since that 18 of June to be left barren by the owner—& there are in it the remnants of a last year compil[e]d.

Standing & musing there remembering how I thought of Mother in that calm ebbing away of life amidst the horrible carnage, I looked down & saw a bullet, & while stooping to pick it up, another & another appeared in sight & I took up *six* within as many feet of each other and of the spot where I fell. You may imagine what the havoc must have been that day. [A]nd for 17 years relic hunters have been carrying away lead & iron from that field—amounting, I was told, to cart-loads. I could easily no doubt have found many more had I searched, or kicked away the earth a little. But these I have, & that other that made so straight a way through me, will do.[102]

You can not imagine, I believe, what thoughts came over me, as I thought of all those who stood there on that day—for & against—& what it was all for, & what would come of it—& of those who on the one side & the other thought there was something at stake worthy of dearest sacrifice.

Such thought never would end, had one time to ponder, & it is well perhaps that the common cares & the inexorable duties of life call us away from too long thoughts.

Another study is this capital. Here are gathered the representatives of all sections & parties & creeds & countries, within little space. It is like a spectacle—a scene in an amphitheater. Here is the little world around which the whole great country moves.

Self-seeking marks too many faces, & all the strifes of peaceful times—less noble often than those of war,—are seen here in their little play, or great one, so the case may be.

All is not evil here, however. I went to a church thronging with earnest people this morning, & heard words of deep impressiveness, & witnessed a wonderful scene of infant baptism which also set me to thinking long of how we are responsible for each other.

I shall hasten home now, & shall hope to see you before long. Trusting you are all well & happy under God['s] protecting love & care.

I am

Your affectionate brother

Lawrence.

[UMO]

102. Chamberlain had kept the distorted minié ball which surgeons cut out of him at Petersburg.

≋ TO HENRY WADSWORTH LONGFELLOW

Bowdoin College,
Feb 27 1882

My dear Mr Longfellow

The faculty of the College remembering this anniversary[103] desired me to telegraph you their congratulations.

It is now so late I cannot reach you in that way tonight. We too hold fast to our part in you, and are only the more proud that we share [you] with the whole world.

Yours as ever
Joshua L. Chamberlain

[HU]

≋ TO OLIVER OTIS HOWARD

Brunswick June 13 1882

Maj Genl. O. O. Howard
My dear General.

This is to be a most interesting Commencement. Especially in the circumstance that we are to open our Memorial [H]all & dedicate it to the memory of the men who fought & fell for the Country. This will take place on July 12th Wednesday. The occasion would fail of its peculiar significance if you should be absent from the service. We want you & *must have you* give a short address on the occasion. There will be some others. But we shall look chiefly to you for the speech that will be most appropriate & most honoring to the College & to the men it thus commemorates.

There will be a great gathering of old graduates & all will wish to see you. I wait your answer with deep interest.

Very truly yours
J. L. Chamberlain

[BSC]

≋ TO JAMES W. BRADBURY

Brunswick June 29 1882

My dear Sir:

I shall have to speak for the College on the occasion of turning over the Hall[104] by the Building Committee. That seems to be inevitable. And the Com-

---

103. Longfellow's seventy-fifth birthday. He died in Cambridge just under a month later.
104. Memorial Hall.

mittee thought you were the person on all accounts to make the report for the Committee & the opening speech. I am then to respond to you, & then others are to be called upon. We must rely on you for this.

As to the hall, it still drags. The carpenters are now behind. I have written & telegraphed Mr Brock that he is in our way with the delay of the floors &c & I have complained to the architect *whose business* it is to see that the work is carried on properly, & I got nothing from any of them.[105]

The gas fixtures are *far short* of the sample Mr Woodman[106] & I selected & I am now complaining to the architect under whose instructions this work has been made in Boston. I shall now inform the architect again that I will not accept this work. You see the torments at every step.

I cant get the Committee together for a meeting & so have to write the members individually.

I think Tibbetts[107] is holden to do a good job. He has not done it. There are leaks everywhere in his work, & have been all winter. I enclose to you his letter & Mr Moses[108] endorsement.[109] Please preserve as part of the history of the case. The visiting committee meet Thursday June 29th. I wish you could be here before that time.

Truly yours

J. L. Chamberlain

Hon J. W. Bradbury LL.D.

[BSC]

105. Brock is unidentified. The architect: Samuel Backus or William Preston.

106. Perhaps former cavalryman John P. Woodman (b. 1843), a Burlington lumber supplier.

107. Thomas Tibbetts did the pointing (the process of finishing masonry joints and corners with mortar or cement). He wanted to be paid to fix his shoddy work.

108. Galen C. Moses (1835–1915), a Bowdoin graduate, was a respected Bath builder and businessman.

109. Chamberlain enclosed Tibbetts's letter and an endorsement by Chamberlain to Moses reading, "Tibbetts said the defects in his work grew out of the wet condition of the walls & that he did the best he could. It remains a question whether as a good workman he ought not to have observed the condition of the walls & governed himself accordingly."

Waterville.

Brunswick Feb 17 '83

Dr. Pepper[110]

My dear President:

I am not neglecting your suggestions, if I seem to be, [in] your letter.

But I am so crowded with cares & worries that I cannot give the time I would to the discussion of the measures you propose.

As to the reduced fares I w[oul]d be in favor of them for *once each term*, & no more. I dont want to facilitate the constant tours the boys are getting up in term time. I will see what our friends of the M.C.R.[111] think of the proposition. I will not neglect the matter.

As to beneficiary aid I am almost sick of it.

Long since, I have made up my mind not to promise absolutely aid to candidates proposing admission.

I have said to them "The Beneficiary funds at Bowdoin College are not intended for electioneering funds. They are for students who *have been admitted*, & have proved themselves needy & deserving."

I was driven to this by frequent letters saying that Bates & Colby had offered — so much: now what will you offer?

I dont like such auction business, & I dont want such men as students here.

I would be glad, & would doubtless be profited to have a conference with you on this.

I am still intending to come to you: though I see how worn I am likely to be. But I feel a drawing to you, & shall enjoy coming, I believe.

I will try & keep you informed of my plans & possibilities.

Faithfully yours

Joshua L. Chamberlain

[YUL]

110. George Pepper (1833–72) was the new, modernizing president of Colby. *National Cyclopaedia*, 37:339.

111. The Maine Central Railroad was the dominant system in southern Maine and one of the state's first lines to switch to standard gauge and connect with the rest of the nation. *Maine*, 317.

(11 85 Washington St. Boston)

19 Ap 1883

Dear Fanny

We have concluded to try the [operation][112] this morning. I apprehend no serious results.

Grace will be ready to provide for you when you come.

May God bless & keep you.

Yours always

J. L. C.

[BSC]

~ TO SAE

Brunswick July 3[d] 1883

Dear Sae:

I went to Boston & spent last week — The Steamer from Bath to Boston my vehicle. They had fitted up the Bridal State room with every comfort & luxury for me & treated me like a prince. I came home the same way Saturday.

Of course coming home as I did while yet weak & tender, the wound also not quite healed & ve[r]y sore, — I mean three weeks ago — the effect on me was not good. So when I went back last week it was not strange that the Dr. put me to bed & made a sick man of me.

But I feel much better now. I can walk out some but find a cane a useful companion. I can walk half a mile without being tired. But I have to be a little careful about walking as it is likely to irritate unhealed portions.

The sea air does me most good, & I try to go down to my seaside place[113] as often as possible. That short ride does not hurt me at all.

Besides I get rest down there, & that almost takes the place of the care, which I cannot well have at home, — there are so many other interests to be looked after.

Still on the whole I am going.

You know there are these things I have to deal with & try to recover from.

1. *The general strength* prostrated by the shock & wear & tear of the spirits [ill.] & other medicines I had to have.

112. In early March, Dr. Joseph H. Warren of Boston discovered that Chamberlain's wounds were in critical need of surgery and ordered him to cease working, submit to surgery, and change climate, preferably in Florida. 1 March 1883, Warren to Chamberlain, YUL. Chamberlain took the rest of the semester off. Wallace, *Soul of the Lion*, 246.

113. Domhegan.

2. The *surgeon's operation* itself

3. The *original wound.*

The first depends on my general, constitutional strength, & just there is where I am going. *That* is something solid to stand on, & I feel it strong under me. The second I get over but slowly—in fact the process of healing is stopped for the present, & I shall have to have another little touch of the surgeon by & by.

The third has been greatly helped, *I think,* by the operation & *may* be entirely overcome. The Doctor says I shall be better than for 20 years: but I take that at a discount, or rather hold my judgment in abeyance on that point. Your letters are very interesting & helpful. Mother wrote me a beautiful letter not long ago. I am coming down to see you before long.

Love to all:

L.

Will Perkins came out the first in his class.[114] Dont you want to "come to Commencement" this year?

[LC]

TO THE TRUSTEES AND OVERSEERS OF BOWDOIN COLLEGE

To the Trustees & Overseers

of Bowdoin College,

Gentlemen:—

I beg to lay before you with feelings of deepest gratitude for your generous support and consideration, my resignation of the office of President of this College.[115]

Respectfully submitted

Joshua L. Chamberlain

Bowdoin College

July 10 1883

[BSC]

114. William A. Perkins (1861–1918) of Brewer, Phi Beta Kappa and 1883 Bowdoin valedictorian.

115. Due to his deteriorating health and some political factors, this third attempt to resign was accepted. See 8 July 1873 and 26 June 1876.

CHAPTER 4 ⌇ NEW FIELDS

With politics foreclosed and academia unappealing, Chamberlain threw himself into the heady world of business. The power of his name made him a valuable commodity for letterheads and capital campaigns. Over the next several years, Chamberlain became the president or senior officer of numerous New York railroad and technological development companies such as the Kinetic Power Company, which made improved urban transit engines, and land development companies in Florida, where he hoped the climate would benefit his health. His involvement in each company varied: for some he only raised seed investment, whereas he actually operated some of his Florida ventures. Lecturing, veterans' meetings and reunions, and his health prevented him from giving his full attention to even one company for any length of time.

Education still held some appeal to Chamberlain, so he took on the presidency of an avant-garde art institute in New York City, but most of his intellectual energies were increasingly focused on Civil War history. He wrote and lectured widely, attended reunions, and was a member of the Executive Committee of the Maine Gettysburg Commission, which produced the commemorative *Maine at Gettysburg: Report of the Maine Commissioners.* Ever an active veteran, he was elected president of the Society of the Army of the Potomac and was awarded a Medal of Honor for Little Round Top.

⌇TO GRACE

Brunswick Jan 1 *1884.*

My first new date to my first-born darling!

Your letter to your Mother this morning lets a good deal of light on several things.

I thought I could not mistake the dashing *M* in the address on the glove package. But I have let other things that belonged to closing a years accounts get themselves out of the way before I took up an account that is never going to close, & gave myself the pleasure of thanking you for your thought.

A glove is more than a covering. It is an *uncovering* as well. It means in bare hand—the true hand—the pledged hand, not for challenge given & taken, only, but for assurance in any & all plighted engagements. That is the glove *off*, you see! The significance of the glove then (you will say) is the *not* having it! Like the small boys definition of salt — "That stuff that makes por-taters taste ser bad when you dont put none on 'em." "Lucus a non lucendo."[1] But the *reason* of the glove taken — *I* think, tho' I never saw it so explained — is that taking off the glove, leaves bare the hand — man's characteristic instru-ment of ownership of himself in his defence — of his right & duty to his own, be it person or property. He takes, he gives, he defends, he holds, he wields in action, for all works & ends.

The glove accordingly was in the orient the token of a contract com-pleted, & of ownership & delivering into possession — in sales, even of land. One threw down his glove upon the land, & it was his! It is easy to see how the glove came to be the token of challenge & acceptance to battle. This comes out of the *generic* significance — as the symbol & token of responsible person-ality — of defence & mastership — of truth & honor, to the uttermost. So you see what my gloves must be to me when I take them from you!

When I *wear* them, they will be even more — a sort of laying-on of hands — & being clothed — upon of another's grace.

Your remarks on the domestic & national situation, have more truth & good sense in them than any thing that has been said in all the platform & *platitudinarianism* speeches of the last 20 years.

So we have got into the miserable habit of "stopping over" (as you say) & we shall get all spilled out if we dont stop it, or have somebody stop it for us.

I hope to see you within the week. I spent Xmas eve with Garkie & made them all handsome presents. Mamma is pretty well, except her eyes.[2]

Yours aff

J. L. C.

[BSC]

⌘ TO JOHN P. NICHOLSON?

[I will send Morrills report, and on having a copy made of my memorandum at the time I made an official report to Rice; but he did not want to stir up the Pennsylvania people by my report.]

Private   Brunswick Jan 25 1884

My dear Colonel:

I had no communication with Col. Fisher[3] at all at Gettysburg. His Regi-

---

1. An etymological contradiction: *lucus* is Latin for a "dark grove," but it is said to derive from the verb *luce*, "to shine."

2. Fannie had always been plagued by eye problems; her eyes now began to degenerate rapidly.

3. Joseph W. Fisher, see 10 Nov. 1865 to Bachelder.

ments did not occupy Round Top until I had been there at least three hours. Crawfords[4] report is false in every particular.

It was Genl Sykes[5] who told Col. Rice to occupy Round Top. We (the 20 Maine) had driven the remnant of Hoods Division[6] in our front over the western spur of Great R Top at about sunset, & it was quite dark when Fisher came up & reported to Col Rice for orders. Rice massed him (his Brigade)[7] in our rear.

When Sykes'[s] order came, [three words ill.] Rice ask[ed] Fisher to make the movement to seize the crest (or western slope) of R.T. He emphatically declined, & I remember his saying that his men were armed with some inefficient rifle — "smooth-bores" it seems to me he said, & especially that the ground was difficult & unknown to his men. He & his men also were much agitated. Rice then turned to me & said, "Col, will you do it?" meaning so much I thought to rebuke Fisher who with a fresh Brigade refused to undertake it, as he did to ask me to do it.

The fact was, I went with only my own Regiment.

After I had fairly taken the crest of R.T., — with several [ill.] & with some loss to my own command, — & had formed a strong line in order to be secure against attack, one of Fishers Regiments, commanded by Col. [Dare][8] came up moving by the flank by some road they had formed, (we now know what it was. I had not found it, because I went up in line in dispersed order taking rocks & all as they came). [Dare] was trying to find me he said, as he was ordered to come to my support. I asked him to form on my right, but as he was "right in front" his attempt to "front" faced him to the rear, & while I was trying to make him face about, the enemy hearing the confusion opened fire & his regiment started like antelopes & went down the road they had come up on, & never stopped till they were behind [ill.] on Little Round Top again.

I then sent for the 83[d] Penna, of our own Brigade,[9] which came out

4. Samuel W. Crawford (1829–92) commanded the 3rd Division, V Corps, at Gettysburg. GB, 99–100; Trulock, 390.

5. George Sykes (1822–80) succeeded Meade as V Corps commander at Gettysburg. GB, 493.

6. Maj. Gen. John Bell Hood (1831–79) commanded a division of Longstreet's I Corps, Army of Northern Virginia, at Gettysburg. CWD, 407–8. Also see 14 Aug. 1903 to Nicholson.

7. Fisher commanded the 3rd Brigade, 3rd Division, V Corps.

8. Lt. Col. George Dare commanded the 5th Pennsylvania Reserves, Fisher's old regiment, at Gettysburg.

9. Capt. O. S. Woodward led Strong Vincent's former regiment, the 83rd Pennsylvania, at Gettysburg. CWD, 637–38; Trulock, 390.

promptly & were formed with me, where we stood all night, — Hoods men being just down in front of us so near we could hear all their movements & some of their conversation even.

Some time during the night some of Fisher's Regiments came around by the left somewhere & formed near the top of the mountain — doing no good & no hurt, as the enemy were not threatening from that position but on our right. In fact there were not so far as I could learn — & I scouted that hill pretty thoroughly — any of the enemy near Fishers Brigade until morning of the 3[d]. I had nothing to do with Fisher, nor he with me.

J L C.

[GNMP]

≈ TO HENRY JOHNSON

Brunswick
Feb. 6 1884

My dear Professor Johnson:

Your letter has had an experience like that of the Apostle to the Gentiles.

Last winter I took it with me to Florida thinking I should have more time & strength there than here to answer it.

I was scarcely able to read it while there, & I came back to Boston in April & went into Hospital & into the valley of the shadow of death.

The letter was sent after me to Boston but I was not able while there to look at it. It was placed among papers that were withheld from me, & in fact it was only last week that on revisiting the scene in Boston I found the letter again, & have brought it home with me.

But I had not forgotten the letter nor you. Occasionally I have inquired of our friends at Dr. Lincoln's[10] & have heard good accounts of you.

My interest in what you are doing is in no wise abated. I still look forward to the carrying out of those ideas & plans for the well-being of the college which you so ably supported in making for the time being so worthy of attention as to hold a place in our revised course.

I thought it best to resign the Presidency at the last Commencement;[11] and I want to say to set a caution against your young ambition, that however pleasant and useful the life of a College Professor may be, that of a President, in I may say any of our common or best New England colleges even, is about the most thankless wearing and wasteful life that can be undertaken.

Very many things have made my experience singularly fortunate and

10. Unidentified.
11. See 10 July 1883 to Trustees and Overseers.

happy. The kindness shown, & the friendships grown on this Alpine precipice have been rare & sweet plants, in flower & fruit.

I shall expect to see you come home richly laden with the best "spoils" of your Gothic campaign & ready to overthrow & set up empires. And I wish to assure you of my constant regard, & of the support I shall still be able to give to your enlightened views of college work.

I think we have held up well the prestige of the Department of Modern Languages but we have no provision as yet for a division of the work in order to give freedom for the administration of the Library.

That is something we must bring ourselves up to. It is a necessity of the College.

There are some things I might like to have you do for me in the way of a private collection of books on Political Science & Public Law.

I am not yet quite ready to say what; for I am not sure what I shall choose to undertake for next year here or elsewhere.

I have had two very attractive Presidencies offered: but no more of that sort of thing for me if I can help it. Other things draw me more, still in the line of my studies & experience.

I would be glad to hear from you again, now that my health will allow me to do my part of the correspondence more ————.

With sincere regards to Mrs. Johnson[12]

I am

as ever

your friend

J. L. Chamberlain

[BSC]

➣ TO CARL SCHURZ

Copy of letter to the Brunswick Feb. 20, 1884.

Hon Carl Schurz

My dear Sir;—

I had engaged to begin a course of Public Lectures here on the 19th inst, & made an effort to defer beginning for a week in order that I might be present at the meeting in Brooklyn on the 22[d].[13] Had I not been detained in New York

12. The former Frances M. Robinson of Thomaston.

13. Liberal Republicans met in New York on Washington's birthday to launch the "Independent Republican Committee" to pressure the main party into nominating candidates they found palatable. The party went ahead and nominated Blaine. An increasingly dubious legend has it that the independents voted as "Mugwumps," electing Democrat Grover Cleveland president.

until last Monday I might have arranged it. As things have turned I find it next to impossible to get away.

I regret it much, for I fully sympathize with the feeling that it is absolutely necessary for the success of the Republican party that their nominations should command the respect of sincere & thoughtful members of that party, who are not self-seekers but are looking to the real interests of the Country.

If I could be present at the meeting I should doubtless find occasion to express my opinion as points came up for ~~decision~~ discussion, but without knowing what questions may arise or what measures may be proposed, I can not say anything here of any value.

I only desire to have all influences brought to bear to hold the Republican party up to its high ideals and make its practical measures correspond with its proposed principles.

With sincere regard
Very truly yours
Joshua L. Chamberlain.

[YUL]

TO CHESTER A. ARTHUR

Copy

Brunswick Maine
March 4th 1884.

To the Honorable
Chester A. Arthur
President of the United States.[14]
Sir:

Your were kind enough to say to me two years ago that you would like to know if any place should open under your administration which would be agreeable to me.

This emboldens me to mention now the vacant Russian Mission.

I am not sure that your remark warrants me in departing so much from the custom in such matters as to write you thus directly; but I prefer to rest this suggestion on your very kind overture, rather than allow my friends to bring the matter forward, as they seem quite disposed to do.

This simple method saves you trouble and possibly embarrassment.

I do not desire even to ask for the place but to submit myself entirely and cheerfully to your good pleasure.[15]

14. Chester Alan Arthur (1829–86), 21st president of the United States.

15. Arthur chose Alphonso Taft (1810–91), secretary of war and attorney general under

With highest respect & regard
your obedient servant
Joshua L. Chamberlain
Copy of letter to President Arthur
March 4th 1884.

[YUL]

≈ TO G. P. PUTNAM'S SONS

Copy

Bowdoin College
March 12, 1884

Messrs.

G. P. Putnam's Sons

Dear Sirs;—

I thank you for the courtesy of sending me a copy of your edition of De Laveleye's Political Economy.[16]

It is a pleasant thing to have this bright book so well put into English, and so handsomely put into form by you. People will enjoy the fresh and clear manner of this exposition of the "orthodox" system of Political Economy as modified by the influence of the modern historic school. M. De Laveleye gives also some views peculiar to himself, which are always valuable for suggestion, if not for adoption.

The book will be welcomed to a place in the library of the student and the lecture room of the instructor. I feel bound to say, however, that one effect of the book on my mind is to call up with new force the doubt I feel about the practical usefulness or even validity of processes of economic reasoning or of exposition which make the leading and the last thought the utmost possible productive power of man in industry.

It may indeed be said that this is to doubt the usefulness or validity of the teachings of economics. But however that may be it is certain that the industrial power of man is given for something else than to be intensified to the last degree for the greatest product of goods.

M. De Laveleye always does well what he undertakes, and he has here so happily exhibited the relation of economic science to the other humane

---

Grant (as well as father of William H. Taft), to succeed the late William H. Hunt. Shavit, *U.S. Relations with Russia*, 208, 91; *EB*, 11:494.

16. Chamberlain was reviewing a new translation of *Élements d'économie politique* by Emile Louis Victor de Laveleye (1822–92), a Belgian socialist economist and international lawyer, published by Brunswick native George P. Putnam's (1814–72) publishing house. Josephson, *Biographical Dictionary of Modern Peace Leaders*, 198–99; *WhoAmH*, 498; *WhoAm*, 1002.

sciences in his early chapters, and has scattered along the course of his exposition such pregnant remarks, that one cannot but wish he might give to these a vital and organic development.

I would be glad if you could include among your valuable economic publications one that should make the goal & glory of the economic art something else than the raising of industrial productivity to its highest pitch. Where that high pitch has been most nearly reached, we still see economic social conditions which demand that the whole subject be traversed on a new line and with a different objective if we would get at the true law of industrial effort as bearing on the well-being of a people.

Surely the matter is too important to be neglected, and too much within the compass of our duty and interest as members of the social body and the "body politic" to be left to the hands of revolutionists, socialists and anarchists.

I should like to see a candid treatment of the subject of the organization of Industry with reference to the welfare of the people.

Very truly yours
Joshua L. Chamberlain
(Lecturer on Political Science
and Public Law
Ex President &c)
Dr Sirs:
I have let myself go on with perfect frankness, as I trust also without offence. I authorize you, if you think best to make use only of what I say on my final page. Please [do] understand that my question is not from the point of view of "Protectionism." It is the aspect of *unequal competition* which moves me. C.

[YUL]

≈ TO UNIDENTIFIED RECIPIENT

copy   Brunswick June 25, '84
My dear Sir;
The question is what measures & what kind of law will best prevent the use of intoxicating [*liquors*] in our State & Land.[17]

Laws against murder & poison-using are not usually nor ever—, so far as I know, put into the form of *constitutional, organic Law*.

It would be no more effective restraint upon the evils & crimes of society

17. In Feb. 1884, the Maine legislature approved the nation's first prohibition amendment (though cider remained legal). It was repealed in 1933. *Maine*, 388.

to put those enactments into that form of law, than to put them into statute law.

The thing is to execute the law.

There is a singular idea that the higher form you give to law the more it will execute itself. That is not so. The more sincere & cordial support a law has among the people, the stronger it is. In fact that is the strength of human law.

Now we have a thoroughly well-organized system of laws,—all sufficient to reach the case within any realizable degree. And it seems to me the true way to effect the good sought for, is to take hold & brace up public sentiment & support and enforce our laws.

I am perfectly willing to try any legal measure that has reasonable promise of advancing this great cause. But I do not think the constitutional amendment is to do any practical good. That will not execute itself any more than other laws. And the danger is that it will draw away our interest from the [personal], living effort, to the idea of mere law to do our work for us.

Of course it may be a matter of pride to the leaders to see their ideas incorporated into the highest form of law; but that will not reach the evil.

Now that this amendment is placed before us in the *name* of a great cause, good men will not want to vote against it. But I regard it as a waste of energy, if what we want is real reformation, & not simply verbal reformation. I cannot go into a full discussion as I have not time. I sent to the Boston Post some of my views in answer to their request, & I have asked them to send a copy for you if you care for it.

What you want is I suppose is my opinion on the question of the efficacy of the amendment & I give to you, upon my reason & conscience, & not as following or fearing any other man.

Yours truly

J. L. Chamberlain.

[PHS]

TO FANNIE

New York 8 Aug. 85

My dear Fanny;

The great scene is over. Grant is laid in his tomb.[18] You may imagine— few others can—how strange that seems to me. That emblem of strength &

18. Ulysses S. Grant died of throat cancer on 23 July 1885 in Mount McGregor, New York. On the eighth, an eight-mile-long funeral procession carried his body from New York City Hall to Riverside Park, where he was buried in a temporary tomb.

stubborn resolution yielding to human weakness & passing helplessly away to dust.

I wish you could have seen the faces of Sherman & Sheridan & Hancock[19] as they stood over that biër before the body was laid away.

What thoughts — what memories — what monitions passed through those minds! The pageant and the tribute of honor were grand — worthy of a great nation. I wish now very much that I had brought Wyllys with me.

This is the last of the great scenes. At least for this generation. I will tell you more about it when I get rested a little, or after I come home. By Genl Hancock's kind attention I was treated with marked distinction — too much in fact.

I had a carriage directly in the group of Cabinet Ministers & the most distinguished men of the Country. It chanced that I was far ahead of the Governors of States & the officers of the Army. I would not have chosen that position because it was too much. But Genl Hancock's staff officer did not seem to understand that I was only a private citizen.

I was also in the same line with the Senators chosen as chief mourners. It strangely happened that *Governor Coburn* of Maine was left out without notice & without provision by carriage for a place in the procession. I stopped my carriage when I saw him & took him & the Commander in Chief of the Grand Army[20] into my carriage & my place — far ahead of that to which they would have fallen if they had had a carriage!

By this means they had a chance to see the whole ceremony & at the burial service they were with me not ten feet from the central scene. The casket before the tomb-door, while the last services were paid — the last prayer offered — the bugler stepped to the front & sounded with trembling lips *the tattoo!* The evening roll call — you remember — the end of day — the signal of silence & darkness. They who stood about — most of them — could not feel all that said to me. I looked in vain for a face that seemed to express what I was feeling. But not till I saw the faces of Sherman & Sheridan & Hancock did I meet that response, & that deepened all my own feelings.

The great men of the nation were there. But nothing seemed great to me — but what was gone; except the multitudes that crowded miles on miles, & the tokens of mourning that overshadowed the city.

Grant himself seemed greater now than ever. And he is.

19. Maj. Gen. Winfield Scott Hancock (1824–86) orchestrated the procession. DAB, 8:221–22.

20. Samuel S. Burdett (1836–1914), an Iowa cavalryman, lawyer, and congressman. *WhoAm*, 166.

I am glad I saw it all, & was admitted to a near place.

Do not think me foolish & egotistic. It is not that spirit that prompts me to speak of myself: but you know I have had great & deep experiences—& some of my life has gone into the history of the days that are past.

I shall probably go to Phila. & West Virginia next. Address care of M.C.C. Church Parkersburg West 2[?]. Good night & all blessings.

Yours

J. L. C.

[MSM]

TO FANNIE

Ocala Oct 20 1885

My dearest Fannie:

Yours of the 14 inst is just received and I am glad enough to have the sight of your hand writing again. It has been a very hot day & I have had a very hard days work & to no small degree an annoying one.

You would be impressed at the amount of business I have had on hand, I am very tired & should no doubt write you a much better letter if I waited until morning but I am so rejoiced to have a word from you I can not help writing you something. The night is glorious—the moon high in the heavens—fleecy cloudlets feathering the blue. All is still except the fine chirps of the cicadas, & a plaintive negro song floating from a distance on the soft air. Still it is dull & lonely here. I do not mean that I miss people, or long for society, for I do not. But nature herself though soft & sweet lacks richness & body, so-to-speak, & fails to fill my spirit to perfect satisfaction. How I should delight to have you here though! & I am sure we should find worthy & profitable themes for converse, & even nature would please me better by having more *body* in it then! There are many set-backs in such work as we have. The worst now is the great expenses that have been run up for the company in my absence— unnecessary it seems to me, & using up our money in a way that embarrasses me in pushing forward my works.

I have been at Homosassa & all over our lands & waters. I walked scores of miles, & never once tho[ugh]t of snakes! Nor have I seen one in all my three weeks of travel & tramping.

It is a trying season of the year & people are dying suddenly & strangely. Several of my Florida friends here have been taken suddenly sick today. I feel entirely well. But I have taken some risks, being obliged to expose myself much to all weathers, & especially to work too hard, once or twice I have had a "queer" feeling in my head, that a small pill of quinine—or what is better a lemon or a [lime]—has immediately put me right.

I am in the midst of my building: just begin[nin]g to put up the first, — having been to Cedar Keys[21] & got my material & also my men. I have got up a beautiful design for a Hotel, & it is to be put up at once, & managed by one of the most successful of Florida Hotelmen. I have been making the terms of contract with him today. I shall have a place for you whenever you can come after Nov 1. Either here or at Homosassa. Only it will be something like camp life for a time. But you will like it I think. The oranges will be ripe by that time. My bananas were very fine. They are about gone now. Everything looks well at our place here. The trees have taken on an extraordinary growth. An old stump I have been trying to save by smearing tar on it, &c, has suddenly put out half a dozen vigorous shafts which have made six feet of growth. One of Wyllys' trees, put out year before last, has many oranges on it, & I am letting them stay on for him to see, though it w[oul]d be better for the tree, perhaps, not to let it bear this year. I wish I could stay at my place when in Ocala, as I dislike extremely to live in the town, & it is so delightful to me on my hill. The log house is commodious and good enough for me. Its open fire-places make good cheer in the cool evenings, & we have had one or two even now, where the mercury stands at 90° by day.

But I am compelled to stay in town & at the hotel, taking my meals at a restaurant! This is because I have to be where I can see men who come in on the evening trains; & then I have to be in the office of the Company nearly all the time. [A]fter a while I shall live, when in Ocala, in my log house. James & Mathie are coming back to the place & it will always be kept in good condition.

You will be sorry to know I had to give up my Huguenot Speech after all. It was impossible to get myself into town for a speech in New York on so great an occasion & then I cannot possibly leave without setting our work back for a whole year. If our warehouse & Hotel don't go up *now*, & are not vigorously pushed ev[er]y day *just now* they will not be ready in season for this winters travel, & we lose the sale of our lands for the entire season & an entire year.

The truth is, no matter how many men are in this thing, my presence is necessary, in order for any thing to go on. I wrote as good a letter as I could to the President of the Huguenot Society, & also one to the Wisconsin & Chicago people. But I must give up the idea of going north for three or four weeks yet. Our enterprises here are full of promise, & really one worthy of my best powers. I feel that we are making history, & good history. Frank Drew[22] ought

21. Cedar Keys is on the west coast of Florida, midway between Tallahassee and Tampa.
22. Bvt. Col. Franklin M. Drew (1837–1925) of the 15th Maine was a Presque Isle lawyer and politician. *WhoAm*, 340.

to have taken my offer of half my place here. I could readily get double for it now, on what I offered it to him for.

There is to be a great "boom" here this season, & I shall sell some of my lands. I expect to come home in November to take you. So be getting yourself ready. I should think it would be the middle of November when I can fairly get away.

Give my best regards to Col. & Mrs Drew & Mrs Record,[23] & invite them to come & see us here. I shall have one "shore room" in my log house, — & Homosassa will be a Paradise even out of doors.

aff yours
J. L. C.

[BSC]

≈ TO GRACE

44 W. 35 st
New York
Dec 13 '86

My dear Gracie:

You & dear Mamma must not think I would willingly let all these long days pass without a word from me.

But I really have not been able to write until now your dear beautiful letter makes it impossible not to do so.

I was not well for several days before our poor tired "little one" went from me to you. When she went I stood on the bridge in the gallery of the Grand Central Depot, and watched the train bearing away, — at first so slowly but so strongly & sure, — my dear one committed to its trust, till it had passed out of sight, and only the circling wreaths of steam told of its track. Then that vanished.

I turned back to the desolate Hotel — only for a moment entering the deserted room — & gave the orders that completed the scattering of the things which outwardly had made our little home for so many weeks & months. The big trunk to an office "down town" & the two handbags to Dr Upham's,[24] to which latter place I afterwards brought myself — depressed in body & in mind.

23. Perhaps Melvina S. Dunn Record, wife of William Clement Record (b. 1837) of Readfield.

24. Prof. Francis W. Upham (1817–95), Prof. Thomas Upham's brother and a Bowdoin graduate himself, practiced law and taught history at Rutgers Female College. Allibone, *A Critical Dictionary*, Supplement, 2:1460.

There was a dinner party there that even[in]g, and all remarked my *peculiarly* "poor looks."

The next day was stormy, the snow gusts whirling in the air, & circling around in eddies & making the fences & posts & yards look like a field of graves. I was here at Dr. Uphams, you understand.

I would have given anything to be able to stay quietly in my room & think & rest. I wanted to write dear Mamma a letter, & did begin one. But I had to come out, & be entertained, & to spend the day in a false position, & had but little rest. I went to dine with the Kendalls[25] & they let me sleep on the sofa an hour or two. It was peaceful & restful there—sort of "Saints Rest."

Monday I went down town & tried to carry forward my work but with little success—still feeling very ill.

Tuesday 7th was my wedding day & I still tried more than ever to write my little letter to "Mamma."

It was a cold north-east-weather day. I went down to the Wall [S]t office, & the moment I had secured the completion of the long pending business—the "Contract." of which Mamma knows—I felt a sudden severe illness—first in my head—then in my limbs—then all over me. I rose to go, but sank into a chair.

The kind friends there—not Wall [S]treet "sharks"—I assure you, nor "Bulls & Bears" to me—took me, or led me, (I could walk) to the nearest station of the Elevated Road[26] & your Mr Upham, of the office, (not a near relative of my host but a son of Dr J. Baxter Upham[27] of the "*Great [O]rgan*") came up with me. Half way up I had to go out on the platform to get the breath of the N.E. stormy air—the atmosphere in the cars made me deathly sick. I was home [none] too soon; for the moment I got out there, I threw up my breakfast (which had been quite simple) & which I perceived was all in its crude state, just as I had swallowed it four hours before. When I got to the house, here, the spasmodic, congestive chills through the body, seemingly from hip to hip, were intensely severe, and my feet & hands grew cold as ice. Everybody of course flew to me. I was enveloped in hot water bottles & flannels, in bed, of course; Young Mr. Upham telegraphed for his father Dr. Baxter Upham, a very skillful physician, Mrs Upham[28] telegraphed my own Doctor

25. The Kendalls are unidentified. Also see the following letter and 23 Jan. 1894 to Fannie.

26. On the Sixth Avenue line. Pullen, 118.

27. Jabez Baxter Upham (1820–1902), a Maine Medical School graduate, was a Boston and New York physician.

28. Elizabeth K. Upham, then fifty-one, wife of Francis Upham. Pullen, 117.

Jackson,[29] who lives 7 miles away but in the line of the elevated road, & Dr Francis Upham ran for Dr Fordyce Barker, perhaps the most eminent physician in this City.[30] I was soon seized with violent fits of vomiting, which made pretty thorough work of my stomach, & they thought afterwards may have "saved my life" — but I think that puts it rather strong.

Young Upham meantime gave me a hot-water-mustard foot bath,[31] and in an hour or more I was in a gentle perspiration, & the pains greatly relieved. But I knew it was a sharp attack; and as the pains crept into the region of the heart, I did not know what was coming, but thought it best to give instructions about many things, & to give your address, & that of my home friends, & of many in this city, who would wish to be near me in case of need.

But I told Mrs. Upham not to send any word unless it became necessary — not at any rate while I was conscious.

I was not in the least frightened, nor afraid, but I was thinking much of dear Mamma, & you & upon Wyllys, I knew not where. Dr Baxter Upham came first of the physicians. He searched for tokens of heart disturbance & of pneumonia — in both of which matters he is an expert. He was soon satisfied there was no pneumonia, & the disturbed action of the heart he believed to be only an effect of the shock & of the pain — which I know was true, for I have no disease of the heart.

While he was with me, Dr Jackson came. I was much easier then, & I felt that Dr Jackson knew about me well enough to give a true diagnosis, & also to put me in the right line.

He said all I had done to meet my case was just right. He said the attack was the result of a long over worked & over worn nerve & vital force, & that he thought the malaria in my blood[32] had rushed out & seized me & dragged me

29. Unidentified.

30. Benjamin Fordyce Barker (1818–91) was perhaps the most eminent physician in America. A graduate of Bowdoin, the Medical School of Maine (where he also taught), and the Sorbonne, he was professor of Obstetrics at New York Medical College and Bellevue Hospital Medical College and president of the American Gynecology Society, all of which he had helped establish, and author of the long-definitive *Puerperal Diseases*. DAB, 1:601.

31. This was a common home health procedure with a variety of uses, such as sedation, or, as here, to promote circulation — "to act as a stimulant when the powers of life seem much diminished in their energy." Mustard grains or table mustard would be mixed with hot water to make a bath. Another method of application was to place a poultice (a cloth soaked in the mixture) on the skin for about twenty minutes, causing inflammation and "much pain." *The Family Doctor*, 274; Lyman et al., *The Practical Home Physician*, 1076.

32. In Florida, Chamberlain had a bad bout of the malaria he had contracted during the war.

down. He did what was right—gave me a little acetate of ammonia & a little quinine, & left me much better. In the eve[nin]g Dr Barker came & added a slight treatment.

Dear, kind Mrs Upham, as Mamma will readily know, was ready to lay the universe at my feet, & in truth did really over whelm, & perhaps over load, me with attentions & suggestions & questions I could not answer for multitude, minuteness & persistency, & this she still does.

So I pulled through three or four days—the three Doctors coming in, out of kindness, every four hours, to keep hold of me, and after that I had only the weakness & wretchedness of the reaction to endure. I have not yet left my bed as a home, but I am sitting up now—for my second essay at sending you a letter. (It is now Tuesday 2 P.M.)

Mrs Upham wanted to write to you, but I wanted to do that myself. And so it is only now that I have thought it best to let you know all about it. Had I needed you, or had things grown worse with me, I would have had you informed at once. But as it was, no good could come of making you anxious & agonized.

Mrs Upham was sure I could come down to a dinner she was to give last Saturday, & to which she had invited several distinguished people to meet me, & I at one time thought I might be able just to go down for an hour, & let her telegraph Horace to send my package of fine clothes from Boston, & that at any rate you would believe I was not having a very bad time if I was sending for my best clothes.

They came: & I thank Horace for his kind & prompt attention.

Now, dears, I am "all right," & hope by tomorrow to go down town a while in the middle of the day. I have every thing done for me that "money," & perhaps "love," could command. So I suffer for nothing except for sight of my own "ones."

I am thankful for all the love & mercy God has shown us, & I think of it much.

How kind it was in Horace to cheer me that lonely Sunday with the telegram! I insisted on keeping it right beside my face, until your letter came. Now, I substitute that for it. Our dear one, I know, is happy, sheltered & cherished in her precious daughter's home. Wyllys is well. My mother & sister are well. So, as Cicero would say, "I am well."

Do not fear or worry for me. I shall go on now, with care & caution, & will keep you informed of my condition. With a heart full of love to you, my dearest ones, I am always yours

J. L. Chamberlain

[BSC]

The Alpine
Broadway & 33^d st.
Feb 15 18[8]7

My dear Gracie:

[Y]ou must not think I could possibly feel that your were indifferent to me, or any otherwise than the best & dearest & most dutiful daughter.

I am now more concerned for you than for my self, & I trust you will plan to take a long & good rest early in the Summer, if not before. I think that is what I need too. The Doctor of course thinks my trouble is simply "*malaria.*"

I know better. It is overwork: or rather that "all work & no play, which makes Jack a dull boy." I am trying now to "favor myself" a little, & think the trip to Florida, now, will do me good.

I hope to be off in about a week.

I live quite a lonely life now. This great new home is only a quarter filled, & things are not going smoothly. But the janitor's wife is a good woman, & sends me a neat little breakfast at 8 am, — a French breakfast, coffee & oatmeal, — & if I do not feel well, she looks after me more.

I am going to get her to look after my clothes — mending & washing, &c, & try to find a little peace, even without a home.

I have many friends within a short distance, & this Building is in a very "central" place: the Broadway, Sixth-Avenue cars, & University-Place cars all crossing at 33^d st, & a [station] of the 6th ave. Elevated, at the same corner. So you see I can get any where in a *few minutes.* Mrs Upham & the misses Kendall are only two blocks off & they come to see me & ask me to their homes often. They are of the very "salt of the earth." Jennie "[A]bbot[t]"[33] is 10 Blocks up & she comes too, with her fine daughter "Helen."

I am about well now: you know I recover so quickly. But I do miss "Mamma" [ver]y much. New York without her is a desolation to me. I dont want to go any where or see anything without her.

But I do have many invitations from choice people. The lady cousins of Lady Randolph Churchill[34] are of those who invite me often. So Mrs Mc-Alpin[35] & many others of my "millionaire" friends. Dont worry about me. I am glad for mamma.

33. Jane Abbott (b. 1833/4), daughter of John Abbott (11 Nov. 1865 to Hodsdon). Smith, *Fanny and Joshua*, 189–90.

34. Jennie Jerome (1854–1921), a flamboyant American heiress, wife of Lord Randolph Churchill (1849–95), and mother of Winston Churchill (1874–1965). Martin, *Jennie.*

35. Perhaps David H. McAlpin's (23 Mar. 1893 to Carnegie) second wife, Adelia Gardiner.

Yours
J. L. C.

≋ TO HIS MOTHER

The Alpine
New York
Sept 8 1887

————

My dear Mother:

This is my birth day and I must write you my letter, as I always do, to bless and thank you for my life; for all your suffer[in]g for me & tender care, and faithful guidance & good instruction.

I trust I have made the life of some good to the world, and a joy to you.

Perhaps I have not made all that was possible of my life: but I trust God has still use for me, and has spared me through so many perils and so many years, for a blessing somewhere yet to be given and received.

I pray that you may be kept in health and peace & that God's peace may rest in your soul.

I thank Him & I thank you, for the happy little meeting we had a few days ago. I trust I can be of some comfort and use to you still in these sweet [evenings] of the years.

Your prayers for me are always in my heart. God has answered them for my good, and will do so still.

It is a day full of gratitude to you & to God for my spirit, & I am happy and ready for anything to which I may be called. May God bless & keep you.

Your loving son
Lawrence.

≋ TO GRACE

New York
Oct 20 1887

————

My Gracie:

The little package which you will receive to night or in the morning I intended to have reached you with among your birthday tokens of remembrance & love.

It happened so that I could not send it until my return from Philadelphia. I have an impression that you fancy the sapphire. I therefore had one

Sarah Brastow Chamberlain (Courtesy of the Brewer Public Library)

placed between diamonds. For the sapphire though deep & rich, needs like some other precious gems I know of, to be set in the midst of lights to show its own beauty best. Things that are sufficient to themselves inspire our admiration: but those that need others, win & hold our love. Accept this little token of my grateful appreciation of your goodness to your mother & to me when we needed such light & love. It but poorly expresses my thoughts to you. I think I would have had a *ruby* to betoken the depth of love I have for you. But the sapphire is the emblem of all the high intelligences, & of Heaven itself. So we may well have that for our bond of sweet memories & hopes.

I do not like the mounting of this ring much; but we can have the stones reset, at your liking. I think them fine ones,—not so large as I could wish, but precious with thoughts.

So with all thanks to God for his gift to me in you, & all blessings prayed for to rest in your heart forever, I am

your much blessed father

J. L. Chamberlain

[BSC]

〰 TO GRACE

433 W. 57th st
New York Sunday Feb. 12 1888

My darling Gracie:

Your sweet letter received this morning as I was on my way to *Grace* church touches me deeply. I long for your companionship too, and can discern even now the heights we should reach in our heavenwork walks and sweet communions. I want you to spend more time with me, and I shall manage to have you do so. At least you can come to New York & spend a few days now & then. I really think you would enjoy the fireside here, & the little circle of friends who brighten the hours still more than the firelight.

You must by all means stay here a few days in your return homeward. I fear that I may be called away before you are ready to come, as I am "called" now to go to Florida the last of the month. I would defer the visit there for the sake of having you here with me a few days. We will have some of the times of old—like those of the dear dreamy days at the Isles of Shoals, or our Indian Summer walks & drives, or rests in the balcony looking out on the white moonlight.

I was a little perplexed—not to say, *hurt*, to hear by round about ways that you had gone to Washington without giving me a chance to spend an hour with you & take you through the city. I understand it all now. I wish you were here now. These have been days of receptions, parties, & gay times, when you would have felt yourself at home, and would have shone "brightest of all the throng." I feel sad that you are not more privileged in Washington. It seems strange that you should have to feel grateful to the wife of one of my staff officers for calling on you. She ought to be proud to be able to do so, and I will do her the justice to doubt not that she is.

I will give you a note to Mrs Grant[36] if you will send it to her, & I know she will give you a warm welcome. I will also think of other friends to put

36. Most likely Julia Dent Grant (1826–1902), Ulysses S. Grant's widow, who had moved back to Washington. McFeely, *Grant*, 519.

you in relations with. I only wish I could be there with you. But do not doubt that your own worth, & ability & rare accomplishments, will make you an honored guest wherever you choose to go. I will send you the letter by next mail. Lovingly, & with "long thoughts." [Y]ours as no other can be,

    J. L. C.

[BSC]

〰️ TO GRACE

New York July 13 88

———

My darling Daisy:

Your dear little letter is with me. I want much to see you, & hope our lives will come together soon. I expect to leave here for the 3 Bs. Boston, Brunswick & Bangor, about the middle of next week.

Business will make me go to Bangor as soon as I can. I hope to have "our little mamma" with me. Shall call & try. But she may refuse me, as she did Horace.

I am much occupied with my business here, but am pretty well, — though needing a yacht trip, or some change of that sort.

The reunion at Gettysburg[37] was remarkably interesting — 25,000 pilgrims returned to their old fields, & many distinguished officers. It was a remarkable honor, on such a field & such an occasion, for one who was only a Colonel on that field to be chosen President of the Society of the Army of the Potomac. I shall have to do something to prove myself worthy of it. But a fellow couldn't get such a recognition unless there was something about him to draw men's minds, or hearts. I was not a candidate; & it was a surprise to me for there were candidates who "ranked" me out of sight.

I made a good many little speeches; but purposely refrained from going into speech-making there.

I can do that sort of thing, when occasion requires.

Thank you for your wise & loving thoughts about it. As to the fan, — if Carrie Sweetser[38] does not want it, I dont believe "our" Carrie could do anything with it. I thought it would be useful to *you*. But never mind; it will find its place.

If I had time I should like to take the Portland Steamer from this City. It is a charming voyage, through the sound, & up the Maine coast. But that

37. Celebrating the 25th anniversary of the battle.
38. Unidentified.

Little Round Top, 2 October 1889. Chamberlain is labeled "2."
(Courtesy of the Maine Historic Preservation Commission)

would take me *by* you, & not *to* you. So I think I shall take the Fall River line, as usual.

But I will not leave you in uncertainty. When I am about to leave here, I will let you know.

Where are you going this summer? *Will you go with me to Brunswick & Brewer?*

Wyllys is well & bright.

aff yours

J. L. C.

[BSC]

〰TO GRACE

New York Jan 18 1889

My dearest little girl:

I have wanted to write you a good letter in response to your dear little note: but no such quiet time has come to me yet. I have had to be out ev[er]y evening to keep myself in good relations with the *gentlemen* I am associated with.

So you must take this sort of a letter for the one I would (& will) write.

I am trying to see my way to come to Boston & give the lecture the "boys" want me to, on the 6th. But it is [very] hard for me to break out & give *one* lecture when my mind is so absorbed in other business.

I have promised to come to the Bowdoin dinner on the 13th Feb. & I cant stay over from the 5th to the 13th, but should have to come back & go to Boston again the next week. It is a great draft on me to do either. They say I made a real Chauncey [sic] Depew speech[39] at the Bowdoin dinner here, & I enjoyed it: but may not be able to do it again.

I want "little Mama" to come here as soon as she can get ready, so she can enjoy the many things that belong to "the season." I shall have to go to Florida last of February. I have an invitation to take a *very important* place in a great Railroad system in the north. I *may do it*. It is a great opportunity, if I can master the "technique" of it, so as to fill the position with credit. People here say I can make myself famous in a new sphere, if I take this. More of the anon.

Full of *brain*, & *brain-work*, but with a little heart kept for my dear ones yours ever

J. L. C.

[BSC]

✎ TO FANNIE

The Grand Pacific Hotel.
Chicago, No 2d 1889

My dear Fanny:

I am so far on my way home: but am so "held on to" by my old army friends & Maine friends here that I shall have to stay over night. That will br[in]g me home Monday night 10 o'clock. I suppose, But dont sit up & listen for me. It may be I cant get there till later & I *may* be detained in Syracuse or Albany.

It is a long [journey] to Rockford[40] & I was very tired; but I had to make up for the disappointment I gave the people in not [coming] when they wanted me.

So I stood up & talked to them for 2 hours & a quarter solid. It seems I didn't get through then; for they insist that I shall give the memorial address

---

39. Sen. Chauncy M. Depew (1834–1928), a famous wit and after-dinner speaker. DAB, 5:244–47.

40. Rockford is about one hundred miles west of Chicago, the farthest west it seems that Chamberlain ever traveled.

then. Chicago is after me too. [A]nd they say they will have me here at the *Maine* association the last of this month.

I have not been able to rest much yet: but these wide awake[41] warm hearted people are very [interesting] to me. It is a good thing to see this great west of [ill.].

They want me to commit myself to Chicago for the worlds fair rather than New York,[42] & the [newspapers] have been interviewing me. But I am conservative on that.

With all good thoughts & hopes

yours

L.

[SL]

〰 TO GEORGE T. LITTLE

New York, June 23[d] 1890

My dear Profr. Little; —

My many movements for the last month have outstripped my mails, — those which were forwarded to Boston last week having alone reached me until now.

I was on my way to Commencement, & expected to have [left] Boston this morning for Brunswick. But urgent telegrams called me back here Saturday night, & I dont see [an]y way this morning to get away even tonight.

Of course I make no objection to your removing the Senior Library, my books & all, to the general Library.[43] The good of the College & of the students is all the object I have or ever had in the matter.

My methods of instruction were peculiar I suppose, & no one is likely to follow them. I had a thought of teaching students how to investigate a subject, & also give them the sight & touch & taste, of the masterpieces of the topics in hand. Hence the presence of the Senior Library was almost a necessity for me in my lectures. But while I feel strong & tender bonds in the memories of the "old time," I do not feel any reluctance to have the wave of oblivion pass over my works & relics, if it is for the good of others (as I am sure it will be) to have new & better ways offered them. You have doubtless anticipated my full concurrence in your proposition.

41. A term often used for Republican Party activists.

42. For the competition between the cities to host the Columbian Exposition, see Larson, *The Devil in the White City*, Part I.

43. As president, Chamberlain had developed and donated to a special library for senior seminars.

I had hoped to be with you before this; & am now, though under great pressure & care & responsibility, trying to get to you. But meantime accept this hasty letter, which I have made long only because of the tender associations wakened by your kind letter.

Sincerely y[our]s

Joshua L. Chamberlain

⤷ TO FANNIE

Friday eve [ca. early 1891, NYC]

My dear Fanny:

I have your beautiful letter that quickens all my great love for you so that I am impatient of any conditions that seem to keep you away from me. All I am doing is with the fixed and undismayed purpose of being able to realize our ideal home & its sweet society. I have patiently and not unwisely planned & toiled to secure the command of the things necessary for this freedom. I have been delayed & baffled as to some of those plans. But I am still active and full of courage, & I cannot but believe some of the things I have in hand will be brought to results before very long.

You well know, my [recent] plan for living included you near me & your place was set apart & prepared. But our dear Wyllys seemed to be providentially brought back to me—for his sake chiefly though as it has turned for my sake too. He has had a hard lot & luck, & of course in one way the brunt of it came upon me. *Patience* has been my prayer and it has been heard & answered. The place I had for you in the house, Wyllys had to take, & all the arrangements made for living limited us to about this number. But still I want you to come & it would be just as well if Dear Daisy would come too, & see at least how we are living. In that case, Wyllys & I could share a room for the happy days & nights thus vouchsafed. Whenever the weather is disagreeable to you, or you feel most drawn to come, then come, & find always a sure welcome. I should like it most when [ill.] the Boston spring air is trying to you, or a little later when the budding spring sweetens the manifold slumbering life-germs in the neighboring Park, where we could walk & talk. Meantime do not feel bitterly that others have of me what you cannot. I do not think that is ever so. It is doubtless an advantage to any who have souls or minds to appreciate, to catch even the overflow of my thoughts and fancies. But all that is best—all that is most mine is kept for you & is most yours. Nor do I indeed [see] many, nor much of the few I most enjoy. Those in the house are good, and faithful, & reverential and careful of me & for me. The patience I have long[ed] for has wrought a strange peace & calm in my spirit and now in the days of my convalescence, which is slow, in that the old wounds were the occasion & location of my illness, I am impelled & inspired to *write* & I do so to the extent of my strengths not allowing anything to tempt me from it. I have a little brochure in hand, on the astral soul or "*In two worlds.*"[44] You will live it.

I send you a little token of one kind to give you freedom to act as you like.

Yours

J. L. C.

[MHS]

≋TO OLIVER OTIS HOWARD

101 West 75th st

New York City.

Feb 17 1891

Maj Genl Howard

My dear General,

If there is no one to represent Maine at the funeral services of Genl Sherman,[45] I will stand in any place proper for such testimonial. Genl Sherman was a very warm and dear friend to me although I know none of his immediate family.

I am well content for myself to appear as a private citizen, & an individual, in this occasion; but I did not know but there may be occasion or opportunity to have the State of Maine represented in some way. I suppose the Army of the Potomac will wish to appear by some representation. Do not take any notice of this, unless the suggestion is appropriate.

I do not wish to trouble you, & am very far (as you know) from wishing to thrust myself into notice.

Yours truly

Joshua L. Chamberlain

[BSC]

44. This refers to "Spiritualism" and mediums.

45. William T. Sherman died on the 14th of pneumonia. Although he was buried in St. Louis, his funeral was held in New York City.

Sunday P.M.
14 Feb. 92

My dear Daisy:

I go to Brunswick to attend [a] meeting of Trustees of Bowdoin College on Thursday next. Genl Hubbard & I go together, passing right through Boston that morning. If your mother is there I shall bring her back with me reaching Brunswick Friday night or Saturday P.M. She may not think she can get ready; but I do not like to have her there, & shall make every effort to take her with me.

I may stay over a night in Boston; and shall come to you, if it is a seasonable hour.

Your assistance may be needed to induce your mother to come away. If you can write her to be ready to come with me, I may be able to get her. I can take her right along with me, unless you prefer to have her stay with you until my return from Florida, where I am going for a week at the end of the month, I think. I have asked her to go with me, & she may like to do so. But I shall be glad to have her away from the lonely house in Brunswick.

aff yours
J. L. C.

[BSC]

≋ TO ANDREW CARNEGIE

101 West 75th st
New York City
Feb. 14 1893

Hon. Andrew Carnegie;[46]
My dear Sir:—

Having well in mind the sentiments of your most interesting chapter on Art in America in your "*Triumphant Democracy*."[47] I cannot refrain from calling your attention to one institution in this City which had it been in existence at the time you wrote would have ~~commanded~~ received, I am sure, your special ~~regard~~ commendation.

This is the School for the instruction of "Artist-Artisans," the object of

46. Andrew Carnegie (1835–1919), was the world's richest man and leading philanthropist. *EB*, 2:880.

47. Chapter 14, "Art and Music," of Carnegie's *Triumphant Democracy, or Fifty Years' March of the Republic* (1885) describes how American art now received even European recognition.

which is to afford means of Art-Culture directed particularly to the "Useful Arts" for the encouragement of native talent, & skill, so that we can supply a home-need by home-workers. In fact, this is a movement towards the emancipation of America from an almost servile dependence on Europe for works of skill & on forms & fabrics of beauty to supply the great & increasing demand which ~~betokens~~ marks our advancing taste & ~~civilization~~ and ampler conception of the art of living. This school has been started by a rare man, of character, culture and heart fitting him for the great work he has projected.

The splendid gifts of Mr Morgan for a School of Trades in the City, of Mr. Drexel of Philadelphia for a School of Arts & Sciences, and of Mr Armour for a similar School in Chicago,[48] still leave one of the most important needs of the Country not provided for. I speak advisedly when I say that I regard the School for Artist-Artisans as second to none in importance whether in an educational, industrial, commercial or patriotic point of view.

#

Your well known character—your word & your works—inspire me with entire freedom in addressing you in this manner. ~~I believe you will be glad to look into this [subject]~~ my [bringing] this object are which will [commend] your [approval] & interest as it has my own. I had ~~intended to give myself~~ the pleasure of ~~calling you in person introduced by a~~ make your acquaintance through the [interceding] of friends who have the advantage of being also personal friends of yours, but I am confined to my room by a rebellion of my old war-wounds & I have to allow my earnestness to express itself by ~~merely writing~~ the pen which in my case is not mightier than the sword, for the effects of the latter compel me to fall back upon the former. I hear that you also are confined to your house by what, I trust, is not a serious disability, & I may therefore hope that you may be able, in the interval of business cares, to look over some of the printed matter explanatory of the object I am here commending which I take the liberty of enclosing.

With sentiments of highest respect & esteem

I am truly yours

Joshua L. Chamberlain

P.S. For purposes of identification I may add that I am a Maine man at present only a sojourner in this City having lately been President of

---

48. John Pierpont Morgan (1837–1913), America's foremost financier, was a trustee of the New York Trade School. *EB*, 8:320–21. Anthony J. Drexel (1826–93), a Philadelphia banker, founded the Drexel Institute, a free technical school offering day and night classes to all in 1892. *DAB*, 5:455–56. Philip D. Armour (1832–1901), Chicago meat packer and grain dealer, established the Armour Institute of Technology in 1893. *DAB*, 1:347–49.

Bowdoin College in Maine & several terms Governor of that State, a General in the War for the Union, & somewhat familiar with other public matters. J. L. C.

#There is no other school like this in the Country, & N.Y. should ~~New York is really behind~~ encourage this. Other Cities in the

Mr Stimson has received had flattering ~~offers~~ invitations & ample assurance of support from at least five other cities ~~to go there with his School~~, but he holds to this City as the proper place for an institution of such ~~a great~~ scope & importance.

[YUL]

≋TO ANDREW CARNEGIE

N.Y.C. Mch 23ᵈ 93.

Dear Mr. Carnegie;

Your very kind reply to my letter of Feb 14ᵗʰ concerning the School of Industrial Arts gave me much encouragement. We are doing all in our power to hold the School together for this year, feeling assured that if we can carry it by this point, our generous citizens will see its value, and see it fairly established ~~beyond fear of failure~~.

Mr. Stimson's heart is so tender towards the earnest souls that have come to him for instruction, that he is giving to many of them all the privileges of the School with little or no charge. Consequently the direct income of the School does not meet the bald, necessary expenses. Neither he nor most of his assistants receive salaries for their labor. It is most truly with them a labor of love. We are trying now to free Mr Stimson from the burden of the rent.

Our friend Mr. D. H. McAlpin[49] owns the building in which the School is held, and if he sees that it is going to be a success, he will no doubt ~~generously~~ assist us.

Can I do anything to facilitate your plans for looking into the [merits] of the School as you kindly intimated you purpose of doing? If so, I beg you will allow me to do so. I am not yet able to be about, but I would make an extraordinary effort, or if need be sacrifice, for the sake of this most worthy cause. ~~Please command me.~~

I fear Mr. Stimson is getting worn out, and I fear disheartened about holding the School here. He is ~~receiving quite lately very tempting most appreciative offers elsewhere and he is~~ the soul of the school & its body too, and he is too rare a man to let go from this city

---

49. David H. McAlpin (1816–1901), tobacconist and educational philanthropist. *National Cyclopaedia*, 33:304.

Very truly yours,
Joshua L. Chamberlain

≈ TO ALEXANDER S. WEBB

101 West 75ᵗʰ St.
New York City, May 18ᵗʰ '93

Dear General Webb:—

I have to thank you for the interest you have so kindly taken in the matter of the medal of honor. The requirement of witnesses I do not regard as unreasonable. The curious transformation of the rear rank to the front now that it is profoundly peaceful and safe there, is quite noticeable all along the line, and makes a fellow of my temperament reluctant to put in any claim for recognition of any kind.

The government is wise, now at last, in requiring some evidence of merit on the part of claimants. I wish it had begun to do so 25 or 30 years ago. But for my particular case; I am unfortunate in the fact that people who could be witnesses of any special acts of mine in battle, fell victims of their "environment." They were mostly killed.

As to Gettysburg, my comrades there are pretty well gone. I have copies of the official reports of my superior officers, and also of their personal letters to me commending my action in that battle. Would this kind of evidence be received? I will quote the concluding lines of Gen. Rice's report to the Division Commander,[50] that you may judge whether that kind of testimony would avail.

Major J. F. Land. of the 20ᵗʰ Regt. is a physician in this City. He was one of my Captains in that battle.[51] Gen'l Ellis Spear of Washington, D.C. is another. I could get their statements, I suppose. I may [be able] to think of others. I have been trying to get over to see you. I hope to do so soon. I shall have to come at about noon, which is not a good time, for you.

Yours ever,
J. L. Chamberlain

50. Brig. Gen. James Barnes (1801–69) commanded Griffin's 1st Division, V Corps, at Gettysburg. CWD, 21.

51. Maj. Joseph F. Land (b. 1838). Baillie, 1678.

[ca. 18 May 1893]

The official reports, if they are still on the files, ought to show that at least in three battles I had a part which could not be expected as matter of course in obedience to orders, and the results of which were of such consequence as to call for special recommendations of my commanding officers for my promotion; failing to receive which, I was in each case, immediately advanced in grade of command, though not of rank.

I refer to the Battle of Gettysburg, July 2^{d} 1863.[52]

of the White Oak Road, March 31st 1865.[53]

and Appomattox Court House April 9th 1865.[54]

In the first, I made a countercharge, when my ammunition was all expended which repulsed a repeated attack of greatly superior force, and broke the enemy's attempt to turn our left at Round Top. Seizing also the Great Round Top. In the second, though at the time "held in reserve," having had a hard battle with heavy loss in my command, and severely wounded myself, but one day before, I vo[l]unteered to recover a field which had been yielded by two Divisions (of my Corps), and with my Brigade and another (Gregory's) sent to report to me, turned the enemy's position, and captured his works covering the White Oak Road, — an event which made possible the success of the battle of Five Forks on the following day.

In the third, on the march to Appomattox, and when near the field, at a direct request from Gen'l Sheridan, I "double-quicked" my command, reaching Sheridan in advance of my Corps, and relieved his cavalry then in action taking the fight into my own hands and driving the enemy before me when the flag of truce came in.

All this was duly recognized by my superior officers at the time; but circumstances, — my own peculiar habit of reticence (in those days) and the absorbing interest which followed the event of Lee's surrender, being among them, — prevented me from thinking much about myself, or others of me; and so my story ended with the war.

For the last Campaign I was recommended by all above me for promotion to full Major General, and, strange to say, actually received the commission of that rank, which for reasons then unknown to me, was asked to be returned

52. To 3rd Brigade, 4th Division, V Corps (reorganized as 1st Brigade, 1st Division on 6 June 1864).

53. Gregory's (see 6 July 1865 to Thomas) 2nd Brigade, 1st Division, V Corps, added to his command.

54. To the 1st Division, V Corps.

in a private letter from the Secretary of War. I since learned that there was another Major General to be appointed from Maine,[55] and so its "quota" would be full.

It appears to me, knowing that the grounds on which some medals of honor have been bestowed would upon any classification of purely *military* service bring me fairly within the category, I seem to be in danger of being [made] conspicuous by being left out.

A few days ago I was surprised and honored by being asked to recommend Major General Howard for one of these medals, with the assurance that this recommendation would be enough to call attention to the General's merits. This reminds me that my influence once obtained for another the Cross of the Legion of honor in France, which I had much more reason to receive one myself, so far as the recognized grounds of such honors went then.

I know of nobody but you, now living, who can give me the proper advice or assistance in this matter.

Faithfully yours
Joshua L. Chamberlain

[YUL]

✎ TO FREDERICK C. AINSWORTH

Brunswick Maine
September 16 1893

Colonel
F. C. Ainsworth, U.S.A.
Chief of the Record & Pensions Office
War Department[56]
Washington, D.C.
My dear Sir:—
I have to acknowledge the receipt of a "medal of honor" in accordance with your notice of August 17 1893,[57] and to express my high appreciation of the honor thus conferred.

Very respectfully
Your obedient servant

---

55. Francis Fessenden (see 23 Jan. 1906 to Merriam), son of Sen. William Pitt Fessenden.

56. Col. Frederick C. Ainsworth (1852–1934). *WhoAm*, 11. See also 24 Sept. 1907 and 21 Oct. 1907 to Ainsworth.

57. Congress awarded Chamberlain the Medal of Honor for "Daring heroism and great tenacity in holding his position on the Little Round Top against repeated assaults, and carrying the advance position on the Great Round Top."

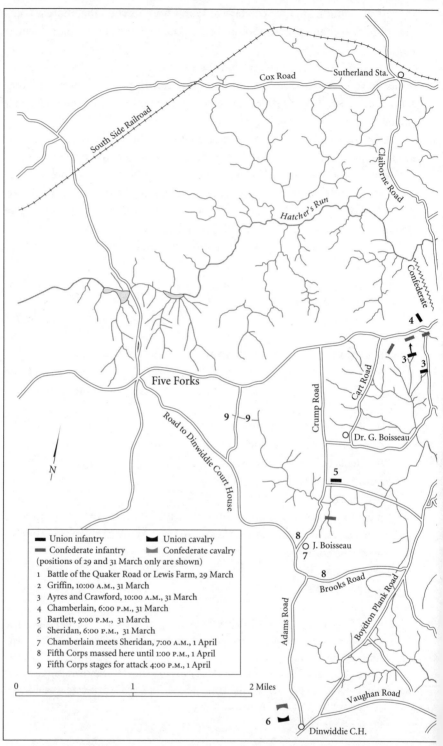

Cox Road   Sutherland Sta.

South Side Railroad

Claiborne Road

Hatcher's Run

Confederate

4

3

3

Five Forks

Crump Road

Cart Road

Road to Dinwiddie Court House

9 — 9

Dr. G. Boisseau

5

N

8
J. Boisseau
7

8

Brooks Road

Adams Road

Boydton Plank Road

- Union infantry
- Union cavalry
- Confederate infantry
- Confederate cavalry
(positions of 29 and 31 March only are shown)
1   Battle of the Quaker Road or Lewis Farm, 29 March
2   Griffin, 10:00 A.M., 31 March
3   Ayres and Crawford, 10:00 A.M., 31 March
4   Chamberlain, 6:00 P.M., 31 March
5   Bartlett, 9:00 P.M., 31 March
6   Sheridan, 6:00 P.M., 31 March
7   Chamberlain meets Sheridan, 7:00 A.M., 1 April
8   Fifth Corps massed here until 1:00 P.M., 1 April
9   Fifth Corps stages for attack 4:00 P.M., 1 April

0   1   2 Miles

Vaughan Road

6

Dinwiddie C.H.

Actions at the Quaker and White Oak Roads, 29 and 31 March 1865, and staging for the Battle of Five Forks, 1 April 1865 (Adapted from Trulock, 232–33)

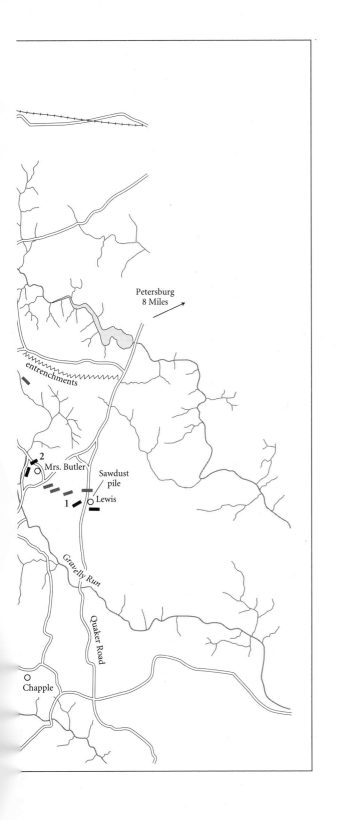

Petersburg
8 Miles

entrenchments

2
Mrs. Butler

Sawdust
pile

1   Lewis

Gravelly Run

Quaker Road

Chapple

Joshua L. Chamberlain
(Lately Bvt. Maj. Genl U.S.V.)

≈ TO FANNIE

101 W. 75th st
New York Jan 23^d 94

———

My dear Fanny:

You have not, I hope, been allowed to know how very hard a time I have had with sufferings and disabilities since Christmas. I have told Wyllys to write you such particulars as he thought proper, and he has no doubt, and rightly, softened the story down so as not to distress you.

But now I am getting up, and shall recover rapidly—having no poison in my blood from miserable drugs.

I dont know how the attack was prompted—probably by a seizure with *grippe*,[58] which caught me by the throat, & then went to the "weak spot."

But now I want you here. You certainly have stayed long enough in Brunswick; & I am much concerned to have you exposed to the inconveniences and uncongenial surroundings that beset you there. You can be made comfortable and happy here, where we shall welcome you with love, and I can give you as much good as you can me. So please be ready to come right away. Make a very short stay with Daisy now, & plan for a longer one when we leave here very early in the season.

Grace & Eleanor have been out into the sunshine, and are reported as wonderfully well. She wrote me the brightest letter I have ever read.

Mr Allen's[59] sudden death was a shock to us all. He was a very wonderful man, with no ordinary endowments. He was very fond of Grace, & she will miss him. The funeral will be Wednesday I believe. I am glad you are not there for that. It would be too much for you. Let me know what money you need.

Lovingly yours

J. L. Chamberlain

Miss George Kendall[60] sent you a nice little pocket-purse;—but I am afraid you have nothing to put in it. Let me know. [P]lease. Wyllys is

---

58. Influenza.

59. Stephen M. Allen (1819–94), a prominent Boston banker, lawyer, and builder of libraries, was Grace's father-in-law and Fannie's lifelong friend. Trulock, 321, 521 n. 79; Baillie, 18.

60. Unidentified, but see 13 Dec. 1886 to Grace.

driving out once a week, or oftener. He is working up his own patents. He *will not* do anything else & must be allowed to stick to this.

[BSC]

TO GEORGE T. LITTLE

101 W 75th st New York City
Feb 20 1894

Dear Professor Little:

I send you Dr Taylor's[61] letter & his [s]igned blank which I really do not know how to fill. Dr. Taylor himself is the man I would vote for. He is an earnest friend of the College. I would nominate him if there were any use in it. Please represent me in filling this blank & depositing it properly.

My attention has accidentally been drawn to the record in the General Catalogue. I suppose the notices there are intended to embrace facts of appointment & service. In my own case the record shows me as follows: (I was never *elected* "Tutor")

I mean now *within* the College.

Instructor in Logic & Natural Theology
Prof. Rhetoric & [W]riting
Instructor in Comparative Philology
Prof. Modern Languages
Prof. Mental & Moral Philosophy
Lecturer, Political Sciences & Public Law.
President.

There are my offices, my election & service. Please also substitute for "Pres. Railroad Co." Prest. Institute of Arts New York.

I resigned the Railroad office & it was not worth mentioning at all, except to *locate me* temporarily.

Let me know if I can be of service to you in any of your work.

Truly you[rs]

J. L. Chamberlain '52

[BSC]

61. Unidentified.

NEW FIELDS { 151

Boston Dec 19 1894

Dear Sadie:

I seem to be strangely hindered in my purpose of visiting you this year. I had to take Fanny to the Eye Infirmary[62] here, last month; & now she will probably remain until she follows her Doctor to New York some time in January. She is at #200 Columbus Ave Hotel Lafayette, & when I cannot be with her she is very lonely. In the meantime business matters will hold me pretty constantly either here or in New York — chiefly the latter, for two more months at least. There is a new start in my Railroad interests which promises extremely well, and I shall have to attend closely to them.

I shall have to go to Brunswick Friday but must be back here by Tuesday or Wednesday. It does not seem quite like giving me a chance to make you the long intended visit. If possible, I will [come] over to catch a glimpse of you, but I may find so much to straighten out in Brunswick that even this will be difficult. I will write you again when I reach Brunswick.

Grace has a severe sore throat. The baby is firmly well & bright. Wyllys is at Gracie['s], still hammering at his invention. I had hoped to get time to write; but if I do anything at this, it will have to be in my odd hours when in New York. That seems my best place for working at this to advantage.

Miss Elizabeth Edmunds has rented for herself apartments at 101 west 75th st (where we all were) & makes me a very generous offer of a home there when I am in New York.

Fanny & I will be there when not at 200 Columbus in Boston. I am unusually well & strong.

With great love to you all
your affectionate brother
Lawrence

[LC]

New York March 19th 95

My dear Sae:

Your letter was so full of calamities it almost made me laugh! When misery passes a certain pitch it becomes ludicrous. Whether this is because of an incongruity between one's deserts and his "environment," or between what he

---

62. Perhaps the free Massachusetts Charitable Eye and Ear Infirmary in Boston, founded in 1827.

has a fair right to expect & what he actually gets—it is certainly not in accordance with the "fitness of things."

But I dare say it was the suppressed humor with which your descriptions are charged that gave the sort of quickening sensation we call the ludicrous. Do you remember when you & I "laughed out loud" at a funeral—where all the mock-solemnity was arranged like a row of graven images?

Well, you seem to have a favorable point of observation for your study of human affairs. Brewer seems (if not the center of radiation for evils) to be the focus which attracts them mightily, & sets them whirling around your point of vision at any particular time. Some unregenerate observer of life says "there is a secret satisfaction in the aspect of other people's discomfiture." I dont accept that, but when "things" get very bad, I am apt to laugh. This has carried me through many rough & dark places.

But I have most deeply & constantly sympathized with you & Charley in the awful trials that have come upon you. I wish Charley could come on here & make a little visit, & take a rest. I think it would be quite convenient for Miss Edmunds.[63] Indeed she suggested it. Fanny will not come until I go after her & that will not be just yet.

I have been quite well this winter. But an abscess in my right inside ear has been a bad thing to put up with. I am better of it now.

Hope to hear good news about Tom. Grace writes that she tried to be polite to Alice, but fears she did not succeed well. I am very sorry Alice should be so broken up in her well-found plans. I thank you for your letter.

aff. yours

J. L. C.

Don't flatter yourself you have all the misery around you in Brewer. There was a little left for New York & vicinity. Just as my ear got so I could *walk*, Miss Elizabeth came down with a roar of pleurisy,[64] so sharp a knockdown in its fantastic play that I had to telegraph Lillian to come at once from Trenton—(where Washington crossed the Delaware in midwinter among the ice cakes). This was ten days ago—Elizabeth is enjoying a season in bed now, & I am at the other end of the "til[l]er"—*up* & *out*! & *off*!

However, we all—the "girls" & I, appreciate your kind remembrance.

They never forget your generous courtesies, & hope to recognize & recompense them in some due form & measure.

Love to all. L.

[LC]

63. Elizabeth Edmunds.
64. A disease of inflammation of the lining of the lungs.

Brunswick, Nov. 27th 1896.

Dear General Spear:—

I have your valued letter of the 25th. I am sure you ought to write out the matters which you suggest as to Bethesda Church and Peebles' Farm.[65] The sketch you send is good enough; but you would prefer to have it in more conventional style. Please take it as a compliment, and not otherwise, if I return it to you for this purpose, as I judge you made no press copy of it. Cant you put [it] into shape, & get it back to me pretty soon?

As to Gettysburg itself: quite a number of things have been put in distorted perspective lately. The influence of Colonel Oates'[s] statements has extended to color the accounts of the whole engagement. This was manifest in Prince's address.[66] I think you have been somewhat affected by this late account. No doubt all th[at] Oates says of his own command is perfectly correct. But to reduce our whole fight to an encounter with his regiment is to falsify history. Th[e]re is no room for question that our right was engaged with the enemy some time before Oates came on us. The time, topography, &c. of the movements make this almost self-evident. The history of the 83[rd] Pa.[67] is explicit on this point. My own recollection is clear. An account I wrote soon after the battle without motive for distortion, puts this truthfully. The status of the prisoners we took corroborates the testimony. Some of the 4th Ala., and of the 4th and 5th Texas were taken.

The Melcher incident is also magnified.[68] He is now presented to the public as having suggested the charge. There is not truth in this. I had communicated with you before he came and asked me if he could not advance his company and gather in some prisoners in his front. I told him to take his place with his company; that I was about to order a general charge. He went on the run, and did, I have no doubt, gallant service; but he did no more than many others did,—you for instance, on whom so much responsibility devolved in bringing up the left wing and making it a concave instead of a convex line in

65. In the first days of Cold Harbor, the federal right flank lay at Bethesda Church. Peeble's Farm was a side action at Petersburg (30 Sept.–2 Oct. 1864). CWD, 62, 162–65; Faust, *Historical Times Illustrated Encyclopedia*, 567–68.

66. Perhaps Prince's address as regimental historian at the 20th Maine reunion at Gettysburg in 1889. See *Dedication of the Twentieth Maine Monuments*; and Pullen, 140–42. Both Spear and Prince had traveled to Washington to visit then-senator Oates.

67. Judson, *History of the Eighty-Third Regiment*.

68. Holman Melcher of the 20th Maine claimed to have suggested and led the charge at Little Round Top and that Chamberlain had stolen credit. See Melcher, *With a Flash of His Sword*.

the sweeping charge. There is a tendency now-a-days to make "history" sub-serve other purposes than legitimate ones. "Incidental" history, even if true in detail can be made to produce what used to be called in our logic "suggestio falsi."

I have been trying, at Hamlin's request, to reconcile the several accounts of the battle which he has in hand to publish, and it is the hardest work I ever did in the literary line. Prince's account is admirable in its historic truth, and is written in masterly style. But I observe the effect of some "ex parte" data[69] he had been furnished with. He did not consult me in the preparation of his address. I have a good deal of data, originating on the spot and at the time, which would have saved much judicial discussion as to matters of fact.

As I have no place in the volume about to be published except in mere addresses, I have no proper opportunity to make "statements." Hence I would like to have those which are to appear, consistent and correct. I have added some foot-notes to some of the papers put into my hands.

I have not done much to your account. The only fault I find with it is that it is too condensed, and somewhat unequal in scale. But what you en-large upon is not found anywhere else, and hence is of utmost value. I wish the whole of it were as full.

Truly yours,

Joshua L. Chamberlain

P.S. Now, it seems, it was Morrill that won the battle. He did good and praiseworthy work. But one might ask why he did not make some demonstration while Oates was advancing on us, and not wait until we had fought him as long as we could stand, and then turned on him and got him running.

The "whole truth" is sometimes quite different in its bearings from what is called truth. But to make a part truth displace the whole is not in accordance with old-fashioned ethics. C.

[Coll. of Abbott Spear, Warren, Maine]

꜠ TO ABNER R. SMALL

Brunswick, Jan. 20th 1897.

Dear Major Small:—

After my long afternoon with Captain Verrill, I went to New York, where I received your list of names of men at Gettysburg, and General Tilden's[70] com-

---

69. *Ex parte*: legal term meaning "on behalf of," here implying untested data.

70. Charles W. Tilden (1832–1914) of the 16th Maine, a member of the Maine Gettys-burg Commission. BBGB, 618.

ments on the rule of leaving off men not then actually in the line of battle. I fully agree with him that the names of men present at the battle even if not "in it," as teamsters, clerks, musicians &c, should be recognized and assigned to their true place in the list. I would not put on the list the names of men sick in Washington, no matter how deserving they may be of mention and remembrance, for character, or for duty elsewhere. But all who were at Gettysburg should, I think, be on your list, with remarks in case of those not expected to be in the line of battle. They were in their places, doing their duty.

But now, on arriving home this morning I find from General Hamlin a list made up, he says, by Lieut. Wiggin; which differs as to the names of men in the several companies from the list we have so widely as to be almost unrecognizable as intended for the same. In some of Lieut. Wiggin's companies, there is a tremendous preponderance of sergeants and corporals, and men we were sure were either off, or on, appear in his lists in quite the contrary categories. What can I do but send both list[s] to you for your final judgment and decision? I do not know enough to undertake to determine such matters. Kindly revise, and return.

How about your map? Captain Verril[l] was expecting it when I left him.

Faithfully yours,

Joshua L. Chamberlain

[MHS]

≈ FRAGMENT TO CHARLES HAMLIN

Brunswick, Jan. 20ᵗʰ 1897.

Dear General Hamlin:—

I have just returned from a week's absence, during a part of which I went over very carefully with Captain Verrill the matters he has so ably undertaken to look after. I now find your valuable letter enclosing a list of men of the 16ᵗʰ Regiment present for duty at the battle of Gettysburg. This you say was made out by Lieut. Wiggin. Not knowing of the existence of such a list I had persuaded Major Small, busy as he is, to aid me in making up such a list, which after much labor is just now [as] complete as he could make it.

But it is a remarkable fact, and one which illustrates the difficulty of arriving at the exact truth even in plain matters of fact in preparing "war-histories." that the two lists so carefully made up differ so much as to [be] almost unrecognizable as intended for the same.

Major Small and I have labored very hard, and long, to get the truth; and in some respects Lieutenant Wiggins'[s] list seems to be most accurate, from the specifications he makes as to detached service on the part of some men of whom we had not discovered this. Still, the list of names is greatly at variance in the two cases. I have returned both to Major Small, and he and I may have to have another sitting over the matter.

I asked Captain Verrill to send you the corrected copy for printer of my address at Gettysburg, which he wished to look over. You do not mention the receipt of it. I hope it is not lost, as I have no copy.

I [am] at work still to make the accounts of these two regiments as

[MHS]

≫ TO ABNER R. SMALL

Brunswick Feb 25 97

Dear Major Small:

I went before the Executive Committee of the "Gettysburg Commission" all day & evening till 11 o'clock yesterday, & presented the papers of the 16th complete. The Committee objected to the speeches of Genl. Hall[71] & me[72] as not proper to go into the Book but finally, I am told, admitted my speech (perhaps out of courtesy to me, as I was present) and also objected to the sketch [made] up from your History,[73] & voted (I think — at any rate I was so informed) to exclude this. I am sorry; for it is a very bright & valuable paper. One objection they made was that we had too much. Well this was because we were called on to make up as much matter as we could for each Regiment, [b]ut in this preparation, I had stricken out all repetition — So each paper had new matter; or at any rate, a new view. I would like much, with your permission, to withdraw my remarks, — if the Committee does not finally exclude them. I will see them published in another "collection," which will give them much wider notice.

They criticised also our placing five or six men [ill.] on the roles as "missing & never since heard from in the list of killed. There may be good reason for this perhaps, and I asked leave to with draw this paper of casualties for correction. In attempting this, I find some further discrepancies, which I submit to you:

71. Former commissioner Bvt. Brig. Gen. James A. Hall (1835–93) led the 2nd Battery, Artillery Brigade, I Corps, at Gettysburg. Charles Hamlin wrote "Hall's Second Maine Battery" in *MAG* (14–36), partly based on Hall's manuscript (15–23). *BBGB*, 254. See 27 Feb. 1897 to Hamlin.

72. Chamberlain's response to the toast "Gettysburg" at a 16th Maine banquet, *MAG*, 63–66.

73. Small, *The Sixteenth Maine Regiment*, with an introduction by Gen. Hall. Small's essay was included in the 16th Maine section at 46–63.

1. Corporal Hosea D. Manly, Co. I. we have as "missing since Gettysburg but in your Book he appears as afterwards *promoted to Sergeant & Sergeant Major!*
2. Corporal George D. Marston Co. I. we put down as *"killed,"* because he had not been heard from since Gettysburg. In your book he appears as "missing since Gettysburg, but also as promoted to sergeant & finally discharged June 19 1865!
3. Francis A. Crane Co. C. we have in our list as killed. You[r] book simply says "prisoner Gettysburg. Promoted Corporal." Was he ever heard from?[74]

There are two or three others whom you & I thought proper to place among the killed as they were seen in battle, never seen again & have been reported "missing" ever since.

I have looked up all I can of this list, but cant be sure. Can you complete the co[rr]ections?

Please return to me not later than Saturday 1.pm. as I have promised all to Hamlin before Monday.

yours (in not very good humor)

J. L. Chamberlain

[MHS]

FRAGMENT TO WILLIAM C. OATES

Brunswick, Maine, February 27th 1897.

Hon. William C. Oates;

My dear Sir:—

I am having some controversy with some of the "Gettysburg Commission" of this State in regard to points of our respective movements on the Round Tops on the afternoon and evening of July 2nd 1863.

They think it impossible that you should intend to say you came over the summit of the Great Round Top to attack our extreme left, ~~then commanded by me.~~ They think you and most of the Confederate commanders called Little Round Top the "mountain"; and their specific argument in your case is that the line of direction indicated by the position of our extreme left, and also the very great difficulty of surmounting the rugged sides of Great Round Top, make it almost certain that it was one of the lower spurs of the Round Top, and

---

74. As published, Manley of Auburn was listed as "missing," Marston of Auburn as "killed or died of wounds," and Crane of Fayett as "missing; never heard from since, probably killed." *MAG,* 53, 57, 59, 61.

not its utmost summit which you crossed in your advance and near approach to our left.

[M]y right was struck some little time before your regiment enveloped my left; ~~some troops, I think the 47th ala.~~ the 47th ~~appeared to have~~ had reached my ~~right~~ front before this. I think also, that the attack of the Texas regiments ~~probably~~ I think extended over so far as to reach my right even before the 47th struck. If I am correct, all the accounts I have seen harmonize. You could not, of course, have struck my line as soon as the regiments which had more favorable ground to pass over, and your attack coming some little time later gave me the impression that it was by what I then called "apparently a new line" that the really heavy blow fell upon me which made me reel and recover so many times

[BSC]

FRAGMENT TO CHARLES HAMLIN

Brunswick, March 5th 1897.

Dear General Hamlin: —

I have been giving particular and laborious attention to the matter of the material for publication in the Gettysburg volume. You now have too great a mass of matter. That of the 20th Regt. will make about 100 pages of manuscript. By doubling the columns for the list of men present in the battle, which can be done by using a smaller type than that of the body of the pages, you can save about six pages. I find the pri[n]ted page holds about 100 more words than the ma[nu]script page: 370 to 270. So at the best, the material of the 16th and the 20th will be about 75 pages as the matter now stands.

It is manifest to me that you will have either to give up your general historical sketch of each regiment, (which having no exclusive reference to Gettysburg could be better spared than some other matter directly pertaining to the battle of Gettysburg), or leave out your lists of men present in the battle, (which is necessarily imperfect, though we have all worked very hard on these), or else leave out some interesting papers from each regiment, or, lastly, cut down, remodel and consolidate all the descriptive papers. I would earnestly advise leaving out the historical sketches. These have no proper place in such a report as this; and they take up more space than any other papers. But you wish to treat all regiments alike in respect to the kind of exhibit allowed them. If a general historical sketch goes in for one regiment, it must go in for all. I dont see how you are going to do it. As to the objectionable parts of Major Small's paper for the 16th; in the judgment of your Committee, I have set out all that I think they would object to, and can offer this in more pruned shape. It presents the incidents of the conflict of the 16th, (which was

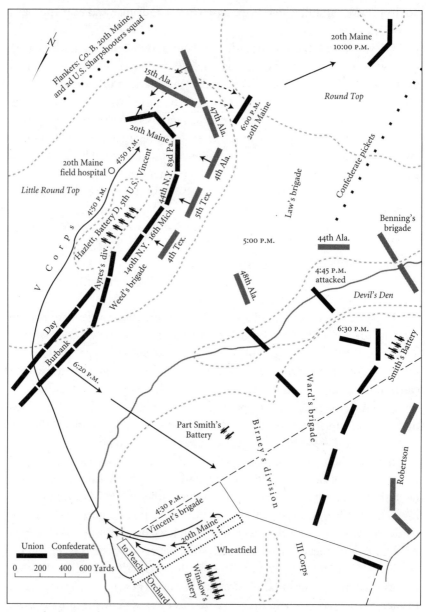

The Twentieth Maine and Vincent's brigade at Little Round Top, 2 July 1863
(Adapted from Trulock, 131)

a remarkable one) in very picturesque light. I do not know whether the Committee think this quality of writing is reprehensible in such a work as yours. If so some other things will have to be cut into in other regiments' accounts.

As to the 20th regiment, we have embarrassment. You desired to get a good bulk of interesting matter pertaining to the battle. I have taken great pains to do so. But now it is manifest to me we have too much. And cutting it down is to be a task; for it has been fitted and dove-tailed together in such a manner that we shall in any case have to perform all the operations of surgery, — cutting and attaching and healing "solution of continuity."

You proposed to put in all our public speeches at the time and place of the actual dedication of the two monuments. Prince's alone will take 24 pages of your book. Mine will be half as much.[75] There is fully half your space, at the start. Hinds[76] account is more systematic and perhaps suitable for a strict account. But it may not be so interesting as [Prince's. I trouble you] with all this, not because I want you to do any work on it, but because all of it having been got together by your express wish and by my long effort in pursuance of this, I want to be guided by you in the final form. There are two lines of policy to fol[l]ow in cutting down:— to make the papers official in character; and to

[MHS]

≋ TO ABNER R. SMALL

Brunswick, Apl 16th 1897.

Dear Major Small:—

You will rejoice with me when I inform you that after truly incredible labor I have succeeded in consolidating the paper made up from your History and that presented by Lieut Wiggin, so as to get them both within the limit required by the Executive Committee of the Gettysburg Commission, and have forwarded them all complete to Gen. Hamlin at Bangor. I had to take this work with me on the road to Washington and set the type-writers at it by dictation wherever I could catch the time, place and them.

The proofs will, I suppose, come to you, and to General Tilden, and you can criticise and correct as you may feel inclined.

I have done my last best, and am only ashamed of my own high-wrought,

75. "The State, the Nation, and the People," Chamberlain's address at the dedication of the Maine Monuments at Gettysburg was included, but Prince's address (see 27 Nov. 1896 to Spear) was not.

76. Perhaps Pvt. David H. Hinds of the 16th Maine or journalist Asher C. Hinds of the executive committee. Nothing attributed to either of them was included in the volume.

but entirely true remarks before your brave and loved survivors, where my affection may have betrayed itself.

Well, God made me so; [I] can[t] help it.

With no little of it to you and yours,

I am ever, faithfully yours,

Joshua L. Chamberlain

P.S. I have a mass of papers out of which this account has been made up. Shall I send them to you? They have all our correspondence &c C.

[MHS]

≈ TO FANNIE

Brunswick

Friday Morning

May 28th 97

My dear Fanny:—

It seems to be my plan now to start by the Saturday evening steamer from Bath & arrive in Boston Sunday [morning], & take Breakfast with you, & then leave for Springfield by Sunday 4 P.m. train. Monday morning train is too late for my appointment in Springfield. Hence I must "travel Sunday." Neither Wyllys nor I seems quite well. In face we are both rather "run down." He is wishing we were at Domhegan. I would rather be here now, — as I have less care here than any where. I shall go to New York from Springfield, to take away what furniture is to be brought home. There is no use in leaving it there longer. In this case I shall probably return by the New York & Portland steamer, to look after the "things." I have not felt much like writing a new Memorial Address,[77] but have had to do it, & I do not feel well pleased with it.

It has rained — rained — here all the week.

Georgie goes down to Domhegan this afternoon.

With great love

L.

[SL]

---

77. "The Two Souls," praised by the *Springfield Republican*: "A more remarkable discourse on such a theme has seldom, if ever, been produced. In the future record of his work, nothing else that Governor Chamberlain has said will take so high a rank as this great consideration of man's duty to his fellow man." Quoted in Herndon et al., *Men of Progress*, 568.

Wednesday Ev[enin]g
Aug 4 '97

My dear Sae:—

Our plans are changed. Fanny does not want to go and be a burden to you situated as you are, and Lillian says she will not go unless you will let her take right hold and help you. So now my plan is this. I want you to go to Bar Harbor as my guest, and let me install you & Fanny there while I go to the Aroostook & then return for you. In order for you to be able to leave home for this, Lillian says she will modify her plans, & come & take your place & look after Dana, if you will only let her. She is entirely competent for this, & is ready to do it, cheerfully & gladly. After that, I will take you all up to the foot of Mount Katahdin for the view I promised you.

If I can possibly do so, I shall come over *Friday* P.m.

P.S. I have just consulted Fanny & she says she will go with me Friday P.m. In this case I shall not be able to go to Bar Harbor *before* I go to Aroostook, but shall go right on there Saturday P.m. & *shorten* my stay there & come back & have the Bar Harbor & Katahdin trips upon my return from the Aroostook. So I can only be with you *now* for Friday night & Sat. prenoon. Lillian will stay here at the house (she is taking care of us here now) until she hears from me about all our plans. I write this in haste.

Yours affectionately
J. L. Chamberlain

[LC]

Brunswick Sept. 20 1897

My dear Alice:

I thank you very earnestly for your most interesting letter. Your habits of observation & powers of description make your letters really valuable [and] informative, as well as delightful to read.

Of course you had no objection to my reading you[r] letter to all our "people" assembled in the big parlor at Domhegan, where we *all* are now, and wish you were. The fall weather is delightful.—The clear bright skies & west winds make a climate all its own—not summer, nor by any means winter, but room enough to be out of doors all day or cool enough to enjoy a big brisk & short-lived fire in the big fireplace in the evening. The two babies[78] make things cheery—although just for a day or two the little one "Beatson"—or

---

78. Eleanor and Beatrice "Beatson" Allen, see Dramatis Personae.

"Birtson" I shd. spell it—is doing what girls have to do pretty early now-a-days, "cutting her eye teeth"![79] This causes some discomfort to her & possibly to the rest of us. The little (junior) [finally] made a swooping visit to your mother, a week or more ago, and had a charming time. I wanted Dana to come back here with them. He deserved a good vacation, but he wrote me in a fine, manly letter that he could not leave just now. I was glad to be at the house when your father got home, & I heard an enthusiastic account of his doings & goings—and yours too. I am glad you are in so good a place, and have such interesting neighbors & companions. It is a good thing to take advantage of the opportunities afforded by the College.[80] You have given me a high opinion of the College & of *society* there. I almost think that if things were a little *greener*, it would be a good place for us all to go to. I may possibly come out to that country this fall & help you eat some of the grapes you describe,—or oranges, perhaps, would do. I have not a very good chance to write here, but will not wait till I get to town—as I go any day or two. Meantime, with much love from us all

your young uncle
J. L. Chamberlain

[LC]

✍ TO WILLIAM P. FRYE

Brunswick, Maine, April 22nd 1898.

Hon. William P. Frye, U.S. Senate,
Washington, D.C.
Dear Sir:—

I beg to submit to you a summary sketch of a plan of organization of the active military forces of New England for the present crisis.[81]

To meet the exigency we should avail ourselves at once of existing militia organizations, in which there may be presumed to be a considerable proportion of men physically able, and well instructed, inured by discipline to the demands of the service, and with the spirit of loyalty and patriotism, who are ready to go at once to the field of action.

These being mustered into the service of the United States with their present familiar organization and officers, others remaining could be made into a camp of instruction, constantly and rapidly preparing men for the service as they might be called.

---

79. An expression meaning to get out of babyhood, to grow up. OED, 5:634.
80. Pomona College in California.
81. The eve of the Spanish-American War.

I speak now on the large scale. I have reason to believe I could organize a Division of New England troops, which would commence at once for such a course, and furnish immediately a goodly number of well-prepared men for the field, while the remainder carefully recruited, would be able to protect our shores against land attacks, and also afford a constant stream of reinforcements for the most exigent points.

I have no perfectly matured plan of details, but offer the suggestion that each of the States of Maine, New Hampshire and Vermont might furnish one regiment; Massachusetts three, Rhode Island one and Connecticut two. These regiments would cons[ti]tute three Brigades, and for purposes of unity and efficiency the Brigades could be organized into a Division. This Division not to be gathered into one camp; but at first the several regiments forming camps of instruction at the respective local centers, then the Brigades, if desirable, to be concentrated, the First at say, Portsmouth, N.H.; the Second, at Boston; and the third at New London, Conn. The head quarters of the Division, for administrative purposes, to be in Boston. The commander of the Division at the beginning, would make the constant tours of the command, to make effective the "touch," the unity, and the "esprit de corps."

Some plan like this should immediately put into shape and train.

From my acquaintance with the men of the New England States, and their acquaintance with me, I believe I could rapidly organize out of the militia of the States a superb Division of United States Volunteers. My motive is by no means that of personal preferment; but wholly for the interests of the public service of the Country in her hour of need. Still, I cannot but think that my day is not yet over for the service of my Country. You gentlemen in Congress and in the offices of the Government are in your right places: I desire to be in mine. And it is not unbecoming in me to express the conviction that by temperament, education, and a peculiar experience of public service, I am capable of taking a part like that suggested. The condition of my wounds is very much better than for years; and while I would not think it advi[s]able for me to go into Cuba at this season of the year, I should be ready, by the time the stress came, and the troops were ready, to take the field wherever called.

I am, with high respect, and regard,

Your friend and servant,

Joshua L. Chamberlain

[NA]

≫ TO RUSSELL A. ALGER

Brunswick Maine
April 22ᵈ 1898

To the Honorable
The Secretary of War:[82]
Sir:—

I hereby tender to the Government in the exigencies of the impending war, my services in any military capacity for which I may be deemed qualified.[83]

    I have the honor to be
    with high respect
    your obedient servant
    Joshua L. Chamberlain

[NA]

≫ TO FRANK A. GARNSEY

Brunswick, Maine [January] 18ᵗʰ 1899.

Com.
Frank A. Garnsey;[84]
Bangor;
Dear Comrade:—

Your kind answer to my inquiry is received as I return from Governor Dingley's[85] funeral. Otherwise I would have answered your suggestions before. I thank you for giving me the address of General Gordon; it happened that I received a letter from him just after I had written you.

    I thank you also for your invitation to the lecture of General Gordon; I will make every endeavor to be with you then.

    Your suggestion about an article from me on the subject of the surrender for publication, touches a proposition now before us for General Gordon and me to give our lectures on the surrender in close connection in various places.

---

    82. Bvt. Maj. Gen. Russell Alger (1836–1907), former senator from Michigan. DAB, 1:179–80.

    83. Alger replied that Chamberlain's offer had been filed for consideration "at the proper time should an opportunity occur making this possible." 30 Apr. 1898, Alger to Chamberlain, NA.

    84. Companion Frank A. Garnsey (b. 1839), a Bangor businessman, had been a junior officer in the 2nd Maine. *Representative Citizens.*

    85. Nelson Dingley (1832–99), former Maine governor and congressman. *BioDictGovr*, 2:616.

It was on this point that I wished to confer with Gen. Gordon before he made more engagements. You know I wrote a lecture on this subject soon after the event,[86] and have given it widely in New England and in other States; not very much, however, within 20 years. The renewal of a demand for this for a new generation, in connection with General Gordon's on the same subject, shows that people still feel an interest to hear the old story, and perhaps to see and hear two actors in that impressive scene. Neither of us knew of the other's writing on the same subject; and I presume it is as true of his as of mine, that nothing is changed in our original account. No new light was needed by either of us. We spoke from knowledge.

Your suggestion raises the question whether such an arrangement might not be possible for you, and perhaps more useful to you than what you suggest. I don't know what your plans and arrangements are about your lectures. By good rights mine ought to precede his, for the sake of observing historical order and scenic "perspective." There may not be time for this, however, and I do not know that this order is absolutely necessary. But I can well see that by having us consecutively, some, perhaps many, would patronize your "entertainment" who might not be drawn to either his or mine alone.

For my part, it would be far easier to give my lectures than to write a "cooked over" paper on the same subject. Besides, I am likely to give my lecture in various places, and I do not quite like to "cut the heart out of it" by publication beforehand.

But I wish to be of all the service to you possible; sympathizing with all your interests, and almost belonging to you, representing my old home.

Kindly let me know what your wishes and plans are touching on this point. I can take any evening after time suffic[i]ent for arrangements and due notice. I venture this suggestion, not for my own advantage, for I have calls enough to lecture, but to serve you in the most effective way. This measure might give new impetus to your patronage of General Gordon's lecture.

With warmest regard,
yours in F.C. & L;[87]
J. L. Chamberlain

[BSC]

86. "Lee's Surrender" was frequently reprinted. See, for example, *Kennebec Journal*, 3 Jan. 1868.
87. Likely "faith, courage, and loyalty."

TO GRACE

Sunday P.M.
Jany 29 1899.

My dear Gracie;

I did not mean to add to your cares or your collection of "girls" by the suggestions of my letter. You need all your strength of body and spirit for [fulfilling] your own sweet trust.

Now that I understand from Lillian's last letter that our dear one will be likely to remain perhaps all winter and I dont know how much longer in Boston, in the hope of help for her eyes, I shall make suitable provision for her comfort without throwing any burden on you beyond that of tender solicitude & cheering sympathy — which you will not feel to be a burden. It was not at all that Lillian is unwilling to take care of our poor little brave sufferer that I make the suggestion of a temporary change. Lillian does not complain. She has a sincere affection and admiration for our "little Mother," and will cheerfully stay with her. But I thought from some complaints on the other side, that it was "dull" & monotonous and tedious for the *patient*, and that what she might regard as a brighter mind, or more cultivated character would be better companionship for her.

More attendance and good care might be easily secured; and some persons might be found who would regard the advantages you refer to as part of the inducement or payment for such service: but our dear one requires spiritual companionship. That is not so easy to command.

What I wish we could do is to bring her home. I have not a doubt that magnetic treatment could be brought here for twice a week, to do her some good & at less expense than where she is.[88]

Dearest of love,
from Father & "Gennie"

[SL]

TO SAE

April 4th 1899

My dear Sae:

I thank you for your beautiful letter. Do not worry about me. I am wonderfully upheld. And am pretty well. As well as I ought to be, considering that I do not spare my strength much.

Fanny is blind: but *will* stay in charge of this magnetic Doctor who dares not tell her that he cannot help her, — if it needs telling. I do not see how Fanny

---

88. Magnetic treatment was a form of alternative medicine.

keeps up. She exhausts all her energies—physical & spiritual—in frantic un-
reconciliation (and who can blame her?) to this affliction. Lillian is wearing
herself out. We fear she will be a confirmed invalid, out of it. I cant get them
home, & Lillian writes me that it would do no good & make me not only
unhappy, but *wretched* to go up there.

Still I am going—as I ought to—soon.

Grace is *well* & her three little ones—all well.

Wyllys & I are well. I am busy and he is. I think he will now get his invention into the market. I am writing a good deal. Have just finished my "book"
of *Memoirs of the Last Campaign*: of the Army of the Potomac & Lee's Army.
Also have written out—what never before has been written—the "*charge at
Fort Hell*[89]—where I was mortally wounded.

The chapters on the "Passing of the Armies"—I think you would like.

Sunday, I wrote for Fanny & Lillian a little "chapter" of the "meaning of
Easter morning," which I shall get them to lend me, for you.

Yes, I saw that [ill.] had gone. It makes me lonely. I had sent him my address you spoke of as soon as I got home. What a beautiful paper that was of
Dr Field's![90]

I am anxious about Charley. Proud of Alice. Also of Dana.

Yours ever.

Lawrence.

[LC]

89. Chamberlain's 18 June 1864 charge at Petersburg, discussed in his "Reminiscences
of Petersburg and Appomattox: October, 1903."

90. Perhaps George W. Field (1818–1900), a Bowdoin- and Bangor-educated teacher
and minister.

As his health and wealth faded toward the end of the century, Chamberlain sought a patronage position and a veteran's pension. Politics played its inevitable role, and Chamberlain's refusal to play partisan games prevented him from receiving what he — and many others — considered his due: retirement in the regular Army and appointment to the top administrative (and patronage) post in the state, that of collector of customs for the Port of Portland. Fully cognizant of Chamberlain's fame and the risks of keeping the office from him wholesale, the Republican Party granted him the number two role, the surveyorship. Disappointed at this turn of events and weakened by his wounds, Chamberlain thrust himself increasingly into a much happier task: Civil War history.

In 1905, Fannie's blindness was complete, and her health failed. Chamberlain tried as he could to nurse her. His final letters to her suggest a renewed closeness in their marriage.

Chamberlain was still protective of his legacy and wistful for his youthful heroics, but his final years were those of an elder sage devoted to honorable, scholarly memory. Even if he felt underappreciated by many and believed he deserved better care from the government, he lived with the knowledge that the public still revered him as the "Grand Old Man of Maine."

〜 TO WILLIAM MCKINLEY

Brunswick, Maine, November 18, 1899.

To the President:[1]

Honored Sir, —

I was formerly an applicant for the Collectorship of the Port of Portland and Falmouth; but cheerfully acquiesced in the appointment of Mr. Milliken, who now fills that office.[2] As the Surveyorship of the port is soon to become vacated I now respectfully apply for appointment to this position.

As Mr. Allen, Representative-elect of this District, is not yet in Washington I beg permission to present this matter thus directly, and to enclose the recommendation of Ex-Governor Cleaves and Ex-Judge Symonds and Judge

---

1. William McKinley (1843–1901), 25th president of the United States.
2. Milliken is otherwise unidentified.

Whitehouse of the Supreme Court of Maine,[3] simply at this time as letters of introduction.

I have a very strong petition in my support, which will be presented through Mr. Allen on his arrival at the Capital. There will doubtless be other candidates whose claims he will desire to consider. I trust the President will pardon me for wishing now to bring my name before him for his consideration.

With highest respect,
Your obedient servant,
Joshua L. Chamberlain

[MHS]

TO EUGENE HALE

Brunswick, November 20th 1899.

Hon. Eugene Hale;
U.S. Senate.
Dear Senator Hale:—

The sudden death of Mr Milliken leaves the Collectorship of the port of Portland vacant. You may perhaps remember that I was an applicant for this position at the time of the last vacancy, and I had reason to think with the general approval of our Delegation in Congress. The complications about the office at that time by reason of Mr Reed's desire to appoint [M]r Milliken, which both of these gentlemen stated to me frankly, led me to withdraw my pretensions cheerfully, and wait for the next chance, as they assured me should not pass me by.

Circumstances have compelled me to look to the Surveyorship, of late; but here too, was complication in the fact that the offices open or soon to become so in the Custom House were promised to men who had helped Mr Allen to his nomination and election. Nevertheless, I have the names and interest of many of the strongest men in our District in my application for that office. Now, however, the way seems to be providentially open, without embarrassment to anybody, that I know of.

I think I am safe in presuming on your interest in my behalf, and your freedom to exercise it. Hence, before others get ahead of me, as is likely to be the case if I do not take the first moment to move, I write you making known

---

3. Henry B. Cleaves (1840–1912) of the 23rd Maine was governor from 1893 to 1897. Joseph W. Symonds (1840–1918), an associate justice from 1878 to 1884. William Penn Whitehouse (1842–1922) of Augusta, later chief justice. *BioDictGovr*, 2:622–63; *WhoAm*, 1212, 1337.

my desire, and the support I can bri[ng] to warrant favorable action towards my present application.

I am humiliated to have to ask for a place; but I know of no reason why I should not have this one. You will help me?

Yours as ever,

Joshua L. Chamberlain

[MHS]

TO AMOS L. ALLEN

Washington, D.C. December 1, 1899.

Hon. Amos L. Allen, M.C.

Dear Sir:

I present herewith sundry papers endorsing my application for appointment, as Collector of Customs for the Port of Portland and Falmouth, Maine.

These are three petitions signed by citizens of Portland: Two petitions signed by 250 prominent citizens of Brunswick: Letters from prominent men in the First Congressional District and other parts of the State of Maine.

I make reference also to other letters which have been sent directly to the President, and are probably on the files of the office of the Secretary of the Treasury.[4]

Several other petitions and papers are on the way addressed to you from other portions of the District and State.

I ask your attention to these papers, and unless you see fit to take favorable action thereupon, I respectfully ask you to secure for me a personal interview with the President, and to be present yourself at this interview, in order that you may be satisfied that any statements I may make to the President are true and warrantable.

Very respectfully yours,

Joshua L. Chamberlain

[MHS]

TO AMOS L. ALLEN

Washington D.C.
Dec. 5th 1899

Hon. Amos L. Allen: M.C.

Dear Sir:—

I herewith place in your hands additional petitions — 81 names from the Town of Brunswick, and 56 from the Town of Harpswell — making the total

4. Lyman Judson Gage (1836–1927), a prominent banker. DAB, 7:85–86.

Chamberlain near the turn of the century
(Courtesy of the Portland Press Herald/Maine Sunday Telegram*)*

from Brunswick, 319, and of Harpswell 56,—all of whom are men of standing. Also additional petitions from Portland embracing the names of officers & employees in the office of U.S. Engineers, and one from Androscoggin County, embracing all the County officers: also letters from chairmen of 2^{d} & 4th Dist. committees and several past Department Commanders of the Grand Army, and from prominent officers of the Voluntary Army, in Maine. I beg to add [these] to those in your hands.

Truly yours
Joshua L. Chamberlain

[MHS]

TO ALEXANDER S. WEBB

Ebbitt House
Washington Dec 7th '99

Dear "Andy Webb";
yes "old Chamberlain [will] help Webb,"—& [pour] his heart.

An hour after receiving your letter this morning, I went into the Senate chamber and laid the matter before Senator Hawley.

He will present your bill—Senate 1901[5]—Monday morning, and will look after it heartily. I move promptly, you know. Somehow, I can do more for you than I can for myself. But this is "my Law and my Gospel," I *love to do it for you.*

Faithfully yours
Joshua L. Chamberlain

The Priest has not yet seen your letter to him about me, but I thank you for it, & will get at it, somehow.

I may be in New York Monday myself. C.

[YUL]

TO SAE

Brunswick Dec 24th 99

My dear Sae:

Wyllys has brought me in two beautiful handkerchiefs marked with a well-cherished hand with my name.

How it suddenly rises upon me what a "name" is, not simply an identifi-

---

5. The bill would restore Webb to his active duty status and then retire him, thus providing him a pension. See 1905 and 1906 letters on Chamberlain's efforts to have such a bill passed for himself.

cation but symbol of a concrete something made up of so many elements & essences that constitute individuality.

It seems to partake of that "worth of personality" which is the reason & basis of "spiritual law,"

He tells me (Wyllys) that you sent him something & Lillian [a] useful instrument for some of her tasks. She has not so much time now to devote to me & my matters; as we have been, & still are, running a big house under her general direction.

You may know that we had all our children here Thanksgiving day, so that an old partitioned table of *twelve* filled the circle, long broken. That is, Horace & Grace & 3 children & nurse: Fanny & I & Wyllys & Miss Edmunds & Miss Hodgdon (the new special attendant of Fanny) & Mrs Curtis, our old smiling-faced rear-guard.

We were beginning to have a good time, but I was called away to Washington right from the table at 4.40 P.m. & went up with Horace & broke the journey by passing the night with him.

But Grace & "Beatsen" stayed until last Monday, when Grace had to go & take charge of her baby[6] (who had gone up a few days before) & was reported to be "sick,"

When I came back from Washington last Thursday I called on her, & found that the baby had *scarlatina*[7] & they were sequestrated in their course — Horace & two other children being with his step-mother. The[ir] baby is now very sick; but they are alarmed for the others, though holding no communication.

We [are] with Grace, but have to [ill.] on others to answer, as she fears infection by [ill.].

We all thank you for remembering us, & wish we could make proper acknowledgment. We are so "busy" — somehow — that there [may?] not seem time to look up these tokens. However, I hope to be better circumstanced in a few weeks. I expect a pretty good office in the Portland Custom House in February. I wish you could see the splendid testimony sent the President by the people of Maine. Almost the whole of the [quality] men of Portland, & 400 citizens of Brunswick among the number. I treasure these.

With greatest love to you all,

yours.

Lawrence

6. Rosamund Allen, see Dramatis Personae.
7. Scarlet fever.

Miss Edmunds says she is going to write you herself as soon as *she gets a moment.*

[LC]

≋ TO AMOS L. ALLEN

carbon copy   Brunswick, Maine, December 25th 1899.

Hon. Amos L. Allen,
Washington, D.C.
Dear Mr Allen:—

I have returned home, and find my friends well pleased that you were able to secure the Surveyorship for me. Of course it was not what we deemed our support to warrant; but we saw how you were placed, and I think most of them think as I do that you did the best you could under the circumstances.

It is true it is difficult to see why, if Mr Moses[8] and I were to have the two offices, I could not have the one I wanted and he the one he wanted. I have no doubt you would have been sustained by, a large majority if you had given me the Collectorship; but it may all be best as it is. At any rate, I am not going to embarrass you; nor are my friends.

Some people in P[o]rtland are pretending that the matter of the Surveyorship is still open. But I tell them I have your positive assurance it is to come to me; and they may rely upon this.

I shall see as many as I can, and the feeling about Portland will soon calm down. You will have some letters to this effect.

With all bes[t] wishes of the season,

I [remain], very truly yours,

Joshua L. Chamberlain

[MHS]

≋ TO JOHN T. RICHARDS

Brunswick, December 26th 1899.

General John T. Richards;[9]
A[u]gusta, Maine.
My dear General:—

Your kind heart suggests a delicate way of congratulation to cheer me in my defeat for a place which I thought it fitting to aspire to, and very many

---

8. The collectorship had been promised to the incumbent appraiser, Charles M. Moses. Pullen, 153.

9. Richards is unidentified.

others of the highest character and station thought me competent for and entitled to. It is this testimony which is my real reward for any service I may have rendered, — this recognition rich in character and volume, which cannot be bought nor held cheaply, nor be given to the exchangers to be traded on or off.

The surveyorship is a good little office, no doubt; and I ought perhaps to be thankful to get it, — whether as a gift of grace or pity, or a sop to tender consciences, or a concession to a popular demand which I could not be wholly ignored on the part of the disposers of pieces and distributors of our rights and liberties. It is s[ai]d to be an easy [place,] no responsibilities, no duties, no power, no prominence, no part in the governmental representation, and requiring no ability. Whether this description of the place should inflate my vanity when I am told that I am "entitled to it," is a question for the meek, who are said to be about to "inherit the earth," To me it suggests a free bed in a hospital.

It has a good salary for such a place,[10] I confess; and that is something of a silencer. This is a reason why many would be glad to get it, to whom it is the highest thing that ever came into their lives. It is a reason why I do not like to disp[la]ce others, — as for instance the good fellow who is the present incumbent, and needs it as much as I do.

What you are thinking of in your straight-forward kindness of heart towards me, is the good salary and the comparative ease and comfort of the surveyorship. These are reasonable grounds. I accept them; and I sincerely thank you.

What I aspired to, and received the splendid support of a large and powerful portion of our citizens for, was the Collectorship. This is a representative office. It is concerned not only with the collections of the customs; but it represents the party in power; it represents the Government in its authority and dignity: it represents the President among the people as the Senators and Members of Congress represent the people in the halls of legislation and government. And this not only in matters of public ceremony and courtesy, but not impossibly in times of public exigency which demand executive ability and experience of great affairs. Hence it has been held not unworthy of the ambition of first-class men. It has been thought promotion even for Governors.[11] I am free to say I thought myself equal to these things.

10. $4,500 per annum. Trulock, 525 n. 99.
11. Lot Morrill and Israel Washburn were collectors for Portland and Daniel F. Davis for Bangor.

The Surveyorship has nothing of this character or history about it. It is essentially an obscure office, tending to keep one out of notice, as well as out of responsibility. I am still conscious of vital activities which welcome heavier tasks, and demand more scope.

But you must know that it was resolved that I should not have either of those places, no matter what my support should be; and this result was forced from the hands of those who in our peculiar republican system of government have the disposal of even the Presidential appointments, by the danger to them of ignoring my strength with the people. I know that,—and they know it. I know some other things,—which they do not; and which are pleasant to think of.

Perhaps I ought to be satisfied with the result as it is. Some people say so. But it will not be for the reason that I have been given the inferior place because I had the strength to command the superior one; not for the reasons that I have been "taken care of" at the public expense somewhat prematurely; but rather that, as some tell me, I have been spared the dire experiences of being the disburser as well as the Collector of "Customs"; and for my own part, that I may please myself with thinking I am on the same retired list with Hawthorne, even if unable out of my own experiences to scrape together the "mosses from an old Manse," or from observation of others to bring out with remorseless truth those "covered ways of conduct" which when exposed inexorable law marks with the "Scarlet Letter,"[12]

I ought to say that I think Mr Allen in his decision did the best he could under the circumstances which were pressed upon him with one motive or another.

You will pardon this rather long letter; but your kind suggestions led to this exposition, which it may be best to treat as entirely confidential.

With constant reg[a]rd, as you well know,

Truly yours,

[MHS]

12. Nathaniel Hawthorne (1804–64), a Bowdoin graduate, had held patronage customs posts at Boston and Salem, where he was surveyor, an experience he satirized in his introduction to *The Scarlet Letter* (1850). His *Mosses from an Old Manse* (1846) is a collection of tales and historical sketches written during his residence at the Old Manse in Concord. DAB, 8:424–29.

TO JOSEPH ROSWELL HAWLEY

Brunswick, Maine, January 12th 1900.

Hon. J. R. Hawley, U.S. Senate;

My dear General:—

I have already written you thanking you for your interest in reviving the bill for the restoration and retirement of General A. S. Webb. I have rested on your assurance that you would bring this bill before the Senate; and indeed, you took measures to prepare it for this purpose while I was sitting beside you in the Senate Chamber.

I hardly understand why I can get no trace of it as yet; as you said you would bring it up on the next Monday, which would be December 11th.

I venture to enclose to you a memorandum of testimony in regard to General Webb's conduct at Gettysburg at a momentous crisis of that battle. I think members of the Military Committee should see this.

General Webb is a man of highest character and of record perfect and complete on every line. No man is more deserving. And the bill now to be brought up does not do justice to him, nor give what he easily might have had before, under existing law. It seems to me that now, he should have the recognition he asks for through friends who know him and his record, as a measure of partial justice, and for the honor of the Country's service.

With warm regard,

Yours as ever,

Joshua L. Chamberlain

[YUL]

TO AURESTUS S. PERHAM

Brunswick Jan 26th 1900

Dear Captain Perham:

I have been in the mood every day since I got home to write you thanking you for your kindness to me while in Washington.

Your letter just received admits no further delay. I have not got over my cold yet, and have had all the work I could do writing & speaking, so I am pretty well tired out. Now I thank you still further for this letter. I am glad you saw Governor Robie,[13] & that Mr Allen[14] confirms what he has said to me. I suppose the appointment will come on about the middle of February.

---

13. Frederick Robie (1822–1912) was governor of Maine from 1883 to 1887. *BioDictGovr*, 2:620.

14. Rep. Amos Allen, see Dramatis Personae.

I would be glad if General Whittaker[15] would write out for me his account of the bringing in of the flag of truce, as he told me in Washington he would do. I will write him and ask him to write it out for me. It is valuable testimony & history. I wish I had while in Washington bought one of Genl Longstreets *"Manassas to Appomattox,"* and got you to ask him to give me his autograph on the fly leaf. I have not met him since "Appomattox Court House," but I have a high regard for him, and his book is written with a spirit of truth & candor that enhances its value as the work of an eminent soldier.[16]

I will see if Spear will not help me get the book & then you might ask the General if he will write in it for me.

Longstreet will not remember me, but as I was a Division Commander he will not hesitate to do me this honor.

I will write you again about this.

Truly yours, and with my best compliments to your wife & your father,[17]

Joshua L. Chamberlain

[MHS]

〜 TO GRACE

Sunday [morning]
Feb 25 1900

———

How the wild storm sweeps in from the sea! Over what tumults of waves oceans — wide & [ill.] what ice — crashings on the shore — this wild south east storm! And how the great trees across the human paths sway and bend — royally in their strength and grace! And see the earth so calm, locked in trea-sure — keeping frost, & veiled in snow (*this*) snow moving — as it were — run-ning, too in waves before the storm! There are the trees where my dear one looked out while growing like them in strength & grace — able also gracefully & strongly to bend before the storms & yet to *stand*! This would be the [morn-ing] to be at home — when you would not wish to be elsewhere, nor be called out by duty or pleasure. But only to sit & look out & think, & look in and love! How the rain pours in streams down the window panes of my study where I

15. Perhaps Edward W. Whitaker (1841–1922) of Connecticut. BBGB, 618; CWD, 913.

16. Lt. Gen. James W. Longstreet (1821–1904) was vilified in the South for his criticism of Robert E. Lee in these 1896 memoirs (as well as for his Republican affiliation).

17. Sidney Perham (1819–1907) succeeded Chamberlain as governor. MSL (repus) (govs).

am at the big table early—before any one else is "up"—meaning "down"! It is I who am *up*. For the storm wakes in me all strengths—to hear & to do. But just to *love* & to sit here & write *you* this little greeting. When they come down, I will bring them into my mood, but I shall not read this letter to them, for it is *yours*.

As to things below, all is going on as well as we could really expect. Our dear one is pretty patient, & keeps a very sweet face, which is a joy to us, & helps us to bear the trouble it is to our spirits to have her eyes sealed to all outward things.

I think she enjoys "looking" over her old pet things. Last evening we spent in looking through her *drawings* she made when a girl. She remembers the finest details of them each & all, & I told her what each one was & we could talk about it. I read to her all the great things others read the little ones. She has a fancy now for *Plato*, & I have been reading those books which tell about Socrates & his last discourses just before his death.

Then for another line I take his wonderful discussion of great subjects, which *are* wonderful and equal to what we call "inspired" writings. I believe these were inspired, as are the thought[s] of [every] seeker after God.

I thank you for the little letter. It did seem that I was at my best that [evening] in Portland. But there is far more *in* me yet.

I trust all is well with you. We are well. Miss H.[18] may go soon & I may have to call Lillian home. But we will keep things in order & peace. I go to Portland April 1st. Wyllys is doing well.

yours with the love of all the worlds
J. L. C.

[SL]

〜 TO ASA DALTON

Brunswick Ma[r]ch 8th 1900

Dear Doctor Dalton[19],

I appreciate your kind letter, as also your generous testimony in my behalf in connection with the Collectorship.

I suppose this little office is to be accepted by me with a good grace, although I feel humiliated at being thought worthy & fit only for this when the other was open.

I value such letters & friendship as yours more than I do the office.

---

18. Assumably Miss Hodgdon, Fannie's new attendant. See 24 Dec. 1899 to Sae.
19. Asa Dalton (b. 1824), pastor of St. Stephen's Church in Portland. *Bib Maine*, 1:339.

Truly yours
Joshua L. Chamberlain

[PHS]

≫ TO OLIVER OTIS HOWARD

Brunswick Mch 22^{d} 1900

Maj. Genl. O. O. Howard, U.S.A.
Dear General;
Mr Rogers[20] has sent me the beautiful little "prospectus" of the *Lincoln Memorial University*,[21] and I wish to say that you have my earnest sympathy in your noble endeavor. It should be supported by all our people. There is no object now before them more worthy.
I recognize it as your work too.
Truly yours
Joshua L. Chamberlain

[BSC]

≫ TO JOHN M. HAY

Regular form	Brunswick, Maine
Sent. 26th	October 25th 1900.

& fee $1.00
To The Honorable,
The Secretary of State;[22]
Washington, D.C.
Sir:—
Desiring to set out on the Seventh of November for a visit to Southern Europe and Egypt,[23] I respectfully apply for a pass[p]ort, and enclose fee of one dollar, required by law.

20. Unidentified.

21. After founding Howard University in Washington, Howard founded Lincoln Memorial University in Tennessee in 1897, claiming that Lincoln had inspired the project when praising the loyalty of eastern Tennessee: "General, if you come out of this horror and misery alive—I want you to do something for these mountain people—If I live I will do all I can to aid, and between us perhaps we can do [them] the justice they deserve." The prospectus was part of a large fund-raising drive. Peterson, *Lincoln in American Memory*, 143.

22. John Milton Hay (1838–1905), Lincoln's personal secretary and biographer. *DAB*, 8:430–36.

23. Advised to seek a warm, dry climate for his health, Chamberlain, a member of several Egyptology associations, chose Egypt and Italy. Trulock, 525 n. 98. See 5 Jan. 1901 to Sae.

I append items of personal description which, as I remember, are required in such case.

 I have the honor to be,
 Very respectfully,
 Your obedient servant,
 Joshua L. Chamberlain
(one enclosure)
[*Enclosure*:]
Notes of description;
Joshua L. Chamberlain,
Brunswick, Maine

Age,	72 years.
Height,	5 feet 9 inches.
Weight,	170 pounds.
Complexion,	fair — (somewhat browned).
Hair,	grey, (nearly white).
Shoulders,	broad.
Forehead,	high.
Face,	square.
Eyes,	grey-blue.
Nose,	medium size, (somewhat Roman).
Chin,	square.
Mouth,	medium size,
	Wound — scars, — right thigh & left hip.

See subsequent sheet:
Regular form.

[YUL]

≋ TO JOHN M. HAY

<table>
<tr><td>Not</td><td>Brunswick Maine</td></tr>
<tr><td>An exact</td><td>October 25 1900</td></tr>
<tr><td>copy _____</td><td></td></tr>
</table>

To The Honorable,
The Secretary of State
Washington, D.C.
Sir:
 Appreciating the importance of having some voucher in addition to an ordinary passport in case of possible contingencies during my proposed visit abroad, I beg to ask, — if it is proper for me to do so, — for some circular letter which might be shown to our Ministers or Consuls.

And for further identification and description, permit me to say that I served during the "War for the Union," as Colonel, Brigadier General, and Major General by Brevet, finally commanding the First Division, Fifth Army Corps, Army of the Potomac, receiving [meantime?] the "Congressional Medal of Honor for "Gettysburg"; serving thereafter for four terms as Governor of Maine, and twelve years as President of Bowdoin College. I was also adjunct U.S. Commissioner to the Paris Exposition of 1878. At present I am Surveyor of Customs for the Port of Portland, Maine, and have applied for a leave of absence on account of the present effects of severe wounds received in the battle of Petersburg June 18 1864.

My purpose in this visit to the Mediter[r]anean is to facilitate my recovery from this present condition, and influenced also by my interest in historical studies, and social and political questions of the day.

I have the honor to be

Very respectfully

Your obedient servant

Joshua L. Chamberlain

P.S. My application for passport has already been made in regular form.
J. L. Chamberlain

[YUL]

≈ TO FANNIE

New York
Nov. 6 1900

My dear Fannie:

If I did not feel that it would be better for you & for me that I should take this trip abroad, I should be very sad at leaving you now, even for so short a time. But it will interest you to keep "the run of me" in your mind and heart as the "little people" trace from day to day [my] very course on the waters and over the lands.

My thoughts will be with you always, and I shall feel charged and commissioned and empowered to see things for you, and bring you whatever of those can be taken into the soul. You can send me word when they write me, what your wish and thought would command me.

I pray God to have you in His holy and healing care. You remember we are "engaged" again, — not to sink down under any evils in our absence, but to keep whole and well, for other days to come. What is it that Dante says. — not this exactly but nearly: "*And other songs in other keys, God [w]illing,*"

Soon again!

J. L. C.

〰️ TO SAE

Portland
Friday noon
7th Nov. [1900?]

Dear Sae:

I am sending you just a word to thank you for your long interesting letter, before I leave at 12:40 for a half-day at Brunswick to look after my affairs there. Lillian enjoys your letters so much, she keeps them for reference and thought — guidance. You take hold of great subjects. I wish I could be with you, and in my library if possible. But the "world" is changing so fast & so much in these days, all old books are behind the times. It seems as if we were about to have a new creed of social ethics, found on "natural law" instead of moral law, — which is now said to be the (imperfect) work of man. But all must admit that the revelation of God is still going on — in His Providence & in the minds of men.

The artists (Sewells) also have been much with us leave tomorrow for their home in *Oyster Bay*.[24] We shall miss them. They are fine people. The portrait is well painted, but is not "*me*," They leave it here in the [ill.] rooms for "show," I am sorry.

Could not you or Alice come over for a while? It is very pleasant here. I am writing up my old war papers.

Love to all

Lawrence

〰️ TO SAE

Jany 5 1901

My dear Sae:

I have just taken a turn among the Pyramids & to the Sphinx, and have come in now (12 n) for a rest from the glare of the sun on the surrounding sands. This is my second visit here. I am to go up the Nile next week on one of the Nile steamers & see all the interesting places so well in your mind.

---

24. The Sewells were otherwise unidentified artists. Oyster Bay is on northern Long Island.

At present I have only visited Heliopolis. "City of the Sun"= *On*, built by Ramses II ([Lesistvis?]), where Joseph got his wife, & Moses his education, & Plato & Pythagoras & so many other of the old scholars & philosophers found it worth their while to stay *years*.

No vestige of the famous city is left now but great heaps of ruins. I could see the brick down among the rubbish, which were some of those (I have no do[u]bt) made by the "Children of Israel," for it was Ramses II you know, who put them at the task of brick-making to build his cities.[25] But I wanted to stand on the spot (though this is 20 feet under ground) or at least under the *sky*, which *endures*, & *think* what history had been wrought there.

I have "timed" myself & have taken passage from Alexandria Feb. 7th, & from Naples Feb 15th, to reach New York on the 26th. I am going rapidly as is my *wont* (or rather my *will*) & shall come home in many ways in better condition than when I left. I wish I had more of your interesting letters. But it takes 3 weeks to get a letter here. Now I go to my camel.[26]

Love to all

Lawrence.

[LC]

〰 TO AURESTUS S. PERHAM

July 2d 1901

Dear Major Perham;

I thank you for your very kind letter. The manuscript of my memorial address[27] is not decipherable and is in no condition to serve as copy of what I said. As soon as I can get time I will try to go over it so that it might serve you in some way. The demand for my addresses I find to be such that I shall have to publish a little volum[e] of them.[28] But it is hard for me to get time for any work of revision & preparation.

I have to keep at it. — Throw[in]g off a lot of new things that are not sufficiently finished to serve a general use as reading matter.

---

25. Heliopolis is an ancient holy city and site of a temple to the sun god Ra whose ruins are about six miles northeast of Cairo. It is debated whether thinkers other than Eudoxus indeed studied there. Ramses II "the Great" governed Egypt from 1279 to 1213 B.C. A great builder, he was probably pharaoh at the time of Moses. EB, 9:927–28.

26. On Chamberlain's foreign adventures, see Pullen, 155–56.

27. Chamberlain gave numerous memorial addresses, such as "The Two Souls" (see 28 May 1897 to Fannie), "Five Forks," and his remarks published in the pamphlet "Not a Sound of Trumpet."

28. It would seem that Chamberlain never did. The historian would love to discover one.

·Mrs. C. being blind, much of my time & my strength goes to sympathy with her.

Genl Whittaker[29] kindly sent me his notes

yours as ever

J. L. Chamberlain

[MHS]

〰 TO L. B. EATON

COPY[30]   Portland, August 1st 1901.

L. B. Eaton, Esq.[31]

Washington, D.C.

My dear Sir:—

I thank you with peculiar pleasure for your fine and appreciative letter of the 30th ulto, and the reference therein to some notice of a simple act of mine at the surrender of Lee's Army.

I had not supposed anybody remembered, or cared, what I said on the occasion referred to. I remember it well; for it was the last flag surrendered there, and it came in borne by a little remnant of a Regiment which had recently been, I think, acting as a Headquarters Guard, and therefore came in late in the ceremony, after being relieved from that detail.

The poor fellows—or I would rather say, the noble fellows—clung to that old flag, battle-smoked and blood-stained, as if it were dearer than life to them—dear as manhood and honor. I felt their feeling, and said to them something like what you have quoted.

You may not know that in forming my lines to receive the surrender of these arms and colors, I had given instructions for the regiments successively, as the [respective] Confederate Commanders and Divisions were passing our front to form for this last act in arms,—to come to the "carry" of the manual (then called the "shoulder") in token of respect for brave men, and in a deep sense comrades; and this being done, was responded to in like manner by the passing column.

Was not this a grand feature of this last meeting in arms of two historic armies? If you are from the "Old North State,"[32] I would like to meet you.

29. Edward Whittaker, see 26 Jan. 1900 to Perham.

30. This letter was printed in the *New York Sun* and in an editorial in the *New Orleans Times-Democrat*. For the latter's text, see Chamberlain Association of America, *A Sketch*, 47–48.

31. Eaton is unidentified.

32. A nickname for North Carolina.

There was no body of men more brave and in all ways manly than those she sent to that great ordeal.

I accept with gratitude your good wishes for that you naturally consider my "declining years," I do not feel as if my years were declining,—except as to their numerical remainder. In all that makes their value I look upon them as mounting. "The best is yet to be,"

God grant it may be so with you.

With high regard

Truly yours,

Joshua L. Chamberlain

[PHS]

≈ TO GRACE

Portland Dec 9 '01

My dearest Grace:

We had a lovely anniversary of our wedding.[33]

I took home a beautiful Arabic seat-cushion & a Persian shoulder-rest for your mother's dining room chair where she spends much time; & two beautiful *aprons* to guard her fine dresses at meals: and I gave her one of the lovely napkin rings you know something about, so as to keep her napkin entirely distinct to her own *feeling*, from all others.

We had a very fine Wedding day dinner & another Sunday. Nappy took *two pieces* of mince pie & a good glass of Sauterne! Salome came in & Mrs. Houghton[34] Saturday P.m; & Prof & Mrs Woodruff & Ed & Mary,[35] Sunday evening. La Lignora goes to the Sherwood House Portland Tuesday. Your mother wants you all to *come down to Christmas*. Can you? If so, let me know. or if *some of you* can come. She sets her heart on it, & everything is so pleasant now in the house I should much like to have you too.

affectionately [yours]

J. L. C.

[SL]

33. Chamberlain and Fannie celebrated their 46th wedding anniversary on December 7th.

34. Mrs. Houghton is unidentified.

35. Frank E. Woodruff (1855–1922), professor of Greek and Religion at Bowdoin. The latter two may have been his children.

⫷ TO WYLLYS

Dec 26 1901

Dear Wyllys;

Thanks for all good messages. Package from #1925 Com. Ave. all right I suppose you find it hard to get into just what you want. But I would keep trying & w[oul]d take what I could get in my line to begin with.

I dont want people here to think you made a failure.

I am pretty slow in my getting about but hope to [rise].

At office half a day at a time, using great care. Rather a strain on my *spirits* to be so disabled. Sae & Alice *sick in bed*. Big quarrel here over the Collectorship—Moses & Emmons.[36] I keep *out* of it,—tho' they tried hard to pull me into it. Things are right at home. Very many presents, tho' not desired. Too many letters to be written in acknowledgment,

Love to all

J. L. C.

[MHS]

⫷ TO AURESTUS S. PERHAM

Portland [Maine]
Jany 21 '02

My dear Major:

Most assuredly Buckingham[37] is right. My Brigade came up along the *face* of the return and with Gregory's Brigade (assigned also to my [command]) I charged that whole "return,"[38] Bartlett[39] with our 3ᵈ Brigade took the enemy more on their flank.

I myself was at the angle before Ayres[40] carried it. The point where he had his first sharp attack was from a work built in front of the white oak road South of it (while the main work & "return" were north of it) about 160 or 200 yards in extent. *There* is where Ayres first was struck, & where he burst the enemy up. My troops were on the right & in touch with Ayres['s] 2ᵈ Brigade

36. Charles Moses, see 25 Dec. 1899 to Allen. Willis T. Emmons (b. 1858), a Saco jurist and mayor, was appointed collector for Maine and New Hampshire, based in Portland. Baillie, 506.

37. Capt. Buckingham is unidentified.

38. 1st and 2nd Brigade, 1st Division, V Corps, respectively. A "return" is a right angle in a line, here in the Confederate line at Five Forks, covering the left flank.

39. Joseph J. Bartlett (1834–93) commanded the 1st Division, V Corps, and 2nd Division, IX Corps, at Five Forks. GB, 23–24.

40. Romeyn B. Ayres (1825–88) commanded the 2nd Division, V Corps, at Five Forks. GB, 13–14.

Harold Wyllys Chamberlain, 1881 (Courtesy of Bowdoin College)

when the angle & the return were carried. I took 1100 prisoners and Ayres more, at that point and mov[emen]t. I have it all circumstantially set forth in my paper & it perfectly accords with what Capt Buckingham says and what Faucette[41] says. I do not see how you can get on without my account; for my line was really part of Ayres['s] line. We went in together. I had before picked up Gwyn's Brigade,[42] & put it in on the return, *before* Ayres'[s] other two Brigades got up to the angle. I moved South at the *first rip of* Ayres fight at the advanced work, & as fast as I could march. So I was on the *return* before Ayres was at the *Angle*, & I was with him there.[43] If I could possibly take out half a dozen sheets of my paper & send you, I would. Perhaps I can before you have to read your paper finally. I wish to send my best greetings to the dear old "*Maryland Brigade*,"[44] whom I hold in honor & affection.

Truly yours

Joshua L. Chamberlain

[MHS]

≈ TO FANNIE

Portland May 13 1902

My dear Fanny:

It was hard for me to come away again last Monday in such a pressure for the train as not to be able to go up and see you. I felt the loss of myself all day & the next. Ever since my return I have been on the "jump" & the "stretch," Monday e[vening] at Judge Putnam's[45] for the "Fraternity" Club; and last Even[in]g at the Anniversary of the "Thacher Post" Grand Army "Banquet" — where I had to make quite an elaborate speech. I wish I had time to give you a sketch of it. My subject was "*Memorial Days*"[46] & I went into the office & reason of *Memory*, & its place in Civilization and life.

As well as constituting the main element in personal identity & in the resurrection & immortality. Contrasting it with "transmigration of souls"[47] &c. If I were not pressed with other things, I would write it out to "keep,"

41. Faucette is unidentified.

42. 3rd Brigade, 2nd Division, V Corps, commanded by James Gwyn (1828–1906) at Five Forks. BBGB, 250.

43. Chamberlain added this sentence in a second draft of the letter.

44. The 1st, 4th, 7th, and 8th Maryland Volunteers comprised the 2nd Brigade, 2nd Division, V Corps.

45. William L. Putnam (1835–1918) of the U.S. Court of Appeals for the 1st Circuit. DAB, 15:285.

46. See note 27 (2 Jul. 1901 to Perham) regarding his memorial day addresses.

47. Reincarnation.

I trust you are bearing up as beautifully as you have been doing. So many people now are praising you & sending loving greetings for your brave & cheery way of bearing this great affliction, you must feel the influence of it coming through the air, or [e]ther, or whatever other queer element our souls are floating in. I am making plans to give you as pleasant a summer as you can have.

This is only a little love-greeting between whiles. I shall soon be home again.

yours affectionately

J. L. C.

[BSC]

≋ PAGES FOUR AND FIVE OF A FRAGMENT
TO UNIDENTIFIED RECIPIENT

[ca. May 15, 1902]

4.

campaign[48] might be brought up in close proximity, and the 1st and 2nd Brigades of the Division, — the 198th Pennsylvania, and the 185th, 187th, 188th and 189th New York, — were so stationed, out not as part of my line. Coulter's Brigade of Crawford's Division[49] was ordered up to the vicinity with their teamsters to take the surrendered property to Burkesville Junction. What was the disposition of the tro[o]ps of the Corp[s] or of Ord's command,[50] I do not know. The latter soon after, or just before, went to Lynchburg, as I understood.

The Confederate camp was in plain sight of us across the valley of the Appomattox. We saw them breaking camp, and forming for this last movement. General Gordon led at the head of his command, composed of several of the remnants of the famous old Rebel Corps.[51] I could not resist the impulse to pay some speci[a]l attention to such a ceremony, — the last token of surrender to the power of the "Union," — and I instructed my Colonels to have their men come from the "order arms" to the "shoulder," or "carry," while each division of the Confederates was passing our front. At my bugle-signal this was done. Gordon quickly caught the meaning of this, and with a graceful salutation himself, gave command to have his own men [to] take the same

48. The Appomattox campaign.

49. At Appomattox, Richard Coulter commanded the 3rd Brigade of Bvt. Brig. Gen. Crawford's (see 25 Jan. 1884 to Nicholson?) 3rd Division, V Corps. CWD, 205; Trulock, 395.

50. Maj. Gen. Edward O. C. Ord (1818–83) commanded the Army of the James. Faust, *Historical Times Illustrated Encyclopedia*, 547–48.

51. II Corps, Army of Northern Virginia.

position of the manual as they passed us. This was done. Arms stacked, colors laid down, each division then passing off to give the paroles prepared by General Sharp[e], [A]sst Provost Marshal, U.S. Army,[52] and then free to go where they will. Teams coming up meanwhile to take away the collected material. Major Ashbrook, Ord[i]nance Officer of our Division[53] having charge of this. Thus successively all the confederate troops acro[s]s the river come up and pass along. It takes all day. At evening, we burn the broken cartridges left in the street, and by

5.

this lurid light the last of Lee's army passes from history.

I spoke with many of the principal officers of the Confederate Army, during this ceremony, and I have memoranda of their remarks.

As to my own part in this, I did not at the time think it of any special importance. Somebody had to be set at this service, and I took it without feeling that a special honor was conferred on me. But the fact was worth remembering; and the incident a conspicuous passage.

If I may refer to any corroborative testimony, I could cite from the official report of the Commander of the Fifth Corps,[54] one passage: "In the last engagement at Appomattox Court House, General Chamberlain had the advance, and was driving the enemy rapidly before him when the flag of truce came in."

General Gordon also speaks of my giving them a respectful salute, in his famous lecture, published in the recent collection of American eloquence.[55]

General Lee, too, refers to my treatment of some war-worn regiments of theirs which begged to be allowed to cut up their old flag and distribute the treasured tokens of service and suffering among their children. This appears, I believe, in the Personal Reminiscences written near the close of his life.[56]

I trust this, too hastily written after all, may not weary you.

Very truly yours,

Joshua L. Chamberlain

[BSC]

52. George Henry Sharpe (1828–1900), chief of the bureau of military information. *BBGB*, 548.

53. Maj. Ashbrook, ordinance officer of 1st Division, V Corps, is otherwise unidentified.

54. Charles Griffin, see Dramatis Personae.

55. See 18 Jan. 1899 to Garnsey. See also Gordon, *Reminiscences of the Civil War*, 444; Chamberlain, *The Passing of the Armies*, 195–96.

56. Lee, *Personal Reminiscences*, 308–9.

Portland July 1 1902

My dear Fanny:

You do not know how much I am thinking of you, and wishing to help you, and be of some good to you.

You were so gentle and patient and receptive and appreciative, and in all ways so sweet, when I left you, a strong tenderness continues to hold me to you ever since. I see that you need me, and I wish, of all things, to meet that need. It is the deepest wish of my heart to be able to bless you — to bring, to be, a blessing, & not merely to pray for one to come, in vain words & vague thought. But when I try to do it, and think & study & plan how best to do it, I do not seem to succeed. Somehow I am turned off — baffled, almost driven to the very contrary of what I so earnestly meant. Your affliction seems to have made you *hard*, rather than *tender*, & I feel as if I were smitten in the most sensitive place in my heart. This I know is a part of your affliction — a symptom of your disease. It is hardest of all to see these physical deprivations affecting the mind and spirit — by nature so bright, so clear, so sweet. This must not be. We cannot let this tendency go on. It will become a new distress — a terrible condition. We must strive to restore that sweetness and clarity I might say in the true sense of the word, that *charity*, which makes you in your real self so lovable.

You need love — most of anything; & that is exactly what you can have if you will receive it — as indeed you sometimes do, even now. But I sometimes see you scorning a service or attention brought to you in love, and for loves sake, & you are missing & losing much by this, which you need & deserve & could have, if you would receive it, you have good & true friends who should be near you in such days as these. I wish you to have them, & to make these dark days full of an inner light. Do not be too critical & expecting, & do not scorn what is brought in love. It makes *you* so unhappy — that is the most of it all, & that makes me so more & more as I see your need.

[SL]

〰 TO FANNIE

Portland
July 10 1902

Dearie:

I have a beautiful letter from our Gracie. She is considerably troubled about my condition as well as yours, and I have written her as reassuringly a letter as I could.

It is true, dear; I am much reduced from my usual condition, & note a serious diminution of my recuperative force. But this contemplated yacht trip will probably keep me up. Dr Shaw says I *must* have a respite, & ought to be off three weeks. That I cannot manage. But if I could feel happy about you— I mean that the best is being done that is possible, and that you are looking more at the blessing-side of things than at the hard & dark side, a very great burden would be taken off my spirit. And it is this, more than any thing, that makes my heart so heavy.

Now you have all your own, old sweetness and brightness, if you could let it appear. And this seems to me your best comfort & compensation. Surely we must not let you fall off into darkness of spirit. It will work fourfold trouble for your physical condition. Think how many are loving you & caring for you, & wishing to come nearer you so as to be of real good. Wyllys is nobly resolved to stay by you now,—much as he needs a change,—while I find it absolutely necessary to be off the "dead line" for a while.

Now, dearest, cherish all you can the things which are "not seen"—& are of the "eternal." They are in *us*—not out of us—& they are yours. May the dear Lord be ever near you with his grace & love.

yours

J. L. C.

[BSC]

TO AURESTUS S. PERHAM

Portland Dec 22^d '02

Dear Major:

Pardon delay in acknowledg[in]g your letter, offering to send me the Chickamauga maps. I have not been well.

I have them already, and therefore will thank you for this suggestion, & excuse the sending.

Am glad to learn that Gwyn[57] is out, & in better health. He was a good soldier, & although Ayres was much incensed against him about "5 Forks," I was able to get Ayres to take a different view of the matter. Gwyn never knew what I saved him from with Ayres. But I always liked Gwyn, & am sorry to know he has not been in [fair] condition.

Am sorry, too, to hear that Mrs Warren[58] has been so ill.

57. For both Gwyn and Ayres, see 21 Jan. 1902 to Perham.

58. Likely Gouverneur K. Warren's wife, the former Emily Chase of Baltimore. *DAB*, 19:473–74.

Mrs [Chamberlain] you so kindly remember, is totally blind. It causes me much unhappiness. I have not been well myself & am quite "poorly" in condition yet, with very much to do.

I do not think I have heard from you since your mother's death.[59] The glimpse I had of you in Washington was not long enough to allow me to express my sympathy.

Truly y[ours]

Joshua L. Chamberlain

[MHS]

≈ TO JOHN P. NICHOLSON

Portland, Maine, January 12th, 1903.

Dear Colonel Nicholson

I thank you for the fine Volume of the Register.

In looking, naturally, at my own name, I wonder why, in your evident cordial intention towards my record, you omitted so important and exceptional an incident as the promotion to Brigadier-General on the Field by General Grant, June 18th, 1864.

I have General Grant's "Special Order No. 39"[60] making this promotion formal (he had verbally communicated on the evening of the 18th or morning of the 19th), and have also the Commission of Brig.-General which copies the record in these words: "For gallant and meritorious conduct in leading his Brigade against the enemy at Petersburg, Virginia, where he was dangerously wounded."

General Grant was kind enough to refer to this in his autobiography.[61] He afterwards (after the promotion) told me it was the only time it had been done in the history of the country. He afterwards promoted General Upton in a similar manner.[62]

It seems to me an important public record like yours should have noted this.

I have all the original correspondence between General Grant and the President, sent me by kindness of the Secretary of War.[63]

59. Almina J. Hathaway Perham. *WhoAm*, 959.

60. *OR*, ser. I, vol. 40, part 2:236.

61. See Grant, *Memoirs*, 601–2.

62. Actually, Grant had promoted Emory Upton (1839–81) (see Chapter 3, note 8) a month earlier for his twelve-regiment charge into the "Bloody Angle" at Spotsylvania on 10 May 1864. Trulock 467 n. 75; *DAB*, 19:128–30; *GB*, 519–20.

63. Edwin M. Stanton, see Dramatis Personae.

Sincerely yours,
Joshua L. Chamberlain

[CWLM]

≋ TO FANNIE

Portland
Feb. 11th 1903

———

My dear Fanny:

As I am not going to Augusta today, & consequently cannot be at home this e[vening], as I thought I might, I write you this little word.

I fear I may have seemed to you almost harsh in my extreme anxiety to have you work out of the gloomy mood which seems so darkly to envelope you, when I urged you so emphatically. I know well such things cannot be brought about by argument, over emphasis of suggestion. Evidently we must *do* something. I am studying this *all* the time.

It happens that the things I think of are not such as suit your feeling. Very naturally, you perceive the disadvantageous things in any proposition intended for your help, quicker and more forcibly than the helpful or agreeable things. In your condition, perhaps, this is inevitable; you are so shut up & shut in, that the relief of surrounding circumstances cannot come in to lighten a vexation, as it can with us who see the whole compass of [things] around us. If you could have a little reading & conversation *"club"* or circle to take up some distinct and continuous line and work up an interest, it would be a good thing! But I am aware you do not see, or have at hand, those whom you would like to form such a circle.

So with a *music* circle, I suppose. Your ideas & cravings are too high, your needs seem beyond ordinary reach.

I cannot see that I can *do* more than to give you pleasant change by bringing you to Portland as often as possible. That I am plan[n]ing to do whenever I myself am able to carry it through. Many demands on my time & strength leave me scarcely an hour to keep my own mind properly fitted for the work I have to do.

The *Chamberlains* here send much cordial regard. They wish you to come freely to them at any time. This we may avail ourselves of. I think you do wonderfully well under your deprivations & positive ills. The material course of time will bring some of these, anyway. I gave a long lecture here last evening when I was not able. But am not much worse for it this [morning].

With great love
yrs
J. L. C.

[BSC]

≋ TO AURESTUS S. PERHAM

Portland March 16 1903

Dear Major Perham:

I have been very busy, having not a half-hour at my disposal for searches
as to evidence, or *proof*, as you call it, of the truth of my statement in regard
to Grant's thought of Warren for Commander of the Army. The ground of
my statement was what *Grant had said to me* in talking of our affairs, after
the war. But I took part of Sunday to see what I could give as proof of my
statement.

I find such a sentence in Grant's "Memoirs" Vol II. page 216.[64]

I think this will satisfy you.

Truly yours
Joshua L. Chamberlain

[MHS]

≋ TO JOHN F. HILL

Portland Maine
April 27th, 1903.

Hon John F. Hill,
Governor of Maine:[65]
Dear and Honored Sir:

I am in receipt of a Commission as Trustee of the Bath Soldiers Orphan's
Home forwarded to me from Brunswick. I thank you for the remembrance;
but had you conferred with me about this appointment I should have begged
to be excused. I am willing to serve you or the State, in any capacity to which
you think my abilities equal; but I hardly like to devote my time (which is very
valuable to me at least) to objects of inferior importance, and which others
could fill in all respects as well as I. If it were something where my previous
experien[c]e or special qualification would render my service of [esteemed?]
value, I should not feel as likely declining if other public duties would permit
acceptance. But as matters are—I have such a demand.

64. See Grant, *Memoirs*, 541–43.
65. John Fremont Hill (1855–1912), a doctor who had turned to banking and politics.
Baillie, 755.

198 } SURVEYOR OF CUSTOMS

Do not think I am unwilling to be disrated in having it made to appear that a trivial place like this is commensurate with my present abilities. I am not worrying about that; but I really cannot afford to give time to objects which many others can care for as well.

So unless you particularly desire me to take this place may I beg you to excuse me from qualifying under this commission, and fill the place with some one equally worthy to fill it.

With very high regard

your obt. servt.

Joshua L. Chamberlain

[MHS]

≫ TO GRACE

Home June 28 1903

My dearest Gracie:

I tried to get time to go out & see you, but when I telephoned you were all *out* and I had to come back Friday 7 P.m.

I have had no time to tell you of the delight I felt at our little heart-talks, & the good you have done me. But I trust we shall have this opportunity before very long.

I was glad to know you were reported "all well," Horace was not in his office when I called. I found the cheque here, which I took with me to return for I cannot think of keeping that. You cannot *pay* for any to see me — in any other way at least, than the task and trial it is to you to have to share my cares and anxieties.

It is very cheerful here to day. Lillian is at home & your Mother is lovely to her, & to us all. I think she feels much helped by Lillian's caring. Now I look for better conditions.

When Florence goes, we shall go to the shore, — although your Mother at present, rebels against it. I have had a great pressure on me for a month, & until July. Then I must take a rest.

I would enclose the cheque but it is fully endorsed, & I fear to risk it. When I get to Portland I will send you mine in exchange.

I am trying to write the critique on "the Gate Beautiful"[66] — under difficulties.

With more love than I can express, & special thanks for you dear letter, I am

---

66. John W. Stimson's revised *The Gate Beautiful: Being Principles and Methods in Vital Art Education, copiously illustrated* (Trenton: A. Brandt, 1903).

yours aff forever,
Joshua L. Chamberlain

[SL]

〰️ TO GRACE

Monday [evening]
Aug 3^{d}, 1903

My dearest Gracie:

Lillian brought your mother in to the City[67] last week & got her a beautiful black dress, fashionable & [very becoming], for an every day dress: also a *beautiful white* silk waist, & a very rich *black* silk waist, and a very fine & (somewhat expensive) [*poplin*] — all much of your mothers delight. They came in and dined with me & spent the afternoon. Then *I* went to the store and selected another dress, black with a delicate white figure in it, — not very expensive but very becoming to her, matching her gray hair &c.

So she is well supplied. But of course the dear little woman following her old & indulged habit; got hold of a very rich black silk skirt, elaborately barred & flowered &c, & insisted that she wanted that, too.

I did not think she needed this, as she has a beautiful new silks [s]he had made at your house, I think, & the opportunities for her to wear this lately desired one are now very rare & unlikely to occur. So I dissuaded her from buying this expensive silk skirt at present. She has waived the matter for a while.

Lillian also got a chance to inspect your mothers *underwear*, & has bought her a good supply which she is *giving* her — to silence objections.

Sae has invited her to go & make her a visit, & Lillian will take her to Brewer some day this week, if I am not able to make the journey (as the Doctors say I am not)

So you see we have moved in the "enemy works," & I hope your Mother will much enjoy the change of scene & surroundings. She is perfectly lovely to Lillian — seems to cling to her almost as much as she does to Wyllys, who gets a chance now to work up some new inventions I think well of & am "backing him" with all the money he needs. I get up but slowly — am at my office half the time.

your loving father.

[SL]

67. Probably Portland.

Brunswick, Maine, August 14th 1903.

Colonel John P. Nicholson,

Chairman, Gettysburg Battlefield Commission:

My dear Colonel: —

I recognize the compliment of your communication enclosing a copy of the request of Hon. Wm. C. Oates, lately Colonel of the 15th Alabama Regiment, asking permission to erect a monument at the point where he says his regiment was stopped on the evening of the second day's fight at Gettysburg, and especially the honor you do me in asking my opinion on the subject.

I should feel no objection to the erection of a monument to the honor of a regiment that had pushed its way so far around the flank of the Union line and made so gallant an attack; but I should expect it to be placed on ground where it actually stood at some time during the battle, — at the extreme point of its advance, if desired, — so that it might not only represent the valor of a regiment but the truth of history.

Some of the statements of Colonel Oates in his letter to the Secretary of War[68] differ widely from the well established record of facts in the case, and very materially from former statements of his in papers published by him and in personal letters in the course of a correspondence with me, in both of which I was much gratified to find so close an agreement between our impressions and recollections as to our contest there.

In occupying Little Round Top my regiment, the 20th Maine, had the advance, and therefore became the extreme left not only of the brigade but of the entire Union line. The other regiments formed in succession, on our right; the 83[rd] Pennsylvania, the 44[th] New York, and the 16[th] Michigan. I was therefore in position to observe the whole formation of the brigade, being with Colonel Vincent and Colonel Rice until the 16[th] Michigan, the extreme right, was e[s]tablished. The rapid advance of the right of Hood's Division had been closely observed by us, and the importance of our position fully understood and prepared for. Our original formation was in nearly a straight line, facing a little to the west of south, — my own position facing the western summit of the Great Round Top.

The formation of the enemy's attack caused its left to strike first, and upon the right of our brigade; the engagement running rapidly to our left as the enemy successively arrived in our front. My right wing was hotly engaged when I fortunately observed a body of the enemy moving still towards our extreme left without facing to engage us; which gave me notice of their inten-

68. Elihu Root (1845–1927), later secretary of state and a U.S. senator. DAB, 22:577–82.

tion to gain our flank, and gave me time to "refuse" the left of my line[69] and at the same moment to extend it to double its ground by coming into one rank formation. Our movement caused redoubled earnestness on the part of those then confronting our original line, now made up of only the right wing of my regiment, but we opposed obstinate resistance to their taking advantage of our attempt to "change front under fire," known by all to be perilous. Our movement was timely too; for it was hardly accomplished when the troops I had observed having, as they perhaps supposed, gained a direction to strike us in flank, burst upon us in great fury. They struck, of course, our center and re-fused left; and the attack became, and for some considerable time continued, truly a mêlée,—a mixed-up fight.

This resulting in a repulse for the enemy, and a momentary clearing of our front, we picked up our wounded and gathered what ammunition we could from the cartridge-boxes of the fallen strewed upon the slopes, and threw up on the more exposed places in our line what could scarcely be called "breast-works," being piles of stone nowhere more than eighteen inches high, but serving to cover a little a man lying down, as some had to do to make any "stand" at all. Most of the enemy's wounded falling into our hands were of the 47th Alabama. We knew the fight was not over, from the general appear-ance of things, and from reasons in our minds. The lull lasted but very few minutes, when a new and formidable onset was made from the direction of our "refused" left,—or more exactly speaking, in the direction of the axis of our "salient," or blunt-wedge-shaped formation. This attack was by a force far greater than we had before encountered, and taken up along our whole front enveloped us completely. We had such advantage of position, however, and of well impressed sense of the necessity of holding that flank now cover-ing the all-important Round Top position, we had been told by Vincent at the beginning must be "held at all costs," that we gave this determined body so confidently assailing us a hard time of it, with repeated rebuffs until our ammunition totally exhausted, there was nothing else for it but the "bayo-net." It was a curious, and what the boys call "cheeky," piece of work making a right-wheel bayonet charge in the faces of such a confro[nt]ing foe.

The brave enemy were astonished at it, and estimated its force by its con-duct rather than its contents. The "charge" swept the slope and valley clear of living foes. Four hundred prisoners fell into our hands. We returned to our position on the slope of Little Round Top. A hundred and fifty of their brave men lay in our front,—100 badly wounded and fifty dead. The latter we buried

69. To refuse a military line is to pivot one end back, creating a "return" to protect a flank.

the next day. Before morning we scaled the Big Round Top, capturing many more of the scattered Alabama and Texas men,[70] — mostly of the latter.

These are the well-established facts; controverted by no authentic claims that I know of. Some inferences must be manifest:

1. Colonel Oates could not have "driven the right of the 20th Maine back upon its left, and attacked the 83rd Penna. and 44th New York." If he had attempted this, he would have been taken in flank and rear by these regiments. In fact the right of my regiment never changed its ground, touching the left flank of the 83rd, for more than a moment during the engagement, until it took up the "charge." The relatively small loss in the 83rd, — 8 killed and 38 wounded, — is enough to show that it was never struck by the fierce onset of the 15th Alabama. This regiment never saw the front nor flank of the 83rd nor the 44th regiments in this engagement. It could have seen only their rear, and that for a brief season in their extreme advance upon us.

2. Colonel Bulger of the 47th Alabama did not "surrender his sword to Colonel Rice," nor see Colonel Rice on that field, — unless in hospital, the day afterwards. Colonel Bulger fell in front of my right wing.[71] Major Robbins of the 47[th][72] (whom Colonel Oates assigns to the 4th) well knows the spot. I came upon the Colonel personally in the wheeling charge, lying badly wounded, and had him carefully taken up and sent to our field hospital. Col. Powell, of the 5th Texas,[73] was soon after cared for in a similar manner.

3. The 15th Alabama made a gallant fight after a needlessly hard round-a-bout march; but never on the slopes of Little Round Top encountered any other line of battle but that of the 20th Maine.

4. To assist in reconciling with fact the statement of Colonel Oates as to his "driving back the right of the 20th Maine upon its left," it should be said that he did drive over the northern slope of Great Round Top a considerable number of the 2nd U.S. Sharpshooters, who had been stationed at the westerly base of the mountain, but fell back before Oates'[s] advance all the way over the northern slope, and so far past

70. For statistics, see Desjardin's *Stand Firm.*

71. Lt. Col. Michael Bulger (1806–1900) was shot through the lung, left for dead, and captured at Little Round Top. Allardice, *More Generals in Gray*, 46–47.

72. Robbins is otherwise unidentified.

73. Robert M. Powell was mistaken for Longstreet and captured at Little Round Top. *CWD*, 666.

my front as to be taken up by my Captain, Morrill, (whom I had sent out at the opening of the fight with his company, towards the eastern end of the valley to guard against a surprise from that quarter,) and formed on his left.

It was these two bodies of troops, formed in a strong skirmish line which, being of different uniform, were regarded by Colonel [Oates] as "two regiments," of which he speaks in his official report of the battle as threatening his right when he gave the order to retire.

I cannot venture to advise as to the erection of the monument proposed by Colonel Oates. That would involve the entire policy of the U.S. authorities in charge of that battlefield. But as to the location of this monument, I should regret to see it placed near the monument to Vincent, who fell near the right of our brigade line, on ground never seen by the 15th Alabama during the battle. Placing their monument there, as I understand Colonel Oates to desire, would indicate that the 15th Alabama had run entirely over the 20th Maine and annihilated it. The facts are, quite curiously, nearly the converse of this.

I have tried to state facts clearly as to the particular points in question, upon which I suppose you desire my testimony. I trust it may [be] acceptable and of service to you.

I am,
wit[h] very high regard,
your friend and servant,
· Joshua L. Chamberlain

[GNMP]

〰 TO JOHN P. NICHOLSON

Portland, Maine, Sept. 2nd 1903

Colonel John P. Nicholson,
Chairman, Gettysburg Battlefield Commission:
My dear Colonel: —

You do me renewed honor in asking my consent to your forwarding a copy of my communication regarding the respective positions of the 20th Maine and the 15th Alabama Regiments during the engagements on Little Round Top, July [2nd], 1863, to the Secretary of War.

While my letter was written as a personal communication to you, and the freedom of its style was influenced by your suggestion of a confidential character to be maintained in this correspondence, I still see no reason to shrink from any scrutiny its contents may have brought to rear upon it, and offer no objection to your placing a copy of it on the files of the War Department. I have only to regret that the form of the communication submitted to me as the subject of our correspondence compelled reference to previous statements of Colonel Oates, which were not in conformity with those in his letter to the Secretary of War you allowed me to peruse.

I am with high regard,
Truly yours,
Joshua L. Chamberlain

[GNMP]

〰TO HENRY JOHNSON

Portland Dec 1 1903

Dear Professor Johnson:

Is Edgren's Italian Dictionary[74] a good one for me? Published by Holt.

I am not quite "up" on Italian & have only Graglia's Italian Dictionary.[75] Also will you give me some advice as to a Provençal[76] Dictionary. Is there any?

Yours with all best wishes.

Joshua L. Chamberlain

[BSC]

〰TO THOMAS R. LOUNSBURY

Portland, Maine.
Jany 21st 1904

T. R. Lounsbury, Esq.[77]
New Haven:
Dear Sir:

I know I am addressing an honored name; but at this moment am unable to assure myself of the appropriate title. Doubtless the "*notum*" would be much more "*pro magnifico*" than the "*i quotum*," I trust I shall be pardoned.

I feel myself honored by the wish of the Yale Graduates Club to hear my simple story of the Surrender of Lee's Army at Appomattox.[78]

74. August Hjalmar Edgren, *An Italian and English Dictionary with Pronunciation and Brief Etymologies* (New York: H. Holt and Company, 1901). Edgren (1840–1903) fought in the Swedish and Union armies before turning to philology. DAB, 6:20–21.

75. Giuspanio Graglia's decades-old *A Dictionary of the Italian and English Languages*.

76. Provençal is one of the dialects of southern France labeled by linguists as "Occitan" (*langue d'Oc*). Chamberlain may have been attracted to its rich medieval literature.

77. Thomas R. Lounsbury (1838–1915) of the 126th New York, a Yale Chaucerian. DAB, 11:429–31.

78. See 18 Jan. 1899 to Garnsey.

It now appears to me possible that I should be able to be with you on some Saturday before the middle of March. As things are just now, I cannot determine the exact date. But I will keep the matter in mind, and will let you know as soon as the way clears.

Thanking you for your kind expressions,

I am truly yours

Joshua L. Chamberlain

〰 TO GRACE

Portland

Aug. 16, 1904

My dearest Gracie:

I had a good letter from Wyllys this morning. I am glad he finds dear Gorgan so much better. I am getting myself together again,—but rather slowly, but able to be in my office all office hours. It is very comfortable & pleasant for me to "live" in the yacht. One of the Wilson girls[79] will be with Lillian. She gives a chowder luncheon to Mr Farnsworth, & daughter, or Miss Rich (of the Customs House) tomorrow.

I do not really feel able to stand the strain of the Chamberlain meeting[80] Friday & doubt if I shall try to go to it. In case I do not go, I shall take the yacht to our shore Friday & be there, & at home, over Sunday. If I *do go*, I shall try to get up to the shore Saturday.

We will not be out of speaking-distance [from] my dear Gorgan any time, & will be within an hours reach of her. When we are at anchor for over a day in any place Wyllys or I will go to Gorgan. I see you are to leave Wednesday— probably, by fast train (12.30 Pm Brunswick). I will meet you at Station at 120 if nothing prevents unless I hear that you will not be on that train. I suppose it will not, however, be of any great account to you to have me come up there just for the few minutes. Perhaps Wyllys will come with you if Gorgan is willing. He may like to go to the Chamberlain meeting if I cannot. I shall be sorry to have to be absent from the meeting, as I wish to insist on relinquishing the Presidency of the association. I wish some good may come to you by your generous visit to Gorgon—you do not know how much good your visit & our heart-talks have done me. Nothing has made me so nearly peaceful and happy for years.

79. The Wilson girls, as well as the Farnsworths and Miss Rich, are unidentified.

80. The Chamberlain Society of America, of which Chamberlain had served as president since 1899.

Chamberlain at the wheel of the Pinafore, *2 August 1905
(Courtesy of Bowdoin College)*

Yours most dearly
Father.

[SL]

TO JOHN P. NICHOLSON

Portland, Maine, March 16, 1905

Dear Colonel Nicholson:

I have your notice of the book of Colonel Oates and also a copy of his letter concerning the monument he proposes to mark the point of his extreme advance on Little Round Top. I am wholly at a loss to know what Col. Oates wants me to do. He seems to have satisfied himself that I am incorrigible on the point he wishes to establish, and that he never can agree with me. As he looks to you to vindicate his rights in the matter of what he thinks our conflicting claims, I infer that you submit the case to me hoping that if possible I may make some modification of something I have said or done. I have never set up any "claims" at all about the action of Round Top. I have simply stated the facts; first in my official report written on the march away from Gettysburg, and since in a more extended account on the same lines, in a lecture, perhaps not quite accurately reported. I cannot change the facts, nor any statement of my own about them. I remember saying in a letter to you some time ago referring to the statements of Colonel Oates then made that his regiment advanced until confronted by the 83rd Pennsylvania and 44th New York, that this regiment never reached that ground, nor encountered a shot from these Union Regiments. My own regiment held by its extreme right, but all the rest of it was pressed back entirely from its ground two or three times, but finally regained its original position. I am more than willing that the monument of the 15th Alabama should be placed inside my lines, for some of these men were doubtless there, and I should feel honored by the companionship of the monument of so gallant a regiment on that historic crest, as I was honored by its presence forty years ago.

The present feeling of Colonel Oates surprises me; for in two letters from him to me some years ago, I was much gratified at the remarkable agreement of our statements and recollections, and in a published account by him, which I have, the same general agreement appears so far as his statements about encountering my line of battle are concerned. His remarks there, about being confronted by cavalry I took exception to as no portion of our cavalry was in that part of the field. What he encountered was a flanking party I had sent out on my left front, together with a company of sharp-shooters which joined them. However [that] is not material, for this body was no doubt more serious an opponent in its flank attack than any cavalry could be on those broken and wooded slopes.

The agreement of the general statements as heretofore made by Col. Oates and myself, I consider remarkable, and I greatly regret that he should now find occasion to accuse me of withholding from him any measure of just recognition of his skillful and bold attack, and the splendid gallantry of the 15th Alabama, for which I have ever felt a peculiar regard.

The matter of monuments is in your charge, not mine. All I could wish is that they be placed in accordance with historic truth.

With very high regard,

Your friend and servant,

Joshua L. Chamberlain

Col. John P. Nicholson,

Chairman, Gettysburg Battlefield Commission,

Gettysburg, Pennsylvania.

[GNMP]

Portland, Maine, May 18, 1905

General William C. Oates,
Montgomery, Ala.

My Dear sir:

Since the receipt of your favor in regard to placing a monument to the 15th Alabama on the slope of Little Round Top, Gettysburg, I have been prostrated by a severe attack resulting from old wounds so that I have not been able to respond promptly.

In this letter I find your impressions place me at a disadvantage in your estimation on two very different grounds; first in that our former correspondence by way of letters made so little impression on you that you are led to deny having such correspondence; and secondly in that you ascribe to my influence with the Government authorities their refusal to permit the erection of a monument to the 15th Alabama on the ground where they fought.

These suggestions compel me to look over my vouchers to see if I have possibly been mistaken on topics of so much importance as to involve my word of honor.

I find that I did receive, in answer to a letter of mine, two letters purporting to be from you, and so regarded by me, and that I based important statements in public addresses on what was given in them very perfectly confirming my own recollection and reports on the minor points of the conflict on Little Round Top.

Looking also at my correspondence with Colonel Nicholson, Chairman of the Gettysburg Commission, I find that in the private correspondence instituted by him on this subject, I made no objection whatever to the erection of a monument by you on the ground attained by the 15th Alabama or any portion of it during the battle, expressing only the wish that this ground be accurately ascertained, and also that Colonel Nicholson in his final communications with me, does not rest the action of the Commission on any testimony or influence of mine, but makes an independent statement of his own as the basis of his conclusions.

To come to present conditions, you will perceive by my personal letters to Col. Nicholson, copies of which it seems he has sent you, the expression of my complete and cordial willingness to have the monument of the 15th Alabama placed within my lines on the slope of Little Round Top, on ground actually reached by portions of that regiment in the sharp passages of the fight. As to exact location, I cannot say from mere description what was the extreme point to which my left was driven by you, but certainly it was not doubled back upon my right, nor was the right driven materially from its connection with the 83rd Pennsylvania; I should say it was to a perpendicular with the line of my right front, that is, a quarter circle. The losses, both in my right companies and in the 83rd, show that they were not very sharply assailed. It is really my desire to have your monument set up, only let us make sure of our ground for the sake of historical fact.

I really do not know what more you could desire as to my present attitude in the matter now at issue. I should be glad to meet you again, after your honorable and conspicuous career of which the trials and tests of Gettysburg were so brilliant a part.

Very truly yours,
Joshua L. Chamberlain.

[GNMP]

〰 TO FANNIE

Portland
Aug 12 1905

My dear Fanny:

I believe this is your birth day, and although your condition is far from being what I could wish and constantly pray for,[81] I cannot help sending you a word of loving greeting with thanks that we have been so long spared to each other, & life has been so rich in blessings.

You have had a useful and honorable, — & I trust on the whole, — a happy life. Your husband & children "rise up & call you blessed" — as the old scriptures represent the crowning grace of a good woman. Every body is send[ing] me letters of sympathy & love for you — more than I can answer for some time. But I am returning greetings for you to them all. The dear little girls have been working at some little tokens of affection for your birth day, & you will have them by this time. I shall soon come to see you & try to cheer you. With all love & prayer for blessing to come to you.

yours
Lawrence.

[SL]

81. In addition to her blindness, Fannie had slipped and broken her hip on the 4th. Smith, *Fanny and Joshua*, 323.

TO AURESTUS S. PERHAM

Portland, Maine
September 6th 1905.

Captain A. S. Perham,
Washington, D.C.
Dear Friend:—

I have to thank you for your kind inquiry for Mrs Chamberlain's health, and for your sympathy with us all in her afflictions.

I regret to have to say that we are not succeeding in bringing her up and I fear the issue. I will convey to her your kindly message.

We are doing all we can, and praying for the best, without much evidence of success.

For my own part, I have better report to make. I am as well as one could expect to be under all I have to do and suffer.

I am glad to hear that your honored father[82] is in better condition than he was last spring, and able to enjoy life.

Kindest remembrances to him, and to all of yours.

Truly yours,
Joshua L. Chamberlain

[MHS]

TO ALEXANDER S. WEBB

Portland, Maine, October 11, 1905

Dear General Webb:—

I have thought much of the suggestions in the paper concerning the proposed retirement of Volunteer General Officers of the Civil War, which you sent me with the request to change it to suit my case. I hardly know what you refer to by this. My service was something over three years and five months; all of it in the field, and three years of it in command of troops. I had the regiment from Chancellorsville, and was assigned to command a brigade[83] August 15th, 1863: June 18th, 1864 was promoted to the corresponding rank by Grant on the field before Rives' Salient, Petersburg. I had my own and Gregory's brigades in the last campaign, and was placed in command of the First Division after the surrender—a day's march out. As you know, I twice narrowly saved my life under wounds.[84]

82. Former governor Sidney Perham, see 26 Jan. 1900 to Perham.

83. 1st Brigade, 1st Division, V Corps.

84. In addition to the injuries he suffered at Petersburg, a Confederate ball at Quaker Road, 29 Mar. 1865, passed through Charlemagne's neck and Chamberlain's bridle arm

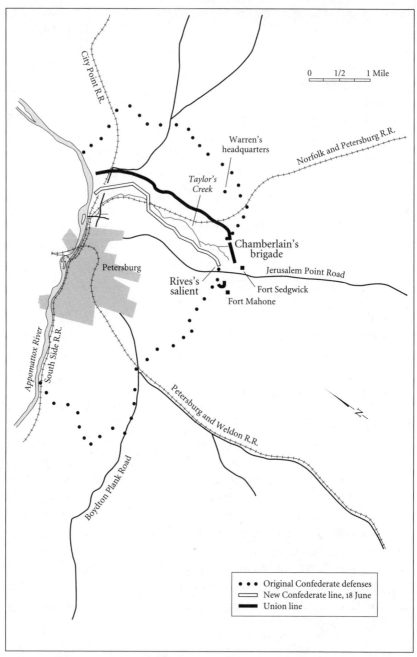

Chamberlain's assault on Rives's salient at Petersburg, 18 June 1864, 3:00 P.M.
(Adapted from Trulock, 197)

Now a word as to the measure proposed. Would it not over-burden the proposed list and defeat the measure, to put in all who attained or received the rank of a general officer? Should it not be of such as commanded troops in the field, — and not of bureaus &c.? Would you put Colonels into the "bill" unless they actually commanded brigades in the field? [A]nd would you include all those who secured brevets of brigadier general, including almost everybody who had a friend at court after the war had ended? It would appear to me that the list should be somewhat discriminating and a roll of honor. Otherwise, I really do not want any part in it. There have been enough of such things. A brevet, which used to cost all the blood that would run out of our bodies, is not worth now a real old brass button: and the medals of honor are no sure token of distinguished service or merit, after the raid on them from the rear. And would you create a separate little nursery or yard to put these "old brigadiers" into as "Retired Volunteers"? The volunteers were "retired" long ago. What I have thought of is just what was done in the cases of Hawley and Osterhaus.[85] Surely some are left who served as much and deserve as much, not to say, need as much, as they.

Would there be no toleration of a measure to place surviving general officers of the Union Army in the Civil War, who commanded troops in the field, on the retired list of the regular army with the rank of the highest commission or command they actually held and exercised in the field in the times of the nation's supreme peril?

If they are not worthy of this or if this would degrade the army either in its history or in its present rare tests and superior estate, then I would accept the situation and be content to be buried in an honorable grave. That is better than to go into an unseemly struggle to obtain recognition and be denied it, and to go down under the shame of it.

I am writing this without having yours at hand at this moment. I will try to give a more politic answer when I come to my desk and to a "realizing sense" of actual life and the probabilities, which some old essayist says, are "the guide of life."

I am writing this now in my changer on the fifth stor[y], at night, looking out on the sea.

---

and body (deflected from his heart by field orders and a pocket mirror), knocking nearby Lt. Vogel off his horse. Chamberlain passed out in his saddle and was brevetted major general for "conspicuous gallantry." Trulock, 234–35, 239.

85. Acts of Congress placed these generals on the retired list as brigadier generals. GB, 353.

Yours with love, old and new,
Joshua L. Chamberlain

[YUL]

≈ TO FANNIE

[ca. 18 October 1905]

It will be best to destroy this ⸺⸺
Fannie,

I cannot but thank you for your confidence—I am aware it is not such as you would show to every one. As to the writings I can *say* nothing. [Y]ou should be happy in such a friend as the one who could thus write. I was thankful that you are so soon to see Him, no matter what it cost me—It is not strange to me—I know what my lot is & I have learned to bear it. Since I have read those writings I hope that you will spare my poor words that I was trying to write you—to you—who have been blessed with this richer boon. I feel that my words will seem dumb & lifeless. I can not dare to write to you, now that I know what you are wont to have for letters. *I* am *nothing* & you will forgive me if I cannot write—you are going where friends dearer & more worthy will love to cluster around you—you can scarcely need to think of one so sad & distant as I shall be. But Fannie—may God bless you—do not think that I can ever forget in my darkest hours the gleam of white light you have shed upon my soul. May God bless you as He blessed me when I was suffered to know you—He *will* bless you—I feel it in these tears—unmanly though they be. He will bless you. My blessing too Fannie, and may peace be yours. May be you can not read this Fannie—no matter. It is not what I would have written. My eyes have not suffered me to see many words that I have written. You see that I am not calm

These stains upon the paper alone can tell you what I could not say. There are other things written here & than what your eyes can read for this will soon be dry. Good bye Fannie—I will be patient till you are gone & the pall shall fall on me, *alone* with buried memories.[86]

L⸺⸺

[SL]

---

86. Fannie died on the 18th of October.

Portland, Maine, October 25th 1905.

General Thomas T. Munford,[87]
Lynchburg, Virginia;
My dear General: —

The death of my wife, who was a broad-minded, and richly endowed woman who loved her whole Country, in peace and in war, and honored brave men who did manly duty as they itin [*sic*] their own hearts, has come upon me since the receipt of your letter, and my delay in acknowledging it is thus to be pardoned.

I am glad to have this word from you, and the honor of your wish to know what I said on the battle of Five Forks some years since is appreciated. I very much wish I could have seen you before I put my recollections into print. As you will see from what I send you, this account is of my own experiences and thoughts, and not an attempt to write history. Most of it is extended from notes I made soon after the surrender at Appomattox. I dare say I have not been perfectly accurate in my references to your command and your brilliant part in the sharp action at Five Forks.

I have been puzzled over the "reports," official and otherwise, which have appeared concerning that day's action. I have been requested to prepare an ac[c]ount of the entire "last campaign" of our two armies. This will give me an opportunity to profit by any criticism[s], corrections or suggestions you may be kind enough to make. I send you a copy of the paper you refer to, with assurance of my very high respect and sincere regard.

Truly yours,
Joshua L. Chamberlain

[DU]

TO THOMAS T. MUNFORD

Portland, Maine,
November 10 1905

Dear General Munford:

I thank you for your letter. Both your generous references to my paper, and your tender sympathy in my deep affliction touched me deeply. Manhood is one of the noblest of God's gifts or manifestations. To nothing do I respond more quickly than to what you have shown me.

I am perfectly aware that in my account, which only claimed to present

---

87. Brig. Gen. Thomas T. Munford (b. 1831), cavalry officer and planter. CWD, 574; Smith, *Fanny and Joshua*, 330.

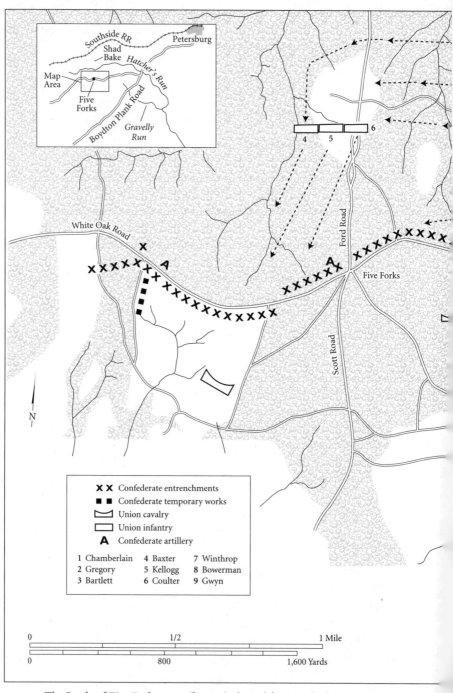

The Battle of Five Forks, 1 April 1865 (Adapted from Trulock, 262–63)

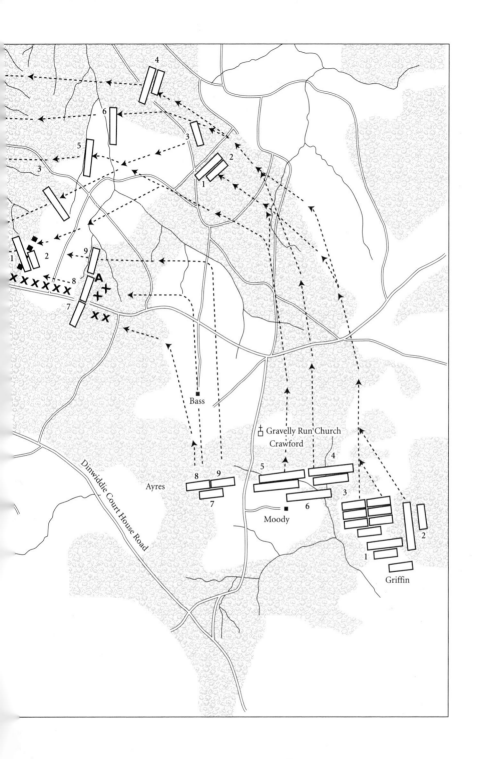

4

6

3

5

3

2

1

1 2

9

8 A

7

Bass

Gravelly Run Church
Crawford

Ayres

8 9

7

5

6

Moody

4

3

2

1

Griffin

Dinwiddie Court House Road

things as they appeared to me,—which is perhaps a narrow point of view, although in some ways useful,—there must be errors even in statements of "past" concerning "the other side." I would be truly and greatly obliged to you if you would freely criticise and correct me on such points. What I wish is to get the truth as far as possible—the "whole truth" I fear is out of reach.

I took some pains to lay out the positions and movements in that field a rude sketch or plate inserted in the pamphlet sent you. This cannot be wholly correct so far as your early position and subsequent movement are concerned. If you will freely mark errors and correct them on the copy you have I will gladly send you another copy, and will have the plate retouched for future use.

Moreover, I will more strongly emphasize the fact that it was *you* in command and not Fitz Hugh Lee.[88]

I had heard of the incident of the "shad dinner" which occupied so much of the attention of three of your generals when the battle came on, & *off*![89] Mrs Pickett,[90] you may know, denies this with indignation.

I take the liberty to send you a copy of a historical address I recently gave,—the tone of which may not displ[e]ase you. The first sentence may possibly apply to other cases than that I had in hand.

Sincerely yours
Joshua L. Chamberlain

[DU]

➤ TO HENRY CLAY MERRIAM

Portland
January 17, 1906

Dear General Merriam:

I thank you very much for your generous interest in my behalf. I thought it likely you would find members of our delegation rather lukewarm in the matter, although I know of no reason why it should be so.

88. Fitzhugh ("Fitz") Lee (1835–1905), Gen. Lee's nephew and cavalry commander. CWD, 475.

89. The embarrassing story continued to be suppressed: George Pickett and Fitzhugh Lee were at a "shad bake" with Brig. Gen. Thomas L. Rosser (1836–1910) when the battle of Five Forks began. Walter Morrill and a squad from the 20th Maine stormed them and forced Pickett to surrender. Once the diners realized that they outnumbered the squad, they fought back hand-to-hand, forcing Morrill to retreat and give up his prize captives. Because of the dinner and the assault, Pickett reacted tardily to the Federal assault at Five Forks and underestimated its power. CWD, 284; Vickery, "Walter G. Morrill," 127–51; also see Freeman, *Lee's Lieutenants*, 3:665–70.

90. LaSalle Corbell Pickett (1848–1931), see 22 Aug. 1913 to Perham.

I do not know which of our Senators would take interest in a bill for me, but will try to find out.

Today I have your second letter. In regard to Webb, he did once ask me to join in a proposed "omnibus bill," but on receiving my reply he retired from advocacy of that bill, and instead (as I understand) voted [for] a private bill. I enclose [a] copy of that letter of mine to Webb, which, may I ask you to preserve, as it is my only copy.

I have written out as brief a sketch as I can without making it a mere "abstract of titles," of the points and passages of my career most likely to be considered "germane to the question" — expanding only the details of my being sent to command the parade at Appomattox, as you especially desired me to do this.

This is not, of course, to be set forth at length in any statement to be published for the use of Congress. I suppose only the barest "headings" would be proper for such a purpose.

This is for you to look over, and see what should be made up. When receiving your corrections and criticisms I will prepare it more properly. I was going to look up the passages in Gordon's and Lee's books and quote pages but I sent it along as it is.

I do not go into many matters of fact in my "career" which, though important to me, must have no bearing on the point now at issue — which, I suppose, is chiefly the military.

Thanking you much,

yours

J. L. Chamberlain

I think the "appropriation bill" passed.

[cc]

≈ TO HENRY CLAY MERRIAM

Portland, Maine
January 21, 1906

Dear General Merriam:

I am followed up closely with rather reproving comments on my declining to join the movement for an omnibus bill retiring General officers and Colonels of Volunteers who have received the brevet of Brigadier General, upon a special basis of Volunteer Retired List. I am now assured by the movers in this that this bill is sure to pass: still I am urged more strenuously than ever to give my approval to the bill.

My reasons for not joining in the movement were chiefly the following:

It is so sweeping in its scope that it seemed to me it could not be favorably received by the Congress; It should have been limited to officers who had not only been "with" troops in the field a year, but had actually commanded troops in the capacity of their brevet rank. You know many of us were all the time commanding in a grade above our actual rank, and this in the case of colonels commanding brigades was a hardship, by reason of the increased expense attaching to the position of command.

Brevets were scattered so promiscuously after the war that they are no indication of service in the field or anywhere else. It seems to me hardly just to base the application of this measure upon the brevet rank rather than on the actual service rendered. This, in fact, is my chief objection to the measure now proposed. I cannot truthfully say I approve this bill. And yet it seems a little ungracious for me to withhold assistance to old comrades deserving consideration, on account of the inclusion of some who do not stand on the same ground.

What would you advise?

Yours

J. L. Chamberlain

[cc]

TO HENRY CLAY MERRIAM

Portland

January 23, 1906

Dear General Merriam:

I sent you a letter stating the embarrassment I am under in declining to join my "comrades" in petitioning for the "omnibus" retiring bill. I showed you my reasons for this declining in the copy of my letter to Webb. I do not however oppose that bill, but being of opinion that it had no chance of a passage, I did not wish to impair any influence I might have in promoting a more limited measure. But "they" will now probably call me selfish and fight me on a personal bill. This is unfortunate. Had I better join them in the present petition, and then if they fail and things look right, put in my personal bill on the Hawley precedent?

You know with Genl Fessenden's death, his retired pay might fairly be claimed by me.[91]

---

91. Stanton had withdrawn Chamberlain's promotion to major general to give it to Francis Fessenden (1839–1906), son of Sen. Fessenden. See ca. 18 May 1893 to Webb. *GB*, 152–53.

I have noted a few points in the draft you were kind enough to prepare—on the whole shortening it. The suggestions I made are:

1) As to the statement that I commanded a brigade in *all* the battles of '64 up to Petersburg. I was not in the "Wilderness" and would you not introduce Genl Grant's testimony in the way I have indicated?[92]

2) Would you not add the fact of being twice wounded in '65?

3) I did actually command the Division till we were leaving Appomattox. The fact was, that as my being so severely wounded in June '64 cost me the old command—the veteran brigade of the Division—and I cheerfully accepted the command of the youngest (and hardiest) brigade in members.[93] Griffin invariably ordered the 2nd brigade to "report to me" in every action after that time, so that my "command" was really equal to my old one [in] importance. It was a case where my cheerful acquiescence in an assignment of *reduced* importance took the attention of my superiors. It is the truth that I "commanded two brigades."

4) I do not like to say Grant honorably designated me. When he left he told the "Commissioners" Gibbon[94] and Griffin (Sheridan had gone) that I was to command that phalanx. So they told me, officially. Would it be proper to add the fact that I was recommended for promotion to *Major General* by all my superiors of the army of the Potomac?

I venture to strike out the "*argumentum ad misericordiam*" in stating how used up I am, and saying how gratifying it would be to me to receive this recognition.

To save you trouble, I have my suggestions embodied in a typewritten form. Whether we shall decide best to do anything with it—you must judge. Genl Raum[95] is at the Ebbitt, trying to push the omnibus bill. Genl Grosvenor[96] is my friend, but he is *in the "Reserve."* So is *Spear.* I hate to set myself up above as distinct from my old *comrades in arms.* The rest of them I do not mind.

92. The Senate bill memorandum did include Grant's testimony. See 14 June 1906 to Warren.

93. 3rd Brigade, which included the 20th Maine, and 1st Brigade, 1st Division, V Corps, respectively.

94. Griffin and John Gibbon (1827–96), commander of the XXIV Corps, Army of the James, at Appomattox, were chosen as commissioners to receive the official surrender of the Army of Northern Virginia. GB, 172.

95. Brig. Gen. Green Berry Raum (1829–1909) of Illinois, a former congressman. GB, 390–91.

96. Bvt. Brig. Gen. Charles H. Grosvenor (1833–1917), a congressman from Ohio. CWD, 363.

Yours as ever,

J. L. Chamberlain

≋ TO HENRY CLAY MERRIAM

Portland

January 29, 1906

Dear General Merriam:

I thank you for your kind interest. I have thought the matter over, and it appears best on the whole for me to aid the "crowd" as far as I can without "going back" on my former statements of opinion. My *opinion* and reasons remain as before, but perhaps the form I have sent Genl Raum may serve him and my letter, frank as it is, ought not to offend them.

Yours as ever,

J. L. C.

I can't see how they can take advantage of my frankness in the letter to Genl Raum of which I enclose a copy. I endorse the *principle* tho' not the particular reasons proposed. If they do not begin to abuse me, my "opinion" enclosed may help them. Yours, J. L. C.

≋ TO HENRY CLAY MERRIAM

Portland, Maine

February 19, 1906

Dear General Merriam:

I thank you for your constant watchfulness, and for the letter just received, telling of the new bill now in progress.

I am glad they place the measure on a basis of service instead of "brevets." But now taking the whole body of officers who were "with" troops a year, runs into one of the obstacles affecting the former bill. There is a legion of those, many of whom, young at the time, are likely to be alive for some time yet, and this will make a big drain on the Treasury. This will be ground of opposition, and defeat, will it not?

Why did they not put it "in command of troops," not less than a brigade? There seems to be a disposition to "carry in" a lot of officers whose real service hardly warrants it.

Of course it is evident now that the "precedents" of Hawley and Osterhaus are not in any way the points to be made.

I don't know what will come of this new bill. But I can afford to wait a while, as you say, and see what turn things take. I greatly prefer to be put on the same basis as Hawley &c. there would be half a dozen others in the same case as I, no doubt. Such a case as that of Curtis[97] should be treated on its own merits.

I hope I shall not tire you out.

Yours as ever,

Joshua L. Chamberlain

[CC]

∽TO ALEXANDER S. WEBB

Portland Maine

Feb. 27th 1906

My dear Webb; —

It is good to see your handwriting. Yes, they sent me a letter to the same purport. I [seemingly] laid it aside. It was an absurdity—a stultification—to ask us to support an attempt to work through a bill we disapproved, and did not wish to have pass, — as they well knew.

The letter we sent was simply approval of the *general principle* — (I mean no pun) & given for the sake of old comradeship. They have given up that bill, you know, and are drawing up another, based on service "*with*" troops — which is also a killing element in the bill. This takes in all sorts Chaplains, doctors, store-keepers & c, as I understand it. I want the basis to be service not less than a year in *command* of troops in the *field*—not less than a brigade.

However, after the sharp attack in the House, on the "retiring" measure lately practiced in the Army, the House will be prejudiced against any & all retiring bills.

This "omnibus" campaign has probably shut off any action that "we" might have secured for officers with a record like yours & Gregg's[98] and others of like grade or merit, — *if there are any.*

But we might well watch the action of the House, & possible put in our private bills by & by if there appears to be any chance for their passing.

I am pretty well; not pulled down with old wounds as last winter.

yours as ever

Joshua L. Chamberlain

[YUL]

97. Newton M. Curtis (1835–1910), colonel of the 142nd New York and a member of Congress, only led a unit larger than a regiment in battle once, but his command of a brigade during the storming of Fort Fisher in January 1865 had earned him a prompt promotion to brigadier general and brevet major general, as well as a Medal of Honor.

98. Maj. Gen. David M. Gregg (1833–1916), a former cavalry division commander. *WhoAm*, 677.

Brunswick, Maine
March 11, 1906

Dear General Merriam:

I deeply feel the kindness and generosity you are manifesting in the inter-est you take in securing my appointment on a "retired list" on status.

Your careful details of procedure set forth in your recent letter, which came to my hands just as I was leaving Portland last week for a few days at home by reason of a sudden "set-back" threatening a bad time of the old sort with my wounds, lets me see the necessity of my seeking immediate response in the best way I can.

1) If the pending bill goes through, although I do not like it, and believe it to be doomed to rejection, I suppose I must accept its conditions—although I confess, this will be with reluctance. But this will, of course, effectually bar any personal action on my behalf forever if it passes. You can perhaps, imag-ine that I am not anxious for the passage of the bill. I never endorsed it, but only the *general principle* of retiring general officers of volunteers.

2) Now, if it does *not* pass, the course you recommend for me may be taken up *if there is any chance for its passage*. Unless we are aware of this, I would feel like letting it all go by. I do not want to be set up just to be knocked down. I would much rather stand on my present record and place.

3) If there *is* a fair chance of its passing I would agree with you that it is best to have it introduced first in the Senate. But I am told that neither of our Senators is friendly to me—for what I do not know. Nor do I know to what *degree* of dislike they entertain this feeling, nor whether it would oblige them to *oppose* my being recognized on military grounds. Perhaps they dislike my conservative political ideas. I think Senators Gallinger, Lodge and Proctor[99] would favor us, and perhaps one of the older Senators from the western states.

By the "rule" or "law" or "courtesy" of the Senate, I suppose any bill for me must emanate from one of the Maine Senators. In this case I must probably write to them both asking them to interest themselves for me, and introduce my bill. Possibly you might find out what their feeling is and advise me.

I think the Maine members of the House would favor a bill for me but would not like to push it with the committees. Mr. Alexander of New York, Mr. Stevens of Minnesota would warmly support me. Perhaps Mr. Capron

99. John H. Gallinger (1837–1918) of New Hampshire; future majority leader Henry Cabot Lodge (1850–1924) of Massachusetts, a Harvard historian; Redfield Proctor (1831–1908), a Vermont colonel and former secretary of war. U.S. Congress, *Biographical Direc-tory*, 1191–92, 1470–71, 1706.

of Rhode Island, also. He is on the Military Committee. The member of that committee from Minnesota is a Maine man,[100] and might favor me. You see how slight a hold I have on the politicians as such. But it is possible that as *men* the congressmen might not be wholly ignorant of me nor ill-disposed towards me.

I dislike more than I can well express, to press you into disagreeable service. But I would be glad if you could find what the feeling would be on the part of Mr. Hull[101] and other members of the House Committee towards a private bill. Or would it be proper or wise for me to write them stating that I had withheld the presentation of a private bill in order not to antagonize the efforts of comrades for a general bill, but now, (that is, after the defeat of this latter-named bill) I desire to make a personal application, or present a private bill, and ask if this would meet their approval. I had at the first, and before the session, written to Congressman Allen of Maine, and Stevens of Minnesota, and had very kindly answers.

You will see by this letter that in spite of my "good intentions" and effort to render myself worthy of your interest, I am in a depressed and dispirited mood, and this may vex you. I am not as well as I could wish, and cannot make myself rally as I wish.

I shall not take it ill if you drop all further effort for me. But I will conform to any suggestions you may make. I do not, however, like to "go to Washington" to press my interests.

Yours with sincere and grateful regard,

Joshua L. Chamberlain

[cc]

---

100. De Alva S. Alexander (1846–1925) of the 128th Ohio, a Maine native and Bowdoin graduate and overseer; Frederick C. Stevens (1861–1923); Bvt. Maj. Adin B. Capron (1841–1911); and Loren Fletcher (1833–1919) of Minnesota, a Kennebec County native. U.S. Congress, *Biographical Directory*, 769, 1165; Congressional Quarterly, *American Leaders*, 300; *WhoAm*, 191.

101. Rep. John A. T. Hull (1841–1928) of the 23rd Iowa. U.S. Congress, *Biographical Directory*, 1347.

TO ANNETTE F. MERRIMAN

Portland
April 23d 1906

Miss Annette F. Merriman:[102]
Dear friend:

Through you, I wish to thank the members of the History class in the Grammar School for their attention and appreciation at my "lecture" on Gettysburg, and for their beautiful token of it so admirably presented. I prize each and all. They will understand that there is something very dear and sacred about "our Country" that makes it worth so dear a cost.

I congratulate you, too, on the opportunity you have, and so nobly improve, to inculcate in these fine young minds principles and sentiments so high.

Sincerely yours
Joshua L. Chamberlain

[PHS]

TO HENRY CLAY MERRIAM

Portland, Maine
May 7, 1906

Dear General Merriam:

Why is it that our friends of the Volunteer Retirement Bill do not see that what is killing their proposition is the large inclusion of officers who were not commanding officers at all to say nothing of their being "General Officers" or not?

As I understand the phrase "with troops," it is expressly intended to take in a lot of brevet brigadier generals, who were colonels and majors on the staff in the field. Deserving as many of them are, I do not think they fairly come into the category of "General Officers" as contemplated in the sentiment justifying the retirement of Hawley and Osterhaus.

I am deluged with circulars, ably drawn, urging the principle of retiring General Officers, which I approve and would endorse; but the application is immediately made to staff brevet brigadiers, who do not logically nor, in my opinion fairly, come under the range of the argument referred to.

Now the statement comes that they are going to carry their scheme over into the next session. This, of course, knocks me out on a special application, for another year. This whole movement has worked directly against me from

102. An unidentified teacher or principal of one of Maine's grammar schools.

the beginning. Yet I am urged often to send them money to pay for this kind of work. It does not seem to me reasonable.

I have pleasant letters from Senator Frye, who thinks my chance much better on a private bill than on such a plan as the proposed. But now, it seems, nothing at all can be done.

I thank you for your patient interest and labor for me.

Yours truly,

Joshua L. Chamberlain

[cc]

≈ TO FRANCIS E. WARREN

Portland, Maine, June 14th 1906

To The Honorable,

Francis E. Warren,

U.S. Senate;[103]

Honored Sir: —

My friends have had a Bill introduced in the Senate providing for placing me on the retired list of the army,[104] which has been referred to your Committee on Military Affairs. I have not been forward in allowing this matter to be presented. But inasmuch as the Congress itself has made the precedent in the cases of Generals Hawley and Osterhaus, as also in that of Captain Boutelle in the navy, presumably upon the military merits of those officers, it seems almost an act of self-respect for me to ask your consideration of the records in my case.

The principle is now well established. The question is how to apply it and preserve just and proper limits. I have not concurred in the belief of some of my old comrades in arms that a sweeping measure, based neither on character of service nor on disabling wounds, and so having not even the grounds of a pension claim, should be expected to meet the favor of the Congress. But the whole question is now before us, and cannot be wholly laid aside. I am aware of the difficulty of discriminating among officers on grounds of merit, but I hardly see what other course can be taken. It may be found practicable to act upon clear cases of merit as they may come up, thus holding the principle in

103. Francis Emroy Warren (1844–1924), a Wyoming cattleman and Medal of Honor winner from the 49th Massachusetts, chaired the committees on military affairs and appropriations. *DAB*, 19:472–73.

104. Senate Bill 6150, introduced by Sen. Frye on 14 May 1906. It and its accompanying memorandum are reprinted in Raymond, "Joshua Chamberlain's Retirement Bill," 341–54.

regard, and taking steps towards a just and reasonable treatment of the whole matter.

I am almost ashamed to seem to be petitioning for recognition. This is a kind of honor that should not be sought. But as the case is, I feel forced to submit my views on the subject, making no doubt of your just recognition when this appears to you wise.

With high regard, yours respectfully,

Joshua L. Chamberlain

[MHS]

TO EUGENE HALE

Portland, Maine, June 26th 1906.

Hon. Eugene Hale, LL.D.,
United States Senator;
Washington, D.C.
My dear Senator:—

Recurring to your very kind letter in regard to the Bill in the hands of the Military Committee of the Senate providing for my retirement in the army of the United States, I beg to ask if the Committee might be disposed to report favorably on the same, and if in that case it might pass the Senate at this session.

As I have before informed you, I have not joined in the measures brought before the Congress by many of my old Comrades in arms, because the basis or conditions proposed therein appeared more like a pension provision than a mark of honor or recognition of service.

At the same time the Congress itself has established such a precedent in the cases of Generals Hawley and Osterhaus and Captain Boutelle, that I cannot but feel myself entitled to some similar recognition.

It would be gratifying to me to be placed on the retired list of the army; but to be included in a sweeping list of beneficiaries with no special reference to character of service would be a different thing. If the bill before the Committee in my case could be passed in the Senate this session, it would meet my wishes in a very grateful degree.

With high regard,
Yours faithfully,
Joshua L. Chamberlain

[MHS]

Brunswick
September 24, 1906

Dear General Merriam:

I am much grieved and not less surprised that you felt hurt, as I judge by the letter sent me by General Mattocks,[105] that I "saw fit" to reply to you on my remarks on the *volunteers* at the Lewiston reunion. I was, in not a thought or word, replying to you, or taking any exception to what you said: I was only supplementing or complementing, your remarks by giving mention to the citizen soldier after your interesting presentation of the Regulars. You suggested (as I said at the time) a *theme* for the hasty words I was called on to utter at the close, or rather breaking up, of the long stretch of talk at the "festival." I had been informed I was to speak first or second in this list, and not being called until everybody was tired out, and many *gone out*, I had all my intended "speech" knocked out of my head. When at so unpropitious a stage of the proceedings I was called up, it struck me that the most appropriate thing I could do at a reunion of *volunteers*, to say a word to *them* and of them, following the tribute so worthily given to the Regulars and suggested by it. I did not "reply" to you, but only followed you. I did not disparage the Regulars, but pointed out, in too hasty a manner no doubt, some of the characteristic differences in the fundamental character of a citizen-soldiery and professional troops. I afterwards pencilled down the line of my remark, for I thought it partly of better interest on some other occasion, and I will look these notes over and see what I was so unfortunate as to say which could possibly have grieved you. You must know that I could not willingly, nor possibly, intend anything to do that.

I am "used up" and "laid up" with a long heavy cold.

Yours as ever,

Joshua L. Chamberlain

[CC]

105. Charles P. Mattocks, see 11 Aug. 1870 to Lane.

1906.
Portland, Maine, November 14.

Hon. William H. Fleming,[106]
Augusta,
Georgia:
My dear Sir:—

My friend, Mr Dana Estes,[107] of Boston, has sent me the fine volume in which he has worthily presented your recent Address on the Race problem in the South[108]

I cannot content myself with thanking him for the favor thus shown me, but must be permitted to express to you the high appreciation of the noble spirit of this utterance and the true statesmanship evinced in th[e] handling of a difficult political problem.

The ability of the argument presented, the high moral ground on which the question is treated, and the judicial wisdom in applying the great principles of human right to the practical treatment of political issues of an exciting character, make a convincing appeal to all to whom the welfare of the Country is dear.

A most difficult practical problem is now laid upon our people of the South, the solution of which as well as the consequences of it, must be mainly undertaken and borne by them, and the sympathy and co-operation of the people of the North should be cordially extended to them.

You have aided greatly in pointing out a ground on which all can meet.

Yours, With very high regard,

[BSC]

106. William Henry Fleming (1856–1944), a former congressman from Georgia. *National Cyclopaedia*, 33:146.

107. Dana Estes (1840–1909), a prominent Boston publisher and native Mainer who accompanied Chamberlain to Egypt and donated antiquities to Bowdoin. *DAB*, 6:188–89; Pullen, 155.

108. "Slavery and the Race Problem in the South, with Special Reference to the State of Georgia," address to the Alumni Society of the State University, Athens, 19 June 1906 (Boston: Dana Estes & Co., 1906). Fleming argued for what was then a very progressive program, supporting freedom (but not complete equality) for blacks, bemoaning the history of slavery, and arguing against the emotional, demagogic fears of "Negro domination."

Portland, Maine, Sept 10. 1907

Hon. Morrill N. Drew,

President, Maine Institution for the Blind;[109]

Sir:—

Being called to service as member of Board of Trustees and Directors of so many institutions and associations that I find my time and attention heavily drawn upon, I am forced therefore to resign those trusts in which my service can best be spared. The interests of your institution are ably cared for, and I feel warranted in presenting my resignation as a Director of the Association; which I hereby do.[110]

Very respectfully,

Joshua L. Chamberlain

[BSC]

Portland Maine

Sept. 24 1907

Major General

F. C. Ainsworth

Adjutant General, U.S.A.[111]

General;

As I understand that is now permissible to receive the new badge of the "Medal of Honor,"[112] without returning the old one (which I value on account of the inscription on it)[113] I beg to be instructed as to the proper course for me to take in making the application.

Very respectfully—

Your obedient servant,

Joshua L. Chamberlain

Brevet Major General, U.S.V.

[NA]

109. Morrill N. Drew (1862–1917), a Portland financier, politician, and philanthropist. MSL.

110. Chamberlain's involvement with the institution was probably motivated by Fannie's blindness. He may have felt that her death rendered his participation obsolete.

111. Frederick C. Ainsworth, see 16 Sept. 1893 to Ainsworth.

112. The medal had originally been a simple upside down five-pointed star, but in 1904 the army added a wreath to the star. *Deeds of Valor*, 1:1.

113. "The Congress to Bvt. Maj. Gen. Joshua L. Chamberlain U.S. Vols. Gettysburg July 2, 1863"

TO FREDERICK C. AINSWORTH

Portland, Maine, October 21st 1907.

Major-General F.C. Ainsworth,
Adjutant General U.S. Army:
Sir:—

I have to acknowledge the receipt at your hand of the Medal of Honor of new design, with rosette and ribbon appertaining to the same, issued to me under provisions of recent acts of Congress, and to express my thanks for your courtesy.[114]

Very respectfully,
Joshua L. Chamberlain
Brevet Major-General U.S.V.

[NA]

NOTE REGARDING LETTER BY JOHN S. MOSBY

Letter from Col. J. S. Mosby[115] to Judge James Keith,[116] Richmond Va says Genl Pickett, in 1870, was very coldly received by Genl R. E. Lee, in a Call the former made on Lee; & that Colonel *Venable*[117] said (1892) to Col Mosby that he, *Venable*, took an order [from] Genl Lee for Picketts *arrest*, & passing Pickett on the retreat from Petersburg, Lee called out with vexation "Is that man still with this army?"

Letter returned to Col A. S. Perham
Sept 11 1908

[BSC]

TO HENRY SWEETSER BURRAGE

Brunswick
Feb. 8 '09

Dear Major Burrage:
I think you may as well make the title
Lincoln in the Field.
Then I can take either paper, for my Philada one is substantially that on

114. The later medal is now in the Hawthorne-Longfellow Library at Bowdoin.
115. John S. Mosby (1833–1916), Confederate cavalry commander. CWD, 571.
116. James Keith (1839–1918), president of Virginia's Supreme Court of Appeals. WhoAm, 600.
117. Charles S. Venable (1827–1900), aide-de-camp to Lee at the end of the war. DAB, 19:245–46.

a rather larger scale than the paper on Lincoln's death and his "funeral in the field."[118]

yours cordially,
Joshua L. Chamberlain

[MHS]

⨊ TO HENRY SWEETSER BURRAGE

Portland
Feb 20 1909

Dear Major Burrage:
I have just got back from Phila. & Washington and th[i]nk the good reception they gave me in both places has rather helped than hurt me. So I can probably meet your wishes as to speaking before our Commandery on the 3^d of March.

I am a little in doubt what paper to read — the one I had some time ago prepared on Lincoln's relations with the Army in the field intending the funeral we held on the day of his public funeral, or to read the substance of my paper in Philadelphia.

I have no notice yet of our meeting which I suppose will be at Riverton.
I sent you a "*subject*," the day I left, which will do in either case.

yours as ever
J. L. Chamberlain

[MHS]

118. Keynote speech at the Lincoln centennial festivities at Philadelphia's Academy of Music, 12 Feb. 1909. Wallace, *Soul of the Lion*, 300. Trulock accidentally dates it 3 Mar. 1909, but this refers to his subsequent delivery of the lecture in Portland. His lecture is variously entitled "Abraham Lincoln" (Trulock); "Abraham Lincoln Seen from the Field" (Wallace); "Oration of the One Hundredth Anniversary of the Birth of Abraham Lincoln" (*Bayonet* and Maine Commandery, *War Papers*, vol. 4); and "Abraham Lincoln Seen from the Field in the War for the Union" (Chamberlain's 1909 Philadelphia private printing). It was also printed in the Pennsylvania Commandery's *Ceremonies in Commemoration of the One Hundredth Anniversary of the Birth of Abraham Lincoln, Philadelphia, February 12, 1909* (Philadelphia: John T. Palmer, 1909) and *The Magazine of History*, Extra Number, No. 32 (1914).

Brunswick Feb 24 '09

Dear Major Burrage:

I found your kind letter and notice in Portland yesterday, and thank you. I was not able to get at Captain Little;[119] but will find him when I go in again, tomorrow. I suppose the companions would prefer that I give the substance of my address at Philadelphia. That would take an hour's time, however; and it might be best to abbreviate it.

Of course we could not invite ladies to the Banquet. I was only questioning whether guests with ladies and the ladies of our Companions who desired, might be admitted when our "supper" is over and the other exercises begin.

Several have spoken to me about this, & I could give no answer. Possibly some notice or intimation may be given by our committee. It would be invidious, perhaps, for me to give a list of those I wish invited,—as so many have made the overture to me. I wish to ask you a[s] to the parliamentary status of the amendment to the Constitution proposed by Gen'l Hubbard, and introduced at our last meeting I *suppose*, under a recommendation of mine.

Genl Hubbard is anxious to have this taken up at the coming meeting. Is it "on the table," or assigned as unfinished business, or must it be brought up anew?

yours as ever

Joshua L. Chamberlain

[MHS]

TO FANNIE HARDY ECKSTORM

Portland April 28 '09

Dear Mrs Eckstorm:[120]

You do me too much honor. But if you insist on your plan I will aid you as I can, in getting at the facts. I understand you desire a letter from me stating that the house you are to have photographed is the one where I was born. This I can do, relying on authoritative testimony, and reinforced by m[y] recollection of earliest days to the limit of some five years.

There is a photograph & crude cut of which I have seen in some local

119. Thomas J. Little, a MOLLUS companion. Possibly the former state representative from Brewer of that name.

120. Fannie P. Hardy Eckstorm (1865–1946), daughter of Chamberlain's childhood friend Manley Hardy, was a Maine naturalist, anthropologist, and folklorist whose works include *The Penobscot Man* (1904) and, with Mary W. Smyth, *Minstrelsy of Maine: Folk Songs and Ballads of the Woods and Coast* (1927). Wallace, *Dictionary of North American Authors*, 133.

paper which might be enlarged, but this would not be so desirable a picture as one you might have had taken before the late obscuration, — or even now this perhaps might be removed for a day in order to get such a picture as you would like. I would contribute to the expense of this, if it is practicable. As to the tablet inscription if anything of my listing is to be mentioned would it not be well to have the leading facts or offices given. I have indicated some of these. The list seems too long, and you can condense it as you think best. The lines might be rearranged. I changed e.g. the LL.D. as I was not "born so."[121]

I am somewhat at a loss how to make the letter of testimony as to the birth-place of substance & form worthy of your proposed plan of preservation & exhibition. I would like at least a better pen than that I now hold in hand. I will try something of this simple sort. But I can do better next time.

Truly yrs

Joshua L. Chamberlain

[UMO]

〰 TO FANNIE HARDY ECKSTORM

Portland Maine
April 28th 1909

Dear Madam:

You wish for my testimony as to the identification of the house in which I was born. I have been audibly informed that this is the one-story house with a little garden in front near the sand-bank on North Main Street, Brewer.[122] What I can remember of these early days is the odor of the roses at the front door. That abides.

Gratefully yours

Joshua L. Chamberlain

[UMO]

〰 TO FANNIE HARDY ECKSTORM

Portland
May 5 1909

Dear Mrs Eckstorm;

You are quite right in correcting "novel" to "noble" in the "copy" I returned. I did not read it intelligently. It occurs to me to ask why you cannot (if

---

121. Bowdoin and Pennsylvania (now Gettysburg) Colleges so honored him shortly after the war.

122. The house, enlarged at the turn of the century, stands at 350 Main Street. Trulock, 404 n. 7.

the result as a picture would be better) *take* the old "Chamberlain house" and say "This House was the *early home*" &c?[123] This may not suit your purpose and idea so well it is true.

Another way must be to wait till the changes in the "Cottage" are completed, & *then* take a new picture of this place for your use in the plan proposed.

I think the photo you have referred to is rather remarkably poor, is it not?

You are [doing] me much honor and I [appreciate] it.

Sincerely y[our]s

Joshua L. Chamberlain

[UMO]

≈ TO FANNIE HARDY ECKSTORM

Portland May 10 1909

Dear Mrs Eckstorm:

The old house was not my birthplace. This was the "Cottage" you speak of. But the old house was in a very true sense my childhood house. It was, and is, the old "Chamberlain Homestead." I think you would be justified in presenting this as my early house. The photo you speak of is under consideration by the State commission for enlargement & to be placed in the State House, is not at all worthy of any respect or regard. It was made "surreptitiously" for a plate I entirely rejected and forbid to be used. There are others proper for use such as you contemplate, — one in particular made by Chickery of Boston. I will try to have a copy made which you can see and judge of.

My sister wishes for one for her house, and I will try to have one made, & sent to her soon.

You are taking too much trouble in doing me this honor.

With best wishes for all

Yours affectionately

Joshua L. Chamberlain

[UMO]

123. By the time Chamberlain was six years old, his father had built a new, two-story frame house on their farm road. Its address is now 80 Chamberlain Street, Brewer. Trulock, 27–28, 404 n. 8.

Portland

June 25 1909

Dear Major:

Frye will come, but does not wish to *promise* to speak.[124] Hale will also come and will speak. Governor Fernald[125] & members of the Council & staff will attend. I have not yet got hold of *King*.[126] He is somewhere about Maine. I am trying to get hold of him.

I had sketched a poem for inscription [on tablet]: but it is a poor one, even after trying to incorporate some lines of yours.

When we begin to be specific in enumerating the offices we are troubled at the space required.

I thought some reference to his robust manhood should be made. I will try again in getting home this evening, and will send result.

yours truly

J. L. Chamberlain

I note with pleasure your personal references, as to our home circle & paper, respectively. yours. C.

[MHS]

❦ TO JOHN P. NICHOLSON

Brunswick Maine

June 28 1909

Dear Colonel:

I am going to take my whole family — son & daughter, son-in-law & three "grand-daughters" — to Gettysburg by way of Baltimore after a Sunday at Newport News, reaching Gettysburg Monday afternoon *July 5th*. Naturally we go to the Eagle Hotel. I am not sure that the commissioners there know me; and a word from you to them might be of assistance to me in letting my people see as much as possible of what has been done on that great field. I trust this may not trouble you too much. Should be glad if you happened to be there too, but am not expecting this as such hot weather as we are likely to have.

---

124. At the centennial celebration of Hannibal Hamlin's birth, to be held in his native Paris Hill, Maine.

125. Bert Manfred Fernald (1858–1926), Republican governor of Maine. *BioDictGovr*, 2:625–26.

126. Perhaps Justice Arno W. King (1855–1918) of the Supreme Judicial Court. *WhoAm*, 677.

Faithfully yours
Joshua L. Chamberlain

[HL]

🙢 TO HENRY SWEETSER BURRAGE

Portland, Aug. 20, 1909

Dear Major Burrage:—

As to the program for the exercises at Paris Hill, I have [no] advice from any quarter. Have you made up one? I should like to form some judgment as to the best order of sequence, and also the time which can be given to the speakers respectively.

Moreover, we wish to know the hour at which it will be necessary to conclude our exercises in order that our people can get home that night. We announce that we begin at 12.30 sharp. If I am to preside, that will be the moment when we begin, unless all is in confusion then, by reason of arriving crowds late for the service. The exercises are likely to consume at the least two hours. We are to have an opening prayer, I suppose: and some music from the band. [W]ith the poem, we are to have five speakers. If Senator Frye is present, (as he told me he would try to be,) h[e] of course must say a few words. I should not take more than five minutes at the introduction, nor more than one minute each in introducing the speakers. This at the strictest reckoning, would use up two hours, giving the average of twenty minutes to each.

But some speakers will inevitably take more time. We shall have to allow for the exercises three hours. This will be tedious, and may crowd the returning visitors in reaching their trains. We need much arranging before hand. I go up on the afternoon of the 26[th].

Kindly give me the judgment of yourself and General Connor;[127] or lay out the matter as you thin[k] it should be, for us to work over a little.

yours truly
Joshua L. Chamberlain
(Brunswick Saturday Ev[enin]g & Sunday)

[MHS]

127. Selden Connor, see 7 Mar. 1876 to Hyde.

Portland
Aug 23 '09

Dear Major Burrage:

Thanks for your letter. You may be sure I "will insist on promptness," But other elements than the *speakers* enter into the problem,—such as I cannot control. If the local committees, or those arranging for the ceremonies or to arriving & seating of guests & the assembly generally, are slack, I cannot "help myself." We cant begin in confusion.

Shall we have one piece by the band between Gov. Long.[128] & Senator Hale? This would be a relief to the audience. The Band should not exceed five minutes. Will there be no printed program? How [to] indicate the unveiling & the Band concert &c? If we do not have the printed program I may have to take some time in announcing & informing &c.

Who is the poet? I took no minute of his name & residence. Have you notified the speakers how & when to come?

yours
J. L. C.

[MHS]

≋ TO JOHN P. NICHOLSON

Portland, Maine,
Sept 4 1909

Dear Col. Nicholson;

I have to thank you for your prompt response to my request for the copies of the Lincoln Memorial [services]. The poem given on that occasion is a remarkable one.

I am honored by your request for two copies of the reprint I had [made] of my own part there.[129] I will send them gladly. I had but few, and only half of them found—the others being in loose sheets for binding in with other papers.

I will try to hold on to two of the bound pamphlets for you. You certainly deserve the best,—if you do me the honor to care for the paper at all.

---

128. Perhaps John D. Long (1838–1915), a former Massachusetts governor and congressman born in Buckfield, Maine, a few miles from Hamlin's birthplace. *DAB*, 11:377–78; *BioDictGovr*, 2:713–14.

129. Chamberlain, "Abraham Lincoln Seen from the Field," see 8 and 24 Feb. 1909 to Burrage.

I should be glad to find myself able to attend the meeting of the Commandery in chief. Am trying to do so.

Yours as ever

Joshua L. Chamberlain

[HL]

TO ROBERT E. PEARY

Portland Oct. 5th 1909

Commander Robert E. Peary:[130]

Dear Friend:

I should have been of the first to greet you on your return from so ard[u]-ous a task triumphant and honored, as you deserve, had I not been entirely disabled by the recurring consequences of my old war wounds. I regret much not to be able to avail myself of the opportunity given by the visit of our Boarding officer's launch this morning to pay my respects to you in person: but have to send my deputy instead who appreciates the privilege.

Be assured I am of those whose faith in your deed as well as your word admits no doubt or [diminution]. The first honors are yours, and we are all proud of you.

I shall take the first opportunity to see you.

Yours as ever

Joshua L. Chamberlain

[BSC]

TO CHRISTOPHER C. ANDREWS

Copy   Portland, Maine, December 4, 1909.

General C. C. Andrews,[131]

St. Paul, Minn.

Dear General:—

I have had under careful consideration the army "retirement" propositions in your several letters recently received, and I appreciate all your suggestions.

The propositions thus far presented to Congress have brought out many difficulties. In the "omnibus" plans the scope was so wide that the Congress

---

130. Robert Edwin Peary (1856–1920) of the U.S. Navy, the Bowdoin-educated explorer who had just led the first successful expedition to the North Pole. "Peary, Robert Edwin" *BOL* (456/39).

131. Bvt. Maj. Gen. Christopher Columbus Andrews (1829–1922), a Minnesota forest commissioner. *GB* 8–9.

shrunk at the total figures called for. The objection was also raised that this scheme was virtually a pension measure. The rank and age limits were also object[ed] to as relatively unjust to merit. In the case of a special list on a basis involving distinction between those of similar rank, this encountered criticism and opposition by others who thought their claims of equal merit with those named, and that this plan deserved to be defeated on its own grounds, unless the list were largely extended to include all of similar army rank. But this, again, would be opposed in Congress as too widely inclusive for practical acceptance.

For my own part, I have looked upon a restoration to the rolls of the army and retirement thereunder as a mark of honor, and quite removed from a mere pension measure. For the conferring of such an honor there must, of course, be a proper bias and reason. This, no doubt, involves making a distinction among those of similar rank, which would probably be objected to by some as unequal and unjust.

There are two qualifications or tests which could not well be regarded as invidious: First, the command of tro[o]ps in the field in actual operations of war; and Second, command exceeding that corresponding to an officer's lineal rank and pay. If a selection is made among these in starting a "retirement" measure, the limit might first be set at the command of a Division in the field. There are substantial reasons for these considerations in equity and justice. The responsibilities and exposures, and in the latter case the pecuniary expenses demanded beyond those contemplated by the laws and customs of the service as appropriate to line rank, which are experienced by such officers are proper grounds of distinction not relating to the character, quality, or ability of any, and therefore not liable to excite criticism as invidious.

I should feel honored in being on such a list of retired officers of the army.

Your suggestion that my name at the head of either of the petitions proposed would give strength to the measure, I take as a compliment. But would not this detract from my "strength" if the proposition were not acceptable to the Congress, and waste or lessen my influence in any other less objectionable plan of action?

I do not like to apply for an increase of pension, although I am doubtless entitled to it. And I must not put myself on a petition which would not be favored by the Senators of my state. I have had considerable correspondence with them first and last, and have acted under their advice. I feel that I must submit any proposal of mine to them before placing it before the Congress. I am now again consulting them on the subject.

I trust that this statement of my views and feelings will be understood by you in its motive, and that it may possibly be of service in laying out a movement to open the way for the recognition of meritorious officers by appropriate action of the Government.

I am, faithfully yours,
Joshua L. Chamberlain

[MHS]

≈ TO ROSAMUND ALLEN

Portland
Dec. 27th 1909.

Dear Rosamund:—

How lovely and dear your letter to Gennie is! I shall keep it among my treasured things. You must come to me in the summer, with the birds and flowers, when all brown-eyed things are building their nests. We will build some too!

Your loving
Gennie.

[PHS]

≈ TO OLIVER W. NORTON

(COPY)

Portland, Maine,
Jany. 15, 1910.

Lieut. O. W. Norton,[132]
Chicago, Illinois,
Dear friend:

It seems like "old times" and the days of great things to see your name and to read your words so calmly and truthfully written, concerning Gettysburg and Vincent.

I thank you for your able gathering of facts and for the conclusions that inevitably follow and which are so clearly and forcibly stated by you.

I regret that these compel us to take account of the incidents connected with the action of the regiment on the right of our brigade, some of the consequences of which led to so great a loss to the service as the fall of Vincent. He was a noble man, and I have not known an abler commander in his grade.

---

132. Oliver W. Norton (1839–1920), a former private in the 83rd Pennsylvania and lieutenant in the 8th U.S. Colored Infantry who wrote numerous works of Civil War reminiscence, including *The Attack and Defense of Little Round Top, Gettysburg, July 2, 1863*, which aroused the Melcher-Chamberlain controversy. His *Strong Vincent and His Brigade at Gettysburg, July 2, 1863* (Chicago, 1909) had just been published. Pullen, 140; *National Cyclopaedia*, 19:153.

Nothing could exceed his skill and energy in taking the position on Little Round Top and the confidence he inspired in his subordinates. To this the result of the fight on the left at Round Top is very largely due.

I shall preserve and value your book on Vincent and Gettysburg, for its intrinsic merit, as well as for your kindness in sending me this souvenir of our personal comradeship.

With all best memories and wishes, yours,

(Signed), Joshua L. Chamberlain.

[CMU]

☙ TO ALEXANDER T. LAUGHLIN

Portland, Maine, Jan. 19th 1910.

A. T. Laughlin, Esq.[133]

My dear Sir:—

The respected and honored names on your circular calling for contributions to enable the Committee acting under the auspices of Messrs Chapman and Alexander[134] to relieve the poor of Portland, lead me to explain why I am unable to respond as you evidently expected me to do.

I am a regular Contributor to several associations which are devoted to this very work, among them The Portland Provident Society, The Salvation Army, and four or five others of like character or purpose.

I have recently doubled my usual contributions to these worthy causes. I do not quite see the occasion for our friends to over-lay this work by measures which might seem to rebuke our citizens for default of duty in this respect.

Those who have not been called upon by other agencies to contribute in this way, may have a duty about it; but I must content myself with going to the very extent of my ability already in the directions named.

With high regard,

Sincerely yours,

Joshua L. Chamberlain

[MHS]

133. Alexander T. Laughlin (b. 1856), a food company president active in Portland charities.

134. Perhaps Henry Leland Chapman, see 20 May 1913 Draft Report; Alexander is unidentified.

Portland

January 27th 1910

Dear Carrie:

I send you the picture of "Sir Galahad" which I have had in my room at the Falmouth Hotel for eight or nine years. It is by Watts.[135] [ill.] It is one of my famous pictures. It represents Sir Galahad when he first perceives the sight of the Holy Grail. You see he has dismounted out of deference in the presence of a superior. And he stands in reverence with bowed head as before the divine, — his hands clasped as in prayer, on his face rapt expression of thanksgiving at the fulfillment of his wish, — the triumph of his quest.[136]

Do you see that the horse also has bowed his head, as partaken of this, reverence & this [gratitude]!

I want *you* to have this picture for your companionship, as it has been for mine.

With all best thoughts and thanks,

yours

Joshua L. Chamberlain

[BSC]

TO EUGENE HALE

Copy

Portland Maine

Jany 29 1910

(*also Senator Frye*)

Hon. Eugene Hale,

U.S. Senator;

My dear Senator: —

As you are aware I have not joined in any of the recent proposals for the "retirement" of Officers of Volunteers in the civil war. This was because I saw that their scope was so large that the Congress could not undertake such a burden for the treasury in its existing condition. I am now again urged to join in an application for the restoration to the rolls of the army and retirement thereunder of certain general officers of volunteers of advanced rank and age.

I hesitate at joining in even this; not thinking that mere rank or mere

135. George Frederic Watts (1817–1904), a London pre-Raphaelite artist. "Sir Galahad," his best known painting, was exhibited at the Royal Academy in 1862. Prints of it were widely available. Girouard, *The Return to Camelot*, 150–53, 175–76.

136. Watts actually intended to portray Galahad resting in a forest during his quest for the Grail.

age, nor both together, with the added circumstance of slender pecuniary resources, would be proper warrant for asking to be placed on "retired" rank and pay on the rolls of the army. I think that merit or service should be a prime consideration. I have suggested to those now about to petition Congress for their restoration to the army as "retired" officers, that two tests or limits might be set for such action: First, a command exceeding that appropriate to the rank and pay of the officer under consideration. The limit might properly be set at Division Commanders, to begin with.

There are grounds of equity and justice in this measure. The added responsibilities and scale and burden of service, and especially, the increased expense demanded by the necessities and customs of the service, for officers commanding in the higher grades, seem to make it reasonable that the pay, or some pecuniary remuneration, should be proportioned to the command exercised, rather than to the mere lineal rank.

On that basis I made an application myself for restoration and retirement on the rolls of the army, two years ago; but withdrew it in order not to interfere with the plans and wishes of my colleagues of the old army, who were proposing general "retireme[n]t" bills to the Congress.

I write now to ask your kind consideration and advice as to what is my duty or best course in regard to proposal for a petition to Congress for the recognition and retirement of a group of officers of high command and service in the war for the Union.

I beg to ask your notice of a copy of a letter recently sent by me in reply to requests from some of my old companions in arms.

With high regard,
yours respectfully,
Joshua L. Chamberlain

[MHS]

TO SAE

February 25th 1910

My dear Sae:

Here I am after an evening with the Bowdoin Boys with an address before the Y.M.C.A. of the College in the Chapel. The snow is two feet deep around my house and as I cant get the key into it I return to the hotel where I spent the night — and very comfortably.

My subject was *The Power of the Cherished Thought*. The boys came out in such numbers that we had to adjourn from the Lecture Room to the Chapel, — the association with which stirred merry thoughts for me. The students received me with most marked & unusual courtesies. [T]he entire assembly rose on my entrance & remained standing until I was seated, & the greeting was repeated with emphasis at the conclusion of my address.

My house does not seem to have been disturbed in any way. How it will be when the snow melts on the roof & the rains come I do not know.

We are all well in our cottage in Portland. Wouldnt it be a good thing for Alice to come over? It is very comfortable here.

I trust you are well; but I am still a little worried about you all. Prof. Robinson is prostrated with over-strain of nervous "system," and will have to give up — probably.[137] I shall try to mail this on the train I meet in going back to Portland. I think I can pretty well; but dont like slippery walking.

Much love to you all, & hoping to see you at #211 Ocean.

your affectionate brother.

Lawrence

[UMO]

≈ TO HENRY SWEETSER BURRAGE

Portland

March 23ᵈ 1910

Dear Major Burrage:

I feel the honor of being so often selected to act on memorial tributes to our deceased companions, & especially do I feel the propriety of my assignment for the paper on Major Small. But besides the preparation of the paper itself, which so largely falls to me, I have to hold correspondence not only with the family, but with each & every associate on the Committee, involving, as in the present case, writing at least six letters, before we get to the final meeting of the Committee.

So you see it is no small task & cost when these sad occasions come so often as they do.

You must have patience with me. I am very busy in these days; &, really, it is not easy to find time & spirit to write a letter. I will try to get at the committee in a few days.

Truly yours,

Joshua L. Chamberlain

[MHS]

137. Franklin Clement Robinson (1852–1910), Josiah Little Professor of Natural Sciences, had taught at Bowdoin since his 1873 graduation. He died that May.

[March 31, 1910]
Boston, Mass.

My Dear Captain; — [138]

I cannot thank you enough for your thoughtful kindness in sending me Col. Haskell's sketch of the battle of Gettysburg which you have made into a beautiful book.[139] It came to my desk while I was under great disability and suffering in my home here, and getting out only yesterday, found it waiting at my office in Portland.

I have now read the book with deepest interest, and cannot delay letting you know how highly I appreciate it. It presents a part of the field and the fight, which I had before no exact or detailed knowledge of, but not only do its graphic descriptions give a vivid picture, but the comments and criticisms of somewhat wider scale so perfectly agree with what I do know of the battle in general, that the perusal gives me peculiar gratification, moreover the presentation of the subject is a masterly piece of scenes in soldierly spirit and [original] suggestions, I do not know its equal in the range of Gettysburg literature. I wish I could have know[n] the man as he was in the field. There was a place for such a man in my heart as well as by my side.

I thank you again for giving me this pleasure, shadowed as it is by the though[t] that his gallant spirit went out free as of dire Cold Harbor. But the book I shall keep by me among cherished things. I would be glad to see the expurgated paragraphs, I know I should [e]ndorse them.

With best regards,
(sgd) Joshua L. Chamberlain

[LC]

138. Perhaps Charles O. Hunt of the 5th Maine Battery, wounded at Gettysburg. MAG, 101, 125.

139. Franklin Aretas Haskell (1828–64) of the 36th Wisconsin was an Iron Brigade staff officer who wrote a narrative immediately after Gettysburg that the Massachusetts Loyal Legion printed in 1908. Several other editions exist. Richard Harwell, *Two Views of Gettysburg, by Sir Arthur J. L. Fremantle and Frank A. Haskell* (Chicago: Lakeside Press, 1964), xxxii–xxxix.

TO CHARLES HUNT

Copy.   Portland, Maine. May 3, 1910.

Captain Charles Hunt,

Boston, Mass.

My dear Captain:—

I thank you for the courtesy shown in your request for my permission to publish my letter commending Colonel Haskell's book.

I had not particularly noticed the strictures on the conduct of Webb's brigade in that battle. General Webb is my very particular friend, and my attention has been called to the charge of a lack of truth in Colonel Haskell's statement in reference to the behavior of his brigade in this battle. Had I known of this being inaccurately given in Haskell's book, I should not have expressed myself precisely as I did in my letter. As my letter stands, I seem to be endorsing Colonel Haskell's criticism of this brigade, and of General Webb, with a knowledge of the facts. Under these circumstances, I should not like to have my letter published, as I should have to explain or partially retract such portions of the letter as might seem to bear upon the conduct of Webb's brigade. This would be unfortunate. I do no[t] like to be drawn into dissensions among my old comrades, and therefore would desire you to consider my letter of March 31st as private and personal,

Very truly yours,

Joshua L. Chamberlain

[LC]

TO AURESTUS S. PERHAM

Portland Maine

July 15, 1910

Dear Major Perham:

I thank you for your letter and for the enclosed copy of your article. I have always been inclined to think well of Col McElroy,[140] and was not aware of his strictures on Genl Warren, or indeed those on Generals Howard and Burnside.[141] He should be willing to correct any mis-statements, or erroneous judgments, if his attention is called to the facts. I dont know what effect on the public mind Gen'l Schurz's reference to Chancellorsville may have. The whole matter of the 11th Corps & Chancellorsville[142] is most unfortunate, for

---

140. Unidentified.

141. Ambrose E. Burnside (1824–81), see 19 Oct. 1910 to Burrage.

142. Howard ignored Hooker's orders to protect his XI Corps' exposed flank, think-

it opens criticism which are not easily rebutted. Your work on the question is well done, and shows the loyal spirit and truth-loving mind.

I am fairly well, & thank you for your kind interest.

yours as ever

Joshua L. Chamberlain

〰️ TO GRACE

Portland

Oct 13, 1910

Dearest Gracie:

Wyllys told me of your accident and present condition last [evening].[143] I had not "dreamed" of this after your splendid mastery of the Gettysburg trip. I was sorry I had sent you a letter seeming peremptory in its demand for information about your time of coming. I only wished to know if I could get over to Bangor and back here before you could come. Now, I dont know how badly off you are; but presume pretty seriously disabled. I fear it, anyway. Never mind! We will have our "good time" at the right time. I am pressed on all sides to make engagements just for those five days; but am not inclined to engage myself for anything just now. We are holding the old house "in commission" as yet, and do not like to disturb its arrangements while it may yet be possible for you to come over in season to enjoy it. We have plenty of "wood and water" & coal there, if we should need to use them.

But do not try to crowd yourself to recover faster than "nature" will advise. [W]e are really not dependent on al[ma]nacs.

But I would much wish to know how you are—if not how you came so.

I dined with Mrs Merriam and *and the General*, yesterday at the Lafayette. I had a "phone" from Mrs M. saying they were at the Hotel for the winter, & I went right up to see them. The General has a surprising "relapse" of good health, and is able to walk about a little—even out of doors. But feebly!

They all sent messages of love & solicitude to you, and hoped yet to see you before very long. Thanks for box for Wyllys & the "things" for me, which I somehow left with you.

Will write you soon again.

---

ing it guarded by thick woods, and was routed by Stonewall Jackson. McPherson, *Battle Cry of Freedom*, 642.

143. Grace had been pinned between an automobile and a stone wall. Her knee was severely injured, leaving her permanently lame. Smith, *Fanny and Joshua*, 339.

Gennie

P.S. The Chicago "Chamberlins" were charmed with all our things—&
us too!

So they said. The Dr. gave me some most excellent advice and
prescriptions. Says he will come over from Chicago to see me at any
moment I need him. Chapman—the Festival Director[144]—praised me in
public—in a most extraordinary manner,—as his temperament leads him
to do in all he does—because he saw me in an audience at the "Rehearsal"
yesterday forenoon. I could not attend the whole course—and only "took
in" the rehearsal. It was fine and all his work in Maine is praiseworthy.

I am pretty well, & getting better. Wyllys well. L not very. G.

[SL]

≋ TO HENRY SWEETSER BURRAGE

Portland
October 19th 1910

Dear Major Burrage:

Returning from a few day's absence from my office, I found on my table
the copy of your account of "*Burnside's East Tennessee Campaign*,"[145] which
you were so kind as to send me. It is an exceedingly valuable and interesting
paper, and I must be allowed to congratulate you on the composition and the
"style" of it.

You have done justice to a most deserving commander also; and I am glad
to see this.

I desire to lose no time in thanking you for the paper and the courtesy in
sending me a copy of it; and hence have to write this rather hurriedly. But it
is not a hasty judgment I have formed. Your paper is every way admirable.

Yours as ever

Joshua L. Chamberlain

[MHS]

144. Chapman is otherwise unidentified.

145. After the disaster at Fredericksburg, Burnside had one of his two Civil War suc-
cesses in defending Knoxville from Longstreet's attack in late summer of 1863. GB, 57–58;
CWD, 107–8.

Portland, Maine, December 9th 1910.

To The Honorable
Frederick W. Plaisted,
Governor Elect of Maine;[146]
Sir:—

I do not know to what extent the records and files of the Executiv[e] Department of the State will acquaint you with the action thus far taken and that further proposed by the Commission on the Fiftieth Anniversary of the Battle of Gettysburg, July 1913.

As this may properly be a matter to which you would wish to call the attention of the Legislature, I beg leave to transmit to you several papers relating to this proposed celebration, including the action there upon by the State of Pennsylvania and that of the Congress of the United States.

Govern[o]r Fernald[147] has so far recognized this proposal as to appoint me as member of this Commission for the State of Maine; which appointment I have accepted. But as our state has not yet had opportunity to confirm the action taken by the Governor, I have not felt at liberty to assume official responsibility as member of this Commission, and have taken such part only as courtesy demanded.

I desire to submit to your direction and wishes all matters concerning the representation of Maine by me on this Commission.

Very respectfully
Your obedient servant,
Joshua L. Chamberlain
Four Enclosures.

[MHS]

146. Frederick W. Plaisted (1865–1943), the first Democrat to govern Maine since his father Harris Merrill Plaisted's term ended in 1883. *Maine*, 375, 377; MSL (govs).
147. Bert Fernald, see 25 June 1909 to Burrage.

Portland Maine
Jany 12 1911

Professor _____
Truman H. Bartlett,[148]
Boston Mass
My dear Sir:

I cannot thank you enough for the instruction and delight you have given me in the article on Lincoln's portraiture. I have studied it with intense interest; and this not only in the subject itself, but in your masterly interpretation. I have hitherto felt an uncomfortable look in all that I have seen of attempts to represent the personality of Lincoln. Your analytical demonstration and high conclusion have given me light and cheer.

Nothing that I have seen of Lincoln portraiture gives the spirituality thereon in his face like the early mask which you show. And the photograph taken before the Gettysburg speech speaks a *presence* of dignity and [honor], of superior [light], although something is lacking in the ~~expression of the~~ face to sustain the impression.

I shall have these sheets so kindly sent me bound up with some pamphlets I am preserving.

To acknowledge my own short-comings, I take the liberty to send you an address I gave ~~a great audience~~ in Philadelphia on the centennial of Lincoln's birth.[149]

Truly yours,

[BSC]

148. Truman Howe Bartlett (1835–1923), a sculptor and former professor of art at MIT, was one of the early students of Lincoln portraiture. His "The Portraits of Lincoln" had been included in a new edition of Carl Schurz's famous essay, *Abraham Lincoln: A Biographical Essay* (Boston, 1907). Myers, *McGraw-Hill Dictionary of Art*, 251; Peterson, *Lincoln in American Memory*, 146, 211, 417 n. 9.

149. See 8 and 20 Feb. 1909 letters to Burrage.

TO SAMUEL ABBOTT

Portland, Maine. January 31, 1911.

Samuel Abbott, Esq.[150]
Boston, Mass.
Dear Friend: —

I thank you for sending me your little book advocating the establishment of the "Order of the Blue and Gray." Your thought is beautifully conceived and expressed. The sentiment appealed to is a noble one, — perhaps the highest in our human nature.[151]

As to the relation of this to other sentiments bearing upon our practical life, and especially involved in our War for the Union, my thought runs like this: We were fighting for our Country, with all that this involves, — not only for the defence of its institutions, but for the realization of its vital principles and declared ideals. The crisis marked not merely an incident of time, but a momentum of force in the nation's life. The fight to preserve it from destruction has a historical, if not moral, value which should not be lost sight of. I am not in sympathy with any movement or proposition which would deny, obscure or ignore that fact.

At the same time, no one must doubt the heartiness and wholeness with which I recognize the manhood, the brotherhood, and the deep unity of a common faith with our own, on the part of those against whom we had to carry our contention to the triumphant end. That has been the spirit of my feeling and action from the moment of the surrender at Appomattox.[152] The meaning of the Old Flag, — the honor of our Country and the love of our fellow men, — holds us broad now, as before.[153] In all that belongs to this I am with you heartily.

Faithfully yours,
Joshua L. Chamberlain

[BSC]

150. Perhaps Samuel A. B. Abbott (1846–1931), a Boston lawyer active in MOLLUS. *DAB*, 1:25–26.

151. In his draft, Chamberlain added, "and the realization of it should be our constant aim."

152. The draft includes the following two sentences: "I welcome forward, on terms of manhood, our returning brethren. Bitterness and narrowness have no place with me."

153. See Chamberlain, "The Old Flag."

~TO GEORGE T. EDWARDS

Draft copy.   Portland, Maine, February 7th 1911.

George T. Edwards, Esq.[154]

Portland;

Dear Mr. Edwards:—

I think the observance of Longfellow Day in our public schools by authority of law, as you propose, would be very profitable for the children and the community.

Its benefits would extend beyond the direct effects. These exercises would invite and involve not only the broadening of knowledge and literary culture; but also the encouragement of noble sentiments,—an important part of education, the object of which is to cultivate the best powers and fit for worthy life and action.

Sincerely yours,

Joshua L. Chamberlain

[BSC]

~TO GRACE

Apr. 26th, 1911.

Dearest Gracie

Thanks for the letter. Am sorry the leg is troubling you:—too much rushing about, or the cold?

As for me I have been "uncommonly well"—as the English would say—and am so still. We have had two or three fine sunny days, but rather cool winds. So it is fine *in the house* looking out into the sunshine flooding the fields.

. . . . .

I shall go over to Brunswick tomorrow & hunt up the paper to quiet [ill.], and may go over to Bath to make some arrangements with the steamer *Alliquippa* & the Hotel Alliquippa at Small Point Harbor to join interests for the season. This boat runs from New Meadows River bridge to Small Point. I am one of the Trustees for the syndicate owning Small Point, you know; and the others think I am the least business man among them!!

We have not fixed on the time for our [Gettysburg] Trip, but it will come towards the last of May.

154. George Thomas Edwards (1868–1932), a Maine author and composer who wrote *The Youthful Haunts of Longfellow* and set many of Longfellow's poems to music. *WhoAm*, 360–61.

The Board of Trade want to join the party making the European excursion (Boston Chamber of Commerce) but I cant, much as I would like it.

Wyllys is doing quite well, but things wear upon him — I can see.

It may not be wholly *business*. We have pleasant callers, & fine music, very often. *Gardening* begins now. There is a green sheen over the fields, & [crocuses] are pushing up.

Rosamunds bright little letters make good cheer. I will answer her soon.

Best wishes for your anniversary. Wish I could come up. W. comes in & sends *love* so do all in the house, [including]

Gennie

[SL]

🌊TO GRACE

Portland, May 6 1911

Dearest:

I must send you Sae's good letter. I wrote her at once on hearing of the fire in Bangor telling her not to work or worry too much, — as I feared she would take occasion to do.

We are all hard a[t] work in these beautiful days, — making a garden & brightening things in and about the house.

Everything seems right in the dear old home. Will have it ready for you when you can come.

I suppose I shall have to go to Gettysburg in a week or two. Really do not want to go now. But by steam to Baltimore it may be not too hard & [paining?].

We are to have a "new girl" — a woman of experience, next week.

I am getting many letters praising my papers on war matters & especially the Lincoln Address.

I am "*quite*" well & in the sense of *very*.

Love always

Gennie

[SL]

✎ TO HENRY SWEETSER BURRAGE

211 Ocean Ave
Portland
Nov 8 1911

Dear Major Burrage,

Your kindly letter—among the first that came to me while prostrated at my sea-side place,—deserves to be, as it is, take[n] up among the first for response at my own hand.

I made myself able to be taken (by aid of automobiles) to my little winter-home here, two or three weeks ago, where Dr Shaw is keeping me close under orders to "*keep still*" in all ways—and *at all costs*!

I say this last, because my temperament & habit incline and almost impel me to use my strength as fast as it comes, in active exercise,—for some good, if possible, to others.

This slow recovery tasks my patience, and so my recuperative energies.

But I think I shall "arrive." Your constant friendship is valued, and as you know reciprocated.

I hope to see you at the next meeting of our Commandery, but am not sure of it—not being quite my own master.

yours as ever
Joshua L. Chamberlain

[MHS]

✎ TO LEON B. STROUT

211 Ocean Avenue
Portland Maine
Dec 9 1911

Mr L. B. Strout,[155]
Brunswick,
My dear Sir;

I found a few days ago on looking in at my office the picture you so kindly left there in the care of my deputy, and I was glad for such a greeting on being able get into my chair there after so long a detention in my bed and house in town.

It is a striking and strong picture; and presents a pose rather new in pictures of me, and gives, I judge, rather a characteristic aspect. If I had been wise, or shrewd, enough not to show so much *neck*, it might have been better

---

155. Strout apparently was a Maine photographer or painter.

for what you wanted to get. However, your work is good, and justifies the pains you took to secure best results.

I am obliged to you and your good wife for your interest and care.

I trust we can have another meeting in my Brunswick house some time in the early summer. I am trying to "get well," although it comes slowly.

Sincerely yours

Joshua L. Chamberlain

[BSC]

〰 TO GRACE

Saturday noon
Dec. 9th 1911

Dearest Gracie:

Yes, they were glorious days, and on the 7th I swung in the Balcony hammocks for a couple of hours, after resting my spirit between the sun and the sea.

Your girls charmed us with their fine personalities, each lovely in her ways and words. Nothing to "Tire" any of us, but much to the contrary.

I took some pains to get acquainted with Eleanor. She is quite a distinct and decided personality, and cannot be judged, & ought not to be treated, by general rules and conventional regulations. She has a pretty well ascertained knowledge of herself, and to a remarkable degree knows as by instinct what is best for her, amidst various possibilities, and ways to attain her ideals. I think she would do well if allowed to follow her own ideas and inclinations pretty much. Her *studies*; at present, seem to engross her interest, and she is naturally impatient of anything that calls her away from her "devotions" in this line. It seems to me it would be well to let her have facilities for study in her own room, so that she could be uninterrupted, unless called to other proper home duties. Then, when with the family, in the home-rooms, she would be free to take part in the amenities of social and home life.

I rather think she should be allowed to "go to College," & have her choice as to which one. This point should soon be determined.

x   x   x

Beatrice does not seem quite well. It would have been well for her to have stayed a week or so more with us.

Gennie

We are expecting Sarah about Wednesday next.

[SL]

Portland Jany 8th 1912

Professor Henry Johnson
Brunswick, Maine,
Dear friend:

The fine verses on Courage so kindly sent me in my time of suffering at my sea-side place, in October last, have been "held in escrow" to await my recovery to a degree to permit acknowledgment. I have especially wished to get strength enough to hunt up (or *out*) some old verses of mine,—written during my feverish attempts at recovering from the "mortal wound," some 46 or more years ago, and now recalled to mind by your stirring suggestions.

I have made the search successful now, at last, and in thanking you for your generous interest, beg to enclose a copy of these old idealized experiences. You will see what notions I had of what might be called courage,—although I do not use the term.

Pardon the presumption in submitting these lines to the scrutiny of a master.

Yours with & for all the best,
Joshua L. Chamberlain

THE TROOPER'S LAST CHARGE.

Halt! grim foregathering host!
  Tested at dearest cost;
Strong with the souls' unlost.
  Ranks death cannot sunder.
Name your high name who can?
  Self ever under ban;
Manhood whose deeds for man
  Waken far wonder.
Rest! steed and rider, rest!
  Search hearts, and bid your best,
Ere the supreme behest
  Voices in roar and rattle.
Brace nerve! and clear brain!
  Hold calm the spirit's strain;
Weld thought in links of chain
  For iron front of battle!
Wrestlings of ages past
  On this the crowning cast:

Flames aloft across the vast
  Man's measureless ideal.
Imaging eternal light;
  Lighting through darkest night;
Charged with compelling might,
  Beckoning to the real.
Soon heaven and earth shall shake
  With the shock your stout hearts
  make,—
Stouter yet for some dear sake
  Your firm lips scarce can
  mutter.—
—What flies so swift and fast?
  What shrills in whirlwind blast?
Hail and Farewell! 'Tis come at last;
  The moment great and utter!
Fleet flag, and bugle shrill;
  Signaling the way and will!

Sabres and sinew thrill,
	Swept as by touch immortal.
Charge now! ye godlike throng.
	Forward! to right the wrong;
Give the pass-word swift and strong,
	Challenged at death's portal.
Straight for the level flash!
	Seething lead, and iron crash;
Right On! The tempest's lash
	And surge of men, too, breasting!
Archangels' trumpets ring;
	Cannon hosannas sing:
This the sword of Christ came to
	bring;—
	Truth so stra[n]gely testing.
Steady sways the blood-red cross;
	Midst where the banners toss;
Earth's joys can count but dross
	Where the soul is master.
Settles deep the darksome fight;
	Wraps in cloud the serried
	might,
Blazoned with young valor's
	light;—
	Defiant in disaster.
Close up! ye steadfast few!
	Where the battering blast cut
	through;
Rally! where your banner flew,—
	Now drenched with strange
	caressing.
Mortal sense is all in vain;
	Deathless hearts, on you the
	strain;

By such loss find life again;
	Turning bane to blessing!
On! let the last be first!
	Quench the fierce front's fiery
	thirst:
Vault the bars of death and burst
	Gates of hell asunder!
In! Let the flame-crests merge!
	Breast the all swallowing surge!
Ring sharp the steel bla[de]s' dirge
	For the brave lying under.
Ha! the cruel, crushing shot,
	Through my life-springs hissing
	hot:
Dark death-angel, beckon not
	Until I see the glory.
High above joy or pain,
	Deathless heart, ride still amain!
Body, bide the soul's disdain,
	Firm-faced tho' pierced and gory.
It is done,—what was to do!
	It is won,—what was the due!
Manhood's worth redeemed anew;
	God's truck of siege and foray.
Clear above my swimming view
	Gleams the guardian glory:
Floats the flag with meaning true:
	Starry white in heaven's blue;
Lanes of light leading thereto;
	Deep-bordered red, the high way
	through.
So runs my life's brief story!

[BSC]

〰 TO HENRY SWEETSER BURRAGE

Portland, March 18th 1912.

Dear Major Burrage;

I have to thank you for the helpful suggestions enclosed with your notification of the appointment of the Committee to raise funds for the Woman's

Memorial in Washingto[n]. I appreciate the courtesy of Commander Cilley[156] in placing me at the head of this committee. But the task laid upon the one expected to be the responsible manager of this very large committee is a heavy and costly one. It involves correspondence with each member to ascertain his convenience as to attending a meeting, and the subsequent call for the meeting, as well as very wide correspondence with other parties, societies, ne[w]spapers, and officials. A place for a first meeting, at least, must be secured, and at some expense, probably. I do not know how, even with the able assistance of the Portland members, I can in my present condition undertake to carry all this work. I have at present no type-writer, as formerly; and my office work exhausts my time and strength just now and for the rest of the month, at least. But I suppose there is some reason to wish me to serve at the first, as chairman; and I will at once try to get the widely scattered and admirably chosen committee together. Probably Portland will be the best, if not the only practicable place for the general meeting. I will try to secure a room suitable for the meeting, with necessary stationery[157] and other material for starting the business. We shall most likely have to get some printing done. Am I expected to pay all costs myself, or what a[u]thorization will be expected?

Could you send me some of the official letter-head paper for the prelimin[a]ry notices and calls?

Thanking you again for your thoughtful courtesy, I am very truly yours.
Joshua L. Chamberlain

[MHS]

≈ TO S. D. WALDRON

499 Ocean Avenue, Portland, Maine.
June 11th, 1912.

S.D. Waldron, Esq.
Gen'l. Passenger Agent.,
Maine Central Railroad Co.[158]
My dear Sir:—
I have to thank you for your courteous letter of the 8th inst. But I am chagrined to have seemed to you to be soliciting an exceptional personal favor.

---

156. Bvt. Brig. Gen. Jonathan P. Cilley (1835–1920) of the 1st Maine Cavalry, a Bowdoin graduate, lawyer, and legislator, was commander of the Maine Loyal Legion in 1912.

157. To read: To Honor the Loyal Women of 1861–1865 By Erecting in Washington, D.C., a Monument to their Memory. THE MOVEMENT HAS BEGUN. 12 May 1912 to Burrage, MHS.

158. Waldron is otherwise unidentified.

My ground was simply this: It is no uncommon thing for commutation tickets for railroad transportation to be sold to persons doing business in the city while residing in near-by towns.

I thought I was fairly of that description,—my home in the summer months being habitually in Brunswick, while my office and work were in Portland. Hence, I asked, as I supposed, for an ordinary privilege granted to citizens so circumstanced.

You say that your Company does not wish to open such privilege to the public, and hence my request is denied. That is "all right," I was not aware of that rule. I was perfectly aware of the State law which you quote; and even without it I have not been in the habit of begging favors for myself of anybody. And I am only mortified to think I seemed to ask for a favor which had to be denied on the ground of being contrary to law or against good morals. But I cannot plead ignorance of the law nor of the gospel; and so must stand rebuked. May I at least ask your pardon?

Sincerely yours,

Joshua L. Chamberlain

[MHS]

≋ TO MARION C. SHARTLE

Portland Maine
August 10th 1912

_____

Mrs. Marion Chapman Shartle;

American Embassy Berlin;[159]

Dear friend:

I have to moderate very much the terms in which I express the feeling with which I received your letter of remembrance and regard. I think I shall have to be permitted to say it was very "dear" in you to send me this message from the midst of the splendid surroundings which must (1) engage your attention and (2) command your interest. Possibly when I see you again I may be able to intimate to you some of the emotions called forth by the train of associations awakened by your kindly words. Many changes have passed around our paths since the meetings of Cairo and Naples;[160] but there are some things which environment and experience cannot change, and I am afraid you would not

159. Capt. and Mrs. Shartle are otherwise unidentified.

160. During his health voyage of 1900. See 25 Oct. 1900 letters to Hay and 5 Jan. 1901 to Sae.

[find] much improvement in me, in the lapse of years and the fleeting course of "things."

You ask me to think of you. You and Captain Shartle have had remarkable opportunities for a certain kind of [four words ill.], and study of different sphere[s] & plans of life. But after all you will have only tested your own ideals and filled out your own [spirited] purposes. You will be more perfectly yourselves. But we will see about all this when we meet again. I am very glad you [are] coming to Portland. I trust this means that Capt. Shartle will be appointed to a station near by.

You speak of "beautiful Brunswick." I shall be glad to welcome you in the storied old home of fifty years of my life which will rejoice to be opened to receive so distinguished & [blessed] guests. My current duties here have compelled me to close that house for a time, & take a modest little cottage-like place in the suburbs of this city, where I am made cheerful and encouraged to hold up long last.

I quite agree with you in your estimate and feeling about our Country & "heritage." The rage seems to be here for what they call the "progressive," but it is [ill.] to know in what [direction] & to what end the "progress" tends—I [ill.] here the things I can "hold fast," [having proved?]—

The photograph I will have for you at your old home, and perhaps would ask you to choose between one [breaking?]—free and easy mood, and one expressing some sober & sterner characteristics. You see I am expecting to see you in person, as well as to send [presentment?] to welcome your coming.

with high respect & regard

yours as ever,

J. L. C.

August 11th 1912
Portland Maine[161]
[SL]

➦ TO ELLIOTT T. DILL

Portland
Dec 13 1912

Dear General;

There were about seventy present at the last meeting of the "20th Maine vols." I should think half of them would "wish" to go to Gettysburg, and if their expenses were paid by the State & U.S., they *would* go.

161. In a margin, Chamberlain added: "You may be very sure I love, love so very much."

yours cordially

Joshua L. Chamberlain

[MSA]

〰 TO ELLIOTT T. DILL

Portland, Maine,
Dec. 17th 1912.

General Elliott T. Dill;—

Dear General;

I thank you for your kindly letter. I have no doubt of your willingness and ability to do everything possible to make things and people go right in the matter of the Gettysburg Fifty year celebration. But it will be impossible to prevent hundreds of old soldiers writing to me to give them some special attention. The mere answering of these letters would be beyond my power. And I need my time and strength for other imperative duties. Even without this Gettysburg business, my old-soldier applications for assist[a]nce in som[e] way or another gave me more than I could carry alone in the way of correspondence. Think of what must be done in the way of keeping account of each and all the men who are finally warranted as entitled and able to go to Gettysburg! And the thousand details connected with tickets, and journeying that must be attended to in some office here at home!

I will not weary you with more of this; but will enclose a letter just received from the Massachusetts Commission.

I have only this old type-writer to work with, and my own unpractised hands, this morning. Please excuse informalities.

Yours as ever,

Joshua L. Chamberlain

[MSA]

〰 TO ELLIOTT T. DILL

Portland, Dec. 20, 1912.

G[e]neral E.T. Dill;

Dear General:—

I see it stated in the New York Times of the 12th inst. that Congress has limited the number of veterans of Gettysburg to be provided for at the celebration next July, to 40,000 for the whole Country.

New Y[o]rk's quota on this basis, is said to be 7,000. I have not the whole number of troops from all the States to reckon Maine's quota from. But it must be much less than I had estimated as the number we should have to care for. You may be able to work this out.

I hasten to let you know about this statement. Can you inform Govern[o]r Haines[162] of this? It might be important for him to know. I have not time to write him this morning.

Yours respectfully,

Joshua L. Chamberlain

[MSA]

≫ TO ELLIOTT T. DILL

Portland, Maine, Jan. 24th 1913.

Dear General Dill; —

I thank you for your courtesy in sending me a copy of the proposed Resolve providing for participation by Maine in the Gettysburg 50th anniversary celebration,[163] as also for your kindly letter of information.

Is there any intention of limiting the application of the appropriation to those residents in Maine who participated in the Battle of G[ett]ysburg? It is not so stated; but might not the claim be set up that this is the meaning and intent of the resolve?

I should say the Resolve is all right, if it is clearly understood or expressed that the necessary official expenses of the State in carrying out the purposes of this Resolve are included in the application of the fund provided. I can ima[g]ine that some difficulty might arise if the amount fell short of providing for all veterans who might wish and be otherwise able to go.

Can we invite guests, such as Loyal [L]egion men, and members of military societies, under the provisions of this Resolve?

Pardon me if I seem too particular,

Ever yours obediently,

Joshua L. Chamberlain

[MSA]

162. William T. Haines (1854–1919), a Republican from Waterville, succeeded Frederick Plaisted as governor of Maine. *WhoAm*, 501.

163. The Resolve was still in the drafting stage. The intent was to provide travel, room, board, and medical care for all Gettysburg veterans then living in Maine, rather than veterans of Maine regiments, and for all head officers of the state organizations. State legislatures funded their own participation and Congress appropriated $150,000 to Pennsylvania's matching funds, but Pennsylvania had to triple its appropriation to properly host the reunion. Dill estimated that Maine would need to contribute $40,000, but the legislature only provided $18,000. 23 Jan., 25 Jan., and 26 Feb. 1913, Dill to Chamberlain, MSA; 23 June 1913, Beitler to Chamberlain, MSA.

499.
Mch 2^d 1913

Dearest Gracie:

It was a bad day yesterday, but I went out to finish up my financial matters on the first day of the month.

"Grace wanted us to have better dining chairs" — so I went and ordered six good pattern chairs which will greet you — & perhaps please you — on your next visit. To day I am trying to answer several letters that have been "lying about" for 3 weeks or more. You see my hand does not very well obey my mind & will in loving letters and words. I have to overcome, as well as I can, a tendency to slack formation of letters — To *indicate* rather than to *represent* what I wish to do. The *"Cosmopolitan"* — I am almost sorry to say, praised my [Gettysburg].[164] I almost hoped they would reject it so that I could have time to prepare it properly & have it published where it would be read by a different class. But there may be an advantage in the present arrangement, as I dont care how much they cut & garble. I shall have a better reason & opportunity to correct & improve. I find my strength strangely lessened. But I think I shall "keep on up" now, for good. The Colbys[165] were here yesterday afternoon, and told me [everything] is going on well about our place & lands &c.

They said "Mary" has made herself very unpopular by the domineering way in which she conducted her "church campaign." I am trying to read [Bergson] & Eucken.[166] Think I shall find great comfort in their views of philosophy & life & religion. I also am looking into the "Emmanuel" Movement in Boston. The Healing Power still practicable by followers of Christ. I have some ideas myself, which one will discuss when we meet again — soon!

Love to all
Gennie.

[SL]

164. "My Story of Fredericksburg" ran in the December 1912 edition of *Cosmopolitan*, but "Through Blood and Fire at Gettysburg" ran in *Hearst's Magazine*, not *Cosmopolitan*, in June 1913. (See 28 Aug. 1913 to Eckstorm.) Hearst owned both magazines and renamed and combined them at various times. Procter, *William Randolph Hearst*, 193; Swanberg, *Citizen Hearst*, 230, 276–77.

165. The Colbys are unidentified.

166. Henri-Louis Bergson (1859–1941) and Rudolf C. Eucken (1846–1926), Nobel laureate philosophers.

499 Ocean Avenue
Portland Maine
April 3^d 1913

Dear Judge Hale:[167]

I am very earnestly considering your very generous wish to have me with you on your visit to Gettysburg in May.

The condition I am in after a season of severe suffering from effects of old wounds rather dampens the ardor with which I should accept the honor of such company as you propose on a visit to a field of such memories and such momentous import in history.

I am somewhat depressed at finding that I cannot be so "sure of myself" as I have hitherto been favored to count upon with confidence. I have been "cut down" suddenly with severe attacks of pain and prostration when least looking for such experience, so I dare not be sure as to what I may be able to do at a given date ahead. But I am thinking of the last suggestion you made,— May 16, I think you said.

I am expected to go to [Gettysburg] officially in June, and would wish to make the proposed pleasant trip as early as we can before that.

I will communicate with you some more clearly and positively.

Sincerely & gratefully yours,

Joshua L. Chamberlain

[MHS]

≋ TO GRACE

[First half of 1913]

Dearest Gracie:

I am having an "*At Home*" season now, for the reception of special friends. Cant move my right arm, except to scribble this; and the pain makes me really sick.

I am summoned to an important meeting of the National Commission of Gettysburg Anniversary celebration, to be in Gettysburg on the evening of *May 14th* So the "Hale" plan so pleasingly arranged has to be modified. Dr Shaw & I to go *first* by the fast conveyance & the [party] of U.S. Judges to come on the 16th & meet us at Gettysb[ur]g. Now Doctor & I would have to leave on the 13^[th] at least or the 12th — if I am able to go at all. He thinks it best for me not to try to stop over in Boston.

---

167. Clarence Hale (1848–1934), a Bowdoin graduate and overseer, was a federal district judge.

Meantime I am not able even to go to my office—for the pain & disability. How long it will be [ill.] we cannot foresee. So you see I cannot come to Boston at present.

The "Thing" is for you to come & see us here, & help to judge whether I am able to go to Gettysburg, or, perhaps, to make me able to do so. So dont mind Lillian's suggestion of waiting a week, but come if you can someday soon. It is [very] hard for me to write.

yours

[SL]

∾ TO ELLIOTT T. DILL

Portland, Maine, April 10, 1913.

General Elliott T. Dill;

Dear General:—

I enclose the important Circular just received from the Pennsylvania Gettysburg Commission. You very likely have received the same. I have notified the Commission that you have kindly undertaken the burdensome part of what we have to do in Maine. But as I am on the official list, papers are likely to come to me, which I shall have to task your courtesy by referring to you for action. To avoid possible embarrassment, I think we, you and I, should have a plan in detail made up to facilitate action on the part of this State.

It might be be[s]ts for me to resign, and let the Governor[168] appoint you in the place. I could not possibly carry on the laborious task you have so kindly and efficiently entered upon. But if there is any advantage whatever for our State or people in having me remain on the Commission, I will so remain and take such part as I am able. I do not like to do so if this will compel us to duplicate our work or papers. I will cheerfully follow the wishes of the Governor and yourself in the matter.[169]

There are several points in this circular which call for immediate as well as continuous action. [I] should be glad to serve as practically your subordinate in this whole business, so far as our work in Maine is concerned.

As I have no other copy of the circular enclosed, I shall be glad, if you have another, to have this returned to me, when you are through with it.

Very respectfully yours,

Joshua L. Chamberlain

[MSA]

168. William T. Haines, see 20 Dec. 1912 to Dill.

169. Gov. Haines appointed Frederick Boothby (see letters below) to assist Chamberlain.

499 Ocean Avenue, Portland, April 25th 1913.

General Elliott T. Dill,

The Adjutant General,

Augusta, Maine.

Dear General:—

I have made diligent search among my books and papers for evidence in regard to the presence in the battle of Gettysburg, of Hosea B. Small, of Newport, and W. C. Keegan, of Lewiston.[170] I am entirely unable to certify as to the fact in either case. I will, however, make a statement of fact possibly bearing on the matter concerning participation in that battle by members of the 20th Regiment, Maine Volunteers.

We had very hard marching two or three days before that battle, and during this time quite a number of men became exhausted or disabled. To such I gave permission to "fall out" of the column of march with instructions to overtake us as soon as they were able, by following the wagon-trains by night, or in any other way they could. Several of these men,—I should say, most of them,—did come up on the morning of July 2nd, at Gettys[b]urg, and took their places in the ranks, and did their best, although by no m[ea]ns in perfect condition for duty. These men deserve special consideration and I hold them in such, whoever and wherever they may now be.

This give a good general ground for the state of the case in these i[n]-stances. It would account for their being reported "absent with leave" or not app[ea]ring for roll-call, on June 30th. They are supposed to be truthful [by] me, and I should give weight to their statements,—especially if these tallied with my notes and clear recollection as to general co[n]ditions. If they were in that battle under such circumstances, it would be a great wrong to them to bar them out of the privileges now offered to veterans of [G]ettysburg. While I cannot vouch for the truth of their claim, I should vote for i[t] in a court of inquiry.

Very truly yours,

Joshua L. Chamberlain

[MSA]

170. Both are otherwise unidentified veterans not of the 20th Maine.

Portland, April 28th 1913.

Dear General Dill: —

I appreciate the valuable work you have been so efficiently carrying forward in the matter of securing advantages for our Gettysburg veterans wishing to attend the Celebration, as also your very kind and courteous attentions to me in connection with this.

I have given close attention to your admirable report to the Governor, and note therein that something will devolve on me as Commissioner to take action upon before long. In conncction with this, I am in communication with the Headquarters of the Commission as to important matters to be attended to as soon as possible, — such as the selection or assignment of ground for location of the Maine Camp, and what facilities there will be for medical treatment, and whether it is practicable to have a field-hospital within these grounds; and if not, what other provisions can be made. It is probable that I shall go on to meet the Commission, and visit the ground with the hope of having some choice about our location. I should be mortified to lose the opportunity of obtaining every prop[e]r advantage through default on my part. I am following closely up every suggestion from the Commission headquarters. My present intention is to go to Gettysburg on about the middle of May, — after we know just about the number of veterans going, and other items bearing upon the scope of our requirements for quarters and subsistence, — not to say, existence, — during those four July days there. I shall be glad to be advised and instructed by you on any points involved in the problem.

I find it already necessary for me to employ assistance in keeping up the increasing correspondence, and an orderly arrang[e]ment of papers pertaining to the preliminary matters now somewhat pressing. I have got the newspapers to publish the circular sent me personally by the Commission Saturday.

With hig[h] regard, Yours,

Joshua L. Chamberlain

[MSA]

≈ TO ELLIOTT T. DILL

Portland, Maine, April 29th 1913.

General Elliott T. Dill;

The Adjutant General;

Dear General Dill: —

I have notice this morning of an important meeting, and the final general meeting, of the Gettysburg Commission at Gettysburg on May 15th and 16th.

I had already signified my intention of making this visit at that time to enable me to act intelligently on matters which are part of the service and trust remaining to me after your kind and able management of everything so far possible.

We ought to have all our returns and other possible data in by the date of this meeting. I enclose a paper with suggestions from Headquarters. I sent the newspapers in this city a general notice as requested by Col. Beitler, last Saturday.

If you desire, I will forward to you all papers I receive from General Headquarters. I presume you have most of them direct. My hands are pretty full of work on this matter now-a-days.

I have promised to be present at the meeting May 15th, although I am suffering something of a down-pull just now. I shall take my old regimental Surgeon, Dr. A. O. Shaw, of Portland with me for attendant and guardian. He was not with the regiment at Gettysburg; but I shall take him as my guest, and at my own private charge. I really do not dare to go without hi[m].

Yours respectfully,

Joshua L. Chamberlain

[MSA]

≋ TO FREDERIC E. BOOTHBY

499 Ocean Avenue, Portland, Maine.

[May 9, 1913]

Dear Colonel Boothby:—

I was so stupid as not to get a clear idea of the nature of your appointment from either your good letter to me or the kind notice sent me by General Dill. He stated that you were to assist me; but I find the exact nature of this assistance is really in the place the General so kindly and ably has hitherto taken. This is an absolutely essential part, which it would be impossible for me, even if in perfect health, to carry on. My own strain has been to keep up communications with the General Commission, and write the innumerable letters ne[c]essitated by the wide preliminary work of the Commission. Having no office force nor typewriter at my disposal, the task has been a personal one, and quite severe.

Now I und[e]rstand that you are to take largely the work hitherto done by General Dill. So I am put in communication with you as to the detail of our Maine quota of veteran visitors.

Just now I am endeavoring with Dr Shaw's daily care, to get myself able to attend the final meeting of the General Commission at Gettysburg on the 15th & 16th of May. It is absolutely necessary that I have Dr Shaw with me, if I am at all able to go. This is for me an official service, and I suppose the State in some way will meet my actual expenses. I cannot expect to have the expense of Dr Shaw's attendance provided by the State. This must be at my personal charge. I have engaged rooms for us both at the Eagle Hotel, Gettysburg, and notified the Commission of the coming of the Doctor and myself on the evening of the 14th. But I have not been able to find out the quickest and best route from N.Y. to Gettysburg. I believe there is an early day train by the New Jersey Central running direct to Gettysburg, without stopping over or going near Philadelphia. I made bold to ask you yesterday, in a very hasty letter ignorantly sent to Waterville, to help me about this. I wish you were going too. You will go in July, no doubt.

Yours as always,

Joshua L. Chamberlain

[MSA]

≈ TO FREDERIC E. BOOTHBY

Personal   Gettysburg May 16 1913

Dear Colonel Boothby: —

I am standing the trip and the task pretty well. I see the importance of my being here in person. Maine seems to be highly regarded by everybody. I write this in haste to let you know I have arranged to *secure quarters and entertainment* for our Governor & party; but you will have to make the *special* arrangements when you are assured of the time of arrival & the number of the party.

I will make a full report of matters decided upon here and to be attended to by us, as soon as I get home the first of next week.

With high regard

yours

Joshua L. Chamberlain

[MSA]

≈ DRAFT OF REPORT TO TRUSTEES AND

OVERSEERS, BOWDOIN COLLEGE

To the Trustees and Overseers of Bowdoin College:

In presenting their report on the Art interests of the College, your committee feel that they may congratulate the College on the remarkable advance made during the occurring year on the lines which you have lately encouraged and supported. The increased attendance of visitors, the still more significant interest of friends and patrons in the gifts and loans of valuable examples of artistic work, the restoration of so many valuable paintings, and their careful re-arrangement in the galleries of the Walker building,[171] the varied usefulness realized in the arrangement of the basement room for exhibitions and familiar lectures on our collections; and especially the successful inauguration of the important course on the history of Art, will, we trust, cause as much satisfaction to the members of the Boards as to your committee, who have long recommended these latter measures, with what may have sometimes appeared too great insistence.

In a review of what has been accomplished, we especially invite attention to the rooms which have been renovated, and to the pictures which have been so carefully restored and brought into presentable condition. We would also call attention to the Edward P. Warren collection[172] received during the year, which Prof. Johnson has arranged with admirable taste and judgment, and to the portrait of our regretted associate, Prof. Chapman,[173] which has been presented by his appreciative friends. We should also mention the Chapman fresco, to which we think worthy the inspection of the board (& something to be inserted here in proof)

We have also to renew our grateful acknowledgments to Dr. Frederick H. Gerrish[174] for his second contribution to the filling of the panels of the Chapel. He has submitted to us the proposition to place here a copy of the celebrated Isaiah of Micha[e]langelo,[175] which met our hearty approval, and the work upon which is now going on. Designs have also been laid before us for an entrance gate to the college grounds which we think an appropriate and imposing piece of architecture, and also of the subject of the Roman centurion for one of the Chapel panels which meets our cordial approval.

In the work of restoration of the paintings in the Walker galleries we have been fortunate in having the assistance of Mr. Moore,[176] who has made his work a labor of love rathe[r] than gain. The work is still unfinished. A con-

171. The Renaissance revival Walker Art Building, designed and built in 1893 by McKim, Mead & White. The original Walker Art Gallery had been in the chapel. Sophia W. Walker was a cousin of President Leonard Woods, whom she helped to build Bowdoin's art collection. Calhoun, *A Small College in Maine*, 197, 111.

172. Edward P. Warren (1860–1928), an Oxford-trained archaeologist and Greek antiquarian honored by Bowdoin.

173. Henry Leland Chapman (1845–1913) had been Professor of Rhetoric and Oratory at his alma mater.

174. Frederick H. Gerrish (1845–1920), winner of all four Bowdoin degrees, was a prominent professor in the medical school.

175. In the Sistine Chapel. The Bowdoin Chapel frescoes and ceiling are designed after Giotto, though many of the figures are more evocative of Brueghel.

176. An otherwise unidentified artist and art restorer.

siderable portion of the appropriation of last year we found it necessary to expend in general measures of preservation, and the result, we are quite sure, will be approved. We therefore ask a continuance of your appropriation of ~~five~~ three hundred dollars for the work of restoration.

We commend the usual appropriation for the current expenses of the Curator of the art galleries.

It is perhaps unnecessary to renew our remarks on the educational mission of art. This department of education has been cordially recognized in numerous institutions through[ou]t the country: and our College which set so early an example in this line deserves not only to be congratulated but to be sustained in its continued endeavor, now that this has been vindicated by manifest useful results.

Prof. Johnson is now visiting some of the art centers of Europe, having especially in view the collection of material for educational purposes and [t]he observation of foreign methods of study in this department. To acquire adequate material for the illustration of Prof. Johnson's lectures on the history of art would probably involve the expenditure of a thousand dollars. We think this would be for the interest of the College, and we feel justified in recommending the appropriation of the sum named to be dra[w]n upon the approval of this Committe[e], as may be required for the purpose stated, and to provide cases for the very valuable collection of photographs and engravings already on hand, and to be acquired during the year.

In closing, your committee would call attention to the instructive report of the curator elsewhere presented, and express the hope that members of the Boards will personally inspect the work of your committee and especially will visit the new lecture room in the basement of Walker Art Gallery. An attendant will be present to give any information which they may desire.

Respectfully submitted
Joshua L. Chamberlain
James Phinney Baxter[177]
Committee
Portland, Maine, May 20, 1913.

[MHS]

177. Baxter (1831–1921), a Maine historian and folklorist, was a former Portland mayor and banker.

Portland, Maine.
May 21, 1913.

Col. Frederic E. Boothby,
Gettysburg Commission,
State House, Augusta, Me.
Dear Colonel:—

In accordance with the terms of my appointment as member for Maine of the National Commission charged with the duty of arranging for the celebration of the fiftieth anniversary of the Battle of Gettysburg, I have the honor to report for the Governor's information that I attended the final conference of the Commission at Gettysburg on the 15th and 16th of May and took such part there therein as the interests of our State demanded. My present object is to report the important decisions of practical questions in regard to the provisions made for the comfort and convenience of visiting veterans in July, with such suggestions of my own as I think will be for the interests of our Maine veterans to consider.

Provision is made by the U. S. Government and the State of Pennsylvania to furnish quarters, subsistence for and medical attendance for visiting veterans of that battle during the celebration from July 1st to July 5th to the extent of 40,000 men. Favorable ground for a great camp has been selected between Confederate Avenue and the Emmitsburg Road, east and west, and between the field of the fight of the first Corps on the first day of the battle and that of Pickett's Charge on the third day. That is probably as convenient a location for the camp of veterans of that five mile front as could be provided. This ground is a mile or more from the railroad station, and, of course, members of the several regiments and batteries will find themselves from one to three miles from their old battle ground. The question of dealing with the distance from the camp to the respective fields is an important one, and as yet no definite provision has been made by the national or local authorities for assisting the veteran in reaching his desired points of interest. It will readily be seen that these trips will task the energies of many of our veterans. Probably means of transportation besides that of the electric road[178] running from the town to

178. An electric railroad connected the town with the battlefield, ending at Devil's Den. Interestingly, the federal government's battle with the Gettysburg Electric Railway Company to protect the battlefield led to a litigation in which the Supreme Court upheld the constitutionality of federal efforts to preserve historic sites. See *United States v. Gettysburg Electric Railway Co.*, 160 US 668 (1868).

Round Top may be brought into requisition; but it would be wise for the old soldiers to be prepared to pay their way, now that they cannot fight their way.

As to the camp itself, it is composed of quite spacious, conical-topped tents something like what were formerly known as "Sibley tents." They are set up in the order of the camp of a division of infantry, with properly located kitchens and other appurtenances of camp. These tents have a capacity of twelve men each, but the present assignment is only eight men to each, so the room is ample. Cots, bedding, water-buckets, candles and toilet utensils are provided, — with the exception that each one is expected to provided his own towels, soap and brushes. Meals are to be served at tables adjoining the kitchen at the end of each company street. The mess-kit is to become the property of the veteran whom it served. Trunks cannot be received, but only hand-baggage which can be handled and cared for by each owner.

The great tent spoken of will seat more than 10,000 persons, and besides its use for general purposes is so arranged as to allow numerous separate compartments for meetings of the several local and regimental organizations at the same time. All desiring to hold such reunions should send notice at once to Col. Lewis E. Beitler, Secretary Gettysburg Commission, Harrisburg, Pa., stating the day and hour such reservation is desired, and the probabl[e] number in attendance. These requests should be in before June 1st and are absolutely necessary in order to secure desired accommodation.

Each State will have its assigned portion of the camp as soon as the number of visiting veterans is assured. I have made requ[i]sition for tents to accommodate six hundred as our Maine quota.

Hospital tents will be er[e]cted in various convenient portions of the field. These are a part of the general provision ~~by the U.S. and State authorities~~. But considering the years that have passed since the youthful service of our veterans, and the consequent diminution of youthful energies, the hard journey from Maine to Gettysburg, and the privations of camp life in the extreme heat of early July, I regard it as highly probable that a considerable number of our veterans will require medical and perhaps hospital treatment in the course of their visit; and I have asked permission to make use of two of our tents for hospital uses if needed. I have no doubt this will be granted, and that the surgeons accompanying our State veteran[s] will find favorable conditions in camp for exercising their care. I beg, however, to remind our veterans that they should be well assured of their ability to stand the strain of this rather trying journey, however agreeable in its idea and purpose.

Each State is requested to send its State flag, to be placed conspicuously to indicat[e] the location of its camp. As to the particular choices our regimental organizations may have by reason of old associations of service in their respective locations within the State camp, this may be arranged during the journey to Gettysburg, and their wish be met on reporting to the orderly or person in attendance at camp.

Our State has already taken careful measures for the proper certification of those entitled the privileges of this Visit. It will be borne in mind that they are guest[s] of the United States and the State of Pennsylvania; and that only actual veterans of this battle are provided for in this camp. No one is entitled to bring other friends for entertainm[e]nt here. Our State has generously provided for the transportation, subsistence and medical care along with the veterans of our own State, of those veterans from other State organizations who are now resident in Maine. No doubt on arriving in camp such will prefer to join their old organizations there. On the other hand, quite as many Maine veterans are now resident in other States which have made similar prov[i]sions; so that this will equalize itself.

To give time for so many arrivals, our generous hosts have arranged to open camp in readiness for the reception of Veterans on Sunday, June 29th, and to hold it open until the following Sunday, July 6th. — the first meal furnished being supper on the first named date, and the last, breakfast on the last Sunday morning. No one under any circumstances will be allowed in the camp before or after these hours.

I would respectfully suggest that our transportation agents endeavor to arrange with the Railroad Companies so as to keep clear of each other the several great trains arriving in Gettysburg at nearly the same time. Great disadvantage and hardship would result from being held for miles and hours away from camp after so tedious a journey.

I will only add that the particular location of our State camp within the grounds now indicated has not yet been determined. I have advised for our location a position near the south-eastern portion of the general camp, as most of our State organizations would find this most convenient for visiting their old battle-grounds.

Awai[t]ing further instructions,
I am very respectfully yours,
Joshua L. Chamberlain
Commissioner for Maine.

[MSA]

499 Ocean Ave. Portland, May 26, 1913.

Colonel F. E. Boothby,
Maine Gettysburg Commission,
Augusta:

My dear Colonel;

I was expecting to see you again before you left. I was free after ten minutes. I did not quite understand in what shape you proposed to publish the circular, in which you [s]aid both our names would appear. It occurred to me after you left that you might for brevity's sake make up a combined paper signed jointly by you and me. I do not think that wo[u]ld be a good way to put it.

My Report addressed to you as representing the Governor as the Adjutant General does, was in fact my official report to him, addressed to you as courtesy and custom require, and was not merely a personal letter giving information. It is the only public record of my service as Commissioner for Maine on the General Commission.

Moreover, to leave this off the record would be a discourtesy both to the Governor and the National Commission. I think the proper way to make out the notice proposed would be for you to recognize the report from me and add to it what belongs to your department of the Commission. Some of the things I say you could not be responsible for, and certainly I could not be responsible for your arrangements and orders from this end of the line. So I am asking this morning that you let me amend my report with reference to my arrangements for hospital tents, &c, and let it be published, if at all, as my official report to the Governor,—still addressed to you as his representative on the Maine Commission, and not appearing to be merely my assistant.

I am submitting a form of a combined circular which seems to me to put the whole matter in the right shape.

"Office of the Maine Gettysburg Commission;
Augusta, Maine. May 26$^{t[h]}$ 1913.

"The following Report of General Chamberlain, representative for Maine on the General Commission on arrangements for the celebration of the Fiftieth anniversary of the Battle of Gettysbu[r]g, is published for the information of veterans proposing to attend."

(Here bring in my report.) (Then bring in your announcement)

"In accordance with the foregoing, information is hereby given of arrangements made by the State of Maine for the proper credentials, transportation, subsist[e]nce and medical care of Veterans visiting Gettysburg on this occasion.

1.

2.

3.

&C.

This, I think, will set forth the whole matter in the clearest and completest way. I want the historical record of Maine in this matter to be of credit to her name,—already honored in the history of that battle.

Yours most cordially, recognizing

you[r] peculiar fitness for this service,

Joshua L. Chamberlain

[MSA]

TO WILLIAM DEWITT HYDE

Portland Maine

June 3^{d} 1913

Dear President Hyde:

The generous salutation of the students of Bowdoin is gratefully acknowledged in behalf of all the noble young men of my early College companionship who inspired by the lofty ideal of a nation's mission to man, offered their best for the Country's life and honor.

I am proud of Bowdoin of the present day, whose young manhood is grounded on the high principles so happily expressed in your cherished message.[179]

Faithfully yours

Joshua L. Chamberlain

[BSC]

TO ELLIOTT T. DILL

Portland, Maine, June 12, 1913,

General Elliot[t] [T.] Dill,

Dear General:—

I have your kind letter, inviting me to be of the Governor's party to Gettysburg, leaving here on the evening of July 1st.

I was just sitting down to ask the Governor if he is particularly desirous

179. Hyde's commencement message in the year of the fiftieth anniversary of Gettysburg.

that I attend the celebration, now that all the arrangements requiring my official participation are complete. If I go, it seems to me that I should be at Gettysburg on the first day, July 1st, so that Maine may have an official representative on the ground from the first. If I do not go, some duly appointed representative should be present to meet the hundreds of questions and complaints that are sure to come.

But the journey by our regular Maine train will be quite severe for me; I found the journey under favorable conditions in May, hard enough; and I had contemplated making a private journey before the "jam," if I have to go. I feel the kindness and courtesy of your invitation on behalf of the Governor; but think it will hardly "do" for me, if I go as Commissioner, not to be present at the beginning. My grave doubts about taking the risks of the trip have been within a few days somewhat affected by the courteous invitation of the Governor of Pennsylvania,[180] as well as other special requests from prominent citizens, and particularly from the survivors of the regi[m]ents that fought at Gettysburg, (of which ten were at some time in my command,) to be with them at this reunion. Your kind letter offering me the comfort and the honor of being of your party puts a new phase on the problem. My decision will depend much on my physical condition two weeks hence, and not a little upon the feeling and wish of the Governor as to the importance of my going. I will place on another sheet some explanations I have already made to him, which I wish you also to know.

With thanks for your kind reference to the 'article,' which is much curtailed and changed by the insertion of "connective tissue" by the Editor,[181] I am sincerely yours,

    Joshua L. Chamberlain

                                   [MSA]

≋ TO ELLIOTT T. DILL

                               Portland, June 12th 1913.

Dear General Dill—

I fear I was chargeable with a lack of official courtesy in reporting my action in the matter of securing quarters for our Governor and Suite at Gettysburg to Colonel Boothby instead of addressing my report to you. Colonel Boothby wrote me at Gettysburg that the Governor had not secured quarters

180. John K. Tener (1863–1946), an Irish-born former professional baseball player and financier. *BioDictGovr*, 3:1318.

181. Perhaps "Through Blood and Fire at Gettysburg," see 2 Mar. 1913 to Grace and 28 Aug. 1913 to Eckstorm.

for that occasion, and requested me to see what could be done about this. I at once interviewed the chief hotel men, and l[ea]rning that there were positively no rooms free for engagement either in the hotels or in any of the principal buildings, I conferred with the President and Secretary of the Pennsylvania Commission, and received the cordial response that our Governor should be worthily taken care of with the General Headquarters at the Pennsylvania College; but they wished to be informed at once how many there would be in our Governor's party. I immediately wrote Colonel Boothby this result, as the request came from him. This was not exactly proper, as this matter was not within the scope of Colonel Boothby's commission, but was under your jurisdiction. I suppose he turned the report over to you. I offer this explan[a]tion, and beg you to accept my apology.

My report to the Governor upon my action as Commissioner for Maine at the General Conference was addressed through Colonel Boothby, because as I understood he was appointed to take charge of the Gettysburg celebration work in Maine, which you had so eff[i]ciently carried through the laborious first stages. I supposed this would be laid before the Governor, and perhaps be published. Reference to my report is made in the circular published, but several items of some importance are not mentioned: such as the statement that I had only asked that in the assignment of State Camps our[s] should be somewhere in the Southeastern portion of the ground, — as this would be most convenient for a la[r]ge majority of our Maine men to reach their old fighting ground. The actual assignment could not then be made. I have not taken any further action on this point; but will, at once, if my suggestion is approved by you, express the wish accordingly so that we may have the definite place and number of our State Camp.

I had expected some advice on this point following my reference to the unfinished matter in the report sent Colonel Boothby.

I noted also the requirements of the Commission that organizations desiring to hold meetings in the available apartments of the Great Tent should make their application without delay in order to secure a place at the time desired. I have seen no notice of this requirement.

The matter of provision for one or two tents fo[r] hospital purposes in the Maine Camp was privately arranged for, and assured. That, I suppose could not be made public, as the Commission granted no such privilege. I have the promise of two extra tents for hospital uses for our State camp.

Other minor matter[s] were referred to in my report which there is no need now to mention.

I write this now that you may not hold me responsible for lack of information on mat[t]ers t[ha]t were entrusted to my charge.

I was very anxious that Maine should be worthily represented in this camp as she was in the great battle, and should be sorry for any default.

Yours with high regard,

Joshua L. Chamberlain

[MSA]

≫ TO AURESTUS S. PERHAM

Portland, June 14th 1913.

my dear Perham:

I highly value your kindness in wishing to see me when in Washington. But I have no purpose of visiting that fine city at the present time, or in the near future.

Our good friend Prince must see farther ahead than I can: but I have no thought that President Wilson[182] will need an interview with me, for any need he may have of aid in running the Government.

And I am not a lobbyist; nor am I seeking favors at [W]ashington.

I should be glad to see you there, or in any good place. I hardly think I shall be able to go to Gettysburg in July.

I have more letters now-a-days than I can answer, or I would write you more fully, but not more gratefully, remembering all your many good offices towards me.

Heartily yours,

Joshua L. Chamberlain

[MHS]

≫ TO FREDERIC E. BOOTHBY

Portland, June 16, 1913.

Colonel F.E. Boothby;

State commissioner for Maine;

Fiftieth Anniversary, G[e]ttysburg;

Dear Colonel:—

One of the best locations on the Gettysburg Field has been assigned to Maine for our State camp;—on Avenue "C," East Range 36th Street; Tents as numbered:

Tents 1 to 37:

2 To 40:

101 to 131:

102 to 132.

---

182. Thomas Woodrow Wilson (1856–1924), 28th President of the United States.

This ground is directly on the Electric Road, & the Emmitsburg Road. Also this Avenue "C" is at the Main Entrance, and the Telephone and Information Station. Nothing could be better.

You will perceive that we have tents enough for all our needs, as the list shows. I perceive that the final requirement is that no less than *nine* men must be assigned to each tent.

A blue print of the whole camp has been sent to me. If you have not the same, I will send you this.

I think it very important that an official State representative should be on the Gettysburg ground at the opening of the camp. It is doubtful about my being able to go to Gettysburg, and it would be well to have some one there a day, or some hours, ahead; so as to be familiar with the camp, and be ready to assist our men to select their particular places and arrange neighbors within the State camp. I wish you might be there yourself. Please confer with General Dill and the Governor on the matters stated herein.

Yours respectfully,
Joshua L. Chamberlain

[MSA]

≈ TO FREDERIC E. BOOTHBY

Brunswick
June 25th 1913

Dear Colonel Boothby;
I find I shall have to give up going to Gettysburg. The Doctor says it will not *do*. So I dont see but you must go, to look after the boys the first two days.

In haste yours,
Joshua L. Chamberlain

[MSA]

≈ TO ELLIOTT T. DILL

Portland, Maine, June 26th 1913.

General Elliott [T.] Dill,
The Adjutant General;
Augusta, Maine.
Dear General;
It is with extreme regret that I have to forego the pleasure of accompanying the Governor and his party of visitors to Gettysburg on the 1st and 2nd of July in response to the invitation with which he honored me through your kind message.

I greatly regret also that under very positive assurance of my surgeon that it would be extremely hazardous for me to undertake this journey and service in my present condition of health and strength, I am forced to relinquish the privilege, and ask release from the duty of attending the Celebration and Reunion for the promotion of which I have gladly served as Commissioner for Maine.

I have notified Colonel Boothby of my inability, and advised that he take the first opportunity to reach Gettysburg in season for the opening of the Camp on the field for the reception of our veterans.[183]

With hearty recognition of your able and efficient service in promoting this meeting of our veterans of the war for the Union, and your great courtesy to me, I remain as ever

Your friend and servant,

Joshua L. Chamberlain

[MSA]

≈ TO FREDERIC E. BOOTHBY

Portland

July 21st 1913

Dear Colonel Boothby:

I was away all the last part of last week, and so only got your kind letter with the interesting & valuable enclosure of the Badge Sunday morning.

I congratulate you on the great success of your good management in the case of our Veterans of Gettysburg on their visit. The State of Maine made as worthy an appearance on this July as she did fifty years ago.

We are all proud to belong to her.

Thanks for your courtesy & friendship.

Joshua L. Chamberlain

P.S. Was anything wrong about my statement of expense account? It seems to me fair that what I actually paid out on account of my Commission service should be made good. C.

[MSA]

183. Chamberlain did see the "boys" off at Portland's Union Station. Smith, *Fanny and Joshua*, 349.

≈ TO AURESTUS S. PERHAM

Portland Maine
Aug 22^d 1913

Dear friend:

I think I acknowledged promptly your kind letter with enclosure of clippings from Mrs Pickett's writings.[184] I have just now seen a very favorable review of her later books in so respectable and authoritative a paper as the *New York Lecteur*—Mrs Pickett sent me a copy of her *"Pickett & His Men,"* I have not quite been able to reconcile some of its statements with the official records, and the testimony of other Confederate officers.

I trust we shall hear good words from Captain Prince. I saw General Ellis Spear at Commencement time at Bowdoin. He was looking poorly; and I have been anxious about him.

I thank you for your continued interest and attentions, and trust "things" are turning well for you in these trying times.

Yours as ever

Joshua L. Chamberlain

Major
A. S. Perham
Washington D.C.

[MHS]

≈ TO FANNIE HARDY ECKSTORM

499 Ocean Ave
Portland
Aug 28 1913

Dear Mrs Eckstorm:[185]

Your good and gracious letter came to a glad hand, and I wrote as best I could in an imperfect knowledge of the situation of the Bird question before the Senate, to our Senator, expressing my view of the importance of protecting our native and visiting birds.

As to your generous feeling and expression concerning my life and actions, your wish is the chief active motive which leads me to try to arrange a meeting with Editor [Greenslet?][186] soon.

184. LaSalle Corbell Pickett (1848–1931) wrote several books adamantly defending her late husband George Pickett, including *Pickett and His Men* (Philadelphia: J. B. Lippincott, 1913) and *The Heart of a Soldier as Revealed in the intimate letters of Genl. George E. Pickett, C.S.A.* (New York: Seth Moyle, 1913). Also see 10 Nov. 1905 to Munford.

185. See correspondence to Eckstorm beginning 28 Apr. 1909.

186. Perhaps Ferris Greenslet (1875–1959), a New York editor and author. Baillie, 1165.

At his request I sent him about a month ago, a lot of my articles which have been privately printed, and some manuscripts dating some time back.

I have had no response to this "entry" or "invoice" as yet.

The Hearst editors mutilated and "corrected" my "Gettysburg" so that I have not tried to get copies of their magazine (Hearst's) in which it appeared.[187]

But I have all my article as I wrote it, and have the right to publish in book form.

Yours with affectionate regard

Joshua L. Chamberlain

[UMO]

TO WYLLYS

499 Ocean Ave. Portland, Oct. 18th 1913.

My dear Wyllys;

I am glad to get your letter. It is a good one. All that is needed is to substitute real values for the value of X in your equation. That is, to get somebody to apply your inventions to actual use.

I do not see why this cannot be successfully started. If so, and the call continues, there is a good prospect ahead for you. You have worked hard, and borne up patiently; and deserve handsome rewards for both outlays.

Now, I should say, [g]o to New York and Conn. as soon as you are fairly ready to make a good show. In a week or so more, I shall be in condition to give you lift. There is no [n]eed of your going to Brewer at present, nor this fall, unless something extraordinary calls, or you find yourself free from other duties or cares. I was made a little anxious when I found Dana working so hard, and so subject to down-pulls. I feared he might have a break-down,— as is so common with people now-a-days. In such a case there is nobody at all who wo[u]ld be interested for him or for any of us, to take up his work. I thought, if you were entirely free, it would be well for you to run over and see how things are, and get the hand of his enterprise, and find what the situation is with the old homestead property, and prospects. There is no need of this visit for some time yet.

But that property is too valuable to be in any way neglected. People (especially the city as[s]essors) say it is very valuable.

I did not think of a partnership. Dana is offered $5,000. by the Mayor of Bangor for a half interest in his plant and good will. I advised him not to accept at present, any way. What Dana proposes to me is to enter with his operations

187. See 2 Mar. 1913 to Grace.

upon my adjoining land, which he is nearing fast. It will be necessary for him to extend his operations to this ground before very long.

You have the best profession or expert preparation in the whole [ill.] world of business just now, and for the long future. The thing to do is to "realize" on it while the tide is rising. Your attention has been absorbed in the inventions in which your brain is so fertile, so that you have not got into the other stratum, or sphere, of making money of it. That is a "worldly way" of looking at things; but it has to [be] regarded. No doubt your present intention is exactly in this line. [Y]ou should have a fair chance to test the essay; and I want to help you to succeed in it. Anything but to undertak[e] manufacturing in competition with established and commanding concerns. We tried that, with a good thing; but found it took too much money, in such times of concentrated capital as these.

I advise you to stick to you[r] line of purpose and achieved knowledge and skill. This seems to be the "time and tide which leads on to fortune."

Nobody can rejoice in your success as I shall. And I will "lend a hand" in your effort to attain it.

Thank you for your able discussion of the situation.

We are enjoying Grace much. Friends are coming to see her. But she needs rest.

With love to your pl[e]asant household, as well as to yourself,

Hopefully yours,

Joshua L. Chamberlain

[MHS]

≈ TO SAE

Jan 20 [1914?]

Dear Sae:

I am passing through deep waters! The Dr thinks I am going to land once more on this shore. I seem to be gaining deliver[a]nce from the particular disease which caused me such unspeakable agony and gaining strength from the condition to which it reduced me. We are gradually discharging Doctors and nurses. My good old Dr Shaw thinks I need an accomplished specialist for a while longer. I greatly appreciate your and Alice's kind wish to come and help me; but my condition is still such that it would not be well for either of us to attempt it just now.

If the dear Lord has appointed me to live a little longer I am resolved it shall be of good to me and others. I am trying to get a little closer to God and to know him better.

With great love to you all.
Lawrence
Dictated to Lillian

[UMO]

≋ TO SAE

February 4, '14.

Your very interesting letter with enclosures gratefully received. Am gaining strength, but slow work. The bed and bed-side chair are still my habitual place. Have to keep trained nurse for a while yet. Love to all.

J. L. C.[188]

[UMO]

188. Reflecting his physical state, this letter is nearly illegible. Joshua Lawrence Chamberlain died just after 9:30 A.M. on 24 February, with his children by his side.

SURVEYOR OF CUSTOMS { 287

[1887?]
on train
Richmond Va.
¼ to 12 Monday morn[in]g

What a good time we had! I was sorry to have to go just when you and I were enjoying ourselves so much, & were of so much good to each other.

You surely must come & see [me] again as soon as I get back.

I woke to a charming spring morning near *Fredericksburg*. As we skirted that field so full of memories of awful scenes, & I looked on that slope where in the darkness I buried my dead, & then took up the dismal retreat with the forlorn remnant amidst the terrible tokens of a lost battle, you can imagine what thoughts took possession of me.

All along our route are haunted fields!

Soon we shall come to *Petersburg*—that will be the culmination for me. It is strange—the peace & beauty of this morning, here amidst such memories—But I see how well & strong I am, & I thank God, and move forward to do my duty.

How I have enjoyed you! [A]nd how do I hope to see you again soon, & in better health & strength! I am glad for all the blessings you have & feel grateful to all who are good to you. Give my love to Horace, & tell him to come & spend a couple of days with you in New York, & leave you a week with me again.

I will write Mamma from Charleston.

I send a *general* note to New York, too, as you may be there & wish to hear. I wanted you to stay a while & rest, but suppose you have started for Boston.

always & more & more, yours
J. L. C.

[BSC]

Nov 5.
Maverick House
East Boston

My darling Daisy:

I thank you much for your dear little letter which I found on my return to Boston. Glad to hear that you & Mamma are enjoying yourselves so well. Let me know all your intentions. I now come into Boston every day & have taken rooms at the Maverick House, East Boston, because I have to sign Bonds of the State which is a hard work. Think of signing my full name *ten thousand* times! Then I have to be very *careful*; for what I have already signed amount to a million and five hundred thousand dollars in value! I came over here in the first place to get Annie (who is making a short visit here) to help me with the bonds & with my letters. Maj Morgan[1] had been doing it, but he went to Maine so there was nobody I could trust. So I get into Boston every morning at about ten & stay here signing Bonds till about four P.M. for I have to lecture *every night* but Sunday. It is doubtful now if I can go home Thanksgiving day. They want me in *Taunton* Mass.[2] that eve[nin]g.

But you & Mamma can come & make me a call when you go "home along," if you go before I do. By next mail I will send you a list of my engagements so you will know just where I am every day. I do not find it very hard to lecture every evening, though few people could stand it. My powerful constitution keeps me up. I hope you are having a delightful time.

I would write Mamma instead of you if the little scamp would answer me. Mrs [Dunning] *wants to come* & keep house for us. What does Mamma say. Let me know your plans.

[SL]

TO JOHN P. NICHOLSON?

My dear Col.

That defence of Little Round Top which Gen. Sykes called in his Report[3] "the key of the field" must be already well known to you. I will, however, give you the facts connected with the particular operations of my command on the extreme left.

The enemy's assault reached us about as soon as we had got into position. It did not seem to me that it was very severe at first. The fire was hot,

1. Unidentified.
2. Taunton, Mass., is located between Boston and Providence.
3. George Sykes's (see 25 Jan. 1884 to Nicholson?) report is printed in OR, 27 (I): 594.

but we gave them as good as they sent, and the Rebels did not so much attempt at that period of the fight to force our line, as to cut us up by their fire. We kept them off however. In the course of a few minutes (perhaps a quarter of an hour) as I was endeavoring to keep myself informed of the enemy's movements, standing upon a high rock in the centre of my line where I could see over the heads of the parties then engaged. I perceived a body of Rebels moving by their right flank towards the smooth valley between us and Great Round Top. I immediately undertook to thwart their design (at least in its full accomplishment) by bringing my right wing into one rank, by side steps, keeping up a strong fire all the while so as to give the enemy no opportunity to break through; while I filed the right wing to the left and rear, and took up a line conforming to the nature of the ground, in outline resembling a horse-shoe, nearly. This hazardous manoeuver in the presence of the enemy, and hotly engaged with them as we were, was successfully accomplished and not a moment too soon. For the Rebels now appeared in a direction which would have struck me almost in rear, and burst on us with a shout.

We opened at once a strong fire, but they still came on returning our fire, and increasing in number and in strength of fire, by the accession of other troops who seemed to be formed (as was natural under the circumstances) *en echelon*, with the outward flank forward. They advanced within a dozen paces of our lines before they broke, and then the struggle became desperate and bloody in the highest degree. We were gradually forced back till we came against the great rocks between us and Hazlett's guns;[4] But we rallied and repelled the fire, and this was repeated twice again with terrible carnage. Our ammunition being totally exhausted and many of our arms unserviceable, I directed that the cartridge boxes of the dead and dying that strewed the field, should be seized as well as more serviceable arms, and with these we met and for a time withstood the enemy's assault; until the ammunition utterly failing; and my losses being so severe that the defensive was no longer possible (I had lost every man of the color guard and two thirds of the color company, for example) it was necessary to take defensive, and I ordered bayonets to be fixed and a charge. This was almost miraculously successful, for we captured 370 of the enemy, and completely routed them, killing and wounding a large number, and driving the remainder of Laws and some of Robertson's men[5] across the slope of Great Round Top; which we afterwards occupied,

4. Capt. Charles Hazlett commanded Battery D, 5th U.S. Artillery, at Gettysburg, where he died in battle. Trulock, 150, 391.

5. Brig. Gen. Evander M. Law (1836–1920) commanded the Alabama brigade that attacked Little Round Top and then its superior division when Hood was wounded. Brig.

following the enemy with some slight brisk encounters and capturing some 25 or 30 more of them on Great Round Top.

In all this we were without support, the "Reserves" up to that time certainly not firing a gun on our part of the field.

Col. Rice praised us very enthusiastically at the time, but as Gen. Barnes[6] was in another part of the field and Gen. Sykes not a witness of our operations, the Reserves managed to give currency to a story that they had done the fighting here. The 83^d Penn. Vols. on our right behaved with admirable steadiness, and though they did not participate in our charge, their heroic fortitude enabled us to accomplish our great results.

While our fight was going on, the right of our brigade had been severely pressed; also the 16th Mich.[7] became somewhat broken, but Vincent rallied them in person, and our line was not fairly broken anywhere but on the left, where indeed there was no help for it. My loss in killed and severely wounded, was three officers and 136 men.

I can't tell you exactly where Vincent was killed. I did not see him after the fight began, nor Rice either until our charge was over, and the assault repulsed for the day.

Very truly yours

J. L. Chamberlain

[NH]

༄ FRAGMENT TO GOVERNOR OF MAINE

The Artillery service requires scientific knowledge & skill beyond what is commonly or easily acquired; & as we have absolutely no Artillery Corps & no instruction in that arm, I think it will be well (while *all branches* of Military instruction, including the highest kinds of engineering, road & bridge building fortification will be fully taught) to make this Corps nominally (& really) an Artillery Corps.

The U.S. Gove[rn]ment will give us every aid, & the State ought not to be behind.

I think it quite probable that some of your existing Companies may not have

[verso] I am

Gen. Jerome B. Robertson (1815–91) commanded Hood's Texas Brigade; two of his regiments joined Law's line at Little Round Top. CWD, 472, 703; Trulock, 139.

6. Brig. Gen. James Barnes, see 18 May 1893 to Webb.

7. Of Vincent's brigade, commanded by Col. Norval E. Welch at Little Round Top. Trulock, 390.

Governor
with high respect
your obdt servt
Joshua L. Chamberlain

[BSC]

≈ FRAGMENT OF TYPESCRIPT DRAFT TO MORRIS SCHAFF

[c. 1911–2]

General Morris Schaff Boston, Mass.[8]

Dear General,—

although I should feel nearer in addressing you as Captain (renewing great days ~~the heart of youth~~,—or Companion or friend, ~~warming our~~ touch ~~together~~ in ~~the~~ life's ~~sunset glow~~;

The ~~richness of your own spirit~~ generosity with which you have referred to me ~~lifted~~ me in the high lights and far-reaching suggestions ~~by your references to me in~~ your great poem of The Sunset of the Confederacy affects me so [ill.] as to, puts it out of my power to offer a worthy word of recognition and response.

The story of those great days which you have given is a wonderful piece of writing, It is a [fine?] poem. It is still more wonderful as a revelation of spirit & character on the part of the writer. ~~I have never seen anything equal to it in the depth of spiritual insight, and wealth of suggestion in the literature of war.~~ It goes beyond Pindars' poem to the victors in the Olympic games, & is [three words ill.]. (And that you should give me so much and such quality of attention in the course of this is a marvel to me.) [Let] me just add that your passage on the "spiritually real of this world," and your association with it of any action or trait of mine, are like a command and consecration to me. I must live up to your appraisal.[9]

8. Morris Schaff (1840–1929), a former Civil War ordinance officer, was a historian who wrote books such as *The Spirit of Old West Point*, *The Battle of the Wilderness*, and *Etna and Kirkersville, Licking Co., Ohio*. Wallace, *Dictionary of North American Authors*, 401. This letter regards Schaff's *The Sunset of the Confederacy*, pages 296–302 of which are highly complimentary to Chamberlain's acceptance of the official surrender of the infantry of the Army of Northern Virginia: "It was not mere chance that Chamberlain was selected, and that he called on that famous corps to salute their old intrepid enemy at this last solemn memorial—. What glorified tenderness that courtly act has added to the scene! How it, and the courage of both armies, Lee's character and tragic lot, Grant's magnanimity and Chamberlain's chivalry, have lifted the historic event up to a lofty, hallowed summit for all people." Ibid., 300.

9. "The selection of Chamberlain to represent the Army of the Potomac was provi-

I am wondering much how you formed your im[a]ge of what you have represented as my action and its motive. I have been very far from publishing myself or my deeds. Especia[ll]y [in] the terrible earnest of our war for the Union. Rejecting almost too sharply the proffers of newspapers reporters to attach themselves to my head-quarters, for which conditions with me offered meager accommodations, I was never "written up"; and my habit of never hanging around [superior] headquarters, not even calling unless especially called, helped to keep me out of notice. What I regret about this last is that it probably deprived me of the [o]pportunity to make your acquaintance, which I have much reason to regret.

I was well content with the notice which I received in the strict relations existing between me and my superiors in the field, trusting the revelations of the future for the rest. It has come, beyond my claim dream. You have set the close in sunset glow. This, too, beyond my thought claim or dream.

One matter more. In the sudden lull after the su[r]render [and] in the following space of my retention in the army after the disbandment of the Army of the Potomac, in that softened mood of adjusting myself to the process of recovery from severe wounds, I turned my attention to writing out my field notes of the [l]ast campaign of the armies of the P[o]tomac and Northern Virginia, — so far as came within my observation. I thought this worth taking some pains to hold fast as they were fresh in time and mind. Some of these cha[p]ters have [b]een given before the Loyal Legion and have been [p]rinted. One of these given before the New York Commandery, you may have possibly have heard or read. It was a brief sketch of incidents of the surrender at Appomattox.[10] I had thought of arranging and publishing thes[e] memoirs of the Last Campaign, to preserve the simple facts of that passing of the armies.

Your splendid poem aff[ect]s this thought in two contrary directions: one on that this moves me to a response by way of echo or antiphony to y[ou]r soul-stirring [paean]: the other, dissuades me fr[o]m the presumption of following your noble portraiture with a matter-of-fact account of operations in the marching and fighting line. I have a vast heap of prose details, — some, possibly of inter[e]st in some ways. But I could perhaps retrench and condense, as I did in the paper before the New York Commandery. I doubt, however, if I shall think it expedient to put forth a paper traversing the same ground over which you have passed with so brilliant a wing. I would rather like to submit

---

dential — in the way he discharged his duty represented the spiritually-real of this world."
Ibid., 296.

   10. Chamberlain, "Appomattox."

to you simply as exchange of friendly confidences, two or three or these crude sketches of mine.

I trust I may before any cloud shuts us quite from each other's sight, persuade you to vi[s]it me in one of my homes in Maine, — the old home of my fifty years in Brunswick, still kept in [commission] which was [the first home of Longfellow as]
[Two lines typed on top of each other]

balcony overlooking the city and a far glimps[e] of the sea; [and?] White Head my counterpart, [an] outpo[s]t of the long way before us.

[YUL]

 GLOSSARY
Terms, Abbreviations, Addresses, and Populations

1st Brigade, 1st Division, V Corps: Previously the 3rd Brigade, 4th Division,
  it included the 121st, 142nd, 143rd, 149th, 150th, and 187th Pennsylvania
  Volunteers. During the Appomattox Campaign, the brigade only included
  the 185th New York and the 198th Pennsylvania.[1]

&c: etc.

Addresses:

  101 West 75th Street — A later home in New York, which Chamberlain had left
    by 1894.

  211 Ocean Avenue — Chamberlain's home in Portland while surveyor of
    Customs. The house had two stories and a clear view of Portland's Back
    Cove, Tukey's Bridge, and the Atlantic. The address was changed to 499
    Ocean Avenue in 1912.[2]

  433 West 57th Street — A home in New York City after the Alpine.

  499 Ocean Avenue — See 211 Ocean Ave.

  The Alpine — A temporary New York home at Broadway & 33rd Streets in the
    1880s.

  Domhegan — Chamberlain's summer home on Simpson's Point, Brunswick,
    which he purchased in 1879. Named after the Indian chief who originally
    sold it to white settlers, it was located between Merepoint Bay and Middle
    Bay. It had its own dock, a large multibedroom house, and several other
    buildings. Chamberlain unsuccessfully attempted to use it as a summer
    school for Stimson's Artist-Artisans Institute. As his use for the property
    diminished, Chamberlain leased it to the nearby Simpson family, who ran
    it as a summer hotel. Grace inherited Domhegan and maintained it until
    she leased it to a Boston hotelier in the 1920s, after which it fell into
    disrepair. The house burned in 1940 and was razed in the 1950s. Little
    remains. Chamberlain's horse Charlemagne is buried on the land.[3]

  The Eagle Hotel — Where Chamberlain always stayed when visiting
    Gettysburg.

  Homosassa — a Florida coastal town about fifty miles north of Tampa and
    forty miles west of Ocala which Chamberlain tried to develop into a resort
    and seaport.

  Ocala — a town in central Florida about forty miles east of the gulf, in the

1. Trulock, 391, 394.

2. Pullen, 159–60; Trulock, 372.

3. Colvin, "Domhegan," 1995.

center of the Tampa-Orlando-Jacksonville triangle, where Chamberlain had various business interests.

Adjt.: Adjutant. An adjutant dealt with administrative matters for a military entity. An adjutant general was the chief administrative officer of his organization.

Aff.: Abbreviation for "affectionate" or "affectionately."

Circular: A document, advertisement, or announcement printed (often as a leaflet) for broad distribution.

Commandery: Like a lodge system, MOLLUS and GAR were comprised of local and state branches called "commanderies."

Companion: A member of MOLLUS or other veterans' organizations.

Council: See Executive Council

Dr.: Abbrev. for either "Dear" or "Doctor" depending on the context.

Encampments: Veterans' reunions that recreated tent cities.

Executive Council: "A vestige of Revolutionary suspicion of centralized power" and the 1819 Massachusetts Constitution, this was a group of seven members elected by the legislature to "advise the governor in the executive part of government." It provided a significant restriction to gubernatorial power until it was abolished in 1975 by the 129th Amendment, partially due to its inconvenience in times of cohabitation.[4].

Fusionists: The alliance of Democrats and Greenbackers in the 1878–81 Maine elections.

GAR: Grand Army of the Republic, the largest Union veterans' organization.

Governor's Council: See Executive Council.

Inst.: Abbreviation for "instant," meaning "of this calendar month."[5]

Loyal Legion: See MOLLUS

MOLLUS: Military Order of the Loyal Legion of the United States, a group formed in Nov. 1865 by an elite set of officers (including Chamberlain) who feared that the peace was fragile. MOLLUS quickly became a fraternal and historical organization. The commandery-in-chief, Pennsylvania, was located in Philadelphia. Chamberlain was a charter member of the Maine Commandery.

Obt., Obdt.: Abbreviations for "obedient"

Pinafore: See Yacht

Servt.: Abbreviation for "servant"

Thot: Abbreviation for "thought"

Ult.: Abbreviation for "ultimo," meaning "of last calendar month"[6]

Wildflower: See Yacht

Yacht: Chamberlain owned two yachts during his lifetime, the *Wildflower*, a six-ton, 26-foot sloop, and the *Pinafore*, a ten-ton schooner, which he bought during the summer of 1879 when he bought Domhegan.[7]

---

4. Palmer et al., *Maine Politics and Government*, 58.

5. *OED*, 7:1041.

6. *OED*, 18:817.

7. Trulock, 347.

Some Population Demographics: From 1865 onward, the northern and western states experienced steady urbanization and industrialization. From the Civil War's end through the 1880s, cities grew at a steady 60 percent. In 1860, America was home to fewer than 400 "urban" places, with populations exceeding 100,000 in only nine; by 1900, these numbers had more than quadrupled. Between 1870 and 1910, the population of New York City rose from 942,000 to 4,700,000; these figures were mirrored in locations including Boston (250,000 to 670,000), Washington (132,000 to 330,000), Portland (31,000 to 58,000), and Augusta (7,000 to 13,000).

By 1900, western and midwestern states had become 40 percent urban, and the Northeast was a full two-thirds urban. Nationwide, the percentage of Americans living in a rural setting dropped from 80.2 in 1860, to 71.8 in 1880, to 60.3 in 1900. By 1890, the populations of New York, San Francisco, and Chicago were 40 percent foreign-born, with the percentage nearly as high in Cleveland and Minneapolis. The age of the compact city had passed into the age of urban transit—except in the South, whose population remained steadfastly 92 percent rural in 1900.[8]

8. Sources: *WhoAmH*, 32–37; Robert G. Barrows, "Urbanizing America," in Calhoun, *The Gilded Age*, 93, 98–99.

U.S. Presidents and Maine Governors and Congressional Delegations, 1865–1914

CONGRESSIONAL SESSION

	1865–1867	1867–1869	1869–1871	1871–1873
President	Andrew Johnson	Andrew Johnson	Ulysses S. Grant	Ulysses S. Grant
Senate	Lot Morrill	Lot Morrill	William Fessenden/ Lot Morrill	Lot Morrill
Senate	William Fessenden [W]	William Fessenden [W]	Hannibal Hamlin	Hannibal Hamlin
1st Dist.	John Lynch	John Lynch	John Lynch	John Lynch
2nd Dist.	Sidney Perham	Sidney Perham	Sam P. Morrill	William P. Frye
3rd Dist.	James G. Blaine	James G. Blaine	James G. Blaine	James G. Blaine
4th Dist.	John H. Rice	John A. Peters	John A. Peters	John A. Peters
5th Dist.	Frederick A. Pike	Frederick A. Pike	Eugene Hale	Eugene Hale
Governor	Samuel Cony	Joshua Chamberlain	Joshua Chamberlain	Sidney Perham

	1873–1875	1875–1877	1877–1879	1879–1881
President	Ulysses S. Grant	Ulysses S. Grant	Rutherford B. Hayes	Rutherford B. Hayes
Senate	Lot Morrill	Lot Morrill/ James G. Blaine	Hannibal Hamlin	Hannibal Hamlin
Senate	Hannibal Hamlin	Hannibal Hamlin	James G. Blaine	James G. Blaine
1st Dist.	John H. Burleigh	John H. Burleigh	Thomas B. Reed	Thomas B. Reed
2nd Dist.	William P. Frye	William P. Frye	William P. Frye	William P. Frye
3rd Dist.	James G. Blaine	James G. Blaine/ William P. Frye	Stephen D. Lindsey	Stephen D. Lindsey
4th Dist.	Samuel Hersey	Samuel Hersey/ Harris Plaisted	Llewellyn Powers	George W. Ladd [F]
5th Dist.	Eugene Hale	Eugene Hale	Eugene Hale	Thompson Murch [F]
Governor	Sidney Perham/ Nelson Dingley Jr.	Nelson Dingley Jr./ Seldon Connor	Selden Connor	Alonzo Garcelon [D]/ Daniel F. Davis

	1881–1883	1883–1885	1885–1887	1887–1889
President	James A. Garfield/ Chester A. Arthur	Chester A. Arthur	Grover Cleveland [D]	Grover Cleveland [D]
Senate	Eugene Hale	Eugene Hale	Eugene Hale	Eugene Hale
Senate	William P. Frye	William P. Frye	William P. Frye	William P. Frye
1st Dist.	Thomas B. Reed	Thomas B. Reed	Thomas B. Reed	Thomas B. Reed
2nd Dist.	Nelson Dingley Jr.	Nelson Dingley Jr.	Nelson Dingley Jr.	Nelson Dingley Jr.
3rd Dist.	Stephen D. Lindsey	Seth Milliken	Seth Milliken	Seth Milliken
4th Dist.	George W. Ladd [F]	Charles A. Boutelle	Charles A. Boutelle	Charles A. Boutelle
5th Dist.	Thompson Murch [F]	District dissolved		

CONGRESSIONAL SESSION

	1881–1883	1883–1885	1885–1887	1887–1889
Governor	Harris Plaisted [F] [a]	Frederick Robie	Frederick Robie	Joseph Bodwell/ Sebastian Marble

	1889–1891	1891–1893	1893–95 & 1895–97	1897–1899
President	Benjamin Harrison	Benjamin Harrison	Grover Cleveland [D]	William McKinley
Senate	Eugene Hale	Eugene Hale	Eugene Hale	Eugene Hale
Senate	William P. Frye	William P. Frye	William P. Frye	William P. Frye
1st Dist.	Thomas B. Reed	Thomas B. Reed	Thomas B. Reed	Thomas B. Reed
2nd Dist.	Nelson Dingley Jr.	Nelson Dingley Jr.	Nelson Dingley Jr.	Nelson Dingley Jr.
3rd Dist.	Seth Milliken	Seth Milliken	Seth Milliken	Seth Milliken/ Edwin Burleigh
4th Dist.	Charles A. Boutelle	Charles A. Boutelle	Charles A. Boutelle	Charles A. Boutelle
Governor	Edwin Burleigh	Edwin Burleigh	Henry Cleaves	Llewellyn Powers

	1899–1901	1901–1903	1903–1905	1905–1907
President	William McKinley	William McKinley/ Theodore Roosevelt	Theodore Roosevelt	Theodore Roosevelt
Senate	Eugene Hale	Eugene Hale	Eugene Hale	Eugene Hale
Senate	William P. Frye	William P. Frye	William P. Frye	William P. Frye
1st Dist.	Thomas B. Reed Amos Allen	Amos Allen	Amos Allen	Amos Allen
2nd Dist.	Nelson Dingley Jr./ Charles Littlefield	Charles Littlefield	Charles Littlefield	Charles Littlefield
3rd Dist.	Edwin Burleigh	Edwin Burleigh	Edwin Burleigh	Edwin Burleigh
4th Dist.	Charles A. Boutelle	Charles A. Boutelle/ Llewellyn Powers	Llewellyn Powers	Llewellyn Powers
Governor	Llewellyn Powers	John Fremont Hill	John Fremont Hill	William T. Cobb

	1907–1909	1909–1911	1911–1913	1913–1915
President	Theodore Roosevelt	William H. Taft	William H. Taft	Woodrow Wilson [D]
Senate	Eugene Hale	Eugene Hale	William P. Frye/ Obediah Gardner [D]	Charles Johnson [D]
Senate	William P. Frye	William P. Frye	Charles Johnson [D]	Edwin C. Burleigh
1st Dist.	Amos Allen	Amos Allen	Asher C. Hinds	Asher C. Hinds
2nd Dist.	Charles Littlefield/ John P. Swasey	John P. Swasey	Daniel McGillicuddy [D]	Daniel McGillicuddy [D]
3rd Dist.	Edwin Burleigh	Edwin Burleigh	Samuel Gould [D]	Forrest Goodwin/ John A. Peters
4th Dist.	Llewellyn Powers/ Frank E. Guernsey	Frank E. Guernsey	Frank E. Guernsey	Frank E. Guernsey
Governor	William T. Cobb	Bert M. Fernald	Frederick Plaisted [D]	William Haines

Note: Unlabeled=Republican, [D]=Democrat, [F]=Fusionist, [W]=Whig.

[a]Maine switched to two-year gubernatorial terms in 1880, partly as a result of the 1879 election count-out crisis.

~~~ DRAMATIS PERSONAE

First-Name, Nickname, and Household Staff Register

Alice: Mary Alice Farrington

Annie: member of Chamberlain's household staff

Beatsen: Beatrice Lawrence Allen

Blanche: member of Chamberlain's household staff

Carrie: Carrie Pennell, member of Chamberlain's household staff

Catherine T. Zell: member of Chamberlain's household staff

Charley (or Charlie): Charles O. Farrington

Mrs. Curtis: member of Chamberlain's household staff

Daisy (or Daise): Grace D. C. Allen

Mrs. Dunning: member of Chamberlain's household staff

Edith: member of Chamberlain's household staff, a table girl

Elizabeth Edmunds: member of Chamberlain's household staff and cousin of
    Lillian Edmunds

Fannie (or Fanny): Frances C. A. Chamberlain

Florence: member of Chamberlain's household staff

Garkie: Wyllys's childhood name for his grandmother Sarah Chamberlain

Gennie (or Genny): Chamberlain, an abbreviation of General

Georgie: member of Chamberlain's household staff

Gorgon (or Gorgan):[1] Fannie, by her grandchildren

Grace: Grace D. C. Allen

Miss Hodgdon: member of Chamberlain's household staff

Horace: Horace Allen; sometimes Horace Chamberlain (d. 1861)

James: member of Chamberlain's household staff in Florida

John: John Calhoun Chamberlain (d. 1867)

Julia: member of Chamberlain's household staff

L: Lillian Edmunds, though sometimes Lawrence

Lillian: Lillian Edmunds, member of Chamberlain's household staff and cousin of
    Elizabeth Edmunds

Little Mamma: Fannie

Lizzie: member of Chamberlain's household staff

Mamma: Fannie

Mathie: member of Chamberlain's household staff in Florida

Nappy: Fannie

Sadie: Chamberlain's sister, Sarah B. C. Farrington

Sae: Chamberlain's sister, Sarah B. C. Farrington

---

1. From Greek mythology: Gorgon was one of the three snake-haired women who could turn men to stone with their gazes, the most famous of whom was mortal Medusa. OED, 6:693.

Sally: Chamberlain's mother, Sarah D. B. Chamberlain

Salome: Salome Field

Tom: Thomas D. Chamberlain

Andrew Tozier: former color sergeant of the 20th Maine whom Chamberlain
recommended for the Medal of Honor for Little Round Top, a member of the
household staff with his family

Wyllys: Harold W. Chamberlain

Catherine T. Zell: member of Chamberlain's household staff

Correspondent Biographies

This is the cast of characters in Chamberlain's correspondence, including both
correspondents and individuals discussed in the letters. The criterion for
membership is to be mentioned in the correspondence more than three times.
Most household employees are included in the First-Name Register only.

Amos Lawrence Allen (1837–1911)
The Bowdoin-educated Maine lawyer who was instrumental to Chamberlain in
securing the surveyorship — though not the collectorship — of Portland upon
his election to Congress.

Beatrice ("Beatsen") Lawrence Allen (1896–1943)
The only one of Chamberlain's granddaughters not to pursue higher education.
She married Lt. David Longfellow Patten of the U.S. Army in 1918.

Eleanor Wyllys Allen (1893–1980)
Chamberlain's eldest granddaughter, a Radcliffe-educated scholar and Foreign
Service officer who worked in Europe and taught at Harvard Law School,
Radcliffe, Yale, and the Université Libre de Bruxelles. Bowdoin awarded her an
LL.D. in 1974.

Grace ("Daisy" or "Daise") Dupee Chamberlain Allen (1856–1937)
Chamberlain's only daughter to survive to adulthood. She lived in Boston with
her husband Horace Allen and their three daughters, Eleanor, Beatrice, and
Rosamund, and often hosted Wyllys or Fannie. She was crippled in an
automobile accident in 1910.

Horace Gwynne Allen (d. 1919)
Son of Fannie's lifelong friend Stephen M. Allen, Allen was a successful Boston
lawyer and council member who married Chamberlain's daughter Grace in 1881.

Rosamund Allen (1898–2000)
Chamberlain's youngest granddaughter, a social worker who specialized in
children's welfare.

John A. Appleton (1804–91)
The influential 6th chief justice of the Supreme Judicial Court of Maine and
reformer of Maine's evidentiary rules. A nephew of Bowdoin's first president,
Appleton was a Bowdoin graduate, overseer, and trustee, and was awarded an
honorary LL.D by the college.[2]

2. Hamlin, "John Appleton."

Romeyn Beck Ayres (1825–88)
  A career soldier from the West Point class of 1847 who commanded the 2nd
  Division, V Corps during the Appomattox Campaign. He finished his career as
  a regular Army colonel.[3]
Lewis E. Beitler
  Secretary of the National Gettysburg Commission for the 50th Anniversary of
  the Battle of Gettysburg in 1913. Chamberlain represented Maine on the
  commission.
James G. Blaine (1830–93)
  Maine political boss, speaker of the Maine and U.S. Houses, U.S. senator,
  secretary of state, and 1884 Republican nominee for president. Known as the
  "Plumed Knight," he was the consummate politician vilified by Schurz's wing
  of the party; he detested Chamberlain. His political memoir *Twenty Years in
  Congress* is considered a classic.[4]
Frederick E. Boothby
  Gov. Haines appointed Col. Boothby of Portland to assist Chamberlain in his
  role as Maine's member of the National Gettysburg Commission in 1913. His
  wife was first vice president of the Maine Branch of the American National Red
  Cross during Chamberlain's presidency.
Charles Addison Boutelle (1839–1901)
  A seven-term congressman, arch-supporter of Blaine, and Civil War naval
  officer. Boutelle was a devoted enemy of Chamberlain, especially during the
  1879 electoral "count-out" crisis. He married a daughter of Maine Adjt.-Gen.
  Hodsdon.[5]
John Marshall Brown (1838–1907)
  Chamberlain's student at Bowdoin and adjutant in the 20th Maine. He later
  served on Adelbert Ames's staff, commanded the 32nd Maine, and was
  brevetted brigadier general. After the war, Brown was a Portland banker and a
  one-term state legislator who was active on Bowdoin boards and in Maine civic
  activities such as the Maine Historical Society.
Henry Sweetser Burrage (1837–1926)
  Historian and active veteran. Burrage studied at Brown, Newton Theological
  Seminary, and the University of Halle, and was briefly a Waterville minister
  before serving with the 36th Mass. and rising to the rank of major and assistant
  adjutant general. From 1873 onward, he was Maine's state historian, writing
  numerous works on Maine and the Civil War, including *Maine at Louisburg in
  1745*, *The Beginnings of Colonial Maine, 1602–1658*, and *Gettysburg and Lincoln*.[6]
Delia Jarvis Chamberlain (d. 1923)
  Wife of Chamberlain's brother John. After John's death in 1867 she married
  Chamberlain's brother Tom in 1870.

3. CWD, 36.

4. *Maine*, 379–81.

5. DAB, 2:487–88.

6. Biography on file in Burrage Papers, MHS.

Frances ("Fannie" or "Fanny") Caroline Adams Chamberlain (1825–1905)
Chamberlain's wife, a former music and art teacher. Fannie was the daughter of Ashur and Amelia Wyllys Adams of the Massachusetts Adams clan. In a somewhat unusual arrangement, the elderly Ashur arranged for his childless nephew Rev. George E. Adams, pastor of the First Parish Church of Brunswick, to adopt Fannie and raise her in Brunswick. She visited her Boston family frequently throughout her life. Rev. Adams married Fannie and Chamberlain on 7 December 1855 in the First Parish Church.

Grace Dupee Chamberlain
See Grace Dupee Chamberlain Allen.

Harold Wyllys Chamberlain (1858–1928)
Chamberlain's son Wyllys, as he was known, graduated from Bowdoin in 1881, studied law at Boston University, and practiced law in Florida where he worked with his father. He considered himself an inventor, ever trying but never successful. He lived in New York, Brunswick, Boston, and, ultimately, Portland, never marrying or quite becoming independent from his family.

John Calhoun Chamberlain (1838–67)
One of Chamberlain's younger brothers, a Bowdoin and Bangor Theological Seminary graduate who briefly worked on the Christian Commission during the Civil War. He married Delia F. Jarvis two years before he died of the same pulmonary disease that killed brother Horace.

Joshua Chamberlain Jr. (1800–1880)
Chamberlain's father, a civically active Brewer farmer.

Sarah Brastow Chamberlain.
See Sarah Brastow Chamberlain Farrington.

Sarah ("Sally") Dupee Brastow Chamberlain (1803–88)
Chamberlain's mother. Her father, Captain Thomas Brastow Jr., had been a private in the French and Indian War and an officer in the Revolution.

Thomas ("Tom") Davee Chamberlain (1841–96)
Chamberlain's youngest brother, a sergeant in the 20th Maine who rose to lieutenant colonel and brevet colonel. After the war, he was a clerk for his brother John (whose widow he married in 1870) in Brooklyn, a merchant in Bangor, an assistant to Chamberlain in Florida, and a pension office clerk in Washington, D.C. He died of chronic lung and heart disease.

Abner Coburn (1803–85)
Republican war governor of Maine, lumber trader, and philanthropist whose firm A&P Coburn was the largest landholder in Maine. One of the state's most wealthy men, Coburn donated large sums to both the University of Maine and Colby, giving a building to each; the Waterville Classical Institute changed its name to the Coburn Classical Institute.[7]

Edward T. Dill
Adjutant General of Maine in 1912 and 1913. He assisted Chamberlain in the administration of Maine's participation in the Gettysburg semicentennial.

7. *DAB*, 4:249–50.

Lillian Amelia Edmunds
>A close family friend who gave up her career as an artist to care for
>Chamberlain. He bequeathed her the use of his Ocean Avenue house and
>permission to be buried in the family plot. She was related to the family who
>kept house after Fannie's death, which included Elizabeth Edmunds.[8]

William Maxwell Evarts (1818–1901)
>Attorney general under Johnson, secretary of state under Hayes, and senator
>from New York. As a lawyer, he acted in the three greatest public cases of his
>generation, defending Johnson in his impeachment trial, representing the
>United States in the USS *Alabama* arbitration in Geneva, and serving as chief
>counsel for the Republican Party in the disputed 1876 presidential election.[9]

Charles ("Charlie") O. Farrington
>A Brewer banker and store owner who married Chamberlain's sister Sarah in
>1867 and helped Chamberlain manage his finances for years.

Dana C. Farrington (1878–1925)
>Chamberlain's nephew, son of his sister Sarah and Charles Farrington.

Mary Alice Farrington (1869–1960)
>Chamberlain's niece, daughter of Sarah and Charles, and a graduate of Pomona
>College.

Sarah ("Sae" or "Sadie") Brastow Chamberlain Farrington (1836–1921)
>Chamberlain's sister. She married Charles O. Farrington in 1867.

William Pierce Frye (1831–1911)
>Republican congressman and senator from Lewiston. A Bowdoin graduate, Frye
>was a strict party man and expansionist who spent four decades in Congress.[10]

James A. Garfield (1831–81)
>20th president of the United States. Garfield was a major general and chief of
>staff of the Army of the Cumberland in the Civil War, a longtime congressman
>from Ohio, and briefly a senator.

John Brown Gordon (1832–1904)
>Confederate general, Georgia governor, U.S. senator, and close friend to
>Chamberlain. Gordon rose quickly through the ranks, eventually reaching
>lieutenant general and commanding the II Army Corps at Appomattox.
>After the war he returned to his law practice until home rule was restored,
>when he beat Alexander H. Stephens for a seat in the Senate. He was the first
>commander-in-chief of the United Confederate Veterans (1890–d.) and an
>early Klansman. His *Reminiscences of the Civil War* (1903), which praises
>Chamberlain, was well regarded for its fairness and lack of sectional rancor.[11]
>Chamberlain "wept bitterly" when he heard of Gordon's death.[12]

8. Trulock, 526 n. 103.

9. "Evarts, William Maxwell," BOL (199/72).

10. DAB, 7:51–52.

11. CWD, 349.

12. See Smith, *Fanny and Joshua*, 316.

Ulysses Simpson Grant (1822–85)
Lieutenant general, general-in-chief of the Armies of the United States from March 1864 on, secretary of war, and the 18th president of the United States. His *Personal Memoirs of U.S. Grant* is considered to be one of the great works of autobiography in the English language.[13]

Charles Griffin (1825–67)
A West Point artillery man who rose to command V Corps when Sheridan relieved Warren at Five Forks. Chamberlain's superior officer and close friend, Griffin died in a yellow fever epidemic in Galveston when he refused to leave his post commanding the District of Texas.[14]

Eugene Hale (1836–1918)
A Republican from Ellsworth who spent twelve years in Congress and thirty in the Senate.

Charles Hamlin (1837–1911)
Son of Hannibal Hamlin, brother of Gen. Cyrus Hamlin, Hamlin was a Bangor lawyer and law lecturer, speaker of the Maine House, and a pioneer in loan associations. During the war, Hamlin was a major in the 1st Maine Artillery and 18th Maine Volunteers, an assistant adjutant general in the 2nd Division, III Corps, and a brevet brigadier general.[15] He was commander of MOLLUS in Maine, chairman of the committee that produced *Maine at Gettysburg*, and author of numerous articles on the war and on Maine jurists.[16]

Joseph Roswell Hawley (1826–1905)
Unlike Chamberlain's, Bvt. Maj. Gen. Hawley's private pension bill passed the Congress—he happened to be chairman of the Senate Committee on Military Affairs at the time. His literary brawl with his former commander Benjamin Butler received nationwide attention.[17]

Rutherford B. Hayes (1822–93)
19th president of the United States. Hayes was a Cincinnati lawyer who joined the 23rd Ohio as a major and rose to division command in the Army of West Virginia. After the war he was a congressman and governor of Ohio until a commission of congressmen and Supreme Court justices appointed him the winner of the disputed presidential election of 1876. The main issues of his presidency were civil service reform, home rule in the South, and resuming silver coinage.[18]

John L. Hodsdon
Adjutant general of Maine at the end of the Civil War. As the state's chief military administrative officer, he would have been in a position to help Chamberlain research his history of the V Corps.

13. CWD, 353; Wilson, *Patriotic Gore*, Chapter 4.
14. Faust, *Historical Times Illustrated Encyclopedia*, 326–27.
15. CWD accidentally conflates Hamlin with his brother Cyrus. See CWD, 369; and GB, 201.
16. DAB, 8:194–95.
17. DAB, 8:421–22; GB, 219–20.
18. "Hayes, Rutherford B.," BOL (263/12); GB, 221–22; CWD, 389.

Oliver Otis Howard (1830–1906)

The Bowdoin- and West Point–educated "Christian Soldier" and major general who commanded XI Corps, ran the Freedmen's Bureau, established Howard University, helped establish Lincoln Memorial University, and was a Trustee of Bowdoin.[19]

Thomas Hamlin Hubbard (1838–1915)

Hallowell and New York lawyer and railroad director, brevet brigadier general who served with the 25th and 30th Maine, and active veteran and Bowdoin alumnus. Hubbard was a munificent trustee, donating Bowdoin's library, Hubbard Hall, in 1903 and Hubbard Grandstand at Whittier Field in 1904. He was president of the Peary Arctic Club, which helped finance his fellow graduate's expedition to the North Pole.[20]

Thomas Worcester Hyde (1841–99)

Founder of Bath Iron Works and president of the Maine Senate. Hyde won a brevet to brigadier general and a Medal of Honor for his service with the 7th Maine and 1st Maine Veteran Volunteers. Hyde earned two degrees from Bowdoin and donated the General Thomas Worcester Hyde Athletic Building (the "Hyde Cage") in 1913 (now renovated as the David Saul Smith Union).

William DeWitt Hyde (1858–1917)

"Hyde of Bowdoin," Chamberlain's successor, was the spectacularly successful, modernizing president of Bowdoin from 1885 until his death. Already a respected speaker, writer, and theologian when he was hired at 26 to energize Chamberlain's reform program, Rev. Hyde wrote many widely read and translated books, taught philosophy, and preached widely, advocating church unity, the socially oriented "new theology," and tariff reform. He turned down numerous college presidencies and a seat in the U.S. Senate. His many reforms include liberalizing Bowdoin's entrance requirements, widening the curriculum, adding electives, focusing upon small groups, introducing more sciences, and procuring new equipment.[21]

Henry Johnson (1855–1918)

Bowdoin professor, librarian, and curator of art. Johnson studied at Bowdoin, Göttingen, Paris, and Berlin and taught at Bowdoin, holding the Longfellow Chair until his death. His greatest contributions to scholarship were his works of art history and his Dante translations, with his *Divine Comedy* standing beside Longfellow's famous translation. As curator of art when the Walker Art Museum was being built, he guided the growth of the college's art gallery and collection. Bowdoin awarded him an honorary doctorate in 1914.[22]

Robert E. Lee (1807–70)

Commander of the Army of Northern Virginia. After the war, he accepted the

19. *GB*, 237.

20. *DAB*, 9:332–33; Calhoun, *A Small College in Maine*, 216–17; *CWD*, 415.

21. Calhoun, *A Small College in Maine*, 187, 195; *DAB*, 9:452–53.

22. *DAB*, 10:101–2.

presidency of Washington College, which after his death changed its name to Washington and Lee.[23]

George Thomas Little (1857–1915)

Bowdoin graduate, college librarian, editor of the general catalogue, professor of Rhetoric and Latin, and chairman of the State Library Commission of Maine.[24]

Henry Wadsworth Longfellow (1807–82)

The most popular literary figure of nineteenth-century America and the best-known living poet in the English-speaking world after Tennyson. A member Bowdoin's famous class of 1825, he returned after a stint studying in Europe to be a professor of Modern Languages and librarian from 1829 to 1835, during which time he lived in the house that Chamberlain later bought. Longfellow was then lured to Harvard, where he taught languages until retiring from teaching in 1854.[25]

George Gordon Meade (1815–72)

The West Point engineer who commanded the Army of the Potomac from Gettysburg onward.[26]

Holman Staples Melcher (1841–1905)

An enlisted volunteer in the 20th Maine who rose to brevet major. After the war, Melcher was a businessman in Portland and twice its mayor. He was an active member of the GAR and the Loyal Legion, and a founder and thirty-year president of the 20th Maine Regiment Association. He claimed to have led the charge at Little Round Top.[27]

Henry Clay Merriam (1837–1912)

A close friend of Chamberlain who tried to guide Chamberlain's retirement bill through Congress. Merriam was a Medal of Honor–winning veteran of the 20th Maine and the 80th Colored Infantry who rose to major general in the regular Army, with prominent roles in the West, domestic defense in the Spanish-American War, and mobilization for the Philippines.[28]

Lot M. Morrill (1813–83)

A Republican boss in Maine and Washington who served as governor, U.S. senator, secretary of the treasury under Grant, and collector of customs for the Port of Portland.

Walter G. Morrill (1840–1935)

A horse trader and horse-race promoter who enlisted in the 6th Maine and rose

23. CWD, 477.

24. Calhoun, A Small College in Maine, 158; WhoAm, 735.

25. Merriam-Webster's Encyclopedia of Literature (Springfield, Mass.: Merriam-Webster, 1995), 693; Calhoun, A Small College in Maine, 64.

26. Faust, Historical Times Illustrated Encyclopedia, 482–83.

27. Melcher, With a Flash of His Sword, viii–xi.

28. Raymond, "Joshua Chamberlain's Retirement Bill," 342; Garraty and Carnes, American National Biography, 15:347–48.

to command the 20th Maine. He was shot in the face at the Wilderness and won a Medal of Honor for Rappahannock Station (7 November 1863). Known as the "Grand Old Man of Harness Racing," he refused to speak or write about his Civil War experiences until his eighties.[29]

John Page Nicholson (1842–1922)

Chairman of the Gettysburg Battlefield Commission and recorder-in-chief of the Loyal Legion. Nicholson had enlisted in the 28th Pennsylvania, fought in several battles in several armies, and rose to brevet lieutenant colonel. He compiled and edited *Pennsylvania at Gettysburg* and *Ceremonies in Commemoration of Abraham Lincoln on the 100th Anniversary of his Birth, at Philadelphia, 1909*; and translated and edited the Comte de Paris's *History of the Civil War in America* and *The Battle of Gettysburg: From the History of the Civil War in America.*[30]

William Calvin Oates (1835–1910)

Commander of the 15th Alabama at Little Round Top. When denied promotion to colonel, Oates took command of the 48th Alabama, rising to general and losing his right arm near Petersburg. After the war he chaired the judicial committee of the Alabama constitutional convention and was elected congressman and governor. During the 1898 war, he commanded regiments at Camp Meade, Pennsylvania. His Civil War writings include "Gettysburg: the Battle on the Right" in *Southern Historical Society Papers* (Oct. 1878) and *The War between the Union and the Confederacy and its Lost Opportunities.*[31]

Peter Joseph Osterhaus (1823–1917)

A Prussian major general who commanded Missouri regiments. A private act of Congress of 17 March 1905 put him on the retired list as a brigadier general.[32]

Alpheus Spring Packard (1798–1884)

Salutatorian of the Bowdoin class of 1816, professor of Latin and Greek, professor of Rhetoric and Oratory, Collins Professor of Natural and Revealed Religion, college librarian, minister in charge of the college chapel, and acting president for the year between Chamberlain's resignation and Hyde's inauguration. His first wife was the daughter of Bowdoin president Jesse Appleton; their son, later a prominent entomologist, briefly taught at Bowdoin. He shared what was later the home of George T. Little and now is the John Brown Russwurm Center with prominent abolitionist Prof. William Smyth and his family; it was an active station on the Underground Railroad. At the 50th reunion of his class of 1825, Longfellow honored the only living member of his college days' faculty in "Morituri Salutamus": Honor and reverence and the good repute / That follows faithful service as its fruit / Be unto him whom

29. Vickery, "Walter G. Morrill," 127–51.

30. *WhoAm*, 897–98.

31. (1905; reprint, Dayton, Ohio: Morningside, 1974); DAB, 13:605; Perry, *Conceived in Liberty*, 276.

32. GB, 352–53.

living we salute. His 65 years of service to Bowdoin may be the longest of any faculty member to an American college.[33]

Aurestus S. Perham (b. 1844)

Pension agent, historian, son of Gov. Sidney Perham, and veteran of the 23rd Maine, 7th Maine Battery, and 1st Maine Light Infantry, rising to the rank of sergeant-major. He was later a major in the Androscoggin Light Artillery and the Lewiston Light Infantry, which he organized.[34]

George Edward Pickett (1825–75)

The dapper and dashing Confederate major general best known for the ill-fated charge at Gettysburg and for graduating last in his class at West Point. He lived his postwar life in near poverty, turning public posts down to remain with his wife LaSalle in Richmond, where he worked as an insurance agent.[35]

John Alfred Poor (1808–71)

A Bangor and Portland lawyer and financier whose advice Chamberlain held in high regard and whom Bowdoin honored. A visionary of sorts, Poor devoted his professional life to developing an independent railroad system for Maine: the European and North American Railroad, a line traveling through Maine that would facilitate sea travel from Europe to America and Canada via Nova Scotia, which was closer to Europe by sea than other major North American ports. It opened in 1871.[36]

Howard Lyman Prince (1840–1920)

A Bowdoin graduate, 20th Maine captain, regimental historian, and federal government clerk.[37]

Thomas Bracket Reed (1839–1902)

The Bowdoin-educated Maine politician who became the unprecedentedly powerful speaker of the House, earning the nickname "Czar Reed."

James Clay Rice (1829–64)

The colonel of the 44th New York who succeeded Strong Vincent to command of the 3rd Brigade, 1st Division, V Corps and was promoted for his efforts to continue Vincent's push to secure Little Round Top. He was killed commanding the 2nd Brigade, 4th Division, V Corps near Spotsylvania.[38]

Carl Schurz (1829–1906)

Brigadier general, senator from Missouri, secretary of the interior, leader of the civil service reform and Liberal and Independent Republican movements, and a

33. Calhoun, *A Small College in Maine*, 107, 158; *DAB*, 14:125–27; American Association of University Women, "From the Falls to the Bay," 8.

34. Biography on file at MHS.

35. *DAB*, 14:570–71; *CWD*, 652.

36. *Maine*, 314–17; Barton, "Chamberlain: Governor of Maine," 20. Chamberlain used the project as part of his scheme to industrialize Maine—railroads would, in his words, "open living streams where there is now stagnation." See ibid., 32–35; *Maine*, 317.

37. Pullen, 140.

38. *CWD*, 696.

leading anti-imperialist spokesman. Schurz was a German revolutionary who had escaped from prison and emigrated to Wisconsin, where he became a prominent editor of German-American publications and was active in the antislavery movement. After Hayes's term ended, Schurz edited the *New York Evening Post* and the *Nation* and wrote several biographies, including his famous *Abraham Lincoln*.[39]

William Henry Seward (1801–72)

Prominent New York governor and senator, Republican party leader and presidential candidate, secretary of state under Lincoln and Johnson, and Lincoln's most influential adviser. He is most remembered for the 1867 purchase of Alaska from Russia for $7,200,000, dubbed "Seward's Folly."[40]

Abner O. Shaw

Portland physician, active veteran, surgeon of the 20th Maine, and the acting surgeon-in-chief of the 3rd Brigade, 1st Division, V Corps, who saved Chamberlain's life at Petersburg.[41] Maj. Shaw remained Chamberlain's Portland physician and was one of his pallbearers.

Philip Henry Sheridan (1831–88)

Along with Grant and Sherman, one of the Union's three most famous generals, succeeding both as general of the Army. He is most known for his Shenandoah Valley campaign, his command at Five Forks, and his blocking of Lee's withdrawal at Appomattox.[42]

William Tecumseh Sherman (1820–91)

Grant's chief lieutenant and successor as commanding general. A West Point graduate, Sherman left the presidency of the precursor of Louisiana State University in late 1860 to rejoin the army, where he rose to command XV Corps, the Department of the Tennessee, all military operations in the West, his Atlanta campaign, his March to the Sea, and his Carolinas campaign. He refused the Republican nomination in 1884.[43]

Abner Ralph Small (1836–1910)

Adjutant and major in the 16th Maine, active veteran, and historian. His historical works include *The Civil War Memoirs of Major Abner R. Small of the 16th Maine Volunteers, with his Diary as a Prisoner of War*; *The Sixteenth Maine Regiment in the War of the Rebellion, 1861–1865*; and a section on the 16th Maine in *Maine at Gettysburg*.

Ellis Spear (1834–1918)

A Bowdoin graduate from Warren who succeeded Chamberlain as colonel of the 20th Maine and was brevetted brigadier general. He became a Washington patent lawyer, commissioner of patents, and commander of the Washington

39. "Schurz, Carl," *BOL (532/4)*.

40. "Seward, William H(enry)," *BOL (539/50)*.

41. *Polk's Medical Register*, 829.

42. *GB*, 437.

43. *CWD*, 750–51; *GB*, 441–44.

Loyal Legion.[44] Spear and Chamberlain were friends until 1912, when Spear accused Chamberlain of historical dishonesty.

Edwin McMasters Stanton (1814–69)

Prominent constitutional lawyer, attorney general for Buchanan, secretary of war for Lincoln and Johnson, and a Grant appointee to the Supreme Court (he died before taking his seat).[45]

Jonathan Ward Stimson (1850–1930)

Founder and educational director of his Stimson Institute for Artists-Artisans from its 1888 foundation until 1900. A former student at the Paris *École des Beaux Arts*, he had also been a lecturer in art at Princeton and director of the Art Department at the Metropolitan Museum of Art.[46]

Thomas Cogswell Upham (1799–1872)

Professor of Mental and Moral Philosophy at Bowdoin for fifty-three years, the son of a congressman, and brother of a judge and a famous professor.[47] Upham was one of the most important American psychologists in the nineteenth century, making significant strides toward weakening Jonathan Edwards's grip on American philosophy and theology. He was hired to refute Kant and his school, which he did through a thesis, regarded as one of the first original American contributions to psychology, that separated the intellect and sensibilities from the will, expounded in *A Philosophical and Practical Treatise on the Will* (1834) and *Outlines of Imperfect and Disordered Mental Action* (1840).[48]

George W. Verrill

Captain of Company C of the 17th Maine at Gettysburg, member of the Maine Gettysburg Commission, a contributor and editor of *Maine at Gettysburg*, and necrologist of his regimental association.[49]

Strong Vincent (1837–63)

The twenty-five-year-old colonel who commanded 3rd Brigade, 1st Division, V Corps at Gettysburg. On Warren's suggestion to secure Little Round Top, Vincent deployed his regiments just as Hood's flank assault began. He was shot down rallying his men and was promoted posthumously.[50]

Gouverneur Kemble Warren (1830–82)

A career soldier who was chief engineer of the Army of the Potomac at Gettysburg and commander of V Corps at Five Forks. For persuading Vincent to protect Little Round Top, a statue honors him there. His career was ruined when Sheridan relieved him at Five Forks, largely due to a personality clash. In

44. Spear, *The Civil War Recollections*, ix–x.

45. *DAB*, 17:517–21.

46. Wallace, *Soul of the Lion*, 279; *WhoAm*, 1188.

47. Francis Upham, see 13 Dec. 1886 to Grace.

48. *DAB*, 19:123–24; Calhoun, *A Small College in Maine*, 108, 150, 157.

49. *MAG*, iii, 193–94, 197, 223, 582.

50. *CWD*, 878; *GB*, 527–28.

1879, the "Warren Court of Inquiry," at which Chamberlain testified on Warren's behalf, exculpated Warren and reprimanded Sheridan.[51]

Israel Washburn (1813–83)

Maine lawyer, congressman, governor, and eldest son of the Washburn congressional family (which included Grant's sponsor Rep. Elihu Washburne). Washburn is considered to be, along with Massachusetts Gov. John Andrews, one of the great "war governors." Washburn became collector for the Port of Portland in 1863 when he declined renomination, but a battle with Blaine cost him the office and a seat in the Senate. He later became a railroad president.[52]

Alexander S. Webb (1835–1911)

Medal of Honor–winning brigade and division commander, Meade's chief of staff, West Point professor, president of the College of the City of New York, and one of Chamberlain's closest friends. Webb's 2nd Brigade, II Corps, was posted by "the little clump of trees" at Gettysburg, where 451 of his men were killed or wounded, himself among the latter. A statue honors him at the Bloody Angle at Spotsylvania.[53]

Francis ("Frank") Wiggin

First lieutenant in Company G, 16th Maine, and author of the regiment's "Historical Sketch" in *Maine at Gettysburg.*[54]

William Willard (1819–1904)

A prominent Massachusetts portraitist of such notables as Senators Daniel Webster and Charles Sumner, who exhibited at the Boston Athenaeum, among other prestigious galleries.[55]

51. *DAB,* 19:473–74.

52. *DAB,* 19:502–3.

53. *GB,* 544–45; *CWD,* 898.

54. *MAG,* "Historical Sketch," 66–79.

55. Groce and Wallace, *New-York Historical Society's Dictionary,* 687–88.

BIBLIOGRAPHY

Sources of Letters Included in This Volume

Augusta, Maine
    Maine State Archives
        Miscellaneous correspondence
    Maine State Museum
Ann Arbor, Mich.
    Bentley Historical Library, University of Michigan
        George S. Morris Collection
Brunswick, Maine
    George J. Mitchell Department of Special Collections & Archives, Hawthorne-
        Longfellow Library, Bowdoin College
        Joshua L. Chamberlain Papers
        Oliver Otis Howard Papers
        Henry Johnson Papers
    Pejepscot Historical Society
        Joshua L. Chamberlain Collection
        Joshua L. Chamberlain Letterbook
Cambridge, Mass.
    Houghton Library, Harvard University
    Schlesinger Library, Radcliffe Institute for Advanced Study, Harvard University
        Chamberlain-Adams Family Papers
Concord, N.H.
    New Hampshire Historical Society Library
        John B. Bachelder Papers
Durham, N.C.
    Rare Book, Manuscript, and Special Collections Library, Duke University
        J. M. Gould Papers
        Noble Papers
        Munford-Ellis Collection, Thomas T. Munford Division
Fremont, Ohio
    Rutherford B. Hayes Presidential Center
        Joshua L. Chamberlain Papers
        Rutherford B. Hayes Presidential Papers
Gettysburg, Pa.
    Special Collections, Musselman Library, Gettysburg College
        Gettysburg College Board of Trustee Records
    Gettysburg National Military Park
        William C. Oates Correspondence Scrapbook
        20th Maine Volunteer Infantry File

Mount Pleasant, Mich.
    Clarke Historical Library, Central Michigan University
        Oliver W. Norton Papers
New Haven, Conn.
    Manuscripts and Archives, Yale University Library
        Civil War Papers
        Frost Family Papers
        Lounsbury Papers
        A. S. Webb Papers   .
New York, N.Y.
    New-York Historical Society
        Paltsits Collection
Orono, Maine
    Special Collections Department, Raymond H. Fogler Library, University of
        Maine at Orono
        Chamberlain Family Papers
        Fannie Hardy Eckstorm Papers
Philadelphia, Pa.
    Civil War Library and Museum
        MOLLUS Collection
Portland, Maine
    Maine Historical Society Library
        Joshua L. Chamberlain Papers, Collection 10
        Henry S. Burrage Papers
San Marino, Calif.
    Huntington Library, Art Gallery, and Botanical Gardens
        John P. Nicholson Papers (NI 713–714)
Washington, D.C.
    Manuscripts and Archives, Library of Congress
        Joshua L. Chamberlain Collection
    National Archives
        Joshua L. Chamberlain Military Pension Records, Military Personnel File,
            and Military Service Records
Waterville, Maine
    Special Collections, Colby College

Books, Articles, Speeches, and Theses

Allardice, Bruce S. *More Generals in Gray*. Baton Rouge: Louisiana State University
    Press, 1995.
Allibone, S. Austin. *A Critical Dictionary of English Literature and British and
    American Authors*. Philadelphia: Lippincott, 1902. Supplement by John Foster
    Kirk, 2 vols., 1902.
American Association of University Women, Bath-Brunswick Branch. "From the
    Falls to the Bay: A Tour of Historic Brunswick, Maine." N.p., n.d.

Bachelder, John B. *John Bachelder's History of the Battle of Gettysburg*. Edited by David and Audrey Ladd. Dayton, Ohio: Morningside, 1997.

Baillie, Laureen, ed. *American Biographical Index*. New York: K. G. Saur, 1993.

Barton, George Thomas. "Joshua L. Chamberlain: Governor of Maine, 1867 to 1871." M.A. thesis, University of Maine at Orono, 1975.

Biographical Encyclopedia of Maine of the Nineteenth Century. Boston: Metropolitan Publishing and Engraving, 1885.

Biographical Sketches of Members of the Senate and House of Representatives of Maine for 1880–1889. Augusta: Howard Owen, 1880–89.

Blight, David W. *Race and Reunion: The Civil War in American History*. Cambridge: Belknap Press, 2001.

Boatner, Mark M., III. *The Civil War Dictionary*. Rev. ed. New York: Vintage, 1991.

Bowdoin College. *Bowdoin College Donations and Funds, 1794–1898*. N.p., n.d.

———. *Catalogue of the Officers and Students of Bowdoin College and the Medical School of Maine, 1847–48*. Brunswick, Maine: J. Griffin, 1848.

———. *General Catalogue of Bowdoin College: A Biographical Record of Alumni and Officers 1900–1975*. Brunswick, Maine: Bowdoin College, 1978.

"Brunswick, Maine: 250 Years a Town, 1739–1989." Town of Brunswick, Maine, 1989.

Brunswick Telegraph, 15 Nov. 1861.

Byrd, Robert C. *The Senate: 1789–1989*. Edited by Wendy Wolf. 4 vols. Washington, D.C.: Government Printing Office, 1993.

Calhoun, Charles C. *A Small College in Maine*. Brunswick, Maine: Bowdoin College Press, 1993.

Calhoun, Charles W., ed. *The Gilded Age: Essays on the Origins of Modern America*. Wilmington, Del.: Scholarly Resource Books, 1996.

Carpenter, John A. *Sword and Olive Branch: Oliver Otis Howard*. Pittsburgh: University of Pittsburgh Press, 1964.

Chamberlain Association of America. *A Sketch: The Original 1905 Biography of Joshua Lawrence Chamberlain*. 1905. Reprint, Bangor, Maine: Brian L. Higgins, 1995.

———. *Joshua Lawrence Chamberlain Supplement: The Twelve Days at Augusta, 1880*. Portland, Maine: Smith & Sale, 1906.

Chamberlain, Joshua L. "Address of Gen. Chamberlain." *Eastern Argus*, 25 Apr. 1866.

———. "Address of General Chamberlain." In Executive Committee of the Maine Gettysburg Commission, *Maine at Gettysburg*, 63–66. 1898. Reprint, Gettysburg: Stan Clark Military Books, 1994.

———. "Address of General Chamberlain." In Maine Commandery, MOLLUS, *War Papers*, 3:28–37. Portland, Maine: Thurston Print, 1908.

———. *Address of Governor Chamberlain to the Legislature of the State of Maine, January, 1870*. Augusta, Maine, 1870.

———. "Appomattox." In vol. 3 of *Personal Recollections of the War of the Rebellion: Addresses Delivered before the Commandery of the State of New York,* by MOLLUS. New York: J. J. Little, 1907. Reprinted in Chamberlain, *"Bayonet! Forward,"* 142–60.

———. *"Bayonet! Forward": My Civil War Reminiscences.* Edited by Stan Clark. Gettysburg: Stan Clark Military Books, 1994.

———. *Education at the Universal Exposition by Hon. Joshua L. Chamberlain.* Washington, D.C.: U.S. Commission to the Paris Exposition, 1878; 1880.

———. "Five Forks." In Maine Commandery, MOLLUS, *War Papers,* 2:220–67. Portland, Maine: Lefavor-Tower, 1902.

———. "Not a Sound of Trumpet." Brunswick, Maine: Bowdoin College Press, 1982.

———. "The New Education." Presidential inaugural address at Bowdoin College, Brunswick, Maine, 19 July 1872.

———. "The Old Flag—What Was Surrendered? And What Was Won?" *Boston Journal,* 4 Jan. 1878.

———. *The Passing of the Armies: An Account of the Final Campaign of the Army of the Potomac Based Upon Personal Reminiscences of the Fifth Army Corps.* 1915. Reprint, with a foreword by James M. McPherson, New York: Bantam, 1993.

———. "Reminiscences of Petersburg and Appomattox: October, 1903," delivered 2 Mar. 1904. In Maine Commandery, MOLLUS, *War Papers,* 3:161–82. Portland, Maine: Thurston Print, 1908.

———. "The State, the Nation, and the People." Address at the dedication of the Maine Monuments at Gettysburg, 3 Oct. 1889. In Executive Committee of the Maine Gettysburg Commission, *Maine at Gettysburg,* 546–59.

———. "The Surrender of Gen. Lee." *Kennebec Journal.* 3 Jan. 1868.

———. *Through Blood and Fire: Selected Civil War Papers of Major General Joshua Chamberlain.* Edited by Mark Nesbitt. Mechanicsburg, Pa.: Stackpole Books, 1996.

———, ed. *Universities and Their Sons.* 5 vols. Boston: R. Herndon, 1898–1900.

Chase, Henry, ed. *Representative Men of Maine.* Portland, Maine: Lakeside Press, 1893.

Cleaveland, Nehemiah, and Alpheus S. Packard. *History of Bowdoin College.* Boston: J. R. Osgood, 1882.

Colvin, Julia. "Domhegan: Chamberlain's Summer Escape." Brunswick, Maine: Pejepscot Historical Society, 1995.

Congressional Quarterly. *American Leaders 1789–1987: A Biographical Summary.* Washington, D.C.: Congressional Quarterly, 1987.

Cooper, John M., Jr. *Pivotal Decades: The United States, 1900–1920.* New York: Norton, 1990.

Davis, Washington. *Camp-fire Chats of the Civil War.* Chicago: A. B. Gehman, 1886.

Dearing, Mary R. *Veterans in Politics: The Story of the GAR.* Baton Rouge: Louisiana State University Press, 1952.

Dedication of the Twentieth Maine Monuments at Gettysburg October 3, 1889. Waldoboro, Maine: News Steam Job Print, 1891.

Deeds of Valor. 2 vols. Detroit: Perrien-Keydel, 1907.

Desjardin, Thomas A. *Joshua L. Chamberlain*. Gettysburg: Greystone Communications, 1999.

———. *Stand Firm Ye Boys From Maine: The 20th Maine and the Gettysburg Campaign*. Gettysburg: Thomas Publications, 1995.

Encyclopaedia Britannica Online. <http://www.eb.com:180>. 1998. (Currently <www.britannica.com>).

Executive Committee of the Maine Gettysburg Commission. *Maine at Gettysburg: Report of the Maine Commissioners*. 1898. Reprint, Gettysburg: Stan Clark Military Books, 1994.

The Family Doctor, or the Home Book of Health and Medicine. New York: Miller, Orton & Mulligan, 1856.

Faust, Patricia L., ed. *The Historical Times Illustrated Encyclopedia of the Civil War*. New York: Harper & Row, 1986.

Foner, Eric. *Reconstruction: America's Unfinished Revolution, 1863–1877*. New York: Harper & Row, 1988.

Freeman, Douglas Southall. *Lee's Lieutenants: A Study in Command*. 3 vols. New York: Charles Scribner's Sons, 1942–46.

Fussell, Paul. *The Great War and Modern Memory*. New York: Oxford University Press, 1975.

Garraty, John A., and Mark C. Carnes, eds. *American National Biography*. 24 vols. New York: Oxford University Press, 1999.

Girouard, Mark. *The Return to Camelot: Chivalry and the English Gentleman*. New Haven, Conn.: Yale University Press, 1981.

Golay, Michael. *To Gettysburg and Beyond: The Parallel Lives of Joshua Lawrence Chamberlain and Edward Porter Alexander*. New York: Crown, 1994.

Gordon, John B. *Reminiscences of the Civil War*. 1903. Reprint, Baton Rouge: Louisiana State University Press, 1993.

Goulka, Jeremiah E. "Defining the Meaning of Their Civil War: J. L. Chamberlain and Northern Veterans Remember." In *Proceedings of the American Historical Association*, 2000.

———. "The First Constitutional Right to Criminal Appeal: Louisiana's Constitution of 1845 and the Clash of the Common Law and Natural Law Traditions." *Tulane European and Civil Law Forum* 17 (2002): 151–96.

"Governor C's Reply." *Kennebec Journal*, 5 May 1869.

Graham, John. "Month of Madness: Maine's Brush with Civil War." M.A. thesis, University of New Hampshire, 1981.

Grant, Ulysses S. *Memoirs*. Edited by Mary Drake McFeely and William S. McFeely. New York: Library of America, 1990.

Groce, George C., and David H. Wallace. *The New-York Historical Society's Dictionary of Artists in America, 1564–1860*. New Haven, Conn.: Yale University Press, 1957.

Hamlin, Charles. "John Appleton." In *Great American Lawyers: the lives and influence of judges and lawyers who have acquired permanent national reputation, and have developed the jurisprudence of the United States: a history of the legal profession in America*, edited by William D. Lewis, 5:41–80. New York: John C. Winston, 1908.

Hatch, Louis C. *History of Bowdoin College*. Portland, Maine: Loring, Short & Harmon, 1927.

Herndon, Richard, et al., eds. *Men of Progress*. Boston: New England Magazine, 1897.

Historical Biographical Dictionaries Master List. Gale Research, 1980.

Hoogenboom, Ari. *Outlawing the Spoils: A History of the Civil Service Reform Movement*. Urbana: University of Illinois Press, 1961.

———. *The Presidency of Rutherford B. Hayes*. Lawrence: University Press of Kansas, 1988.

———. *Rutherford B. Hayes: Warrior and President*. Lawrence: University Press of Kansas, 1995.

Huizinga, Johan. *The Waning of the Middle Ages*. 1924. New York: St. Martin's Press; Doubleday, Anchor Books, 1949.

Hunt, Roger D., and Jack R. Brown. *Brevet Brigadier Generals in Blue*. Gaithersburg, Md.: Olde Soldier Books, 1990.

Johnson, Allen, ed. *Dictionary of American Biography*. 30 vols. New York: Charles Scribner's Sons, 1928.

Josephson, Harold, ed. *Biographical Dictionary of Modern Peace Leaders*. Westport, Conn.: Greenwood Press, 1985.

Judd, Richard W., Edwin A. Churchill, and Joel W. Eastman, eds. *Maine: The Pine Tree State from Prehistory to the Present*. Orono: University of Maine Press, 1995.

Judson, Amos M. *History of the Eighty-Third Regiment Pennsylvania Volunteers*. Erie, Pa.: B. F. H. Lynn, 1865.

Keller, Morton. *Affairs of State: Public Life in Late 19th Century America*. Cambridge: Belknap Press, 1977.

LaFantasie, Glenn. "Joshua Chamberlain and the American Dream." In *The Gettysburg Nobody Knows*, edited by Gabor S. Boritt, 31–55. New York: Oxford University Press, 1997.

Larson, Erik. *The Devil in the White City: Murder, Magic, and Madness at the Fair That Changed America*. New York: Crown, 2003.

Lee, Robert E. *Personal Reminiscences of Robert E. Lee*. Edited by J. William Jones. 1874. Reprint, Baton Rouge: Louisiana State University Press, 1994.

Leitch, Alexander. *A Princeton Companion*. Princeton, N.J.: Princeton University Press, 1978.

Little, George T., ed. *General Catalogue of Bowdoin College 1794–1894*. Brunswick, Maine: Bowdoin College, 1894.

———. *General Catalogue of Bowdoin College 1794–1912*. Brunswick, Maine: Bowdoin College, 1912.

Longacre, Edward G. *Joshua Chamberlain: The Soldier and the Man*. New York: Da Capo, 1999.

Lyman, Henry M., et al. *The Practical Home Physician*. Albany: Ross Publishing House, 1888.

Maine Commandery, Military Order of the Loyal Legion of the United States. *War Papers*. 4 vols. Portland, Maine: various publishers, 1897–1915.

Malone, Bartlett. *Whipt 'Em Everytime: The Diary of Bartlett Yancey Malone, Co. H, 6th North Carolina Regiment*. Wilmington, N.C.: Broadfoot, 1987.

Marten, James. "Exempt from the Ordinary Rules of Life: Researching Postwar Adjustment Problems of Union Veterans." *Civil War History* 47 (March 2001): 57–70.

Martin, Ralph G. *Jennie: The Life of Lady Randolph Churchill*. 2 vols. Englewood Cliffs, N.J.: Prentice-Hall, 1971.

Mattocks, Charles Porter. *"Unspoiled Heart": The Journals of Charles Mattocks of the 17th Maine*. Edited by Philip N. Racine. Knoxville: University of Tennessee Press, 1994.

McConnell, Stuart. *Glorious Contentment: The Grand Army of the Republic, 1865–1900*. Chapel Hill: University of North Carolina Press, 1992.

McFeely, William S. *Grant: A Biography*. New York: W. W. Norton, 1981.

———. *Yankee Stepfather: Gen. O. O. Howard and the Freedmen*. New Haven, Conn.: Yale University Press, 1968.

McHenry, R. Lewis. "Dawning of a New Elizabethan Age: The Presidency of Joshua Lawrence Chamberlain." Independent study paper, Bowdoin College, 1977.

McPherson, James M. *Battle Cry of Freedom: The Civil War Era*. New York: Ballantine Books, 1988.

———. *For Cause and Comrades: Why Men Fought in the Civil War*. New York: Oxford University Press, 1997.

———. *What They Fought For, 1861–1865*. New York: Doubleday, 1994.

McPherson, James M., and William J. Cooper Jr., eds. *Writing the Civil War: The Quest to Understand*. Columbia: University of South Carolina Press, 1998.

Melcher, Holman S. *With a Flash of His Sword: The Writings of Major Holman S. Melcher 20th Maine Infantry*. Edited by William B. Styple. Kearny, N.J.: Belle Grove Publishing, 1994.

Murdock, Eugene C. *The Civil War in the North: A Selective Annotated Bibliography*. New York: Garland Publishing, 1987.

Myers, Bernard S., ed. *The McGraw-Hill Dictionary of Art*. 5 vols. New York: McGraw-Hill, 1969.

The National Cyclopaedia of American Biography. 79 vols. New York: James T. White, 1892–1979.

Nevins, Allan, James I. Robertson Jr., and Bell Irvin Wiley, eds. *Civil War Books: A Critical Bibliography*. 2 vols. Baton Rouge: Louisiana State University Press, 1967.

The New Encyclopaedia Britannica. 15th ed. 29 vols. Chicago: Encyclopaedia Britannica, 1997.

Nolan, Cathal J., ed. *Notable U.S. Ambassadors since 1775*. Westport, Conn.: Greenwood Press, 1997.

O'Leary, Cecilia Elizabeth. *To Die For: The Paradox of American Patriotism*. Princeton, N.J.: Princeton University Press, 1999.

Palmer, Kenneth T., et al. *Maine Politics and Government*. Lincoln: University of
Nebraska Press, 1992.

Paludan, Phillip S. *A People's Contest: The Union and Civil War 1861–1865*. 2nd ed.
Lawrence: University Press of Kansas, 1996.

Perry, Mark. *Conceived in Liberty: Joshua Chamberlain, William Oates, and the
American Civil War*. New York: Viking, 1997.

Peskin, Allan. "Lucretia Garfield." In *American First Ladies: Their Lives and Their
Legacy*, edited by Lewis L. Gould, 230–42. New York: Garland Publishing, 1996.

Peterson, Merrill D. *Lincoln in American Memory*. New York: Oxford University
Press, 1994.

Polk's Medical Register and Directory of North America. Detroit: R. L. Polk, 1910.

Pressly, Thomas J. *Americans Interpret Their Civil War*. Princeton, N.J.: Princeton
University Press, 1954. Reprint, New York: Free Press, 1962.

Procter, Ben. *William Randolph Hearst: The Early Years, 1863–1910*. New York:
Oxford University Press, 1998.

Pullen, John J. *Joshua Chamberlain: A Hero's Life and Legacy*. Mechanicsburg, Pa.:
Stackpole Books, 1999.

———. *A Shower of Stars: The Medal of Honor and the 27th Maine*. Philadelphia:
J. B. Lippincott, 1966.

———. *The Twentieth Maine: A Volunteer Regiment in the Civil War*. Rev. ed.
Dayton, Ohio: Morningside, 1991.

Raymond, Harold B. "Joshua Chamberlain's Retirement Bill." *Colby Library
Quarterly* 7 (Dec. 1966): 341–54.

Representative Citizens of the State of Maine. American Series of Popular
Biographies, Maine Edition. Boston: New England Historical Publishing, 1903.

Rotundo, E. Anthony. *American Manhood*. New York: Basic Books, 1993.

———. "Body and Soul: Changing Ideals of American Middle-Class Manhood,
1770–1920." *Journal of Social History* 16 (Summer 1993): 623–38.

Royster, Charles. *The Destructive War: William Tecumseh Sherman, Stonewall
Jackson, and the Americans*. New York: Alfred A. Knopf, 1991.

Schaff, Morris. *The Sunset of the Confederacy*. Boston: John W. Luce, 1912.

Sewall, John S. *Conditional Subscriptions to the Endowment of Bowdoin College,
1873–1875*. N.p., n.d.

Shavit, David. *U.S. Relations with Russia and the Soviet Union: A Historical
Dictionary*. Westport, Conn.: Greenwood Press, 1993.

Sherman, William T. *Memoirs of General W. T. Sherman*. Reprint, New York:
Library of America, 1990.

Silber, Nina. *The Romance of Reunion: Northerners and the South, 1865–1900*.
Chapel Hill: University of North Carolina Press, 1993.

Simpson, J. A., and E. S. C. Weiner. *Oxford English Dictionary*. 2nd ed. 20 vols.
New York: Oxford University Press, 1989.

Small, Abner. *The Sixteenth Maine Regiment in the War of the Rebellion, 1861–1865*.
Portland, Maine: B. Thurston, 1886.

Smith, Diane Monroe. *Fanny and Joshua: The Enigmatic Lives of Frances Caroline*

Adams and Joshua Lawrence Chamberlain. Gettysburg: Thomas Publications, 1999.

Smith, Jennifer L. "The Reconstruction of Home: The Civil War and the Marriage of Lawrence and Fannie Chamberlain." In *Intimate Strategies of the Civil War: Military Commanders and Their Wives,* edited by Carol Bleser and Lesley J. Gordon, 157–76. New York: Oxford University Press, 2001.

Smith, Page. *Trial by Fire: A People's History of the Civil War and Reconstruction.* New York: McGraw-Hill, 1982.

Sobel, Robert, ed. *Biographical Dictionary of the United States Executive Branch 1774–1989.* Westport, Conn.: Greenwood Press, 1990.

Sobel, Robert, and John Raimo, eds. *Biographical Dictionary of the Governors of the United States.* 7 vols. Westport, Conn.: Meckler Books, 1978.

Spear, Ellis. *The Civil War Recollections of General Ellis Spear.* Edited by Abbott Spear et al. Orono: University of Maine Press, 1997.

Sproat, John G. *"The Best Men": Liberal Reformers in the Gilded Age.* New York: Oxford University Press, 1968.

Swanberg, W. A. *Citizen Hearst: A Biography of William Randolph Hearst.* New York: Charles Scribner's Sons, 1961.

Trulock, Alice Rains. *In the Hands of Providence: Joshua L. Chamberlain and the American Civil War.* Chapel Hill: University of North Carolina Press, 1992.

Tucker, David M. *Mugwumps: Public Moralists of the Gilded Age.* Columbia: University of Missouri Press, 1998.

Unger, Irwin. *The Greenback Era: A Social and Political History of American Finance, 1865–1879.* Princeton, N.J.: Princeton University Press, 1964.

U.S. Congress. *Biographical Directory of the United States Congress, 1774–1949.* Washington, D.C.: Government Printing Office, 1950.

———. *Biographical Directory of the United States Congress, 1774–1989.* Washington, D.C.: Government Printing Office, 1989.

U.S. War Department. *The War of the Rebellion: A Compilation of the Official Records of the Union and Confederate Armies.* 128 vols. Washington, D.C.: Government Printing Office, 1880–1901.

Vickery, James R. "Walter G. Morrill: The Fighting Colonel of the Twentieth Maine." In *A Handful of Spice: A Miscellany of Maine Literature and History,* edited by Richard S. Sprague, 127–51. Orono: University of Maine Press, 1968.

Wakelya, Jon L. *Biographical Dictionary of the Confederacy.* Westport, Conn.: Greenwood Press, 1977.

Wallace, Willard M. *Soul of the Lion.* 1960. Reprint, Gettysburg: Stan Clark Military Books, 1991.

Wallace, William Stewart. *A Dictionary of North American Authors Deceased Before 1950.* 1951. Reprint, Detroit: Gale Research, 1968.

Warner, Ezra J. *Generals in Blue: Lives of the Union Commanders.* 1964. Reprint, Baton Rouge: Louisiana State University Press, 1992.

Who's Who in America, 1910–11. Chicago: A. N. Marquis, 1911.

Who's Who in New England. 2nd ed. Chicago: A. N. Marquis, 1916.

Who Was Who in America. 13 vols. Chicago: Marquis Who's Who, 1981.

Wilder, Philip S., ed. *General Catalogue of Bowdoin College and the Medical School of Maine: A Biographical Record of Alumni and Officers, 1794–1950*. Sesquicentennial ed. Portland, Maine: Anthoensen Press, 1950.

Williamson, Joseph. *A Bibliography of the State of Maine, 1821–1888*. 2 vols. 1896. Reprint, Augusta: Maine State Library, 1985.

Wilson, Edmund. *Patriotic Gore: Studies in the Literature of the American Civil War*. London: Andre Deutsche, 1962.

Woodward, C. Vann. *Reunion and Reaction*. Boston: Little, Brown, 1951.

———. *The Strange Career of Jim Crow*. New York: Oxford University Press, 2001.

economic development policy, 21–22, 25, 30n; and criminal justice, 23–24; and war claims, 23–24; patronage appointments, 33–34; effort to establish naval station, 37

—health, xxix, xxxvii, 95, 114–15, 126, 128–32, 150, 152–53, 162, 184, 189, 195, 247, 254, 256–57, 266–67, 270–71, 282; Civil War wounds, xxxvii, 4–7, 109–10, 114–15, 128–31, 141, 143, 165, 169, 183, 209, 211, 223–24, 240, 258, 289; need for surgery, 4–7, 114–15, 119

—honorary degrees, 18, 235

—investments in shipping, 44, 59

—languages, xviii, 205

—lectures and speeches: to veterans groups, 12, 15, 100, 138–39, 166–67, 191, 294; political, 32

—military career: offers of military service, xxx, 33, 164–66, 292; promotion to major general, 4–7, 11, 146, 220–21; promotion to brigadier general, 196

—physical characteristics, 59, 183, 256–57

—political and social thought, xxxi, xxxiv, 31, 79, 81, 122–24, 185, 230, 262; and Greenback movement, 88–89

—political appointments offered or desired, xx, xxvii–xxx, 78, 83, 86–90, 121–22, 198–99, 281; collectorship and surveyorship of customs, xxx, 170–78, 180–81

—politician and leader: self-analysis, xxv–xxx, 17, 42–43, 96; campaign for governor of Maine, xxvi, 12, 15–18, 29–30; campaigns for U.S. Senate, xxvii–xxviii, 34, 71–72, 101–3; on partisanship, 39, 42–43, 99

—relationship with Fannie, xxxvii–xxxviii, 126, 129, 132, 140–42, 150–52, 168–69, 184–85, 188, 192, 194–95, 197; returning from war, 15; difficulties while governor, 26–28, 32; care for Fannie later in life, 194–95, 199, 210–11, 214, 231n

—relationship with Grace, xxxvii, 40–41, 72, 116–17, 128–31, 133–36, 180–81, 206, 249

—relationship with grandchildren, 242, 255, 257

—relationship with parents, xxxvii, 34, 41, 133

—relationship with siblings and siblings' children: with Sae, xxxvii, 135, 286; on Tom's career, xxxvii, 34–35, 42, 44, 59; with Alice, 163–64, 169, 287; with Dana, 164, 169

—relationship with Wyllys, xxxvii, 13, 135, 140; expectations and encouragements for, 13, 150–52, 189, 200, 255, 285–86

—religion and faith, 28, 133, 141, 181, 185, 191–92, 214, 244, 265, 286

—threats and insults against, 28, 38, 69–70, 77, 96, 103–7

—tragedy and humor, thoughts on, 152–53

—travels and vacations, 44, 163, 199, 206, 289; to England and France, xxviii, 86–90; holidays, xxxvi, xxxviii, 34, 84, 175, 188, 290; to Illinois, 138–39; health trip to Europe and Egypt, 182–86, 261–62

—Victorian masculinity, thoughts on, xvii–xviii, xxxv, 215, 258, 278; duty and honor as guides to behavior, xvii, 23–24, 69–70, 82, 95, 117, 225, 237; duty and honor as guides in career choices, xvii, 29, 33, 52, 60; word as bond, xxxiv, 24, 64, 94; honor in war, 7, 33, 187–88, 192; duties of citizenship, 24, 81, 117; and sectional reconciliation, 187, 253; awards, 213, 220, 228

—yachts, 35, 40–41, 71, 195, 206, 298

Farrington, Charles O. (brother-in-law), 101–2, 153, 164, 303, 307
Farrington, Dana (nephew), 163–64, 285, 307
Farrington, Mary Alice (niece), 31, 35, 42, 153, 163–64, 185, 286, 303, 307
Farrington, Sarah (Sae) B. C. (sister), xxxvii, 13, 66, 90, 200, 255, 303, 307; letters to, 42–44, 109–10, 114–15, 152–53, 163, 168–69, 174–75, 185–86, 245–46, 286–87. *See also* JLC—relationship with siblings
Fernald, Bert M., 237, 251, 302
Fessenden, Francis, 4n, 147, 220
Fessenden, William P., xxvii, 4n, 147n, 301
Fifteenth Alabama Vols. *See* Little Round Top
Fifth Corps, Army of the Potomac. *See* JLC—Civil War historian
Fish, Hamilton, 82
Fisher, Joseph W., 8, 117–19
Five Forks, 189–91, 195; shad dinner, 218. *See also* Civil War
Fleming, William H., 230
Fletcher, Loren, 225
Flint, Ephraim, Jr., 102–3
Forty-fourth New York Vols., 202–3, 208
Forty-seventh Alabama Vols., 159, 202–3
Frye, William P., 164–65, 227, 237–38, 244–45, 301–2, 307
Fusionists. *See* Count-out crisis of 1879

Gage, Lyman J., 172
Gallinger, John H., 224
Garcelon, Alonzo, xxviii, 91, 93–94, 301
Garfield, James A., 107–8, 301, 307
Garfield, Lucretia, 107
Garnsey, Frank A., 166–67
Gerrish, Frederick H., 272
Gettysburg: fiftieth anniversary reunion, xxi, 251, 254–55, 262–83 passim; battle of, 8, 117–19, 201–5,

209–10, 247, 290–92; Maine Gettysburg Commission, 155–62. *See also* JLC—Civil War historian; Civil War; Little Round Top; Veterans groups
Gibbon, John, 221
Gilmore, Charles D., 11
Gordon, John B., 166–67, 192–93, 219, 307
Gould, Albert P., 53
Grant, Julia D., 135
Grant, Ulysses, xx, xxvii, 6, 7n, 78, 198, 221, 301, 308; on JLC's muster out, 7n; on JLC's promotion to major general, 11; funeral of, 124–26; field promotion of JLC to brigadier general, 196, 211, 221
Green, John C., 68
Greenback movement of Maine, 88–89. *See also* Count-out crisis of 1879
Gregg, David M., 223
Gregory, Edgar M., 5, 146, 189, 211
Griffin, Charles, xx, 193, 221, 308
Grosvenor, Charles H., 221
Gwyn, James, 191, 195

Haines, William T., 264, 267, 277–83, 302
Hale, Clarence, 266
Hale, Eugene, 171–72, 228, 237, 239, 244–45, 301–2, 308
Hall, James A., 157
Hamlin, Charles, 155–61, 308
Hamlin, Hannibal, xxviii, 21–22, 301; centennial celebration, 237–39
Hancock, Winfield S., 100, 125
Harris, Clifton, xxvi–xxvii, 26
Harris, Samuel, 77
Haskell, Franklin A., xxiii, 247–48
Hawley, Joseph R., 174, 179, 213, 220, 222–23, 226–28, 308
Hawthorne, Nathaniel, 178
Hay, John M., 108n, 182–84
Hayes, Rutherford B., xxi–xxii, xxvii, 79–87, 90–91, 108n, 301, 308